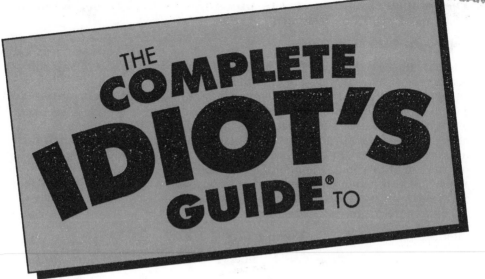

THE COMPLETE IDIOT'S GUIDE® TO

Microsoft® Windows®
2000 Professional

Paul McFedries

A Division of Macmillan USA

201 West 103rd Street, Indianapolis, Indiana 46290

The Complete Idiot's Guide® to Microsoft® Windows® 2000 Professional

International Standard Book Number: 0-7897-2129-5

Library of Congress Catalog Card Number: 99-63003

Printed in the United States of America

First Printing: January, 2000

01   00   99   4   3   2   1

Trademarks

Warning and Disclaimer

Associate Publisher
Greg Wiegand

Acquisitions Editor
Chris Will

Development Editor
Nicholas Goetz

Managing Editor
Thomas F. Hayes

Project Editors
Tricia Sterling
Tom Stevens

Copy Editor
Linda Seifert

Indexer
Bill Meyers

Proofreader
Maribeth Echard

Technical Editor
Jim Cooper

Illustrator
Judd Winick

Team Coordinator
Sharry Lee Gregory

Interior Designer
Nathan Clement

Cover Designer
Michael Freeland

Copy Writer
Eric Borgert

Production
Steve Geiselman
Liz Johnston
Louis Porter, Jr.

Contents at a Glance

Part 1: Why 2K: An Introduction to Windows 2000   **5**

1   New News Is Good News: New Windows 2000 Features   7
*The new and noteworthy niceties that Microsoft stuffed
into the Windows 2000 box.*

2   A Field Guide to Windows 2000 for the Uninitiated   17
*Working with programs, menus, toolbars, dialog boxes, and
other Windows 2000 flora and fauna.*

Part 2: Getting Work Done in Windows 2000   **39**

3   Using My Computer to Work with Files and Folders   41
*Fabulous file and folder fun, including copying, moving,
renaming, deleting, searching, and more.*

4   Prose Programs: Windows 2000's Writing Tools   57
*Getting your words from your brain to your screen using the
Notepad text editor and the WordPad word processor.*

5   From Vapor to Paper: Printing Documents   71
Installing a printer and then convincing it to spit out your stuff.

6   A Movable Feast: Windows 2000 and Your Notebook
Computer   83
*Get the skinny on using Windows 2000's new notebook
knickknacks.*

7   Picture Programs: Windows 2000's Graphic Tools   97
*Creating your own digital masterpieces with Paint, and
copying someone else's masterpieces using a scanner or
digital camera.*

8   The Sights and Sounds of Windows 2000 Multimedia   113
*Playing sounds, movies, audio CDs, and DVD movies,
plus how to create your own sound files.*

Part 3: Getting Connected I: The Web, Email, and More   **129**

9   Modem Operandi: Setting Up Your Modem   131
Getting your modem's mojo working.

10   Using Your Modem for Faxing and Phone Dialing   149
*Putting your modem to work by sending and receiving faxes
and by dialing your phone for you.*

11   Getting on the Internet   167
Using Windows 2000 to jump on the Net bandwagon.

12   Weaving Your Way Through the World Wide Web   179
Hitchin' a ride around the Web with Internet Explorer.

13 Everybody's Doing It: Sending and Receiving   195
    Email Messages
    Using Outlook Express to yakety-yak via email.

14 More Online Conversations: Newsgroups and Internet   213
    Phone Calls
    Chewing the fat in newsgroups and with Internet-based phone calls.

Part 4: Tailoring Windows 2000 to Suit Your Style   229

15 Redoing the Desktop   231
    *Setting the background, changing the colors, and other
    rugged desktop individualism.*

16 Revamping the Start Menu and Taskbar   245
    Giving the Start menu and taskbar an efficiency makeover.

17 Making My Computer Your Own   259
    *More "have it your way" fun, including changing the view,
    sorting files, and customizing folders.*

18 Installing Software and Hardware   273
    *Welcoming programs and devices into your system (and
    giving the boot to programs and devices that have worn out
    their welcome).*

Part 5: Taking Care of Your System   289

19 Backing Up Your Data (The Better-Safe-Than-Sorry   291
    Department)
    Practicing safe computing by backing up your precious files.

20 Painless System Maintenance Chores   305
    *Deleting useless files, checking for errors, getting a speed
    boost, and other hard disk maintenance.*

**Part 6: Getting Connected II: Windows 2000 and   321
Networking**

21 Using Windows 2000 to Set Up a Small Network   323
    *Everything you need to know to get your small office or
    home office networked.*

22 Using Windows 2000's Networking Features   339
    *Learning how to play nicely with the other people on
    your network.*

23 Road Scholar: Using Dial-Up Network Connections   359
    Making the move from road worrier to road warrior.

    Glossary: The Jargon Jar: The Complete Archive   369
    *Build your Windows 2000 vocabulary and learn how to
    speak like a geek.*

Index   377

Contents

Introduction   **1**

    The Parts Department: What's in the Book 2
    Features for a Fun and Fulfilling Read 3

Part 1: Why 2K: An Introduction to Windows 2000   **5**

    1 New News Is Good News: New Windows 2000 Features   **7**

        The "Look-and-Feel" Looks and Feels a Bit Different...........8
        The Internet Is Closer Than Ever 12
        Windows 2000 Gets Along with Notebook
            Computers (Finally!) 13
        New and Improved Hardware Support 14
        Shiny, New Networking Features 15
        What Happened........................16

    2 A Field Guide to Windows 2000 for the Uninitiated   **17**

        Taking a Look Around........................18
        A Quick Mouse Course 21
        Making Things Happen........................23
            Getting Programs off the Ground 23
            The Multitasking Thing: Switching from One Program
                to Another 24
            Pushing Around a Program I: Using Drop-Down Menus 26
            Pushing Around a Program II: Using Toolbars........................27
            Pushing Around a Program III: Using Dialog Boxes..............28
            Shutting Down a Program 31
        What It's All About: Windows 2000's Windows................31
        Dealing with Documents........................33
        Shutting Down Windows 2000........................36
        What Happened........................37

Part 2: Getting Work Done in Windows 2000　　**39**

3 Using My Computer to Work with Files and Folders　　**41**

Getting to Know Your Computer Using My Computer 42
  To and Fro: Navigating My Computer.................................44
  Easier Navigating with the Folders List.............................46
Some Routine File and Folder Maintenance 47
  Creating a New File or Folder 47
  Selecting Files and Folders 47
  Copying and Moving Files and Folders 49
  Renaming a File or Folder..51
  Deleting Files and Folders..51
Searching for Long-Lost Files 52
How Web Integration Changes My Computer 55
What Happened..56

4 Prose Programs: Windows 2000's Writing Tools　　**57**

Using Notepad for Garden-Variety Text Files 58
Using WordPad for Fancier Word Processing Files 60
  WordPad and Word-Processing Files 61
  Tip Sheet: Text-Selection Tricks.......................................62
  Fancy-Schmancy Formatting I: Fonts 62
  Fancy-Schmancy Formatting II: Paragraphs 64
  Fancy-Schmancy Formatting III: Bullets 66
  Fancy-Schmancy Formatting IV: Tabs................................67
Finding and Replacing Text..68
Using Character Map for Foreign Characters and
  Other Symbols 69
What Happened..70

5 From Vapor to Paper: Printing Documents　　**71**

Got a New Printer? Tell Windows 2000 About It! 72
Setting Up Your Pages for Printing 76
Doing the Printing Thing 77
  The Basic Printing Steps...77
  Other Ways to Print Stuff..79
Playing Around with Print Jobs 80
What Happened..81

**6 A Movable Feast: Windows 2000 and
Your Notebook Computer**   **83**

Better Battery Life Through Power Management 84
Synchronizing Files Between Your Notebook and
   Another Computer 86
Working with Those Little PC Card Doodads....................89
   Popping In a PC Card Device *90*
   Yanking Out a PC Card Device...............................*91*
Setting Up a Direct Connection Between the
   Two Computers 91
   Step 1: Configure the Host Computer *92*
   Step 2: Configure the Guest Computer *93*
   Making the Connection *94*
   Direct Connections and the Briefcase *94*
   Disconnecting from the Host *95*
What Happened...95

7 Picture Programs: Windows 2000's Graphic Tools   **97**

Giving Your Right Brain a Workout with Paint 98
   A Tour of the Paint Studio *98*
   Tool Time: How to Use the Paint Tools...................*99*
   I've Got a Cutout—Now What? *104*
   Big, Bigger, Biggest: Seeing More of Your Drawing *106*
   Setting the Image Attributes *107*
   Taking a "Picture" of the Screen *107*
Being Digital: Using Scanners and Digital Cameras..........108
   Installing a Scanner or Digital Camera...................*109*
   Capturing Digital Images *109*
What Happened...111

**8 The Sights and Sounds of Windows 2000
Multimedia**   **113**

We Are Merely Players: Playing Multimedia Files.............114
   Using Media Player to Play Movie and Sound Files *115*
   Using CD Player to Play Audio CDs.......................*117*
   Using DVD Player to Play DVD Movies *120*
Getting the Volume Just Right 122

Assigning Sounds to Things Windows 2000 Does 124
On the Air: Recording Your Own Sound Files 125
What Happened..127

Part 3: Getting Connected I: The Web, Email, and More 129

9 Modem Operandi: Setting Up Your Modem 131

Lines and Transfers and Bits, Oh My! 132
Getting Your Modem Ready for Action 136
Installing the Modem *137*
Modems and Phone Cables..*138*
A Checkup: Running the Modem Diagnostics *139*
Modem Modifications: Some Settings You Hopefully
Won't Need to Set *139*
Where You're At: Setting Up Dialing Locations 143
Area Code Rules, Dude! *145*
Using Long Distance and Calling Card Dialing.................*146*
What Happened...148

10 Using Your Modem for Faxing and Phone Dialing 149

Stop the Presses! Modem Dials Phone! 150
How to Turn Your PC into a Fax Machine 153
Shipping Out a Fax *153*
Creating a Fax Cover Page *156*
Receiving a Fax *159*
Using Imaging to Annotate a Fax *163*
A Few Fax Options..*165*
What Happened...166

11 Getting on the Internet 167

Interstate I1: Setting Up a New Account 168
Interstate I2: Transferring an Existing Account 170
Interstate I3: Setting Up an Existing Account Manually ..170
What You Need to Know Before Getting Started *171*
What You Need to Do After Getting Started *172*
Not Done Yet: Setting Up Your Internet Email Account *173*
Making the Connection 174

Now What? Windows 2000's Internet Features 176
What Happened...176

12 Weaving Your Way Through the World Wide Web 179

Exploring Internet Explorer 180
Basic Web Navigation Techniques 181
Techniques for Efficient Web Gallivanting.....................183
   Saving Sites for Subsequent Surfs: Managing
    Your Favorites 183
   Order Out of Chaos: Searching for Sites 185
   Bread Crumbs in Cyberspace: Using the History List..........188
   The Unwired Surfer: Reading Pages Offline 190
"What If I Want to Use Netscape?" 192
What Happened...193

13 Everybody's Doing It: Sending and Receiving Email Messages 195

Getting Started with Outlook Express...............................196
Using Outlook Express to Send an Email Message 197
   Composing the Message 197
   Populating the Address Book 200
   Creating Signatures 201
   Inserting Attachments and Other Hangers-On............202
   Some Useful Sending Options 203
Using Outlook Express to Get and Read Email................204
   Receiving Incoming Messages 205
   Reading Your Messages...205
   Dealing with Attachments 207
   What to Do with a Message After You've Read It 207
   Using Rules to Filter Out Boneheads and Bores 209
What Happened...210

14 More Online Conversations: Newsgroups and Internet Phone Calls 213

Using Outlook Express to Participate in Newsgroups 214
   Setting Up a News Account.......................................214
   Understanding Newsgroup Nomenclature 216
   Subscribing to a Newsgroup 217
   Downloading Newsgroup Messages..........................218
   Posting a Message to a Newsgroup 219

Using Phone Dialer to Make Phone Calls over the
Internet 220
Using NetMeeting to Make Phone Calls over the
Internet 222
Some Relatively Painless Configuration Chores 222
Placing a Call 225
NetMeeting SpeedDialing 226
Other Things You Can Do After You're Connected..............227
What Happened...228

Part 4: Tailoring Windows 2000 to Suit
Your Style   229

15 Redoing the Desktop   231

Background Check: Changing the Desktop Background ..232
Wallpapering the Desktop 232
Creating Your Own Wallpaper 233
Something a Little Different: A Desktop Pattern 234
Makeover Time: Changing the Desktop Colors
and Fonts 236
The Active Desktop: Your Desktop As a Web Page 237
"Effectations": Changing Desktop Icons and
Visual Effects 239
Changing the Screen Area and Color Depth 242
What Happened...244

16 Revamping the Start Menu and Taskbar   245

A Smart Start: Reconstructing the Start Menu 246
What's with These Crazy New Menus?..............................246
Toggling Some Start Menu Settings On and Off..................247
Adding Your Own Start Menu Items (and Removing
Them, Too) 249
The "Advanced" Route (Not!): The Start Menu Folder........251
Even Easier Ways to Mess with the Start Menu..................253
Renovating the Taskbar 253
Shifting the Taskbar Around..253
Some Useful Taskbar Options 254
Refurbishing the Quick Launch Toolbar 255
Displaying and Tweaking Taskbar Toolbars 256
Creating Your Own Toolbars..257
What Happened...257

17 Making My Computer Your Own   **259**

Points of View: Changing the My Computer View 259
  Bar-Gains: Toggling My Computer's Bars On and Off 260
  Customizing the Standard Buttons Toolbar 261
  Views You Can Use: Changing How Folders and Files
    Are Displayed 264
  Ordering My Computer Around: Sorting Files 265
  Start Spreading the Views: Applying a View to All Folders ..266
A Folder Face-Lift: Customizing a Folder 266
  Refurbishing the Folder Background and Text 267
  Adding a Folder Comment 268
  Changing the Web View Folder Template 269
What Happened 270

18 Installing Software and Hardware   **273**

From There to Here: Installing a Program 273
From Here to Nowhere: Uninstalling a Program 275
Adding On: Installing a Hardware Device 277
  Understanding Hardware Types 278
  Running the Add/Remove Hardware Wizard 281
  Troubleshooting a Device 284
  Upgrading a Device Driver 284
  Removing a Device 286
What Happened 286

Part 5: Taking Care of Your System   **289**

**19 Backing Up Your Data (The Better-Safe-Than-
Sorry Department)**   **291**

Backing Up: Some Things to Consider 292
Creating and Running a Backup Job 295
  Using the Backup Wizard 296
  Creating a Backup Job with Your Bare Hands 297
  Saving and Reusing Backup Jobs 298
Staying Regular: Scheduling Backup Jobs 299
Preparing for the Worst: System Recovery Options 301
  Creating an Emergency Repair Disk 301
  Recovering Your System 301

Recovering Files from a Backup Job 302
 Using the Restore Wizard *302*
 Restoring Files by Hand *303*
What Happened...304

20 Painless System Maintenance Chores   305

Cleaning House: Using Disk Cleanup to Delete Junk
 Files 306
Keeping Your Hard Disk Humming with Check Disk 308
Tidying Up Your Hard Disk with Disk Defragmenter.......310
Setting Up a System Maintenance Schedule.....................313
Keeping Up with the Windows Joneses: The Windows
 Update Web Site...317
What Happened...319

**Part 6: Getting Connected II: Windows 2000
          and Networking   321**

21 Using Windows 2000 to Set Up a Small Network 323

Basic Network Know-How..324
Stuff You Need: Understanding Network Hardware..........324
 The Connection Point: The Network Interface Card............*325*
 The Connection: The Network Cable *326*
Deciding How to Structure Your Network 328
 The Star Structure *329*
 The Bus Structure...*329*
Decisions, Decisions: What Route Should You Take?........330
Getting a Machine Network-Ready.....................................331
 Some Notes About Networking and the Windows
 2000 Setup..*331*
 "Look, Ma, No Hands!" Networking *332*
 The Five-Step Network Setup...*333*
What Happened...337

22 Using Windows 2000's Networking Features   339

Startup Stuff: Logging On to Your Computer....................340
Your Starting Point: The My Network Places Folder..........341
Workgroupies: Notes About Permissions and Users 342

Sharing Your Resources So Other Folks Can Play
with Them 343
   Sharing Folders and Disks 344
   The "In" Crowd: Setting Permissions 345
   Sharing a Printer 347
   Sharing an Internet Connection 349
Playing with Other Folks' Shared Resources 350
   Setting Up Network Places 351
   Making Network Folders Look Like Drives on
     Your Computer 352
   Printing over the Network 352
You *Can* Take It with You: Working with Offline Files......354
   Making Network Files Available Offline 354
   Synchronizing the Offline Files with the Network Files 355
What Happened..356

23 Road Scholar: Using Dial-Up Network Connections   359

Setting Up a Network Computer to Accept
Incoming Calls...360
   Running the Network Connection Wizard...........................360
   Making Adjustments for Incoming Connections 361
Creating a Dial-Up Connection to Your Network 362
   The Network Connection Wizard Redux 363
   Making Adjustments for the Dial-Up Connection 363
Making the Connection 366
What Happened..367

Glossary   369

About the Author

Paul McFedries is a freelance writer who has worked with (yelled at, kicked) computers since 1975, yet still manages to keep his sanity relatively intact. He is the author of more than 30 computer books that have sold nearly two million copies worldwide. His other titles include the Que books *The Complete Idiot's Guide to Windows 98*, *The Unauthorized Guide to Windows 98*, and *The Complete Idiot's Guide to Creating a Web Page*, as well as the Sams Publishing books *Paul McFedries' Windows 98 Unleashed* and *Paul McFedries' Microsoft Office 97 Unleashed*.

Dedication

To Karen, the latté of my life.

Acknowledgments

I've always loved Joseph Addison's description of an editor as someone who "rides in the whirlwind and directs the storm." The hard-working editors at Que are definitely whirlwind-riders and storm-directors, and they have my heartfelt gratitude for always making me look good on paper. Can I be bold and ask you to take a second and look near the beginning of the book for the list of all the people who worked on this project? It's quite a list, isn't it? They're all wonderfully dedicated people who enjoy the craft of book publishing.

However, there are a few people whom I worked with directly, so I'd like to single them out for praise. I'll begin with the book's two Executive Editors—Angie Wethington and Chris Will—both of whom are great fun to work with, but only one of which is good-looking (sorry, Chris!). I worked most closely with Nick Goetz, the Development Editor, and he was the source of tons of large and small improvements to the text. Thanks, Nick: You made this a better book. Copy Editor Linda Seifert had the unenviable task of cleaning up my shoddy grammar and recalcitrant spelling (is it calvary or cavalry?), so she gets extra thanks in lieu of danger pay. Technical Editor Jim Cooper's job was to try out all my steps to ensure that what I say will happen really does happen. So, if there's anything wrong in the book, blame him (I'm kidding, Jim!). Project Editor Tom Stevens did yeoman work pulling the whole book together and shepherding it through the production process. That's no small feat and I appreciate all your hard work. Finally, I'd also like to thank Maribeth Echard who worked extra hard to ensure things looked right and that all those finicky cross-references would steer you in the right direction. A thousand thanks to one and all!

Tell Us What You Think!

As the reader of this book, *you* are our most important critic and commentator. We value your opinion and want to know what we're doing right, what we could do better, what areas you'd like to see us publish in, and any other words of wisdom you're willing to pass our way.

As an Associate Publisher for Que, I welcome your comments. You can fax, email, or write me directly to let me know what you did or didn't like about this book—as well as what we can do to make our books stronger.

Please note that I cannot help you with technical problems related to the topic of this book, and that due to the high volume of mail I receive, I might not be able to reply to every message.

When you write, please be sure to include this book's title and author as well as your name and phone or fax number. I will carefully review your comments and share them with the author and editors who worked on the book.

Fax: 317-581-4666

Email: consumer@mcp.com

Mail: Greg Wiegand, Associate Publisher
          Que
          201 West 103rd Street
          Indianapolis, IN 46290 USA

Introduction

To err is human, but to really foul things up requires a computer.

—Anonymous

The ancestors of Windows 2000—the various incarnations of Windows NT—always seemed like the stronger and smarter big brothers of Microsoft's "consumer" Windows versions—Windows 95 and 98. Stronger and smarter, yes, but friendlier? No way. Windows NT was often prickly, temperamental, and just plain hard to get along with.

Microsoft, tired of its top operating system acting so curmudgeonly, decided to do something about it. They set about making a new operating system that would be easier to use, would recognize notebook computers, would install hardware without complaining, and so on. The result, after a great many years of pizza-fueled programming, was Windows 2000.

Is this a kinder, gentler Windows? Actually, for the most part, it is. There are lots of improvements, big and small, that make Windows 2000 a more pleasant computing experience. On the other hand, this is still Windows you're dealing with. That means there are still plenty of maddeningly cryptic error messages; lots of obscure features within easy reach and crucial features buried behind endless menus and dialog boxes; and far too many features that should be easy-as-pie to use, but are still hair-pullingly convoluted and confusing. In other words, Windows 2000 can still make any normal person feel like a complete idiot.

Welcome, therefore, to *The Complete Idiot's Guide to Microsoft Windows 2000 Professional*.

This is not a book for nerds, geeks, or anyone else who regards a pocket protector as the height of fashion. Instead, this book is aimed squarely at people who, through no fault of their own, have ended up with Windows 2000 installed on their computer and they want some guidance on how to tame this new beast. They don't want to learn fancy-schmancy tricks, they don't want to know absolutely everything there is to know about Windows 2000, and they certainly don't want to wade through pages that are knee-deep with long-winded technical discussions. This book shuns all of that and, instead, just shows you the easiest ways to accomplish the most common Windows 2000 tasks.

You'll also be happy to know that I avoid getting overly earnest about any of this stuff. Sure, computers are an integral part of most people's lives these days, but that doesn't mean you have to furrow up your brow every time you sit down at the keyboard. Instead, keeping your sense of humor at the ready and engaging in a little fun at Windows 2000's expense (both of which I try to do throughout this book) are the best ways to survive your computer sessions with your sanity still intact.

The Parts Department: What's in the Book

The Complete Idiot's Guide to Windows 2000 Professional isn't meant to be read cover-to-cover, although by all means you're free to do so. Instead, most of the book's chapters are self-contained, so you can usually just dive in and start learning. (In those sections that require some background, I've put in pointers back to the relevant material.) To get you started, this section offers quickie summaries of the major sections of the book:

Part 1: Why 2K: An Introduction to Windows 2000

This is the dip-your-toes-in-the-water-before-diving-in section. It's short and sweet (as far as anything related to computers can be described as *sweet*, that is) and it serves as your introduction to the world of Windows 2000. Chapter 1 runs through everything that's notably new in Windows 2000, and Chapter 2 runs through a list of chores that any Windows 2000 neophyte should be comfy with.

Part 2: Getting Work Done in Windows 2000

This is one of the longest sections in the book, and that's as it should be because getting your work done is what it's all about. To that end, the six chapters in Part 2 cover lots of workaday tasks, including dealing with files and folders (Chapter 3), using Windows 2000's writing programs (Chapter 4), printing documents (Chapter 5), working with graphics (Chapter 7), and handling multimedia files (Chapter 8). I also devote an entire chapter (Chapter 6) to the new notebook computer features that are a welcome part of the Windows 2000 package.

Part 3: Getting Connected I: The Web, Email, and More

There are plenty of days when it seems that our computers are just one giant communications terminal. Electronic communication in all its forms is a huge part of our daily lives, and Part 3 devotes no fewer than six chapters to Windows 2000's communications goodies. You'll learn about setting up your modem (Chapter 9) and using your modem to send and receive faxes (Chapter 10). I then turn your attention to that huge, amorphous mass that is the Internet. You'll learn step-by-step how to get connected (Chapter 11), how to surf the World Wide Web with Internet Explorer (Chapter 12), how to exchange Internet email with Outlook Express (Chapter 13), and how to participate in newsgroups and make Internet-based "phone calls" (Chapter 14).

Part 4: Tailoring Windows 2000 to Suit Your Style

Like people living in row houses who paint their doors and windowpanes to stand out from the crowd, most Windows users like to personalize their computing experience by adjusting the screen colors, changing the background, and performing other individualistic tweaks. The four chapters in Part 4 show you how to perform these customizations in Windows 2000. You'll learn how to customize the desktop (Chapter 15), the Start menu and taskbar (Chapter 16), and the My Computer program (Chapter 17). I also show you how to install (and uninstall) software and hardware (Chapter 18).

Part 5: Taking Care of Your System

Thanks to higher-quality parts and improved manufacturing, modern computers are fairly reliable and will often run for years without so much as an electronic hiccup. However, that doesn't mean some disaster—be it a nasty computer virus, an ill-timed power failure, or some other spawn of Murphy's Law—can't strike at any time. The two chapters in Part 5 can help you to prepare for problems. You'll get the goods on backing up your precious-as-gold data (Chapter 19) and on using Windows 2000's collection of system maintenance tools (Chapter 20).

Part 6: Getting Connected II: Windows 2000 and Networking

The final part of the book takes you into the mysterious and arcane world of networking. However, you'll see that for the small networks that Windows 2000 Professional is ideally suited for, networking doesn't have to be an esoteric pursuit. On the contrary, I even take the fairly radical step of actually showing you how to put together your own small network (Chapter 21). From there, you learn how to use the Windows 2000 networking features (Chapter 22) and how to dial up your network from remote locations (Chapter 23).

Features for a Fun and Fulfilling Read

In a book such as this, I believe that it's not only important *what* you say, but also *how* you say it. So, I've gone to great lengths to present the info in easy-to-digest tidbits that can be absorbed quickly. I've also liberally sprinkled the book with features that I hope will make it easier for you to understand what's going in. Here's a rundown:

➤ Stuff that you have to type will appear in a `monospaced font`, like that.

➤ Menus, commands, and dialog box controls that you have to select, as well as keys you have to press, appear in a **bold font**.

➤ Whenever I tell you to select a menu command, I'll separate the various menu and command names with commas. For example, instead of saying: "Click the Start button, then click Programs, and then click Windows Explorer," I'll just say this: "Select Start, Programs, Windows Explorer."

➤ Many Windows 2000 commands have equivalent keyboard shortcuts, and most of them involve holding down one key while you press another key. For example, in most Windows programs, you save your work by holding down the **Ctrl** key, pressing the **S** key, and then releasing **Ctrl**. I'm *way* too lazy to write all that out each time, so I'll just plop a plus sign (+) between the two keys, like so: **Ctrl+S**.

 As you'll see in Chapter 1, there's a lot that's new and improved in Windows 2000. To help you find the new stuff, I use this special "New to 2000" icon in the margin.

I've also populated each chapter with several different kinds of sidebars:

Check This Out

These asides give you extra information about the topic at hand, provide you with tips for making things work easier, and generally just make you a more well-rounded Windows 2000 user.

Techno Talk

These boxes provide you with technical explanations, definitions, and know-how related to the current topic. Skipping this stuff will in no way diminish your life because all of it is readily ignorable. However, you might find some useful tidbits to toss off casually at the water cooler and impress your colleagues.

Caution

These notes warn you about possible Windows 2000 pitfalls and tell you how to avoid them.

Cross Reference

Each of these elements points you to another section of the book that contains related material. For example, to learn more about cross-references, see "Features for a Fun and Fulfilling Read," p. 3.

Finally, I close each chapter with a "Crib Sheet" section that runs through a list of several techniques and tips that you learned in the chapter.

Part 1

Why 2K: An Introduction to Windows 2000

Before exercising (stop laughing!), fitness experts recommend that you spend a few minutes stretching and loosening up your muscles to prepare for the effort to come. This book exercises your brain (you did know that, right?), so it's only proper that you do a bit of a warmup before getting your neurons in full workout mode. The two chapters in Part 1 serve to do just that. Chapter 1, "New News Is Good News: New Windows 2000 Features," is designed for people who have used some flavor of Windows in the past (or who are still deciding whether to take the Windows 2000 plunge) and who want to learn about the new Windows 2000 stuff they'll be tripping over. If you've never used Windows before, then you'll get good use out of Chapter 2, "A Field Guide to Windows 2000 for the Uninitiated." Okay, lift those legs...

Chapter 1

New News Is Good News: New Windows 2000 Features

In This Chapter

➤ Changes to the Windows 2000 interface

➤ New Windows 2000 programs and tools

➤ A look at what's new with Windows 2000 and the Internet

➤ The brave new world of Windows 2000's notebook computer features

➤ Windows 2000 finally gets with the hardware program

➤ A review of the new networking stuff in Windows 2000

➤ A sneak preview of the new Windows 2000 attractions

To those of us who monitor the wheeling and dealing of the computer industry on a daily basis, the release of Windows 2000 was a relief, indeed. For the past few *years*, we've had to run the gauntlet of Microsoft's greatest-thing-since-sliced-bread hype, and the doom and gloom of pundits who viewed each new Windows 2000 delay (and there were plenty of them) as a bad omen that would bring down the entire infrastructure of North American commerce.

Fortunately, the rest of the world carried on computing, blissfully unaware of this long-winded struggle for "mindshare." If they heard anything at all about Windows 2000, they just shrugged and said, "Sounds great. Lemme know when it ships."

Now that Windows 2000 *has* shipped, you might be wondering what all the fuss was about. This chapter will help as it describes some of the many new and noteworthy features that Windows 2000 brings to your desktop. You'll be happy to know that I completely ignore all the high-end features that would warm the cockles of those hearts found only in system administrators, IT jocks, and other geeks. Instead, my focus here (as it is in the entire book) is on those features that are helpful and useful for normal people who just want to get their job done. This will be, by necessity, only a brief overview of these features. Happily, everything I discuss here is explained in more detail elsewhere in the book.

If you're just starting out with Windows, then *everything* in Windows 2000 will seem new to you. You can still read this chapter to get some idea of what to expect. However, you might find that your time is better spent poring over Chapter 2, "A Field Guide to Windows 2000 for the Uninitiated."

The "Look-and-Feel" Looks and Feels a Bit Different

When you fire up your machine for the first time after Windows 2000 has been foisted upon it, you'll notice a few differences right away (see the following figure):

➤ The most obvious change is the desktop, where the old teal motif has been painted over with a rather nice slate blue.

➤ The desktop's icon collection has changed, as well. There are several brand-new icons (such as My Documents and My Network Places) and old icons such as My Computer and Recycle Bin have a fancier look.

➤ The taskbar has been invaded by a new Quick Launch toolbar at the right of the Start button. These icons give you one-click access to some Windows 2000 features. See Chapter 2 for the details.

Cross Reference

To learn more about the Quick Launch toolbar, see "Taking a Look Around," p. 18.

Other look-and-feel tweaks become evident after you start messing around a bit. For example, on most systems, you'll notice that menus and ToolTips (the little yellow banners that appear when you hover the mouse over icons and toolbar buttons) fade in and out, and the underlined letters in menu names and commands don't appear until you press Alt. Here's a list of a few other changes you'll be tripping over:

➤ **Personalized menus** After you've used Windows 2000 for a while (usually a few days), the various Start menus will suddenly shrink to the point where they show only those commands that you've used so far. Chapter 16, "Revamping the Start Menu and Taskbar," has the details.

➤ **Easier Start menu customizing** Rearranging the Start menu is a great way to improve your productivity. Windows 2000 helps by making it possible to customize most Start items directly, and by offering a large number of new customization settings. I talk about all this in Chapter 16.

➤ **Web integration**   This new feature brings some elements of the World Wide Web to Windows 2000. For example, folders are displayed as though they were Web pages, you can set things up so that you can launch icons and files just by single-clicking them, and more. The nitty-gritty on this can be found in Chapter 3, "Using My Computer to Work with Files and Folders."

➤ **The Active Desktop**   This is another feature of Web integration. It enables you to view your desktop as a Web page and to add "active" items such as a stock ticker or clock to the desktop. Chapter 15, "Redoing the Desktop," tells you all about it.

First looks: Windows 2000 sports a slightly different desktop.

Quick Launch toolbar

My Computer is your Windows 2000 tool-of-choice for fooling around with files and folders. To help out with those chores, My Computer comes with some useful new features:

➤ **My Computer's toolbars**   My Computer gives you a choice of toolbars to display. Also, the main toolbar is now fully customizable, as shown in the following figure. Chapter 17, "Making My Computer Your Own," has the details.

➤ **My Computer's Explorer bars**   My Computer comes with several panels that appear on the left side of the window and give you access to more features. For example, the Folders bar displays a tree-like list of the drives and folders on your computer. Again, head for Chapter 17.

➤ **Easier file searching**   One of those Explorer bars is called *Search* and it offers an easier file and folder searching experience. I show you how it works in Chapter 3.

*You use this dialog
box to customize My
Computer's main toolbar.*

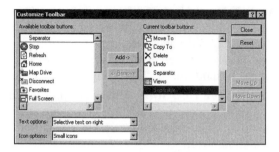

➤ **Viewing image thumbnails**   If you have some folders that have tons of images, you'll love My Computer's new Thumbnails view. Instead of displaying just the filename, it shows you an actual preview of the image, as shown in the following figure. Turn to Chapter 17 to find out more.

*The new Thumbnail view
shows previews of each
graphics file.*

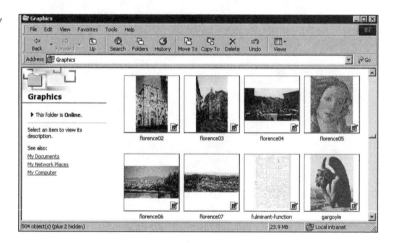

Cross Reference

Read more about thumbnail viewing in "Views You Can Use: Changing How Folders and Files Are Displayed," p. 264.

➤ **Easier file copying and moving**   Although you can still use the standard cut-and-paste or drag-and-drop methods to copy and move files, Windows 2000 offers new Copy to Folder and Move to Folder commands that I think are a bit more straightforward for new users. I talk about them in Chapter 3.

On the multimedia front, Windows 2000 offers three new and/or improved programs for playing files:

➤ **Media Player**   This is an all-purpose player that can handle regular sound files, MIDI files, movies, and more. I show you how to use it in Chapter 8, "The Sights and Sounds of Windows 2000 Multimedia."

➤ **CD Player**   Windows 2000's CD Player is a big improvement over the one in Windows NT 4.0 (see the following figure). For example, it enables you to download a CD's track information from the Internet. You learn how to work it in Chapter 8.

Windows 2000's improved CD Player.

➤ **DVD Player**   Windows 2000 supports DVD, and it offers the DVD Player so you can watch DVD movies on your machine. Again, Chapter 8 is where you learn all about it.

Windows 2000 also boasts a long list of new and improved programs for communications and system maintenance:

➤ **Fax service**   Faxing is now built right into Windows 2000, so you can easily use your modem to send and receive faxes, as described in Chapter 10, "Using Your Modem for Faxing and Phone Dialing."

➤ **Phone Dialer**   Windows 2000's version of Phone Dialer is more polished and feature-rich than the one in Windows NT 4.0. I talk about it in Chapter 10.

➤ **Backup**   The new Backup program has wizards to take you through backup and restore procedures, it can back up to disk drives and network folders (not just tape drives), and it offers a number of other small improvements. The place to be for this is Chapter 19, "Backing Up Your Data (The Better-Safe-Than-Sorry Department)."

➤ **Disk Cleanup**   This new program enables you to rid your system of unnecessary files (see the next figure). I show you how to run it in Chapter 20, "Painless System Maintenance Chores."

Cross Reference

To play your DVD movie now, see "Using DVD Player to Play DVD Movies," p. 120.

Cross Reference

If you're ready to read about phone dialer, see "Stop the Presses! Modem Dials Phone!," p. 150.

➤ **Check Disk**   This program delves deeply into your hard disk's innards to look for problems. It's an important tool and it's covered in Chapter 20.

➤ **Disk Defragmenter**   Over time, your hard disk slows down because the files get all chopped up. To beat this *fragmentation*, as it's called, use the new Disk Defragmenter program, as shown in Chapter 20.

Use the new Disk Cleanup program to trash unnecessary files from your hard disk.

Cross Reference

Disk cleanup is discussed in "Cleaning House: Using Disk Cleanup to Delete Junk Files," p. 306.

➤ **Task Scheduler**   You use this handy tool to set up programs to run at a certain time or on a certain schedule (such as once a week). Once again, Chapter 20 is the place to go for more on this.

➤ **Windows Update**   This is a new Web site that enables you to download Windows 2000 components that have been fixed, updated, or added. It should come as no surprise by now that you can turn to Chapter 20 to find out more.

The Internet Is Closer Than Ever

The Internet has been a Big Deal for a while now, and Windows 2000 reflects that because all of its Internet tools are "mature" (that is, they've been through a number of versions) and most experts rank these tools among the best in the business. Here's a summary of what to expect:

➤ **Internet Connection Wizard**   This wizard takes you step-by-step through the often tricky process of connecting your computer to the Internet. I show you how it works in Chapter 11, "Getting on the Internet."

➤ **Internet Explorer 5**   This version of Microsoft's World Wide Web browser is faster and has lots of little improvements (better searching, easier Favorites, and so on). I take you through all the new features (and plenty of the old ones, too) in Chapter 12, "Weaving Your Way Through the World Wide Web."

➤ **Outlook Express 5** This is Windows 2000's Internet email program. Among many other improvements, it offers easier methods for handling multiple accounts, blocking and filtering messages, and working with stationery and signatures. See Chapter 13, "Everybody's Doing It: Sending and Receiving Email Messages." Outlook Express is also used for Internet newsgroups, as described in Chapter 14, "More Online Conversations: Newsgroups and Internet Phone Calls."

Cross Reference

To learn about Windows Update, see "Keeping Up with the Windows Joneses: The Windows Update Web Site," p. 317.

➤ **NetMeeting** You use this program to set up Net-based "phone calls" where you communicate with other users through your sound card and a microphone. I describe this and other NetMeeting talents in Chapter 14.

Windows 2000 Gets Along with Notebook Computers (Finally!)

The knock on Windows NT was that it wouldn't know a notebook computer if it tripped over one. Aside from the weird image of an operating system with legs, this was a valid charge. Happily, Windows 2000 refutes that charge in the best way possible: by recognizing that notebooks aren't just luggable desktop machines and that they have special requirements and need special tools. Here's a rundown of just some of the notebook support that comes built into Windows 2000:

➤ **Power management** Most notebooks usually end up on batteries at some point, and Windows 2000's new power management features enable you to monitor the battery status and to manage the power used by some components (such as the hard disk; see the following figure). You'll find out more about this in Chapter 6, "A Movable Feast: Windows 2000 and Your Notebook Computer."

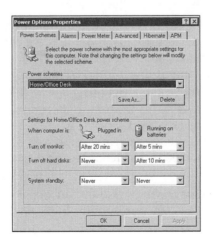

Windows 2000 now has some welcome power-management features.

➤ **Synchronization and the Briefcase**   If you need to move files between a desktop computer and a notebook, Windows 2000's new Briefcase feature makes it easy to keep everything synchronized. Chapter 6 fills you in on the details.

➤ **PC Card support**   The only way to upgrade most notebooks is by inserting those credit card–sized devices called *PC Cards* (formerly known as PCMCIA cards). Windows 2000 now recognizes PC Card sockets and lets you insert and remove the cards while the computer is still running. There are some caveats to this, however, so see Chapter 6.

➤ **Exchanging files along a cable**   You can string a special cable between a notebook and a desktop machine (or whatever) and exchange files along the cable instead of using a floppy disk. Again, pop over to Chapter 6 to see how this works.

New and Improved Hardware Support

Previous versions of Windows 2000 (when it went under the guise of Windows NT) didn't have the greatest of relationships with the hardware side of things. Oh, sure, there was a long list of hardware devices supported by Windows NT, but you were usually left to your own devices (sorry!) when it came to installing them. And if you tried to install some hardware gewgaw that wasn't on the "approved" list? Hah! There was a fool's errand is there ever was one.

Cross Reference

The Add/Remove Hardware Wizard is discussed in "Running the Add/Remove Hardware Wizard," p. 281.

So, when Microsoft announced that Windows 2000 would offer improved and easier hardware support, it was met with unconcealed glee in the NT community. Yes, there's still a list of approved devices that must be consulted before purchasing any hardware, but Windows 2000 does a much better job of recognizing and managing that hardware. Let's take a look at some of the new device support in Windows 2000:

➤ **Plug and Play**   This is the really big news on the hardware front. Plug and Play means that, given the right devices (that is, those that are Plug-and-Play–compatible), Windows 2000 automatically sniffs out any new device in the system and configures it for use without much intervention on your part. I talk about this in greater depth in Chapter 18, "Installing Software and Hardware."

➤ **Add/Remove Hardware Wizard**   This wizard can detect new hardware and install the necessary software to make it work (see the next figure). And just in case your hardware proves elusive, the wizard can also present you with a list of the devices with which Windows 2000 is on friendly terms. Check out Chapter 18 to see how it works.

➤ **Support for new mouse species**   Windows 2000 can work with those mice that have the extra wheel in between the two buttons. I talk about this briefly in

Chapter 2. Windows 2000 is also conversant with Microsoft's new "explorer" mouse that features a few extra buttons.

➤ **Disk drives galore** Windows 2000 goes beyond the run-of-the-mill disk drive types—floppy drives, hard drives, and CD-ROM drives—and provides support for many next-generation drives, including zip drives, JAZ drives, and DVD-ROM drives.

➤ **Support for image scanners and digital cameras** The prices of image scanners and digital cameras have come down quite a bit, so lots of people have one or the other. So it's good news that Windows 2000 now supports these types of devices.

Cross Reference

To learn about acquiring digital images, see "Being Digital: Using Scanners and Digital Cameras," p. 108.

Shiny, New Networking Features

Most Windows NT computers were latched onto some kind of network, so the Microsoft programmers spent quite a bit of time tweaking and adding new networking features for Windows 2000. In fact, most of the prelaunch Windows 2000 hoopla focused on the many highfalutin networking treats that were soldered onto the Windows 2000 frame. However, things such as "Active Directory" and "roaming profiles" apply only to big-time networks, so they're beyond what this book is about. Even so, there are still tons of new network goodies for you to play with:

➤ **The Network and Dial-Up Connections window** This new window acts like a one-stop networking shop. It contains icons for your local network connection, your remote network connection, and any Internet connections you've set up.

➤ **Easier remote connections** Windows 2000 makes it easier than ever to connect to your network from remote locales. You can even set up a plain Windows 2000 machine to accept incoming connections. And thanks to the ministrations of the Network Connection Wizard, setting up all this requires only a few steps. See Chapter 23, "Road Scholar: Using Dial-Up Network Connections."

➤ **A new way to get to your workgroup** The new Computers Near Me folder offers a straightforward route to the other computers in your workgroup. Find out more in Chapter 22, "Using Windows 2000's Networking Features."

➤ **Network places** These are icons that represent shared resources from other computers on your network. They're handy because they let you access resources without having to wade through endless network folders. Once again, see Chapter 22.

Cross Reference

For information on offline files, see "You *Can* Take It with You: Working with Offline Files," p. 354.

15

➤ **Offline files**   These are local copies of network files that you can work with while not connected to the network. Windows 2000 complements this with a new "synchronization" feature that helps you keep the local copies and the network originals in sync. Chapter 22 has the specifics.

➤ **Sharing an Internet connection**   This is one of the most useful of Windows 2000's new networking features. It enables you to set up an Internet connection on one workgroup machine, and then let the other machines in the workgroup share that connection. Yup, Chapter 22 has the details.

What Happened

This chapter gave you the lowdown on the new Windows 2000 features that I discuss in this book. I gave you a preview of those features in five categories: the interface, the Internet, notebook computers, hardware support, and networking.

A Field Guide to Windows 2000 for the Uninitiated

In This Chapter

➤ A 50-cent tour of Windows 2000

➤ Some common mouse maneuvers you need to know

➤ Understanding the windows that give Windows 2000 its name

➤ How to launch programs and use their menus and toolbars

➤ Mundane yet oh-so-vital document chores

➤ How to shut down Windows 2000 safely

➤ A guide to some of Windows 2000's native flora and fauna

If this is your first foray into the world of Windows, the territory will no doubt seem a bit strange, even downright alien. (That's a perfectly normal reaction, and it proves you have the requisite amount of sanity to get through all this stuff.) Before lighting out for parts unknown, you should take a few moments to get your bearings and learn some of the pathways you'll be traversing and some of the landmarks you'll pass along the way.

To that end, this chapter will serve as your guide to the surrounding Windows 2000 area. I'll point out some of the features, take you down a few trails, and offer up lots of tips for surviving in the Windows wilderness.

Taking a Look Around

When you slam the power switch on your computer, Windows 2000 will start pulling itself up by its own bootstraps. The entire sequence takes a few minutes, so this is a bad time to be holding your breath in anticipation.

Booting Your Computer

This bootstrap metaphor is actually a pretty good way to describe the whole process of Windows starting itself up, and it's the source of the verb *to boot*, which means "to start a computer."

If you use Windows 2000 at work, there's a good chance your computer will be joined at the hip (electronically speaking, of course) with a bunch of other computers as part of a *network*. If that's the case, it's likely that you'll eventually see a box telling you to press **Ctrl+Alt+Delete** to begin. What this means is that you hold down both the **Ctrl** key and the **Alt** key, tap the **Delete** key, and then release Ctrl and Alt. Type in your network password (your network administrator should have told you what it is) and then press **Enter**.

After another few seconds, Windows 2000 finally gets its act together and is ready to roll. You might see yet another box on your screen, this one titled "Getting Started with Windows 2000." You don't have to deal with this now, so press **E** to get rid of it.

Getting Rid of Getting Started

The "Getting Started with Windows 2000" box shows up each and every time you start your computer. If you find this annoying, you can tell Windows 2000 to cut it out. The next time the box appears, use your mouse to click the **Show This Screen at Startup** text in the lower-left corner (or you can press **S**) to get rid of the check mark.

With the "Getting Started with Windows 2000" box out of the way, you get your first full view of the Windows 2000 screen. There's not a whole lot to see, is there? That's a good thing because it means Windows 2000 is smart enough not to overwhelm you right off the bat (that Ctrl+Alt+Delete weirdness notwithstanding). However, the screen isn't completely empty. The next figure points out a few of the highlights.

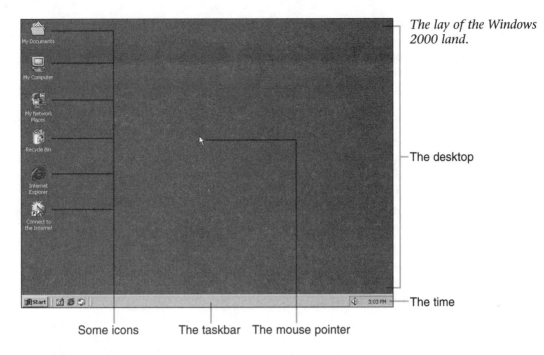

The lay of the Windows 2000 land.

The desktop

The time

Some icons   The taskbar   The mouse pointer

Most of the screen is covered in a soothing sea of blue. This not-quite-barren expanse is the Windows 2000 *desktop*.

Why the Heck Do They Call It Desktop?

That's just Microsoft indulging in a bit of metaphorical license. The idea is that just as you pull out real documents and work with them on the top of a real desk, in Windows you "pull out" electronic documents and work with them on the desktop.

The most intriguing elements of the desktop are those cute little pictures over on the left. In Windowspeak, these are called *icons* and they represent Windows 2000 features. I'll be talking about each of these icons in other parts of the book, but here's a quick summary of each one's place in the Windows 2000 universe:

19

➤ **My Documents**   This icon represents a portion of your computer's hard disk that you can use to store the documents you create. I'll talk about documents in a bit more detail later in this chapter. Also, you'll learn more about storing documents in Chapter 3, "Using My Computer to Work with Files and Folders."

➤ **My Computer**   This icon represents the program that you use to work with all the files that are stored on your computer. Chapter 3 is the place to go to get all the details.

➤ **My Network Places**   You use this icon to access your network, although it appears even if your computer isn't plugged in to a network. Go figure. Connect to Chapter 22, "Using Windows 2000's Networking Features," and Chapter 23, "Road Scholar: Using Dial-Up Network Connections," for the networking nitty-gritty.

➤ **Recycle Bin**   This icon represents the section of your computer where things end up after you delete them. Check out Chapter 3 to learn more.

➤ **Internet Explorer**   This icon represents the Internet Explorer program, which you use to get around on the Internet's World Wide Web. I will show you how it works in Chapter 12, "Weaving Your Way Through the World Wide Web."

➤ **Connect to the Internet**   Before you can use Internet Explorer, you have to get hooked up to the Internet, of course. That's the job of this icon, as you'll see in Chapter 11, "Getting on the Internet."

The final element to consider is the gray strip that spans the bottom of the screen. This is called the *taskbar*, and it sports the following three chunks (as shown in the next figure):

The taskbar is home to several key Windows 2000 features.

Start button   Quick Launch icons   System tray

➤ **Start button**   This harmless-looking rectangle might well be the most important feature of the Windows 2000 screen. That's because, with the exception of the icons on the desktop, the Quick Launch icons (discussed next), and the system tray icons (discussed afterward), you use the Start menu to access just about everything in Windows 2000. See "Starting Programs," later in this chapter, to see how it works.

➤ **Quick Launch icons**   Like their desktop cousins, these icons also represent Windows 2000 features:

This is the Show Desktop icon, and it clears everything off the desktop. (See "What It's All About: Windows 2000's Windows," later in this chapter.)

This is the Launch Internet Explorer Browser icon, and it offers yet another way to start up Internet Explorer.

This is the Launch Outlook Express icon, and it starts up Outlook Express, which is Windows 2000's Internet email program. (See Chapter 13, "Everybody's Doing It: Sending and Receiving Email Messages.")

➤ **System tray**   Windows 2000 populates this area with even more icons. In this case, these icons tell you a bit about what's happening with your machine. For example, the icon that looks like a small speaker shows up if your computer has sound capabilities. This area also shows the time.

Displaying the Date

The system tray's clock can also show you the date. To try it, move your mouse pointer until it sits over the time. After a second or two, the date miraculously appears. If you ever need to change the time or date, double-click the time.

A Quick Mouse Course

If you're unfamiliar with Windows, then there's a good chance that you're also unfamiliar with the mouse, the electromechanical mammal attached to your machine. If so, this section presents a quick look at a few mouse moves, which is important because much of what you do in Windows will involve the mouse in some way.

For starters, be sure the mouse is sitting on its pad with the cord facing away from you. Rest your hand lightly on the mouse with your index finger on (but not pressing down) the left button and your middle finger on the right button (or the rightmost button). Southpaws will need to reverse the fingering.

Earlier in this chapter, I showed you a picture of the Windows 2000 screen that included the *mouse pointer*. Find the pointer on your screen and then slowly move the mouse on its pad. As you do this, you'll notice that the pointer moves in the same direction (although it will stop dead in its tracks when it hits the edge of the screen). Take a few minutes to practice moving the pointer to and fro using slow, easy movements.

To new users, the mouse seems an unnatural device that confounds common sense and often reduces the strongest among us to tears of frustration. The secret to mastering the mouse is twofold. First, use the same advice as was given to the person who wanted to get to Carnegie Hall: Practice, practice, practice. Fortunately, with Windows 2000 being so mouse-dependent, you'll get plenty of chances to perfect your skills.

Second, understand all the basic mouse moves that are required of the modern-day mouse user. There are a half-dozen in all:

➤ **Point**   This means that you move the mouse pointer so that it's positioned over some specified part of the screen. For example, "point at the Start button" means that you move the mouse pointer over the taskbar's Start button.

Slow and Steady Wins the Race

All this emphasis on slow and deliberate mouse movements isn't accidental and, in fact, should be the hallmark of *everything* you do with your computer. There's an old saw that says, "Never let a computer know you're in a hurry." That's good advice because, otherwise, some twisted new variant on Murphy's Law inevitably comes into play to ruin your day.

➤ **Click**   This means that you press and immediately release the left mouse button to initiate some kind of action. Need a fer instance? Okay, point at the Start button and then click it. Instantly, a menu sprouts up in response to the click. (This is Windows 2000's Start menu. See "Getting Programs off the Ground," later in this chapter, for more on this all-important feature. For now, you can get rid of the menu by clicking an empty section of the desktop.)

➤ **Double-click**   This means that you press and release the left mouse button *twice*, one press right after the other (there should be little or no delay between each press). To give it a whirl, point at the time in the lower-right corner and then double-click. If all goes well, Windows 2000 will toss a box titled Date/Time Properties onto the desktop. You use this box to change the current date and time (see "Using Dialog Boxes," later in this chapter). To return this box from whence it came, click the button labeled **Cancel**. If nothing happens when you double-click, try to click as quickly as you can, and try not to move the mouse while you're clicking.

➤ **Right-click**   This means that you press and immediately release the *right* mouse button. In Windows 2000, the right-click is used almost exclusively to display a creature called the *shortcut menu*. To see one, right-click an empty part of the desktop. Windows 2000 displays a menu with a few common commands related to the desktop. To remove this menu, *left*-click the desktop.

➤ **Drag**   This means that you point at some object, press and *hold down* the left mouse button, move the mouse, and then release the button. You almost always use this technique to move an object from one place to another. For example, try dragging any of the desktop icons. (To restore apple-pie order to the desktop, right-click the desktop, click **Arrange Icons**, and then click **By Name**.)

➤ **Scroll**　This means that you turn the little wheel that's nestled in between the left and right mouse buttons. (The wheel is a relatively new innovation, so your mouse might not have one.) In programs that support scrolling, you use this technique to move up and down within a document.

Click Confusion

Okay, so clicking initiates some kind of action, but so does double-clicking. What's the diff?

The whole single-click versus double-click conundrum is one of Windows' most confusing and criticized traits, and I'm afraid there's no easy answer. Some things require just a click to get going, while other things require a double-click. With experience, you'll eventually come to know which clicking technique is needed. Note, however, that Windows 2000 has a feature that can eliminate most double-clicking. In Chapter 3, see the section titled "How Web Integration Changes My Computer."

Making Things Happen

You (or your company) didn't fork out the big bucks to buy a computer just so you could stare at the desktop all day. To get the most out of that investment, you've got to make things happen, which means launching programs and then working with the program's features. This section takes you through all the basics.

Getting Programs off the Ground

I mentioned earlier that the Start button was one of Windows 2000's most important features. That's because you use it to *start* (hence the name) the programs that are installed on your computer. (It's also used to start a few Windows 2000 features.)

Go ahead and click the **Start** button. In response, Windows 2000 displays the Start menu. Each of the menu items you see represents some kind of program or Windows 2000 feature. From here, click the menu item you want. One of two things will happen at this point:

➤ If the item represents a program or Windows 2000 command, the program or command launches.

➤ If the item represents a submenu, another menu appears with a new set of items. The items that have right-pointing arrows are the ones that will toss submenus at you.

To make this more concrete, here's a sample procedure to follow that opens WordPad, Windows 2000's word processor:

1. Click the **Start** button to unfurl the Start menu. (You can also get the Start menu to show up by pressing **Ctrl+Esc** or by pressing the Windows logo key that's available on most modern keyboards.)

2. Click **Programs** to open the submenu.

3. Click **Accessories** to open yet another submenu.

4. Click **WordPad** to launch the program.

In the future, I'll abbreviate the instructions for launching a program by using a comma (,) to separate each thing you click, like so: **Start**, **Programs**, **Accessories**, **WordPad**.

No-Click Menus

You don't have to click those Start menu items that display submenus. Instead, just point the mouse at the item and, after a second or two, the submenu will show up.

The Multitasking Thing: Switching from One Program to Another

In the digital equivalent of walking and chewing gum at the same time, Windows 2000 is coordinated enough to handle having a couple of programs (or more) running at once. You might not need to do this all that often, but it's nice to know that it's possible. In higher geek circles, this capability is called *multitasking*.

If you do have multiple programs on the go, you need to know how to switch from one to the other. The most straightforward method involves the taskbar. As you can see in the following figure, I have both WordPad and Calculator up and running (for the latter, select **Start**, **Programs**, **Accessories**, **Calculator**). Notice how each running program gets its own button displayed on the taskbar. The active program (that is, the program you're currently working in—Calculator in the figure) has a "pressed" button whereas all the other buttons appear normal.

Personalized Menus

After you've used Windows 2000 for a while, it will change the menus so that programs and features you haven't used are hidden from view. To get to those hidden items, click the downward-pointing double arrow at the bottom of most menus.

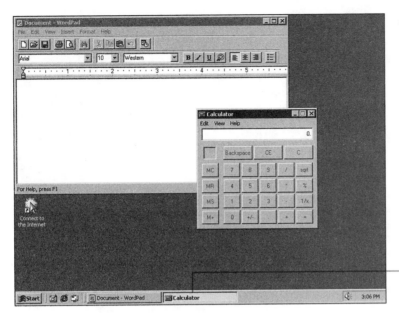

Each running program boasts its own button in the taskbar.

The active program has a pressed button.

To switch to another program, click its taskbar button. For example, the following figure shows what happens when I click the WordPad button. As you can see, the WordPad window is now "on top" of the Calculator window, and WordPad's taskbar button now appears pressed.

Here are a few other methods that Windows 2000 offers for switching programs:

➤ **Click inside the program's window.** Use this method if you can see a piece of the other program's window. Note, however, that you should try to avoid clicking things that are "live," such as menus and toolbar buttons (explained in the next two sections).

➤ **Hold down the Alt key and tap the Tab key.** This method displays a small window that contains icons for all your running programs. Each time you press Tab, a different icon is highlighted. When the icon for the program you want is highlighted, release **Alt** and Windows 2000 will switch to that program.

➤ **Hold down the Alt key and tap the Esc key.** With this method, each time you press **Esc**, Windows 2000 displays the window of the next running program. When you get to the one you want, release **Alt**.

> **Check This Out**
>
> ## Switching Between Running Programs
>
> If you're the type who likes to use the keyboard, listen up. Pressing **Alt+Tab** will switch between running tasks, too.

Click the taskbar buttons to switch between running programs.

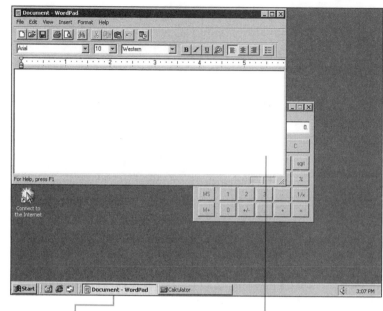

Clicking WordPad's button... ...brings the WordPad window to the front.

Pushing Around a Program I: Using Drop-Down Menus

After you have a program running, you'll need to access its commands and features, most of which are available via the program's *drop-down menus*. To see how they work, open My Computer by double-clicking the desktop's **My Computer** icon. The drop-down menus are hidden inside the *menu bar*, which is the gray strip that runs across the window near the top. Each of the words in the menu bar—such as File, Edit, and View in My Computer—represents a drop-down menu. To open a menu, you have two choices:

➤ Click the menu name.

➤ Press and hold down **Alt**, and you'll see one underlined letter in each menu name. With **Alt** still held down, press the underlined letter on your keyboard, and then release **Alt**. For example, you can pull down My Computer's View menu by pressing **Alt+V**.

The following figure shows My Computer with the View menu pulled down.

From here, click the menu command that you want to run. (Throughout the rest of this book, I'll use a comma to separate menu names and menu commands. For example, if I want you to yank down the View menu and run the Refresh command, I'll say "select **View**, **Refresh**.") When you select a command, one of the following things will happen:

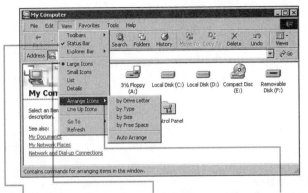

*Click **View** in the menu bar to pull down My Computer's View menu.*

The check mark lets you know this feature is on.

The option mark lets you know which feature in this group is activated.

The arrow means this command displays a submenu.

➤ **The command runs.** In this case, the command carries out its duties without any muss or fuss. For example, selecting **View**, **Refresh** updates the My Computer window.

➤ **A dialog box shows up.** If the command needs more input from you, it will display a dialog box. (Commands that have an ellipsis (...) after their names always display a dialog box.) See "Pushing Around a Program III: Using Dialog Boxes," later in this chapter.

➤ **A submenu slides into view.** In this case, you click on the command you want from the submenu. Commands that have a right-pointing arrow (such as Toolbars and Explorer Bar in My Computer's View menu) always display a submenu.

➤ **A feature is activated or deactivated.** Some commands toggle program features on and off. When the feature is on, a check mark appears beside the menu command; when the feature is off, the check mark doesn't appear. See, for example, the Status Bar command in the previous figure.

➤ **An option within a group of related options is activated.** If the program has a feature with three or more possible options, they'll often appear together as a group on the menu. In My Computer's View menu, for example, the following commands form a group: Large Icons, Small Icons, List, and Details. Only one of these options can be activated at a time, and an option mark tells you which one is currently activated.

Pushing Around a Program II: Using Toolbars

Most programs come with a toolbar (or two or three) located just below the menu bar. The toolbar consists of various buttons that give you (usually) one-click access to common program features. Here are a few things to bear in mind when working with toolbars:

➤ **Toolbar text**   Most toolbar buttons advertise what they do using nothing more than an icon. Rather than trying to decipher the icon, some toolbars let you display text that at least gives you the name of each button. In My Computer, for example, select **View**, **Toolbars**, **Customize** to display the Customize Toolbar dialog box, select **Show Text Labels** in the **Text Options** list, and then click **Close**.

➤ **Button banners**   If the toolbar doesn't offer text labels, you can still find out the name of a particular button by pointing at it with your mouse. After a second or two, a banner (sometimes called a *ToolTip*) with the button name pops up.

➤ **Hiding and showing toolbars**   In most programs, you toggle a toolbar on and off by selecting the **View**, **Toolbar** command. If a program offers multiple toolbars (as does My Computer), select the **View**, **Toolbars** command to display a submenu of the available toolbars, and then select the one you want.

➤ **Drop-down buttons**   You'll occasionally come across toolbar buttons that are really drop-down menu wannabes. For example, see the View "button" shown in the next figure. Click the downward-pointing arrow to see a list of commands.

Some toolbar buttons act like drop-down menus.

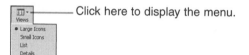 —— Click here to display the menu.

Pushing Around a Program III: Using Dialog Boxes

Dialog boxes are a fact of life in Windows 2000, so it's important to know how they work. This section examines the full variety of dialog box doodads (they're called *controls* by those in-the-know) and explains how they work.

The WordPad program offers a variety of dialog boxes, so I'll use it for most of the examples in this section. If you're following along, begin by selecting WordPad's **View**, **Options** command to have the Options dialog box report for duty, as shown here.

I'll use WordPad's Options dialog box for the first example.

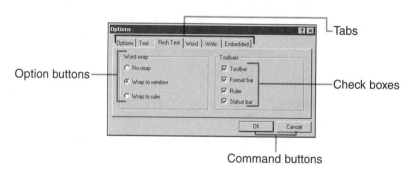

28

Okay, let's get started:

➤ **Command buttons**   Clicking one of these buttons executes whatever command is written on the button. The three examples of the species shown in the Options dialog box are the most common. Click **OK** to close the dialog box and put the settings into effect; click **Cancel** to close the dialog box without putting the settings into effect; click **Help** to open the program's Help system.

➤ **Check boxes**   Windows uses a check box to toggle program features on and off. Clicking the check box either adds a check mark (meaning the feature will get turned on when you click **OK**) or removes the check mark (meaning the feature gets turned off when you click **OK**).

➤ **Option buttons**   If a program feature offers three or more states, the dialog box will offer an option button for each state, and only one button can be activated (that is, have a black dot inside its circle) at a time. You activate an option button by clicking it.

➤ **Tabs**   Click any of the tabs displayed across the top of some dialog boxes and you'll see a new set of controls. (You don't need the Options dialog box anymore, so click **Cancel**.)

➤ **Text boxes**   You use these controls to type text data. To see some examples, select WordPad's **Format**, **Paragraph** command to get to the Paragraph dialog box, shown next. The **Left**, **Right**, and **First line** controls are all text boxes. (The Paragraph dialog box has served its purpose, so click **Cancel**.)

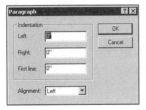

Some sample text boxes.

➤ **List boxes**   These controls display a list of items and you select an item by clicking it. An example can be seen if you select WordPad's **Insert**, **Date and Time** command, shown in the following figure. (After you've played around a bit, click **Cancel** to close this dialog box.)

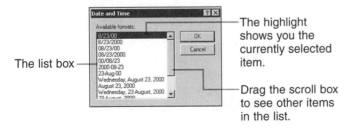

The list box ⟶

⟶ The highlight shows you the currently selected item.

⟶ Drag the scroll box to see other items in the list.

As its name implies, a list box presents a list of choices.

➤ **Combo boxes**   These hybrid controls combine a list box and a text box. You can either select the item you want from the list or type it in the text box. In the next figure, WordPad's Font dialog box shows several examples (select **Format**, **Font**).

WordPad's Font dialog box offers several examples of both combo boxes and drop-down list boxes.

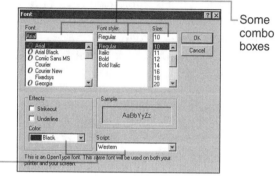

Some combo boxes

Some drop-down list boxes

➤ **Drop-down list boxes**   These controls represent yet another example of the list box genre. In this case, at first you see only one item. However, if you click the downward-pointing arrow on the right, the full list appears and it becomes much like a regular list box. (That's enough of the Font dialog box, so click **Cancel**.)

➤ **Spin boxes**   These controls enable you to cycle up or down through a series of numbers. To see an example, select WordPad's **File**, **Print** command to wake up the Print dialog box, shown next. The spin box is named **Number of Copies**. The left part of the spin box is a simple text box into which you can type a number; however, the right part of the spin box has an up and a down arrow. You click the up arrow to increase the value, and you click the down arrow to decrease the value. (When you're done, click **Cancel** to return the Print dialog box from whence it came.)

Click the spin box arrows to cycle up or down through a range of values.

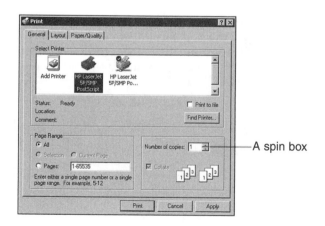

A spin box

Shutting Down a Program

Although Windows 2000 supports multitasking, that doesn't mean you should just fire up all your programs and leave them running all day. The more programs you have on the go, the slower each one will run because Windows 2000 has only a limited amount of resources to go around. So, if you no longer need a program, you should shut it down by using any of the following methods:

➤ Pull down the **File** menu and select the **Exit** (or sometimes **Close**) command.

➤ Click the **Close** button (the "×" in the upper-right corner; see the next figure) in the program's window.

➤ Press **Alt+F4**.

What It's All About: Windows 2000's Windows

When you launch a program, it shows up inside a *window* and everything you do with that program happens inside that window. Because Windows 2000 has the word "window" in its name, you might think that these window things will play a big role in everything you do with your computer, and you'd be right. Therefore, let's take a second to examine windows and run through a few techniques for controlling them.

You've been working with WordPad for a while, so let's try a different program for some variety. Notepad (select **Start**, **Programs**, **Accessories**, **Notepad**) is Windows 2000's text editor, and it presents a nice, simple window without any distractions (see the following figure).

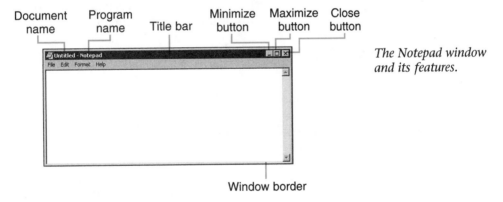

The Notepad window and its features.

The best way to learn what the various nuts and bolts do is to run through all the window techniques you'll use during the course of your Windows career:

➤ **Moving a window** If you have multiple windows open and one of them is in the way, try moving it. You do this by using your mouse to drag the window's title bar.

➤ **Sizing a window**   If you find that you don't have enough room to maneuver inside a window, you can increase its size. Similarly, if a large window is taking up more than its share of screen real estate, you can decrease its size. Either way, you size a window by using your mouse to drag any of the window's four borders. For example, you can make a window wider by dragging the right border to the right.

The Mouse Pointer for Sizing

When you move the mouse pointer over a window border, it changes into a two-headed arrow.

➤ **Minimizing a window**   If you'd rather not deal with an open window right now, but you don't want to close the program, the solution is to *minimize* the window. This means the window disappears from view temporarily. To try this, click the **Minimize** button in the upper-right corner. (Bonus tip: If you want to minimize all your open windows in one fell swoop, click the **Show Desktop** button in the Quick Launch section of the taskbar.) To get the window back onscreen, click its taskbar button.

➤ **Maximizing a window**   If you need to get the most elbow room possible in a window, you need to *maximize* it. This enlarges the window so that it covers the entire desktop (although the taskbar remains conveniently visible). To maximize a window, click the **Maximize** button in the upper-right corner. To return the window to its previous size, click the **Restore** button, which is what the Maximize button turns into (see the following figure).

When you maximize a window, the Maximize button gets replaced by the Restore button.

The Restore button

➤ **Scrolling inside a window**   If the window isn't big enough to hold all of its contents, you need some way to navigate through the document to see the rest of it. One way to do this is to use your keyboard navigation keys: the arrow keys, Page Up, and Page Down. Alternatively, you can use your mouse to control the window's *scrollbars*, as shown in the next figure. Here are the techniques you can use:

➤ To scroll up one line at a time, click the up scroll arrow. To scroll continuously, move the mouse pointer over the up scroll arrow and then press and hold down the left mouse button.

➤ To scroll down one line at a time, click the down scroll arrow. To scroll continuously, move the mouse pointer over the down scroll arrow and then press and hold down the left mouse button.

➤ To jump one screen at a time, click inside the scrollbar between the scroll box and the scroll arrows. For example, to scroll up one screen, click inside the scrollbar between the scroll box and the up scroll arrow.

➤ To scroll to a specific part of the document, drag the scroll box up or down.

➤ You'll rarely need to scroll right or left, but if you do, the application will offer a horizontal scrollbar along the bottom of the window. You use the same basic techniques.

Mouse Wheel Scrolling

If you have a mouse with a wheel, you can scroll up or down inside the window by turning the wheel forward or backward. In some programs, you can also click the wheel and then move the mouse forward and back to scroll up and down.

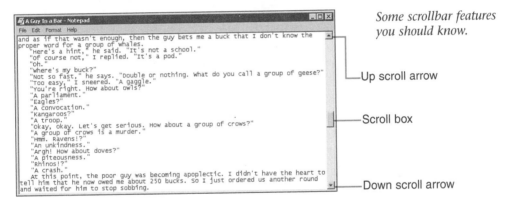

Some scrollbar features you should know.

Up scroll arrow

Scroll box

Down scroll arrow

Dealing with Documents

Fiddling with windows and dialog boxes is a necessary evil in the Windows way of doing things, but it's not what computing is all about. No, the real purpose of that beige beast on your desk is to *create* things: memos, letters, presentations, reports, email messages, Web pages, and so on. (Let it also be said that a second and equally important purpose of your digital domestic is to help you *do* things: play games, surf the Internet, research, and so on.) Anything you create on your computer can be described using the generic term *document*. This section provides a few basic pointers and techniques for working with documents in any program:

➤ **Creating a spanking new document** WordPad, Notepad, and most other Windows programs will display a fresh document automatically when you start the program. If you need another new document later on, select the program's **File**, **New** command (pressing **Ctrl+N** also works in most programs).

➤ **Saving your new document**   When you work on a document, your changes take place within your computer's memory. Unfortunately, the contents of memory are wiped out each time you shut down the machine, so if you're not careful, you could end up losing all your work. To prevent that, you need to save your new document to the safer confines of your computer's hard disk, the contents of which remain in place even when the computer is shut down for the night. To save the new document, select the **File**, **Save** command (the usual shortcut key is **Ctrl+S**). This displays the Save As dialog box, shown as follows. Click the **My Documents** icon, enter a name for the document in the **File Name** text box, and then click **Save**.

Use the Save As dialog box to save your new document.

➤ **Opening an existing document**   After you've saved some documents, you might need to work on one of them again down the road, so you need to open the document. To do this, open the program you used to create the document in the first place, and then select **File**, **Open** (**Ctrl+O** also works in most cases). Use the Open dialog box (which is almost identical to the Save As dialog box) to find your file, click the file to highlight it, and then click **Open**.

➤ **Saving an existing document**   You'll be happy to know that saving an existing document takes far less work than saving a new document. All you have to do is select the **File**, **Save** command (or press **Ctrl+S**).

➤ **Using "Save As" to make a copy of a document**   What do you do if you need to create a document that's similar to another document that you've already created? You could just start from scratch, but Windows 2000 gives you an easier way. It's called the *Save As command* and it enables you to make an exact copy of an existing document under a different name (or in a different location). To give it a go, open the original document and select **File**, **Save As**. Then use the Save As dialog box to pick out a new location or enter a new name (or both), and then click **Save**. When you return to the program, the cloned version of the file will be open and you can make changes at will.

These techniques cover the various actions you can take with the document as a whole, but what about working within the document itself? Here's a list of some common editing chores that you'll use day in and day out:

➤ **Highlighting text using the mouse**   If you want to format or delete a section of text, you first need to *highlight* it. To do this with a mouse, position the mouse pointer just to the left of the first character you want to highlight, and then drag the mouse over the rest of the characters. As you do this, the highlighted characters appear white on a black background.

Watch What You Press When Text Is Highlighted!

If you press a letter, number, or symbol on your keyboard while text is highlighted, the text disappears and is replaced by the character you typed! In some cases, this might be exactly what you want, but you should otherwise be careful about what keys you press while text is highlighted. If you do happen to accidentally blow away some text, immediately select the program's **Edit, Undo** command (discussed later in this section).

➤ **Highlighting text using the keyboard**   If you prefer to use your keyboard to highlight text, position the cursor to the left of the first character, hold down the **Shift** key, and then press the right-arrow key until the entire selection is highlighted. If you need to select multiple lines, use the down-arrow key or the Page Down key (depending on how far you have to go).

➤ **Making a copy of highlighted text**   You can copy highlighted text to another part of the document (or even to a document in another program) by first selecting the **Edit, Copy** command (or by pressing **Ctrl+C**). Move the cursor to where you want the copy to appear (again, this could be in another program), and then select the **Edit, Paste** command (or try **Ctrl+V**).

➤ **Moving highlighted text**   To move highlighted text to another part of the document (or to a document in another program), first select **Edit, Cut** (or tap **Ctrl+X**). The text vanishes, but Windows 2000 is keeping it safe in a hidden place called the *Clipboard*. Move the cursor to where you want the text to appear (again, this could be in another program), and then select **Edit, Paste** (or press **Ctrl+V**).

Where Does Cut and Copied Stuff Go?

All this cut, copy, and paste moonshine is a bit mysterious. Where does cut text (or whatever) go? How does Windows 2000 know what to paste? Does Windows 2000 have some kind of digital hip pocket that it uses to store and retrieve cut or copied data? Actually, that's not a bad analogy. This "hip pocket" is actually a chunk of your computer's memory called the Clipboard. Whenever you run the Cut or Copy command, Windows 2000 heads to the Clipboard, removes whatever currently resides there, and stores the cut or copied data. When you issue the Paste command, Windows 2000 grabs whatever is on the Clipboard and tosses it into your document.

➤ **Deleting text**   Whatever your typing skills, you'll still need to delete extraneous characters and words. If the text is highlighted, press the **Delete** key to expunge it. If you're dealing with just a few characters, you can delete them without the highlighting part. Use one of the following keys:

Backspace   Press this key to delete the character to the left of the cursor.

Delete   Press this key to delete the character to the right of the cursor.

➤ **Recovering from a mistake**   Accidental deletions can make you go gray before your time, but accidental copying, moving, and other changes can also be a problem. If you make a mistake when editing a document, immediately select the **Edit**, **Undo** command (or press **Ctrl+Z**) to restore everything to the way it was before you made your blunder. Note that in most programs Undo undoes only your most recent action, so run the command before you do anything else.

Shutting Down Windows 2000

There's no problem leaving your computer on all the time. It doesn't harm anything, and it won't drain a lot of power. (Although to really minimize electricity consumption, you should shut off the monitor when you're not using it.) The big advantage of leaving your machine on is that Windows 2000 is always ready for action.

If you feel more comfortable with the machine off, please insert the following into a safe and readily accessible section of your brain: *Never, ever, ever shut off your computer while Windows 2000 is still running.* Otherwise, I guarantee that at some point you'll lose data or wreak havoc on your Windows 2000 configuration.

With the scaremongering out of the way, here's the proper procedure to follow to tuck Windows 2000 into bed at night:

1. Shut down all your running programs.

2. Select **Start**, **Shut Down**. Windows 2000 displays the Shut Down Windows dialog box.

3. Use the **What Do You Want the Computer to Do?** list to select one of the following options:

   ➤ **Shut Down**   Choose this option if you're going to turn off the computer's power.

   ➤ **Log Off** *User*   Choose this option if you want to log back into Windows 2000 as a different user.

   ➤ **Restart**   Choose this option if you want to start Windows 2000 all over again.

4. Click **OK**. Windows 2000 shuts down all of its systems, which will take a few seconds.

5. If you chose the **Shut Down** option, wait until you see a window that says It is now safe to turn off your computer. When you do, switch off the power.

What Happened

This chapter gave you a just-the-basics look at Windows 2000. You took a tour of the Windows 2000 screen and saw sights such as the desktop, taskbar, Start button, and lots of inscrutable icons. You also learned how to start programs, switch between running programs, and boss around programs using their drop-down menus, toolbars, and dialog boxes. From there, you found out how to work with windows, deal with documents, and shut down Windows 2000.

Crib Notes

➤ **Starting programs**   Click the **Start** button to display the Start menu, and then click the command or submenus required to launch the program.

➤ **Switching between running programs**   Click the taskbar buttons, or press **Alt+Tab**.

➤ **Dialog box command buttons**   Click **OK** to put dialog box settings into effect; click **Cancel** to bail out of a dialog box without doing anything; click **Help** to view the program's Help system.

➤ **Shutting down a program**   Select **File**, **Exit** or press **Alt+F4**.

Getting Work Done in Windows 2000

Now that you've been properly introduced to your computer's new boss, it's time for the two of you to get better acquainted. That's the job of the half dozen chapters in Part 2. You learn about such workaday chores as dealing with files and folders (Chapter 3), using Windows 2000's writing programs (Chapter 4), and printing your documents (Chapter 5). Subsequent chapters cover Windows 2000's new and improved notebook features (Chapter 6) and its graphics programs (Chapter 7). Part 2 closes with a look at multimedia in Windows 2000 (Chapter 8).

Using My Computer to Work with Files and Folders

In This Chapter

➤ Using My Computer to navigate your system

➤ Copying, moving, renaming, deleting, and creating new files and folders

➤ Searching for files

➤ Understanding this Web integration thing

➤ Your field guide to file and folder flora and fauna

Procrastination is the art of not putting off until tomorrow that which can be put off until the day after tomorrow. Time-management gurus tell us that the best way to avoid procrastination is to create a to-do list and put the *least* attractive chores at the top. Sounds like dubious advice to me, but I'll wait until tomorrow to try to come up with something better. In the meantime, I've taken Part 2's six-chapter to-do list and put what I'm sure would be most folks' least attractive topic up front: dealing with files and folders.

Why the top priority? Well, time-management flapdoodle aside, file and folder maintenance chores are important pieces of the computing puzzle, and are matched in their importance only by their inevitability. Yes, you should be focusing most of your energies on producing high-quality memos and presentations and such, but the better your file and folder skills, the more time you'll have to do *real* work. Happily, as you'll see in this chapter, Windows 2000 boasts quite a few features that make wrestling with files and folders a relatively "no-tears" affair.

Techno Talk

What's a Folder?

I'll be using the term "folder" throughout this chapter, so let's be sure you know what I'm blathering on about: A folder is a storage location on a disk (such as your computer's hard disk). It's used to store files and even other folders (which are known as subfolders).

Getting to Know Your Computer Using My Computer

As you work with Windows 2000, you'll notice that it assumes a certain level of self-absorption on your part because it seems like everything is "My This" or "My That." There's the My Documents folder that you're supposed to use to store your documents, the My Pictures folder for—you guessed it—your picture files, and on and on. The Big Kahuna in this My-opic point of view is My Computer. Although its name implies that it represents your entire computer, My Computer really represents only the bits where files can be stored: your hard disk, your floppy disk, your CD-ROM or DVD-ROM drive, "removable" disks such as those that work with zip or JAZ drives, and network drives.

To see this for yourself, double-click the My Computer icon on the Windows 2000 desktop. The following figure shows the My Computer window that shows up on, well, *my* computer. Because your machine will most likely sport a different configuration, the My Computer window that you see will no doubt look a bit different.

Brain twister: Your My Computer will probably look a bit different from my My Computer.

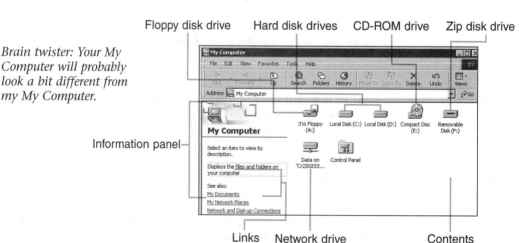

Floppy disk drive   Hard disk drives   CD-ROM drive   Zip disk drive

Information panel

Links   Network drive   Contents

The bulk of the My Computer window is divided into two sections:

Contents   The right side of the window displays the contents of the current folder. The My Computer folder stores your computer's disk drives (plus a few other things), so that's mostly what you see in the contents area. Under each icon, you see the type of disk (or, in some cases, the name of the disk), followed by the letter used by the disk drive. For example, Local Disk (C:) tells you that the disk is a hard disk and that its drive letter is C.

Information panel   The left side of the window is used as an information area. For example, if you highlight drive C, the information panel shows you the capacity of the disk and how much free space you have left. This area is also usually sprinkled with some *links*. A link is blue, underlined text that, when clicked, takes you to a specific folder. For example, clicking the My Documents link takes you to the My Documents folder.

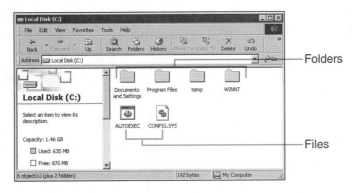

Opening a disk drive reveals the contents of that drive.

To see the contents of a disk drive, double-click it. (If you plan on doing this for a floppy drive, CD-ROM or DVD-ROM drive, or a removable disk drive, be sure you have a disk inside the drive or Windows 2000 will reprimand you.) For example, the previous figure shows the contents of my drive C.

As you can see, this drive contains some files as well as a few folders (storage locations). To see what's inside one of these folders, just double-click its icon. For example, the next figure shows the contents of the WINNT folder (this is where Windows 2000 stores most of its possessions).

An Extra Step for the WINNT Folder

Microsoft would rest easier at night knowing that the likes of you and me weren't poking around in its precious WINNT folder. Therefore, when you first try to open WINNT, you see a warning message. The sky won't fall if you simply view WINNT, so go ahead and click the **Show Files** link. Note, however, that unless you're given specific instructions, under no circumstances should you play around with any of the files in WINNT.

The WINNT folder: more subfolders and more files.

The type of file

Some file stats

A preview of the file

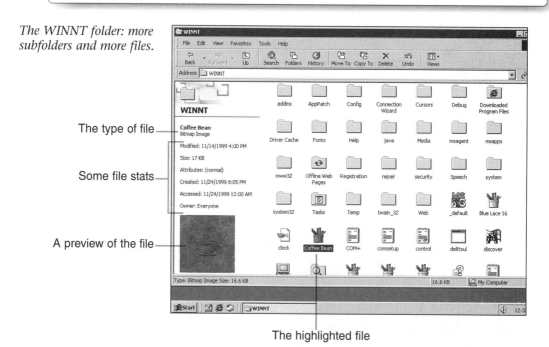

The highlighted file

Note, in particular, that when you highlight a file, the information panel lights up with all kinds of data: the full name of the file; the type of file; some stats about the file, such as when it was last modified and its size. For some files—particularly images—the information panel also shows a preview of the file.

To and Fro: Navigating My Computer

Here are a few pointers for navigating from folder to folder in My Computer:

➤ To go back to the previous folder, either click the **Back** button in the toolbar or select **View**, **Go To**, **Back**. (There's also a keyboard shortcut that you can use: **Alt+Left Arrow**.)

Add Text to the Toolbar

My Computer's toolbar is chock-full of one-click wonders, but it's sometimes difficult to tell which button does what. To help out, you can force My Computer to display the name of each button. To do this, select **View**, **Toolbars**, **Customize** (or right-click the toolbar and then click **Customize**). In the Customize Toolbar dialog box, use the **Text Options** list to choose **Show Text Labels**, and then click **OK**.

➤ After you've gone back to a previous folder, you can move forward again either by clicking the **Forward** button or by selecting **View**, **Go To**, **Forward**. (The keyboard shortcut for this is **Alt+Right Arrow**.)

➤ Rather than stepping back and forward one folder at a time, you can leap over multiple folders in a single bound. To do this, click the downward-pointing arrow beside either the **Back** or **Forward** toolbar button. In the list that appears (see the next figure), click the folder you want to visit. (You also can do this by selecting **View**, **Go To** and then choosing the folder from the list at the bottom of the menu.)

Click this arrow to display this list.

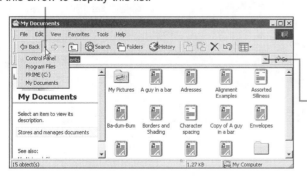

The Back and Forward buttons maintain lists of the places you've been.

Click this arrow to display the Address list.

➤ You can use the Address list to select other locations to go to. To see the list, click the downward-pointing arrow on the right side of the Address bar (or press **F4**). Note, too, that if you know the full name of the folder you want to see, you can type it in the Address bar and then click **Go** (or press **Enter**).

➤ If a folder has subfolders, the folder is called the *parent* and each subfolder is called a *child*. (Strange terms, I know. The irony is that they were probably made up by some geek who couldn't even get a date.) If you're viewing a child folder, you can go to its parent folder either by clicking the **Up** button in the toolbar or by selecting **View**, **Go To**, **Up One Level**. (Keyboard fans can press **Backspace**, instead.)

Easier Navigating with the Folders List

The thing I dislike the most about My Computer is that it shows only one folder at a time, so you often end up "drilling down" through a series of subfolders to get where you want to go. Too slow! To speed things up, activate My Computer's Folders list either by clicking the Folders toolbar button or by selecting **View**, **Explorer Bar**, **Folders**. (To get rid of the Folders list, repeat the same procedure.)

As you can see in the following figure, the result is a list of folders on the left side of the window. When you highlight a folder in this list, the folder's contents appear on the right side of the window. To view subfolders within the Folders list, use the following techniques:

➤ **To view subfolders** Click the **plus sign** (+) beside the folder name. The plus sign changes to a minus sign (-).

➤ **To hide subfolders** Click the **minus sign** (–) beside the folder name.

My Computer modified to show the handy Folders list.

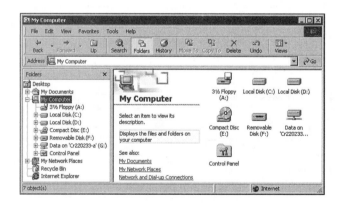

Some Routine File and Folder Maintenance

Now that you and My Computer are getting along famously, it's time to put this digital domestic to good use. Specifically, I'll show you how to use My Computer to perform no fewer than five workaday chores for files and folders: creating, copying, moving, renaming, and deleting.

Creating a New File or Folder

If you want to manufacture a shiny, new file for yourself, the best way to go about it is to run the appropriate application and select that program's **File**, **New** command. (Note, too, that most programs—including Windows 2000's WordPad and Notepad accessories— create a new file for you automatically when you start them up.) You then select the **File**, **Save** command to save the file to your hard disk.

Don't Mess with the Rest

Three of these chores—moving, renaming, and deleting—ought to have a "For Your Stuff Only" label on them. That's because you should never use these techniques on files or folders that you didn't create yourself. If you do, Windows 2000 or one of your programs might blow a gasket and refuse to run.

However, it *is* possible to create a new file within My Computer. Here's how:

1. Open the folder in which you want to create the file.

2. Run the **File**, **New** command. This displays another menu with a selection of file types, including Bitmap Image, WordPad Document, and Text Document.

3. Select the type of file you want. Windows 2000 creates the new file and displays a generic name (such as "New Text Document") in a text box.

4. Edit the name and then press **Enter**.

To create a new folder, follow the preceding steps but, when you get to Step 3, select **Folder** in the menu.

Selecting Files and Folders

Before getting to the rest of the file-maintenance fun, you need to know how to select the files or folders that you want to horse around with.

Let's begin with the simplest case: selecting a single file. How you do this depends on whether you're using Windows 2000's new Web integration feature (see "How Web Integration Changes My Computer," later in this chapter):

➤ If Web integration isn't turned on, click the file or folder you want to work with.

➤ If Web integration is on the job, you select a file or folder just by pointing at it with your mouse.

So far, so good. However, there will be plenty of times when you'll need to deal with two or more files or folders. For example, you might want to herd several files onto a floppy disk. Rather than doing this one item at a time, you can do the whole thing in one fell swoop by first selecting all the items and then moving (or copying, or whatever) them as a group. Windows 2000 offers the following methods:

Selecting the Whole Caboodle

If you want to select everything inside a folder, run the **Edit**, **Select All** command.

➤ **Selecting consecutive items** If the files or folders you want to select are listed consecutively, say "Ooh, how convenient!" and then do this: Select the first item, hold down the **Shift** key, select the last item, and then release **Shift**. Windows 2000 will kindly do the dirty work of selecting all the items in between.

➤ **"Lassoing" items** Rather than trying to coordinate the mouse with one hand and the Shift key with the other, Windows 2000 offers a mouse-only technique in which you "lasso" a group of files or folders. To try it, first move the mouse pointer just to the left of the first item. Now hold down the left mouse button and then move the pointer down and to the right. As you do this, a box appears, and every item touched by the box gets selected (see the following figure). When you've selected everything you need, release the mouse button.

Lassoing Depends on the View

This lassoing technique works if My Computer is in Large Icons view (select **View**, **Large Icons**). However, if you're in Small Icons, List, or Details view, My Computer uses a slightly different lassoing technique (just to keep us all thoroughly confused, I guess). In this case, you have to start to the *right* of the first item, and then drag the mouse down and to the *left*.

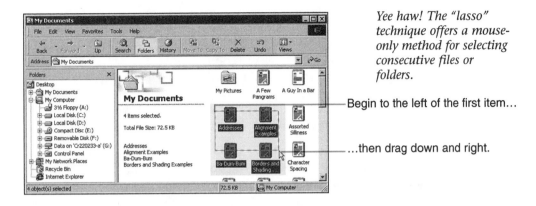

Yee haw! The "lasso" technique offers a mouse-only method for selecting consecutive files or folders.

Begin to the left of the first item...

...then drag down and right.

➤ **Selecting nonconsecutive items** If the files or folders you want to select are listed willy-nilly, say "Oy!" and then do this: Select the first item, hold down the **Ctrl** key, select each of the other items, and then release **Ctrl**.

Copying and Moving Files and Folders

A copy of a file or folder is an exact replica of the original that you store on another part of your hard disk or on a removable disk (such as a floppy disk). Copies are useful for making backups or if you want to transport a file or folder to another computer.

Note, too, that the location of the files and folders you create isn't set in stone. If you're not happy with the current location, there's no problem moving a file or folder somewhere else.

Windows 2000 offers two basic methods for copying and moving files and folders: the Copy to Folder and Move to Folder commands, and the "drag-and-drop" mouse technique.

To use the Copy To Folder or Move To Folder command, follow these steps:

1. Select the files or folders you want to transport.
2. Pull down the **Edit** menu and choose one of the following commands:

   Copy to Folder This is the command to choose if you're copying files or folders. Alternatively, click the **Copy To** toolbar button.

   Move to Folder This is the command to choose if you're moving files or folders. Another route you can take is to click the **Move To** toolbar button.

3. Either way, you end up with a version of the Browse for Folder dialog box onscreen. Use the folder "tree" to locate and select the destination folder or disk drive.
4. Click **OK**.

49

Using the Send To Menu to Copy Quickly

Windows 2000 has a special Send To menu that contains commonly used destinations such as your floppy disk or your My Documents folder. To see this menu, either select **File**, **Send To** or right-click an item and then click **Send To**. Now select the destination you want and Windows 2000 copies the selected items lickety-split.

Mouse fans will enjoy the alternative drag-and-drop method. To use this method successfully, you need to do three things to set up the My Computer window:

➤ Be sure My Computer is displaying the Folders list.

➤ Use the Folders list to select the folder that contains the files or subfolders you want to work with.

➤ Use the Folders list to display (but not select!) the destination folder or disk drive.

So, now you should have the items you want to copy or move in the contents list on the right, and the destination folder in the Folders list on the left.

Here's how drag-and-drop works:

1. Use the contents list to select the files or folders you want to copy or move.

2. Move the mouse pointer over any selected item and then use your non-mouse hand to hold down one of these keys:

   Ctrl This is for copying items.

   Shift This is for moving items.

3. With the key held down for dear life, hold down the left mouse button and move the mouse pointer toward the destination folder in the Folders list (the is "dragging" part).

4. Move the mouse pointer over the destination folder (wait until you see it highlighted), release the mouse button (this is the "dropping" part), and then release **Ctrl** or **Shift**.

Mouse-Only Copying and Moving

To avoid having to hold down either Ctrl or Shift when doing the drag-and-drop thing, hold down the *right* mouse button as you drag. When you release the right button to drop the items, Windows 2000 displays a shortcut menu. Click **Copy Here** or **Move Here**, as appropriate.

Speaking of the right mouse button, if you right-click a file or folder, Windows 2000 tosses a shortcut menu onto the screen. This menu contains a number of commands, including Delete and Rename.

Renaming a File or Folder

Windows 2000 supports file and folder names up to about 250 characters long, so you don't have to settle for boring monikers on the files and folders you create. If you don't like a name, feel free to rename it.

Here are the simple steps to follow to rename a mismonikered file or folder:

1. Select the file or folder you want to rename. (You can work with only one item at a time for this.)

2. Run the **File**, **Rename** command. Windows 2000 creates a text box around the name.

3. Edit the name as you see fit.

4. When you're done, press **Enter**.

Character Constraints

Bear in mind that although Windows 2000 likes long filenames (up to about 250 characters) and will accept most keyboard characters (including spaces), there are nine characters that are strictly *verboten*:

$$* \mid \setminus : " < > ? /$$

Deleting Files and Folders

Although most of today's hard disks boast a mammoth amount of real estate, you'll still run out of room one day if you don't delete the detritus that you no longer use.

Deleting unwanted files and folders is pretty easy:

Recycle Bin

This is the place where Windows 2000 stores deleted files. If you trash a file accidentally, you can use the Recycle Bin to recover it.

Drag to the Recycle Bin

Another way to delete a file or folder is to drag it from My Computer and drop it on the desktop's Recycle Bin.

1. Select the files or folders you want to blow away.

2. Run the **File**, **Delete** command, or click the **Delete** toolbar button. Windows 2000 asks whether you're sure you want to consign these poor things to the cold, cruel Recycle Bin.

3. Say, "But of course, my good fellow!" and click **Yes**.

What happens if you nuke some crucial file or folder that you'd give your right arm to have back? Assuming you need your right arm, Windows 2000 offers an alternative method to save your bacon: the Recycle Bin. Here's what you do:

1. Open the desktop's Recycle Bin icon. The folder that appears contains a list of all the stuff you've expunged recently.

2. Select the files or folders you want to recover.

3. Run the **File**, **Restore** command (or click the **Restore** button in the information panel). Windows 2000 marches the items right back to where they came from. Whew!

Searching for Long-Lost Files

Bill Gates, Microsoft's Big Cheese, used to summarize his company's mission of easy access to data as "information at your fingertips." We're still a long way off from that laudable goal, but there are a few things you can do to ensure the info you need is never far away:

➤ **Use the My Documents folder**   The most inefficient way to store your documents is to scatter them hither and yon around your hard disk. A much better approach is to plop everything in a
single place so that you always know where to look for things. The perfect place for this is the My Documents folder that Windows 2000 provides for you.

➤ **Use subfolders to organize your documents**   Using My Documents is a good idea (if I do say so myself), but you shouldn't just cram all your stuff into that one folder. Instead, create subfolders to hold related items. Windows 2000 starts you off with a My Pictures subfolder that's the ideal place for your graphics files. Feel free to add other subfolders for things such as letters, memos, projects, presentations, spreadsheets, and whatever other categories you can think of.

➤ **Give your files meaningful names**   Take advantage of Windows 2000's long filenames to give your documents useful names that tell you exactly what's inside each file. A document named "Letter" doesn't tell you much, but "Letter to A. Gore Re: Inventing the Internet" surely does.

➤ **Dejunk your folders**   Keep your folders clean by deleting any junk files that you'll never use again.

If you're like most people, then you'll probably end up with hundreds of documents, but if you follow these suggestions, finding the one you need shouldn't be a problem. Even so, there will be times when you don't remember exactly which document you need, or you might want to find all those documents that contain a particular word or phrase. For these situations, Windows 2000 offers a new Search feature that can help you track down what you need.

To get started, you have two choices:

➤ To search within the current folder in My Computer, either select the **View**, **Explorer Bar**, **Search** command, or click the Search toolbar button. (Pressing **Ctrl+E** also works.)

➤ To search all of My Computer (that is, all your disk drives), select **Start**, **Search**, **For Files or Folders**.

The following figure shows the window that appears if you use the latter technique.

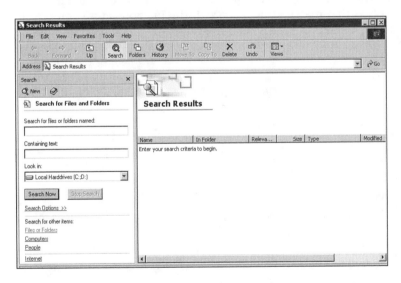

Windows 2000's new search feature helps you find AWOL files.

Let's see what happens from here:

1. Use the **Search for Files or Folders Named** box to search for a file by name. Note that you don't have to enter the entire name of the file; just a word or even a few letters will do.

2. Use the **Containing Text** box to search for a file by content. Enter a word or part of a word.

3. Use the **Look In** list to select the folder or disk drive in which you want to search.

4. Search also provides the following options that might occasionally come in handy. Click the **Search Options** link to see the following check boxes:

    Date   If you activate this check box, Search displays some extra controls that enable you to specify a date range for the file you want to find.

    Type   If you activate this check box, Search displays a drop-down list from which you can select the type of file you want to find (such as a Text Document).

    Size   If you activate this check box, Search provides a couple of controls that enable you to locate a file according to its size in kilobytes.

    Advanced Options   If you activate this check box, you get three more check boxes for your searching pleasure. The most useful of these are **Search Subfolders** (which tells Search to examine not only the folder shown in the **Look In** list, but also all of its subfolders) and **Case Sensitive** (which tells Search to match the exact uppercase and lowercase letters you use in the **Containing Text** box).

5. When you're ready to roll, click the **Search Now** button. Search scours your machine and then uses the right side of the window to display the Search Results: the list of files that match your criteria. (If the file you want comes up right away, click **Stop Search** to tell Search to hold its horses.)

Faster Searches

When you're searching for content, it can take Windows 2000 quite a while to trudge through all the files. To help speed things up, use the new Windows 2000 Indexing Service. This service monitors your documents and maintains an index for them behind the scenes. To run the service, click **Search Options** to open the link, click the **Indexing Service** link, activate the **Yes, Enable Indexing Service and Run When My Computer Is Idle** option, and then click **OK**.

How Web Integration Changes My Computer

Web integration is a new Windows 2000 feature. Its purpose—theoretically, at least—is to make your computer easier to use by incorporating certain features from the Internet's World Wide Web. For our purposes in this chapter, Web integration affects three things:

> ➤ **How you view folders**   As you've seen, Windows 2000's folders appear with an information panel on the left, and that panel contains images, text, and even links to other folders. In other words, the folder acts more or less like a Web page.

➤ **How you launch files and icons**   You normally launch something (such as a document or a desktop icon) by double-clicking it. Web integration changes that so you launch files and icons by single-clicking them.

➤ **How you select a file or folder**   As you saw earlier, selecting a file or folder using Web integration involves just hovering the mouse pointer over the item.

Happily, you can toggle these Web-integration features on and off. To do this, select My Computer's **Tools**, **Folder Options** command to display the Folder Options dialog box. The General tab, shown in the following figure, offers these Web-integration settings:

➤ **Enable Web content in folders**   Activate this option to get the information panel when you view a folder.

➤ **Use Windows classic folders**   Activate this option to do away with the information panel.

➤ **Single-click to open an item (point to select)**   Activate this option to crank up the single-click launching and no-click selecting features. If you do this, the following option buttons arise from their slumbers:

> ➤ **Underline icon titles consistent with my browser**   Activate this option to tell Windows 2000 to underline all the filenames and icon titles using the same style as defined within Internet Explorer. This usually means that file- and folder names and icon titles appear in a blue, underlined text. This is a good idea because it gives you a visual reminder that Web integration is on.

> ➤ **Underline icon titles only when I point at them**   Activate this option to have Windows 2000 underline filenames and icon titles only when you point at them. This is a bit tidier-looking than having everything underlined.

➤ **Double-click to open an item (single-click to select)**   Activate this option to use the old-fashioned mouse techniques for launching and selecting stuff.

Use the General tab to set various Web-integration options.

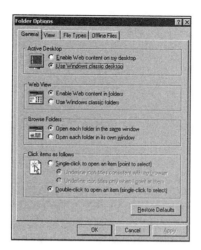

What Happened

This chapter got your Windows 2000 workday off the ground with a look at My Computer and how you can use it to perform basic maintenance chores such as copying, moving, renaming, deleting, and creating new files.

Crib Notes

➤ **What *not* to do**   Don't muck about with anything inside the sacred WINNT folder (unless someone, like me, has given you very explicit instructions) and don't move, rename, delete, fold, spindle, or mutilate any files that you didn't create yourself.

➤ **Selecting a file or folder**   If Web integration isn't on, you select an item by clicking it; otherwise, you select an item by moving the mouse pointer over it.

➤ **Drag 'til you drop**   To drag and drop something, move the mouse pointer over the item, hold down the left mouse button, move the mouse pointer over the destination, and then release the button.

➤ **Rename restrictions**   When renaming a file (or naming a new file), don't use the following characters:

   * | \ : " < > ? /

➤ **Don't forget the right mouse button**   If you can't remember whether to hold down Ctrl or Shift when dragging, use the right-drag method, instead, and then select Move Here or Copy Here from the menu. Also, many file and folder commands are available from the shortcut menu, which you display by right-clicking the selected item.

Chapter 4

Prose Programs: Windows 2000's Writing Tools

In This Chapter

➤ Using Notepad for simple text tasks

➤ Using WordPad for full-bore word processing

➤ Techniques for automatically finding and replacing text

➤ Inserting ã, ö, ¢, ©, and other oddball characters

➤ Becoming a word pro, from go to whoa

Back in the days before a personal computer was *de rigueur* on every corporate desktop and in every household den, people used to put them down as "glorified typewriters." And, in fact, it *was* true that most folks were using their computers for basic writing tasks (and, of course, for playing games). However, anyone who had actually used a computer to compose a letter or a memo knew the truth: that the PC went *way* beyond anything that some clunky old typewriter could do.

And so it came to pass that computers ruled the Earth, but one thing didn't change: Most people still use their computers primarily for writing stuff (and, of course, for playing games). So, it's good news indeed that Windows 2000 comes with just about all the writing tools you'll ever pine for, whether you just need to dash off a quick to-do list or whether you need to compose a professional-looking letter or résumé. This chapter gives you the goods on these writing tools.

Before getting started, you should know that the written documents you deal with will come in two flavors:

➤ **Plain**   This kind of document contains characters that have no special formatting: just plain, unadorned, text. So, unshockingly, these types of documents are called *text files*. In the Windows 2000 world, you read, edit, and create text files by using the Notepad text editor.

➤ **Formatted**   This kind of document contains characters that have (or can have) formatting such as **bold** or *italic*. These types of documents are called *word processing files*. In Windows 2000, you read, edit, and create word processing files using the WordPad word processor.

Notepad is the subject of the first part of this chapter, and I discuss WordPad's eccentricities a bit later (see "Using WordPad for Fancier Word Processing Files").

Using Notepad for Garden-Variety Text Files

If text files are so plain, why on earth would anyone want to use them? Here are a few good reasons:

➤ You just need a quick-and-dirty document without any formatting frills.

➤ You want to send a document to another person and you want to be sure they can open it. Most of the personal computers on the planet can deal with a text file, so that's your safest bet. If you used WordPad, on the other hand, your friend has to have WordPad (or a relatively recent version of Microsoft Word) installed to open the file.

➤ You want to create a document that *must* be plain text. For example, if you want to create a Web page from scratch, you have to save it as a text file; a word processing file won't work.

Web Page Creation Made Easy

Creating your own Web page from scratch sounds like a daunting task, but it's really not that hard. In fact, I tell you everything you need to know in my book *The Complete Idiot's Guide to Creating a Web Page, Fourth Edition*. If you have Web access, you can find out more about the book here:

    http://www.mcfedries.com/books/cightml/

Just about anyone using just about any PC can read a text file. This universality means that you'll get a lot of text files coming your way. For example, if you examine the installation disk of most programs, you'll almost always see at least one text file with a name such as "Readme" or "Setup." This file usually contains information about the installation process (such as how to prepare for the install and how the install operates), last-minute changes to the manual, and so on.

You can identify these and other text files by the icon they use in My Computer. The following figure points out a couple of text files. When you see the text file icon, double-click the file to open it in Notepad.

These are text files.   These are WordPad files.

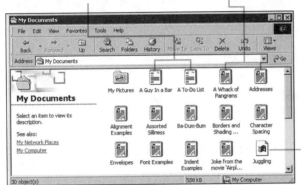

My Computer shows text files using a special icon.

This icon means Windows 2000 doesn't know what the file is.

Techno Talk

Opening Any Text File in Notepad

Once in a blue moon, you'll come across a text file that doesn't have the proper icon and, in fact, has Windows 2000's beats-me-what-the-heck-this-thing-is icon (pointed out in the figure). As long as you're sure it's a text file, you can still talk Notepad into opening the file. To do this, select the file and select **File**, **Open With** to get to the Open With dialog box. Highlight **Notepad** in the list, and then click **OK**.

If you need to create a text file, begin by opening Notepad: **Start**, **Programs**, **Accessories**, **Notepad**. The following figure shows the window that materializes on your screen.

59

Notepad: a simple window for a simple file.

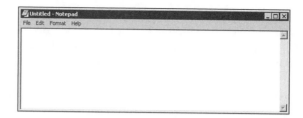

As you can see, Notepad sports a plain, no-frills, look that perfectly matches the plain, no-frills, text files you work with. There's nary a bell or whistle in sight, and even the menus contain, for the most part, just a bare-bones collection of commands: New, Open, Save, Cut, Copy, Paste, and so on. Dullsville. That's okay, though, because that's the nature of the Notepad beast. You just fire it up and then read, type, and edit as necessary.

However, Notepad is not without its small quirks and one-of-a-kind features. Here's a summary:

➤ **Inserting the date and time** To plop the current date and time into your text file, select the **Edit**, **Date/Time** command (or press **F5**).

➤ **Wrapping text** When you type in most normal programs and the cursor hits the right edge of the window, the cursor automatically jumps down one line and starts again on the left edge of the window (this feature is known as *word wrap*). But not, Notepad, no. It just blithely continues along the same line for exactly 1,024 characters, and only *then* will it wrap onto the next line. Dumb! To avoid this annoyance, activate the **Format**, **Word Wrap** command.

➤ **What's up with the Font command?** Despite what I said about text files not using formatting, Notepad sports a Font command on its Format menu. What gives? I assure you I wasn't lying: That command can and should be ignored because regular text files *don't* use fonts. However, Windows 2000 does support a special type of text file that can use fonts. So if (and only if) you'll be sending your text file to another Windows 2000 user, you can select a font (it applies to the entire document). When you go to save the file, be sure you open the **Encoding** list and select **Unicode**.

Using WordPad for Fancier Word Processing Files

Like Dorothy getting whisked from the black-and-white world of Kansas into the Technicolor world of Oz, we turn now to WordPad, Windows 2000's word processor. To get this program down the yellow brick road, select **Start**, **Programs**, **Accessories**, **WordPad**. The next figure shows the WordPad window. Unlike the spartan expanse of Notepad, the WordPad window offers a well-appointed interior with lots of word-processing amenities.

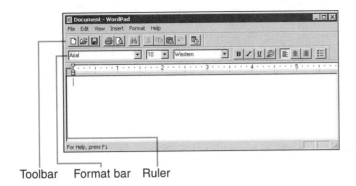

The WordPad window gewgaws include a couple of toolbars and a ruler.

Toolbar   Format bar   Ruler

WordPad and Word-Processing Files

Here are a few notes to bear in mind when working with WordPad and its word-processing files:

➤ **The WordPad file icon**   Like text files, WordPad files also have their own unique icon, as shown earlier. When you see a file with this icon, double-click it to load the file in WordPad.

➤ **What type of document do you want?**   When you select the **File**, **New** command, WordPad winds up and delivers the New dialog box to you. WordPad is wondering what type of document you want to create. You have four choices:

   Word 6 Document   This format is based on the one used by Microsoft Word, Microsoft's flagship word-processing program. (In fact, WordPad's design and most of its features were taken directly from Word.) This is a good choice if you'll be sharing the document with other WordPad users or with Microsoft Word users.

   Rich Text Document   This produces a file in the Rich Text Format (RTF, for short), which accepts all kinds of formatting. It's a standard format in computing circles, so it's readable by many other word-processing programs. This is a good choice if you'll be sending the document to someone and you're not sure what program they'll be using.

   Text Document   This gets you a plain text file.

   Unicode Document   This is a relatively obscure type of text file that can be safely ignored.

➤ **Opening documents: Are you my file type?**   As you've seen, there are several different types of files that fall under the aegis of WordPad. Unfortunately, when you select the **File**, **Open** command, the Open dialog box only shows RTF files. If you're trying to open a different type (such as Word or text), you need to open the **Files of Type** list and select either the type you need (such as **Word for Windows** or **Text Documents**) or **All Documents**.

➤ **Working on two files at once** WordPad's one-track mind means that it can have only one file open at a time. However, there will be plenty of times when you need to work with *two* files at once. For example, you might want to compare text in the two files, or you might want to copy or move text from one file to the other. No problem. All you have to do is open up a second copy of WordPad and use it to open the second file.

Tip Sheet: Text-Selection Tricks

Before you can format, cut, or copy text, you first have to select it. I showed you the basic text-selection maneuvers in Chapter 2, "A Field Guide to Windows 2000 for the Uninitiated," but WordPad has a few extra techniques that can make your life a teensy bit easier:

➤ **To select a word** Double-click it.

➤ **To select a line** Click inside the narrow strip of white space to the left of the line (that is, between the line and the WordPad window's left border). In word processing circles, this strip is called the *selection area*.

➤ **To select a paragraph** Double-click the selection area beside the paragraph. (Those with energy to burn also can select a paragraph by *triple*-clicking inside the paragraph.)

➤ **To select the whole document** Hold down **Ctrl** and click anywhere inside the selection area. (You can also choose **Edit**, **Select All** or press **Ctrl+A**.)

Fancy-Schmancy Formatting I: Fonts

The whole point of using a word processor (as opposed to a text editor, such as our pal Notepad) is to turn dull-as-dishwater text into beautifully formatted prose that other people will be clamoring to read. Happily, WordPad offers quite a few formatting features that can turn even the plainest file into a document with text appeal.

In this section, you begin with the most common formatting makeover: the font. A *font* is a style of text in which a unique design and other effects have been applied to all the characters. To begin, you need to decide whether you want to format existing text or text that you're about to type:

➤ **To format existing text** Select the text to which you want to apply the font.

➤ **To format new text** Position the cursor at the spot where the new typing will appear.

With that done, here are the steps to follow to apply the font:

1. Select WordPad's **Format**, **Font** command. The Font dialog box puts in an appearance, as shown here.

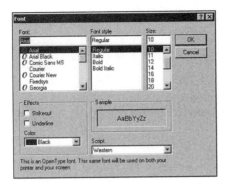

Use the Font dialog box to put some oomph in your text.

2. Use the **Font** list to choose a typeface. The *typeface* is what most people think of when they use the word "font." It represents the distinctive design applied to all the characters. See the next figure for some examples. (Wondering what's up with all those typefaces that have the stylized "O" beside them? Those are *OpenType* typefaces and they generally display better than the other typefaces.)

3. Use the **Font style** list to select a style for the text (see the next figure).

4. Use the **Size** list to choose the font height you want to use. The various values are measured in *points*, where 72 points equals an inch (again, see the next figure for an example or two).

5. The **Effects** group is populated with three check boxes: activate the **Strikeout** check box to get ~~strikeout~~ characters; activate the **Underline** check box to format characters with an <u>underline</u>; and use the **Color** text box to change the color of the text.

6. The **Script** list tells you which language scripts are available for the selected typeface. You use these scripts to create multilingual documents. If you plan on using only English, leave this list set to **Western**.

7. Click **OK** to put the new font into effect.

Serif and Sans Serif

A serif font has small cross strokes at the extremities of each character and is good for regular text in a document. A sans serif font doesn't have the cross strokes and is most often used for titles and headings that require a larger type size.

Note, too, that WordPad offers a few toolbar shortcuts for many of these font tricks. The following figure points out the relevant lists and buttons and shows a few fonts in action.

Some examples of the various font features.

Font (typeface)

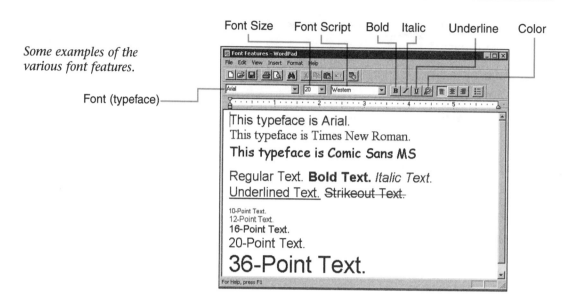

Speaking of shortcuts, you'll be pleased to hear that WordPad also offers a small collection of keyboard combos for easier font fiddling:

Shortcut Keys for Fonts

Press...	To Format Text As...
Ctrl+B	**Bold**
Ctrl+I	*Italic*
Ctrl+U	<u>Underline</u>

Fancy-Schmancy Formatting II: Paragraphs

Few things are as uninviting to read as a document that's nothing but wall-to-wall text. To give your readers a break (literally), divide up your text into separate paragraphs. (Press **Enter** once to start a new paragraph; press **Enter** twice to give yourself a bit of breathing room between each paragraph.)

As a further measure, consider formatting your paragraphs. WordPad enables you to indent entire paragraphs, indent only the first line of a paragraph, and align your paragraphs with the margins. Here's how it works:

1. Place the cursor within the paragraph that you want to format.

2. Either select the **Format**, **Paragraph** command, or right-click the paragraph and then click **Paragraph**. WordPad coaxes the Paragraph dialog box onto the screen.

Installing New Fonts

Windows 2000 brings 20 or so fonts to the formatting table, which isn't bad. However, there are plenty of font collections available on the market, and they generally cost only pennies a font. If you purchase one of these collections, you have to install it. To do that, select **Start**, **Settings**, **Control Panel**, and then launch the **Fonts** icon. When the Fonts folder appears, select **File**, **Install New Font** to open the Add Fonts dialog box. Insert the font disc and select the appropriate drive in the **Drives** list. After a few seconds, the available fonts on the disc will appear in the **List of Fonts**. Highlight the ones you want to install, and then click **OK**.

3. Use the **Left** text box to set how far (in inches) that the text is indented from the left margin.

4. Use the **Right** text box to set how far (in inches) that the text is indented from the right margin.

5. Use the **First Line** text box to set how far (in inches) that the first line of the paragraph is indented from the left margin.

6. Use the **Alignment** list to align the paragraph relative to either the left margin or the right margin. You can also select Center, which centers the paragraph evenly between both margins.

7. Click **OK**.

The following figure demonstrates a few of WordPad's paragraph-formatting options.

Rather than messing around with inches for the various paragraph indents, try WordPad's ruler. The ruler has various markers that set the paragraph indents (see the following figure). Here's a rundown of what they do:

➤ **Left indent for first line**   Indents the paragraph's first line from the left margin.

➤ **Left indent for the rest of the paragraph**   Indents the rest of the paragraph from the left margin.

➤ **Left indent for entire paragraph**   Indents the entire paragraph from the left margin.

➤ **Right indent for entire paragraph**   Indents the entire paragraph from the right margin.

Align Left Center Align Right

Some examples of WordPad's sundry paragraph formats.

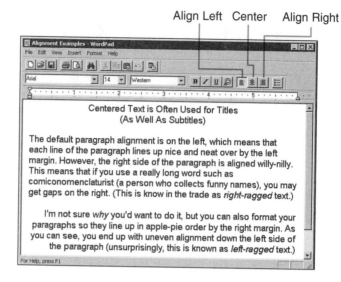

To use these markers to format a paragraph, place the cursor inside the paragraph and then use your mouse to drag the appropriate marker left or right.

Left indent for the first line

WordPad's ruler can make paragraph formatting a breeze.

Left indent for the rest of the paragraph

Left indent for the entire paragraph

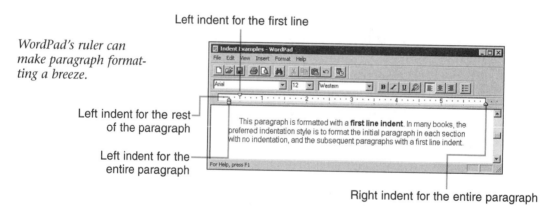

Right indent for the entire paragraph

Fancy-Schmancy Formatting III: Bullets

When you need to include a list of points or items in your document, it's best to separate those items from the regular text by displaying each one in a separate paragraph. To make these items even easier to read, format them with a *bullet* out front, as shown in the next figure. To use bullets, follow these steps:

1. If you want to turn an existing paragraph into the first item in a bulleted list, first place the cursor anywhere within the paragraph. If you want to convert several paragraphs to bullets, select the paragraphs.

2. Turn on bullets by activating the **Format, Bullet Style** command. (You can also click the **Bullets** toolbar button or right-click the paragraph and then click **Bullet Style**.)

3. To create a new bulleted item, move to the end of the last bulleted item and press **Enter**. WordPad dutifully creates another bullet.

4. Enter the text for the new bullet.

5. Repeat Steps 3 and 4 until you've entered all your bulleted items.

6. Press **Enter** twice to tell WordPad to knock off the bulleted style.

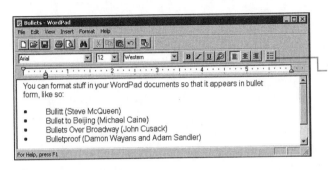

An example of a bulleted list.

The Bullets button

Fancy-Schmancy Formatting IV: Tabs

If you place the cursor on a blank line and press **Tab**, you'll notice that the cursor leaps ahead by exactly half an inch. Press **Tab** again, and you get another half-inch jump. These half-inch intervals are known as *tab stops*, and they're great for making columns or tables that line up like a precision drill team.

WordPad goes one better by enabling you to set your own tab stops anywhere you like. To begin, place the cursor inside the paragraph that you want to mess with. Here are the techniques to use:

The Ruler Rules

Don't forget to use WordPad's ruler when setting indents and tabs. It's much easier to drag the indent markers or click and drag tab stops than to do everything via the dialog boxes.

➤ **To set a tab stop** Move your mouse pointer into the ruler at the spot where you want the tab stop to appear, and then click. WordPad adds what looks like a small "L" to the ruler; that's your tab stop.

➤ **To move a tab stop** Use your mouse to drag the tab stop marker left or right.

➤ **To delete a tab stop** Use your mouse to drag the tab stop marker off the ruler.

Just for the record, there *is* a hard way to set the tabs: Select the **Format**, **Tabs** command to display the Tabs dialog box. In this case, you enter the position (in inches) where you want the tab to appear, and then click **Set**.

Finding and Replacing Text

Back in Chapter 3, "Using My Computer to Work with Files and Folders" (see "Searching for Long-Lost Files" on page 52), I showed you how to use Windows 2000's Search feature to find a file needle in a hard disk haystack. However, what if the haystack is a huge, multipage document and the needle is a word or phrase? Not to worry: Windows 2000 has a solution. It's called the Find feature and it's part of both Notepad and WordPad.

Here's how it works:

1. In Notepad or WordPad, open the document you want to search, if it isn't open already.

2. Select the **Edit**, **Find** command (or press **Ctrl+F**). The Find dialog box punches in.

3. Use the **Find What** text box to enter the word or phrase you want to find.

4. (WordPad only) Activate the **Match Whole Word Only** check box to force Find to match only the exact word or phrase you entered in Step 3. If you leave this option deactivated, Find looks for text that *includes* the word or phrase. For example, if your search text is waldo and this check box is deactivated, Find will match not only the name *Waldo*, but also words such as *Waldorf* and *Oswaldo*.

5. Activate the **Match Case** check box to run a *case-sensitive* search. This means that Find matches only those words or phrases that exactly match the uppercase and lowercase letters you used in your search text. For example, if your search text is **Bill** and you activate this check box, Find will match the name *Bill* and will ignore the word *bill*.

6. Click the **Find Next** button to let Find loose. If it finds a match, it highlights the text. If that's not what you wanted, click **Find Next** again to resume the search; otherwise, click **Cancel** to shut down the dialog box. If Find fails to ferret out a match, it will display a dialog box to let you know the bad news.

7. If you end up back in the document and realize that the found text was not the instance you needed after all, you don't have to fire up the Find dialog box all over again. Instead, either select the **Edit**, **Find Next** command, or press **F3**. Find simply repeats your last search from the current position.

Instead of merely finding some text, a more common editing chore is to find some text and then replace it with something else. For example, you might have written "St." throughout a document and you want to change each instance to "Street." The Replace feature makes these kinds of adjustments a snap:

1. In Notepad or WordPad, open the document you want to work with, if necessary.

2. Select the **Edit**, **Replace** command. (Alternatively, you can press **Ctrl+H**. This gets you face-to-face with the Replace dialog box.

3. The Replace dialog box is pretty much the same as the Find dialog box, except that it has an extra **Replace With** text box. You use this text box to enter the word or phrase with which you want to replace whatever's in the **Find What** text box.

4. Enter the other searching options, as needed.

5. You now have two choices:

   ➤ If you want to replace only selected matches, click **Find Next**. Again, Find highlights the text if it zeroes in on a match. To replace the highlighted text with what's in the Replace With box, click **Replace**. Repeat this until you've finished all the replacements.

   ➤ If you prefer to replace every instance of the Find What text with the Replace With text, click **Replace All**.

Replace All with Caution

The Replace All feature can save you oodles of time, but use it with care. For example, you might think it's safe to replace all instances of "St." with "Street," but the sentence "He went last." might end up as "He went lastreet." (This is a good example of when the Match Case option would come in handy.)

Using Character Map for Foreign Characters and Other Symbols

If you need to use a symbol such as © or £ in a document, or if you want to spell a word such as résumé with the requisite accents, don't go hunting around your keyboard because you won't find what you need. Instead, spread open the Character Map program and use it to copy all the strange and exotic symbols and characters you require. Here's how it works:

1. Select **Start**, **Programs**, **Accessories**, **System Tools**, **Character Map**. This opens the Character Map window shown in the next figure.

2. Use the **Font** list to pick out a typeface to work with. (Hint: For foreign characters and some common symbols, select any regular typeface; for other symbols, try the Webdings, Wingdings, or Symbol typefaces.)

3. Select the symbol you want by clicking it and then clicking **Select** (you can also double-click the symbol). The symbol appears in the Characters to Copy box.

4. Click the **Copy** button to copy the character.

5. Return to WordPad or Notepad, position the cursor where you want the character to appear, and select the **Edit**, **Paste** command (or press **Ctrl+V**).

Use Character Map to get foreign characters, currency signs, zodiac signs, and lots more silly symbols.

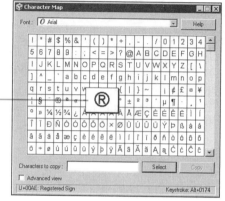

Clicking a symbol gets you this magnified view.

What Happened

This chapter showed you how to get your thoughts down on paper (electronically, at least). You saw that computer-based writing goes way beyond the old "glorified-typewriter" charge. Even a humble program such as Notepad can run rings around a typewriter. And toss WordPad into the mix with its fonts and indents and bullets, and word-processed writing is the only way to go.

Crib Notes

➤ **Smooth versus crunchy** Use Notepad (**Start**, **Programs**, **Accessories**, **Notepad**) for plain-text files, and use WordPad (**Start**, **Programs**, **Accessories**, **WordPad**) for formatted word-processing files.

➤ **Wrap Notepad text** To avoid frustration in Notepad, always activate the **Format**, **Word Wrap** command to ensure that text wraps inside the Notepad window.

➤ **The ruler rules** Don't forget to use WordPad's ruler when setting indents and tabs. It's much easier to drag the indent markers or click and drag tab stops than to do everything via the dialog boxes.

➤ **Map those characters** Use the Character Map program (**Start**, **Programs**, **Accessories**, **System Tools**, **Character Map**) whenever you need foreign characters or symbols that aren't on your keyboard.

Chapter 5

From Vapor to Paper: Printing Documents

In This Chapter

➤ Getting Windows 2000 up to speed with your printer

➤ Playing with page-printing parameters

➤ The standard printing steps

➤ Controlling print jobs

➤ Everything you need to know to get your words down on paper

The book you hold in your hands spent its entire prebook life as nothing more than a bunch of well-ordered electrons. I wrote it on my computer and shipped it to my publisher via email. The editors fixed my atrocious grammar on their computers, and then the production team made everything look nice and neat on *their* computers. The book didn't achieve its current solid, physical, form until it was spat out and bound at the printer.

The moral of this story isn't that someone with atrocious grammar gets to be an author of books (that's a subject for an entirely different discussion), but that, eventually, much of the stuff we create with our computers will eventually end up on paper. So, it helps to know the ins and outs of coaxing your printer into providing you with hard copies of your precious prose. To that end, this chapter gives you the details on setting up a printer, sending documents to the printer, and controlling those print jobs.

Got a New Printer? Tell Windows 2000 About It!

Windows 2000 acts as a kind of middleman between your programs and your printer. When you tell a program to print a document (more on this a bit later), the program shrugs its electronic shoulders and gives Windows 2000 a call. The latter, in the digital equivalent of the old if-you-want-something-done-right-you've-gotta-do-it-yourself maxim, grabs the document and carefully shepherds it to the printer.

There's just one catch: Windows 2000 can't perform its duties as a printing intermediary if it doesn't know anything about your printer. If you're lucky, your printer will have already been set up properly during the Windows 2000 installation process. To check this, select **Start**, **Settings**, **Printers** to open the Printers folder. If you see an icon for your printer, you're set; if not, then you need to tell Windows 2000 about your printer. There are three possible routes:

➤ **Easy—The Plug-and-Play Way**   Many of the latest printers are *Plug-and-Play compatible*. This means that Windows 2000 can recognize the printer automatically. In this case, all you have to do is run the printer cable from the printer to the printer port in the back of the computer, turn on the printer, and restart your machine. You'll eventually see a little dialog box titled Found New Hardware. Say "Yes!" and watch Windows 2000 install the printer automatically. (Note that you might be asked to slip the Windows 2000 CD into the CD-ROM drive.)

Plugging In a Printer

The back of any computer is usually an ugly mess with cables strewn about in tangled knots and all kinds of mysterious receptacles—or *ports* as they're properly called—lurking about. Like most devices, the secret to a successful plug-in is to ignore most of the ports and find the only one that fits the cable. The vast majority of printer cables come with a plug that has 25 pins arranged in two rows. Luckily, the vast majority of computers come with a printer port with an identical shape and with 25 holes arranged in two rows. Be sure the plug is oriented properly with the port, and then carefully slide it in as far as it will go.

➤ **Medium—The install-the-printer-disk way**   Many printers come with a disk or CD-ROM that contains an installation program. Run that program to install your printer.

➤ **Hard—The Add Printer Wizard way**   If Windows 2000 fails to recognize your printer automatically, and if you don't have a printer disk, there's a third route you can take, but it involves clearing a few more hurdles. Fortunately, Windows 2000 offers the Add Printer Wizard, described next, to guide you through the steps.

Here's how to use the Add Printer Wizard to tell Windows 2000 about your printer:

1. Select **Start**, **Settings**, **Printers** to open the Printers folder (if it isn't open already).

2. Launch the **Add Printer** icon to shove the Add Printer Wizard into the limelight.

3. The first dialog box is just a welcome screen, so just click **Next**.

4. If your machine is part of a network, the wizard will next ask whether you're installing a "local printer" (one that's attached directly to your machine) or a "network printer" (one that's attached to some other machine on the network). This chapter assumes you're working with your own printer, so be sure the **Local printer** option is activated.

5. Earlier, I mentioned that Windows 2000 can detect some printers automatically at startup. If you've attached your printer but you haven't restarted the computer, you can still convince Windows 2000 to try to figure out the printer automatically. To do this, be sure the **Automatically Detect and Install My Plug and Play Printer** check box is activated.

Cross Reference

To learn how to install and use a network printer, toddle over to Chapter 22 and read the "Printing over the Network" section on page 352.

6. Click **Next**. One of two things will happen:

   ➤ If you activated the check box, the wizard will warn you that if your detection is a bust, you'll have to run the wizard all over again. If this is cool with you, click **Yes**. Windows 2000 then busies itself with its printer detective work. If you see a New Hardware Found dialog box, you're in luck: It means the detection was successful and your printer will be set up in a few seconds. You can skip the rest of the steps.

   ➤ If you didn't bother with the automatic detection routine, the wizard displays its next dialog box. In this case, proceed to step 7.

7. Now the Add Printer Wizard pesters you to select the printer port, as shown in the following figure. Your printer almost certainly uses the port called LPT1, so be sure that's highlighted. If you know your printer uses one of the other listed ports, highlight the appropriate one. Click **Next** when you're ready for more.

Windows 2000 needs to know the port to which your printer is hanging on for dear life.

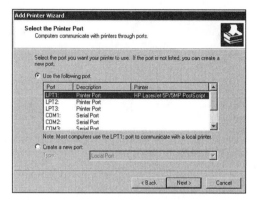

8. The wizard now offers up a list of printers. Use the **Manufacturers** list to highlight the name of the company that made your printer, and use the **Printers** list to highlight your printer. Click **Next** to move on. (If, at this point, the wizard tells you that a "driver" is already installed, just click **Next**.)

No Printer Present?

If you don't see your printer listed, you have two choices:

➤ Crack open the printer's manual and see whether it tells you anything about which printer is *compatible* with yours. If it does, then select the compatible printer in the list.

➤ If you have an inkjet printer, select **Generic** as the manufacturer and **MS Publisher Color Printer** as the printer; if you have a dot-matrix printer, select **Generic** as the manufacturer and **Generic/Text Only** as the printer; if you have a laser printer, select **HP** as the manufacturer and **HP LaserJet** as the printer.

9. The next wizard dialog box offers two options (click **Next** when you're done):

   ➤ **Printer Name**   Use this text box to enter a catchy name for your printer.

   ➤ **Do You Want Your Windows-Based Programs to Use This Printer As the Default Printer?**   This just means that your programs will automatically use this printer when you go to print documents. (However, as you'll see later on, it's easy to change from one printer to another.) Activate **Yes** (unless you know for sure that you don't want to use this printer as the default; in that case, activate **No**).

10. If you're on a network, the wizard will now ask whether you want to share your printer with your network colleagues. Again, I'll leave this to Chapter 22, so just be sure the **Do Not Share This Printer** option is activated and click **Next**.

11. The relentless wizard now wonders whether you want to print a test page. This is a good idea, so be sure **Yes** is activated and click **Next**. (This would be a good time to be sure that your printer is turned on, that it has paper, and so on.)

12. The final wizard dialog box displays a summary of the arduous road you just followed. Click **Finish** to wrap things up.

13. If you elected to print a test page, Windows 2000 lobs the test at the printer. You should get the page within 30 seconds or so. In the meantime, Windows 2000 displays a dialog box asking whether the test was successful. If so, click **OK**; if not, click the **Troubleshoot** button and answer the questions supplied by the Print Troubleshooter.

Whatever method you use, you'll eventually end up with a new icon for your printer in the Printers folder, as shown in the next figure.

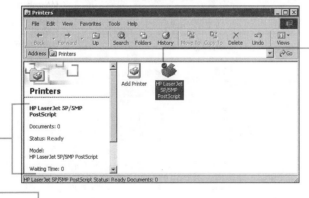

The Printers folder stores an icon for your printer.

This check mark tells you this is the default Windows 2000 printer.

Highlight the printer to see some info about it here.

Setting Up Your Pages for Printing

Before we get down to the brass printing tacks, let's take a quick look at the print-related formatting options available in WordPad and Notepad.

The Margin Minimum

You might think that you could maximize the amount of text on a page by setting the margins to 0. Sounds nice in theory, but in practice? Nope. The problem is that most printers cough up a lung if you set any margin to less than 0.25 inch.

For WordPad (**Start**, **Programs**, **Accessories**, **WordPad**), select the **File**, **Page Setup** command to display the Page Setup dialog box shown in the following figure. You have the following options:

➤ **Size**   Use this list to choose the size of the sheets or envelopes that are currently loaded in your printer.

➤ **Source**   Use this list to specify which paper tray contains the paper you picked in the Size list. In most cases, your best bet is to leave this one as **Automatically Select**.

➤ **Orientation**   These options determine how the text is splattered onto the page. In **Portrait** orientation, the text runs left-to-right along the short side of the page; in **Landscape** orientation, the text runs left-to-right along the long side of the page.

➤ **Margins (inches)**   These text boxes determine how much white space appears between the edges of the paper and the text. You can set the Left, Right, Top, and Bottom margins.

Use WordPad's Page Setup dialog box to monkey around with the print-related settings.

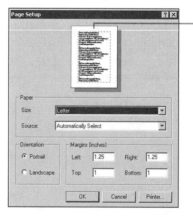

Watch this mock page to get a preview of how things will look.

Notepad, our text-only friend (**Start**, **Programs**, **Accessories**, **Notepad**), offers a similar array of settings. Again, select the **File**, **Page Setup** command to display the Page Setup dialog box. Notepad's version offers the same controls, except that it includes extra Header and Footer text boxes. A *header* is text that appears at the top of every page, whereas a *footer* is text that appears at the bottom of every page. You can enter any text you want, and Notepad is also on friendly terms with the following codes:

This Code...	Tells Notepad To...
&f	Print the name of the file.
&p	Print the page number.
&d	Print the current date.
&t	Print the current time.
&l	Align the text that follows on the left.
&c	Align the text that follows in the center.
&r	Align the text that follows on the right.

Doing the Printing Thing

At long last, you're finally ready to publish your documents for all the world (or, at least, Biff in the cubicle next door) to see. The first thing to do is be sure your printer is at the ready. To that end, be sure that:

➤ The printer is turned on

➤ The printer is ready to receive information (most printers have some kind of "Online" indicator, a button that you can push)

➤ The printer has lots of paper

You also might want to check out a preview of the printout before proceeding. Many programs offer a Print Preview feature that shows you exactly how things will look on the printed page. In WordPad, for example, select the **File**, **Print Preview** command. From here, you can Zoom In or Zoom Out, go to the Next Page or the Prev Page, try the Two Page view to see two pages at once, Print the document, or Close the preview and return to WordPad.

The Basic Printing Steps

Here are the basic steps to follow to print some or all of a document:

1. Open the document you want to print.

2. If you want to print only a chunk of text (or whatever), select that chunk; if you want to print only a single page, put the cursor somewhere inside that page.

3. Select the **File**, **Print** command. (Most programs accept the **Ctrl+P** combination as a substitute for the Print command.) The program displays its Print

dialog box. The next figure shows the version that comes with most of the Windows 2000 programs.

Use the Print dialog box to spell out your printing particulars.

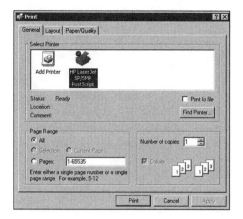

4. The layout and settings found in the Print dialog box vary from program to program. However, most offer the same controls as those found in the standard Windows 2000 dialog box:

   ➤ **Select Printer**   Use this list to choose which printer to use. Note, too, that you also can use the Add Printer icon to launch the Add Printer Wizard from here.

   ➤ **Page Range**   These options let you specify how much of the document to print. Choose **All** to print the whole enchilada; choose **Selection** to print only the currently selected text (or whatever); choose **Current Page** to print only whatever page the cursor is currently blinking away in; choose **Pages** to print a range of pages. (If you choose the latter, use the text box to enter the range using the format *x-y*, where *x* is the number of the first page you want to print and *y* is the number of the last page you want to print.)

   ➤ **Number of copies**   Use this box to tell Windows 2000 how many copies of the document you require.

   ➤ **Collate**   This check box is available only if you're printing multiple copies. When the check box is activated, Windows 2000 prints the entire document (or whatever range you selected), goes back and prints the whole thing again, and repeats until all the copies are done. If you deactivate this check box, Windows 2000 prints all the copies of the first page, then all the copies of the second page, and so on.

5. The standard Print dialog box also boasts a Layout tab where you get the following options:

➤ **Orientation**   You can choose either **Portrait** or **Landscape**, as described earlier.

➤ **Page Order**   Choose **Front to Back** to print the pages from first to last; choose **Back to Front** to print the pages last to first. The latter is handy if your printer spits out each page facing up.

➤ **Pages per Sheet**   Use this list to specify how many pages you want printed on each sheet of paper.

6. The **Paper/Quality** tab lets you select the **Paper Source** that the printer should use.

7. When you've finished fiddling with the options, set the print job in motion by clicking the **Print** button.

At this point, Windows 2000 takes over and begins doling out the document to the printer. (This process is called *spooling* by those in-the-know.) If you keep an eye on the right side of the taskbar, you should see a little printer icon appear beside the time (see the following figure). This tells you that Windows 2000 is hard at work negotiating with the printer.

The printer icon

The taskbar's printer icon lets you know that Windows 2000 is printing your document.

Other Ways to Print Stuff

The Print command is the most straightforward way to print a document, but, in an ongoing effort to keep the country's programmers employed, Windows 2000 offers a whack of other methods. Here's a summary:

➤ **Drag-and-drop**   First, two preparatory chores: Open the Printers folder and use My Computer to find the file you want to print. Now drag the file from My Computer and drop it onto the printer's icon in the Printers folder.

➤ **Toolbar printing**   Most applications have a Print button in the toolbar, and clicking that button is usually the same thing as selecting the Print command. Note, however, that many applications use the Print button as a way of *bypassing* the Print dialog box. That is, after you click the Print button, the application sends the document to the printer immediately without displaying the Print dialog box.

➤ **My Computer's Print command**   You can print from My Computer by highlighting the file and selecting the **File**, **Print** command. (You can also right-click the file and then click **Print**.)

➤ **Deferring printing**   If you're on the road or if your printer isn't available, you can still "print" documents and have Windows 2000 save them until you can hook up your printer once again. To do this, select **Start**, **Settings**, **Printers** to open the Printers folder. Highlight your printer icon and then activate the **File**, **Use Printer Offline** command. (You can also right-click the printer icon and then click **Use Printer Offline**.) When you're ready to print, select this command again to deactivate it and start printing the saved jobs.

Playing Around with Print Jobs

When you heave a document at your printer, Windows 2000 creates a *print job* that represents the printing task. The specifics of the print job are of little concern to normal people and everything happens behind the scenes anyway, so you can usually just forget about it until your pages come slithering out of the printer. Occasionally, however, you might need to interfere with the printing process: You might want to pause the print job to insert different paper into the printer, or you might want to cancel a print job entirely. For these and other print job manipulations, you have to sneak behind the scenes yourself and make some adjustments.

To do this, you first need to display the list of pending print jobs (known in the trade as the *print queue*). Here are a couple of methods you can use:

➤ **The shortcut**   Double-click the **printer icon** in the taskbar. This is the preferred method because Windows 2000 processes print jobs fairly quickly, so you have no time to lose. (If you don't see this icon, it means your print job has been sent to the printer, so there's nothing you can do.)

➤ **The longcut**   Select **Start**, **Settings**, **Printers** to open the Printers folder, and then double-click the printer icon.

The next figure shows an example of the printer window that shows up. Here's what all the columns mean:

Document Name   The name of the document that's printing.

Status   The present status of the print job. This usually shows Spooling when you first send the print job and Printing after the document is on its way to the printer. If there's a problem, this column shows Error.

Owner   The username of the person who initiated the print job.

Pages   The total number of pages to be printed.

Size   The total number of bytes printed and the total number of bytes in the document.

Submitted   The time and date that the print job was initiated.

Port   The printer port being used.

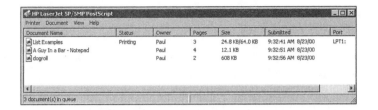

Use the printer window to see and manipulate the pending print jobs.

Here's the lowdown on a few things you can do with the print jobs:

➤ **Pause a print job**   If you need to change paper or perform some other task that requires a temporary stoppage, highlight the print job and then select the **Document**, **Pause** command. When you're ready to resume the print job, highlight it and select **Document**, **Resume**.

➤ **Pause all print jobs**   If you have multiple print jobs and you want to pause them all, activate the **Printer**, **Pause Printing** command. To resume printing, deactivate the **Printer**, **Pause Printing** command.

➤ **Starting a print job over**   If you didn't pause a print job in time and one or more pages have already printed, you can start the job from the top by highlighting it and selecting the **Document**, **Restart** command.

➤ **Cancel a print job**   If you need to bail out of a print job, highlight it and select **Document**, **Cancel**. The Status column shows Deleting and the print job disappears in a minute or two.

➤ **Canceling all print jobs**   If the printing process is a total mess, you can nuke all the pending print jobs by running the **Printer**, **Cancel All Documents** command.

What Happened

This chapter took you through a few methods for setting up a printer and printing documents. You also found out the various ways you could control print jobs by doing things such as pausing them, restarting them, or altogether canceling them.

Crib Notes

➤ **Setting up a printer**   The easiest way to set up a printer in Windows 2000 is to let Plug and Play work its magic. Barring that, you can use the installation program on the printer's disk. If that's a no-go, run the Add Printer Wizard from the Printers folder (**Start**, **Settings**, **Printers**).

➤ **Page setup**   To play around with print-related things such as paper size and margins, run the application's **File**, **Page Setup** command (if it has one).

➤ **The basic printing procedure**   Be sure your printer is on, open the document you want to print, and then run the **File**, **Print** command. (In most programs, you can also either press **Ctrl+P** or click the **Print** toolbar button.) Fill in the Print dialog box and then click **Print**.

➤ **Displaying the list of print jobs**   Double-click the taskbar's printer icon. Alternatively, select **Start**, **Settings**, **Printers** and then double-click the printer icon.

Chapter 6

A Movable Feast: Windows 2000 and Your Notebook Computer

In This Chapter

➤ Using power management to extend the life of your notebook's battery

➤ Keeping files in sync when sharing them between your notebook and another computer

➤ Proper procedures for inserting and removing PC Card devices

➤ Using a direct cable connection to get your notebook to exchange pleasantries with a second machine

➤ A tour of Windows 2000's new notebook features

Previous versions of Windows 2000 (which was then known as Windows NT) wouldn't have known a notebook computer if they suddenly sprouted legs and tripped over one. NT pigheadedly assumed it was running on a desktop computer, and no amount of cajoling or cursing could make it think otherwise. The stark truth was this: If you had a notebook computer, you were wise to avoid NT completely and treat your machine to the more tender mercies of Windows 95 or 98.

Thankfully, that's all changed. I'm pleased to report that Windows 2000 has shed not only the NT name, but also its notebook nincompoopery. Windows 2000 offers power management for sensitive notebook batteries and support for PC Cards. It also can help you synchronize files between a notebook and another machine, and even enables you to set up a direct cable connection between them. I discuss all of these welcome new capabilities in this chapter.

PC Card

A small, credit card–like device that slips into a special socket on your notebook. There are PC Card devices for modems, network adapters, hard disks, and much more.

Better Battery Life Through Power Management

When using batteries to run your notebook computer on an airplane or some other no-power-plug-in-sight location, a worried mind becomes your natural state. That's because the battery can last only so long, so you have a limited amount of time to work or play before your electronic world goes dark. Windows 2000 can help relieve some of that worry thanks to its newfound *power-management* features. For example, one of these features enables the system to shut down idle components (such as the hard disk) to prevent them from gobbling up battery power unnecessarily. Another feature lets you monitor how much power is left in the battery. This section takes you on a tour of these and other Windows 2000 power-management knickknacks.

The first stop on our tour is the taskbar. When you're running under battery power, Windows 2000 can display an icon that shows you how much battery power is left. If you don't see this icon, you have to follow these steps to display it:

1. Select **Start**, **Settings**, **Control Panel** to open the Control Panel folder.

2. Launch the **Power Options** icon to open the Power Options Properties dialog box.

3. In the **Advanced** tab, activate the **Always Show Icon on the Taskbar** check box.

4. If you see a tab named APM, display it and activate the **Enable Advanced Power Management Support** check box. (This isn't necessary for the icon, but it will come in handy a bit later when I show you how to work with power schemes.)

5. Click **OK**.

You'll see a new icon in the taskbar's system tray. If your notebook is running on AC power, the icon will look like a plug. If your machine is on batteries, you'll see the icon shown in the following figure. This icon gives you several visual clues about the state of the battery:

➤ When the battery is fully charged, the icon is blue from top to bottom.

➤ As the battery gradually loses its steam, the level of blue in the icon falls. For example, when there is 50% of battery life remaining, the icon shows as half blue and half gray.

➤ If you move your mouse pointer over the icon, a small banner shows up with the percentage of power remaining.

The Power Meter icon

The Power Meter icon tells you how much juice is left in your battery.

The Power Meter icon is useful, but it's too easy to forget to check it when you're hard at work. To help ensure that you don't power down without warning, Windows 2000 maintains two different "alarms"—called Low and Critical—that can notify you when your battery's goose is almost cooked. To work with these alarms, follow these steps:

1. Select **Start**, **Settings**, **Control Panel** to open Control Panel, and then launch the **Power Options** icon.

2. In the Power Options Properties dialog box, display the **Alarms** tab, shown in the following figure.

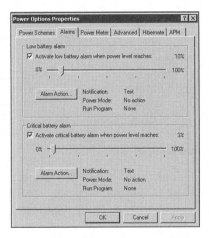

Use the Alarms tab to control when Windows 2000 warns you about a low battery.

3. The Low Battery Alarm group gives you three things to play with:

   ➤ Use the check box to toggle the alarm on and off.

   ➤ Use the slider to set the power level percentage at which the alarm goes off.

   ➤ Click the **Alarm Action** button to display the Low Battery Alarm Actions dialog box. From here, you can request that Windows 2000 **Sound Alarm** or **Display Message** when the alarm goes off. You can also activate the **When the Alarm Goes Off, the Computer Will** check box, and then select either **Standby** or **Shutdown** in the list. Click **OK** when you're done.

4. The **Critical Battery Alarm** group offers the same choices.

5. Click **OK**.

85

As I mentioned earlier, Windows 2000 cheerfully shuts down some system components in an effort to keep your battery on its feet longer. Follow these steps to control which components get shut down and when:

1. Select **Start**, **Settings**, **Control Panel** to open Control Panel, and then launch the **Power Options** icon.

2. The Power Schemes tab gives you two ways to proceed:

   ➤ To use one of the predefined power schemes, select it from the **Power Schemes** list.

   ➤ To create your own power scheme, use the lists in the **Running on Batteries** column. Use the **System Standby** list to specify when your system goes on standby. Use the **Turn Off Monitor** list and the **Turn Off Hard Disks** list to select the amount of time the monitor and hard disk must be idle before they get shut down. After you've done that, click **Save As**, enter a name for your new scheme, and click **OK**.

3. Click **OK**.

Please Stand By

During *system standby*, Windows 2000 powers down everything temporarily. To resume normal operations, you usually either jiggle the mouse or press a key. If that doesn't work, quickly poke the power button. (Don't press the power button for long or you might end up totally shutting down the machine!)

Synchronizing Files Between Your Notebook and Another Computer

Do you have to deal with both a notebook computer *and* a desktop computer? If so, then I'm sure you know all too well the problems that arise when you try to share files between them. For example, if you transport a few files to the notebook and you end up changing a couple of those files, it's crucial to be sure that the desktop machine gets a copy of the updated files.

In other words, you want to be sure that the notebook and the desktop remain *synchronized*. To help you do this, Windows 2000 offers a new feature called Briefcase. To understand how it works, let's examine how you use a real briefcase to do some work at home. You begin by stuffing your briefcase full of the files and documents you want to work with. You then take the briefcase home, take out the papers, work on them, and put them back in the briefcase. Finally, you take the briefcase back to work and then remove the papers.

Windows 2000's Briefcase feature works in much the same way, except that you don't work with the original documents. Instead, you work with special copies called *sync copies*. A Briefcase is really a special type of folder. The basic idea is that you place the documents you want to work with inside a Briefcase, and then lug around the Briefcase using a floppy disk, zip disk, or some other removable disk. You can then copy the documents from the Briefcase to the notebook and work on them. The key thing is that the Briefcase "remembers" where the documents came from originally, and it automatically tracks which ones have changed. You can update the original files with just a couple of mouse clicks.

Before getting started, you need to create a Briefcase. The best place to create the Briefcase is on the removable disk you'll be using to transport the files. Here are the steps to follow to create a Briefcase:

1. Insert the disk you want to use.

2. Use **My Computer** to display the disk.

3. To create a new Briefcase on the disk, either select **File**, **New**, **Briefcase**, or right-click the folder and then click **New**, **Briefcase**. Windows 2000 adds an icon named New Briefcase to the disk.

4. Rename the Briefcase (this is optional).

With the briefcase created, follow these specific steps to transfer and synchronize documents between a desktop and a notebook computer:

1. Copy the files you want to work with from the desktop computer to the Briefcase. (If you're using drag-and-drop, you don't have to hold down Ctrl because Windows 2000 will automatically make sync copies of the files that you drop.)

2. The first time you copy anything to the Briefcase, Windows 2000 displays an overview of how Briefcase works. Just click **Finish** to get rid of this dialog box.

3. Remove the disk and insert it into the notebook.

4. On the notebook, use **My Computer** to open the removable disk and then open the **Briefcase** folder. Copy the files from the Briefcase to the notebook computer.

Don't Move or Rename the Files!

As I mentioned earlier, the Briefcase keeps careful tabs on its files: both where they came from originally on the desktop computer and where you copy them to on the notebook. Therefore, don't move or rename the files after they're safely stowed on the notebook, or you'll break the synchronization.

5. Work with the files on the notebook.

6. When you're done, insert the disk into the notebook and open the **Briefcase** folder. The Briefcase then checks its files with the copies you sent to the notebook. As you can see in the following figure, the Briefcase's **Status** column tells you which files have been changed. (To get the various columns, activate the **View**, **Details** command.)

This column tells you which
files have been changed.

The Briefcase folder keeps track of which files you changed on the notebook.

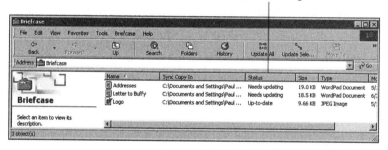

7. To update the Briefcase copies of the changed files, either select **Briefcase**, **Update All**, or click the **Update All** toolbar button. Briefcase displays a list of the files to be updated.

8. Click **Update**. Briefcase grabs copies of the changed files.

9. Insert the disk into the desktop computer and open the Briefcase folder. This time, the Briefcase compares its files with the original one on the desktop machine. Again, the Status column tells you which files have been changed.

10. To update the desktop computer's original copies of the changed files, either select **Briefcase**, **Update All**, or click the **Update All** toolbar button. Briefcase displays a list of the files to be updated.

11. Click **Update**. Briefcase copies the changed files to the desktop computer.

Working with Those Little PC Card Doodads

For years, hobbyists, power users, and geeks of all shapes and sizes have been cracking open computer cases and tickling their machines' innards to add things such as modems, hard disks, CD-ROM drives, networking cards, and more. Your average Joe and Josephine, on the other hand, might have wanted to upgrade their machine, but they lacked the technical wherewithal to pull it off.

Fortunately, notebook computers have changed all that. Notebooks are, by definition, small and lightweight to ensure easy luggability. Their relatively Lilliputian size means that there just isn't enough internal room to "expand" a notebook in the same way that you can a desktop machine. That's good news for non-nerds because it meant the notebook engineers had to find some other way to enable users to "add on" to their machines. The result was the PC Card: a small, credit card-sized wafer that plugged into a special slot—or *socket*—on the *outside* of the notebook. So, now even the digitally maladroit can upgrade their machines with little or no effort.

A Big Name for a Small Thing

PC Cards were originally known as PCMCIA cards, where PCMCIA stood for Personal Computer Memory Card International Association. Doesn't exactly trip lightly off the tongue, does it? Unfortunately, Windows 2000 hasn't clued in to the fact that the PCMCIA designation is more or less obsolete, so it still uses it. I'll mostly use PC Card in this section, but just remember that PC Card and PCMCIA are the same thing.

Windows 2000 helps by recognizing your notebook's PC Card sockets (most machines have at least two), and by supporting *hot swapping*, which sounds like some sort of swinging singles party, but is really just the capability to insert and remove PC Cards without having to shut down the system.

Popping In a PC Card Device

To use a PC Card device, insert it gently and as far as it will go into any free PC Card socket. (You should feel a slight "click" at the end.) Windows 2000 recognizes that a new device is in the socket and beeps the speaker. One of two things now happens:

➤ If you've used the device before, it will be ready for use within a few seconds.

➤ If you've never used the device before, you'll see the New Hardware Found dialog box and Windows 2000 will proceed to install the necessary software to make the device run. You might see the New Hardware Found Wizard, which will take you through the appropriate steps.

After the device is up and at 'em, Windows 2000 displays a special Unplug or Eject Hardware icon on the right side of the taskbar, as shown in the following figure. (Note, too, that this icon will also appear if you have certain other devices—such as an external modem—plugged into the machine.)

When you wedge a PC Card device into your notebook, Windows 2000 displays this icon in the taskbar.

The Unplug or Eject Hardware icon

If you want to see a list of all your PC Card devices, double-click the **Unplug or Eject Hardware** icon. Windows 2000 displays the Unplug or Eject Hardware dialog box shown in the next figure.

*Double-click the **Unplug or Eject Hardware** icon to see a list of all your plugged-in devices.*

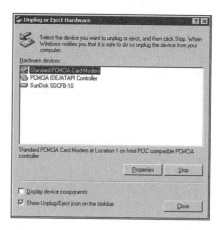

Yanking Out a PC Card Device

This hot-swapping thing should really be called *tepid swapping* because you can't just grab out a PC Card device by the scruff of the neck and drag it out of the slot. Such willy-nillyness is frowned upon. Instead, you need to tell Windows 2000 which device you're giving the heave-ho. This gives Windows a chance to shut down the device. Here's the easiest way to go about this:

Removing the Icon

If you'd rather not clutter your taskbar with the Unplug or Eject Hardware icon, deactivate the **Show Unplug/Eject Icon on the Taskbar** check box in the Unplug or Eject Hardware dialog box.

1. Click the **Unplug or Eject Hardware** icon. Windows 2000 displays a list of the devices attached to your system.

2. Click the device you want to remove. Click the device and then click **OK**. Your computer beeps and Windows 2000 displays a message telling you it's okay to remove the device.

3. Click **OK** and then remove the PC Card device. (On most notebooks, you do this by pushing a button beside the socket.)

Note, too, that another way to go about this is to display the Eject Hardware dialog box (as described in the previous section), highlight the device you want to spit out, and then click **Stop**.

Setting Up a Direct Connection Between the Two Computers

Earlier in this chapter, I showed you how to use a Briefcase to exchange files between your notebook and another computer using a floppy disk or some other removable disk. However, using a floppy disk to transport files back and forth between a desktop computer and a notebook isn't a great solution because floppies are pretty pathetic as a storage medium: They can hold only so much data and they're teeth-gnashingly slow. Zip disks are larger (100 megabytes) and faster, but you might not have a zip drive on both machines.

The solution to easier file transfers between your notebook and another machine is to connect them with a cable and then perform the transfers along that cable. What kind of cable do you need? Windows 2000 gets along with two kinds:

Cross Reference

If you need to access your network while traveling with your notebook, see Chapter 23, "Road Scholar: Using Dial-Up Network Connections," p. 359.

How to Get a DirectParallel Cable

DirectParallel cables are available from a company called Parallel Technologies: (800) 789–4784 or (425) 869–1119. If you have Web access, see http://www.lpt.com/.

Cross Reference

Another way to connect two computers is to network them. See Chapter 21, "Using Windows 2000 to Set Up a Small Network," p. 323, and Chapter 22, "Using Windows 2000's Networking Features," p. 339.

➤ **A null-modem cable** This is a special cable that attaches to the serial port in the back of both machines. Null-modem cables are common and are available from any decent computer or electronics store. Note, however, that this is *not* the same as the cable you use with your modem.

➤ **A DirectParallel cable** This cable attaches to the parallel (or printer) port in the back of the computers. This kind is preferred because it can transmit data quite a bit faster than the null-modem variety. Unfortunately, at the time of writing, these cables were available only directly from the manufacturer.

After you've attached the cable to both machines (they don't need to be turned off while you make the attachments), you're ready to begin the setup. This involves setting up the host and guest computers and configuring both machines so that they can converse with each other. The *host computer* is the one that will be sharing its resources, while the guest computer is the one that will be accessing those shared resources.

The next three sections take you through the necessary steps.

Step 1: Configure the Host Computer

Here's how to configure the host machine:

1. Select **Start**, **Settings**, **Network and Dial-Up Connections**. Windows 2000 displays the Network and Dial-Up Connections window.

2. Double-click the **Make New Connection** icon to launch the Network Connection Wizard.

3. Click **Next**. The wizard asks what kind of connection you want.

4. Activate the **Connect Directly to Another Computer** option, and then click **Next**.

5. In the next wizard dialog box, activate **Host** and click **Next**.

Future Connections

After you've created a connection, selecting **Start, Settings, Network and Dial-Up Connections** displays a submenu of the items in the Network and Dial-Up Connections window (including the Make New Connection icon). If you need to access this window in the future, you have to go the long way: **Start, Programs, Accessories, Communications, Network and Dial-Up Connections**.

6. The wizard now asks you to choose which communications port you'll be using. Select the port to which your cable is attached, and then click **Next**.

7. Your next chore is to select which users are allowed to make the connection from the other machine. Activate the check box beside each user you want to have access. (If the user isn't listed, click **Add** and enter a User name, Full name, and Password (twice), and click **OK**.) Click **Next** when you're done.

8. In the final wizard dialog box, adjust the connection name, if desired, and then click **Finish**.

Step 2: Configure the Guest Computer

To set up the guest computer, follow steps 1–4 in the previous section, and then do this:

1. When the wizard asks whether this machine is to be the host or the guest, activate **Guest** and click **Next**.

2. Select the port to which your cable is attached, and then click **Next**.

3. The wizard next asks whether you want to make this connection available **For All Users** or **Only for Myself**. Make your choice (if in doubt, select the latter) and click **Next**.

4. In the final wizard dialog box, adjust the connection name, if desired, and then click **Finish**.

Making the Connection

To establish the connection between the two computers, you need to do the following:

1. On the guest computer, select **Start**, **Settings**, **Network and Dial-Up Connections** to rustle up the Network and Dial-Up Connections window.

2. Double-click the icon for your direct connection (the default name is **Direct Connection**). Windows 2000 pastes up a Connect dialog box similar to the one shown in the following figure.

Use this dialog box to make the connection to the host.

3. Fill in the **User Name** and **Password**. These should be the same as one of the users you specified during the host setup. If you want Windows 2000 to keep an internal sticky note for the password, be sure the **Save Password** check box is activated.

4. Click **Connect**. Windows 2000 accesses the cable and alerts the host that a guest is knocking on the door. The host authenticates the incoming user, and then displays the Connection Complete dialog box. Click **OK**.

From here, you use the usual networking techniques to access data on the host (see Chapter 22, "Using Windows 2000's Networking Features").

Direct Connections and the Briefcase

After you have a direct connection established, you might want to use a Briefcase to coordinate the exchange of files. Here's how it works:

1. Be sure that the host folder containing the files you want to work with is either shared directly or resides in a shared folder.

2. Use the guest computer to access the shared folder.

3. Copy the files to the guest computer's Briefcase.

4. Use the guest computer to work on the files directly from the Briefcase folder. (There's no need for a connection at this point.)

5. When you're done, connect again and then open the guest's Briefcase folder.

6. Select **Briefcase**, **Update All** to update the host computer's files with the changed files in the guest computer's Briefcase.

Disconnecting from the Host

When you feel you've imposed upon the host computer quite enough, it's time to take your leave. Windows 2000 gives you the following ways to bid goodnight:

➤ On the host or guest, right-click the connection icon in the system tray, and then click **Disconnect**.

➤ On the host, open the guest user's icon in the Network and Dial-Up Connections window, and then click **Disconnect**.

➤ On the guest, open the connection icon in the Network and Dial-Up Connections window, and then click **Disconnect**.

In each case, Windows 2000 asks you to confirm the disconnect. Click **Yes**.

What Happened

This chapter took you on a road trip to discover Windows 2000's new notebook niceties. You learned how to monitor your battery and how to use power management to save battery life; how to use a Briefcase to keep the files on two machines in sync; how to work with PC Cards; and how to configure a direct cable connection between two computers. That's a lot of learning for such a little machine!

Crib Notes

➤ **Use the Power Meter icon** When running your notebook on batteries, be sure you display the Power Meter icon to keep a close eye on the battery level.

➤ **Manage your power** To maximize battery life, create a power scheme that shuts down the monitor and hard disk within a minute or two of idle time.

➤ **Lug the Briefcase** The easiest way to use a Briefcase is to move it onto a removable disk and keep it there. You can then add files to the Briefcase, copy those files to the other machine, and use the update feature to keep the files synchronized.

➤ **Hot swap PC Cards** You can insert a PC Card and Windows 2000 recognizes it right away (and, if necessary, installs the required files). Before removing a PC Card device, tell Windows 2000 to stop it.

➤ **The direct connection** String a null-modem or DirectParallel cable between two machines and then set up one as the host and the other as the guest.

Chapter 7

Picture Programs: Windows 2000's Graphic Tools

In This Chapter

➤ Getting to know the Paint window

➤ A complete look at all of Paint's drawing and editing tools

➤ Capturing images of the Windows 2000 screen

➤ Installing and using a document scanner or digital camera

➤ About five thousand words that tell you how to get pictures worth a thousand words

Before Windows became a ubiquitous feature of dens and cubicles throughout the land, words ruled the computing roost. Memos to the boss and letters to the editor were composed entirely of text, with nary an image in sight.

The graphical underpinnings of Windows are slowly changing all that because now the tools for creating images are no longer the sole province of the "dog-collar worker" (jargon for a graphic artist). For example, while it's probably still true that your memos and letters are text-only, Windows has the tools that enable you to design your own logo and so create a kind of ad hoc stationery.

Similarly, Windows has enabled us to go beyond the workaday world of letters and memos to documents that positively cry out for image enhancement: business presentations, flyers, newsletters, and Web pages, to name only a few. Again, Windows has various tools that let you create images from scratch, mess around with existing images, and capture digital images from an outside source (such as a scanner). None of these tools is good enough for professional artists, but they're more than adequate for amateur dabblers whose needs aren't so grandiose. This chapter shows you how to create and modify images using the Paint program, and how to capture and manipulate digital images from a scanner or digital camera.

Giving Your Right Brain a Workout with Paint

Scientists tell us that, for most people, the left side of the brain is verbal, analytic, abstract, rational, and linear, while the right side of the brain is nonverbal, synthetic, analogical, intuitive, and holistic. The left brain enjoys words, but the right brain revels in images, so it's the latter that will get a kick out of Paint, Windows 2000's main graphics program.

Even if you're a nonartist (that is, someone who hears "Leonardo" and thinks *Titanic*), Paint has plenty of easy-to-use tools that can help you get the job done.

A Tour of the Paint Studio

To get Paint running, select **Start**, **Programs**, **Accessories**, **Paint**. The next figure shows the Paint window that materializes.

The Paint canvas.

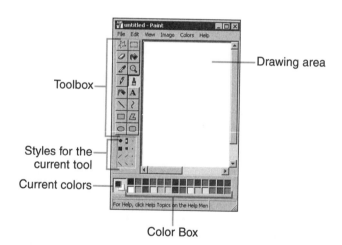

The Paint window is loaded with interesting-looking buttons and lots of color. Here's a rundown of the major features:

> **Toolbox**   This box holds the various tools you use to create or edit your artwork. There's a "pencil," a "brush," an "eraser," and all sorts of utensils for drawing lines and shapes. I describe the individual Toolbox tools in more detail later in this chapter.

➤ **Tool styles**   This box shows the styles that are available with most of the tools. You use these styles to add some variety to your drawings. For example, the Brush tool offers a selection of brush sizes and shapes.

➤ **Color Box**   This box holds all the colors and patterns you can use for drawing or filling shapes. It's just like having your own personal 28-box of Crayola crayons (minus that creepy flesh-colored crayon) that never need sharpening.

➤ **Current colors**   This area contains two boxes that display the currently selected foreground color (the top box) and background color (the bottom box). Selecting a new foreground color is a simple matter of clicking one of the color rectangles in the Color Box. If it's a new background color you're after, right-click a color swatch.

➤ **Drawing area**   This white expanse is your Paint canvas. It's where you perform the mouse moves that lead to the creation of your digital drawings. It is, in other words, the place where all the fun happens.

Tool Time: How to Use the Paint Tools

The best way to tackle Paint is simply to enjoy yourself by experimenting with various tools, styles, and colors. Feel free to let yourself go, toss off those inhibitions, and free yourself from the shackles of adult responsibilities. Give yourself permission to regress to an immature, to-heck-with-it-I'm-going-to-be-at-one-with-my-inner-child state. (It might be a good idea to close the door for this.)

When you're ready to go, roll up your sleeves, pick out a tool, and just start playing. However, just so you know, there *is* a basic four-step method you use for each tool:

1. In the Toolbox, click the tool you want to play with.
2. Click a tool style (if the tool has any).
3. Use the Color Box to choose a foreground and background color.
4. Move the mouse pointer into the drawing area and then draw the shape you want. (The specifics of the drawing process vary from tool to tool, as you'll see in a second.)

Erasing Paint Mistakes

While you're on the steep part of the Paint learning curve, you'll end up with lots of botched lines and mutinous shapes that you won't want in your final drawing. Here's how to get rid of these things (see also the Eraser tool, discussed later in this chapter):

➤ Most of the Paint tools operate by holding down a mouse button and then dragging the mouse. If you make a mess during the drawing, you can start again by clicking the other mouse button *before* you release the button you're drawing with.

➤ If you've already completed the shape, select **Edit**, **Undo** (pressing **Ctrl+Z** will also get you there).

➤ If the drawing is a complete write-off, you can start over by selecting **Image**, **Clear Image** (or by pressing **Ctrl+Shift+N**).

Right-Drag for the Background Color

For most of the Paint tools, a left-drag or a left-click draws a shape using the current foreground color. If you'd prefer to use the current background color, right-drag or right-click, instead.

Here's a review of the drawing-related tools you can grab from the Toolbox:

Pencil You use this tool to draw freehand lines. After selecting this tool, move the mouse pointer into the drawing area, hold down the left mouse button, and then wiggle the mouse around. Paint draws a freehand line that follows your every twitch and shimmy.

Brush This is another tool for drawing freehand lines. It differs from the Pencil tool in that it gives you a selection of brush shapes and sizes (in the tool styles area).

Line You use this tool to draw straight lines (the tool styles offer five different widths for your line-drawing pleasure). To create a line, drag the mouse pointer within the drawing area. You can make Paint draw a perfect horizontal or vertical line, or a line pitched at a 45-degree angle, by holding down the **Shift** key while you drag the mouse.

Rectangle   This tool draws rectangles. The point where you hold down the mouse button defines one corner of the rectangle, and you create the rest of it by dragging the mouse. Need to draw a perfect square? No problem: Just hold down the **Shift** key while dragging. The Rectangle tool offers three styles: a "border only" style that draws only the border of the shape; a "border and fill" style that draws a border (using the foreground color) and fills it with a color (the background color); and a "no border" style that leaves off the shape's border and draws only the fill.

Ellipse   You use this tool for drawing ovals. Again, you do this by dragging the mouse inside the drawing area. If what you really need is a perfect circle, hold down the **Shift** key while doing the dragging thing.

Rounded Rectangle   This tool combines the Rectangle and Ellipse tools to produce a rectangle that has rounded corners.

Curve   Use this tool when you need a wavy line. This one works a little differently than the others you've seen so far. You begin by dragging the mouse pointer until the line is the length you want, and you then release the button. To curve the line, drag the mouse again and then release the button. If you're feeling spunky, you can add a second curve to the line by dragging the mouse once again and then releasing the button when you're done.

Polygon   You use this tool to create a polygon. (In case you can't remember back to high school geometry, a *polygon* is a succession of straight lines that forms an enclosed object. A triangle and a rectangle are examples of polygons.) To wield this tool, begin by dragging the mouse pointer until the first side is the length and angle you want, and then release the mouse button. To create the next side, move the pointer to where you want the side to end, and then click. Paint dutifully draws a line from the end of the previous line to the spot where you clicked. Repeat this move-and-click procedure to add more sides. To complete the polygon, click the start of the first side to enclose the shape.

Fill with Color   This tool looks like a can of paint being poured, and that's more or less what it does. That is, it fills an enclosed shape with a specified color. To use it, just click anywhere inside the shape (be sure it's completely closed!) and Paint fills it up with the current foreground color.

Airbrush   This tool resembles (and works like) a can of spray paint, so I'm not sure why it's called an Airbrush. No matter, it's loads of fun to use because as you drag the mouse, Paint "sprays" the current foreground color. (Drag the mouse quickly to get a light spray; drag the mouse slowly to get a heavy spray.)

Text   If your left brain is feeling thoroughly ignored by now, you can toss it a bone by using the Text tool to add text to your drawing. The first step is to drag the mouse inside the drawing area to create a box to hold your

101

text. When you release the mouse button, Paint places a cursor inside the box, so you can just start typing. Paint also displays the Fonts toolbar (see the following figure). To change the font of the text, select the typeface, size, and other font options. Note, too, that this tool offers two styles: opaque (the text is the foreground color and the text box is filled with the background color) and transparent (the text is the foreground color and the text box background is transparent).

Text Gets Set in Stone

You need to be extra careful when typing your text with the Text tool. Why? Because after you enter the text and then click outside the box to finish up, the text becomes uneditable. If you try to click inside the box to make changes, Paint annoyingly ignores the existing text completely and starts a new text box. So, if you make a mistake, the only thing you can do is undo or erase the text and start over.

A Paint file demonstrating the opaque and transparent text styles.

The Paint Toolbox offers a few other nondrawing tools to enhance your creativity:

Pick Color You use this tool to select an existing color from the currently open image. This is handy, for example, if the image has a color that doesn't appear in the Color Box. You select the color by clicking it.

Eraser This not-to-be-wielded-lightly tool enables you to erase parts of your image. The tool styles offer various widths, and dragging the mouse in the drawing area wipes out everything in the mouse pointer's path.

The Color Eraser

Rather than obliterating everything with the flick of the mouse, you might prefer to erase only a particularly ill-chosen color and replace it with something else. That's the job of the Color Eraser tool. First, set the foreground color to the color you want to wipe out, and set the background color to the color you want to use in its stead. Now select the Eraser tool and then right-drag the mouse inside the drawing area.

Magnifier   You use this tool to zoom in on your drawing and get a closer look at things, which is handy for doing detail work. When you select this tool, use the tool styles box to choose a magnification: 1x (normal size), 2x, 6x, or 8x. (The last gets you so close that you can see the *pixels*.) Then click the section of the drawing that you want to magnify. The following figure shows this tool in action.

Pixels

The individual pinpoints of light that make up a Paint drawing (and, for that matter, everything you see on your screen). Pixels is short for picture elements.

Select   This tool lets you select a rectangular chunk—called a *cutout*—of the drawing, which you can then copy or cut out (hence the name). As you might expect, you use the Select tool much like you do the Rectangle tool. That is, you move the mouse pointer to the corner of the area you want to select, and then drag the mouse until the box encloses the area.

Free-Form Select   This tool is similar to Select, but it lets you mark an area using a free-form line. Click the tool, move the pointer into the drawing area, and then drag the mouse pointer around the area you want to select.

Other Ways to Zoom

Here are a few other zoom-related techniques:

➤ To magnify the image to 400%, select the **View, Zoom, Large Size** command (or press **Ctrl+Page Down**).

➤ To return to the regular size, select **View, Zoom, Normal Size** (or press **Ctrl+Page Up**).

➤ You can also select the **View, Zoom, Custom** command, activate a magnification percentage in the Custom Zoom dialog box, and then click **OK**.

➤ You can see the individual pixels more easily if you activate the grid (shown in the next figure) by selecting **View, Zoom, Show Grid** (pressing **Ctrl+G** also works).

➤ You can display a separate "thumbnail image" that shows the drawing at regular size (see the following figure) by selecting **View, Zoom, Show Thumbnail**.

Use the Magnifier tool to see the pixel trees in the image forest.

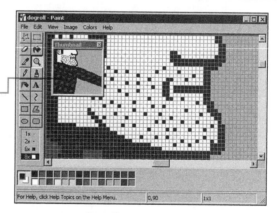

The thumbnail image

I've Got a Cutout—Now What?

Paint gives you all kinds of cutout maneuvers that range from the mundane to the marvelous. Here's a rundown:

➤ **Cut the cutout** Select **Edit, Cut** (or press **Ctrl+X**) to pluck the cutout from the drawing.

➤ **Copy the cutout** Select **Edit, Copy** (or press **Ctrl+C**) to copy the cutout to the Windows 2000 Clipboard.

➤ **Paste the cutout** After you've cut or copied the cutout, you can paste it into the same drawing or a different drawing by selecting **Edit, Paste** (or by pressing **Ctrl+V**). The cutout appears in the upper-left corner of the drawing. Use the next technique to drag the cutout to the spot you want.

➤ **Move the cutout** Position the mouse pointer inside the cutout and the pointer changes into a four-headed arrow. This means that you can drag the cutout to another part of the drawing.

➤ **Move a copy of the cutout** If you hold down **Ctrl** while dragging a cutout, Paint leaves the original intact and moves a copy.

➤ **Save the cutout to a file** Select the **Edit, Copy To** command to save the cutout in its own file. In the Copy To dialog box that appears, select a location, enter a **File Name**, and then click **Save**. (If you want to use the saved cutout in another drawing, open the drawing and select the **Edit, Paste From** command. In the Paste From dialog box, highlight the cutout file and then click **Open**.)

➤ **Use the cutout to create a sweep** This is one of Paint's best effects. Choose the Transparent style, hold down the **Shift** key, and then drag the cutout around the drawing area. As you do this, Paint leaves behind copies of the cutout, as shown in the following figure.

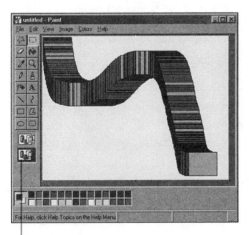

*Hold down **Shift** while you drag a cutout to create the psychedelic sweep effect.*

Activate the Transparent style.

➤ **Flip the cutout** To flip a cutout, select **Image, Flip/Rotate** (or press **Ctrl+R**) to display the Flip and Rotate dialog box. Activate either the **Flip Horizontal** option (left becomes right, and vice versa) or the **Flip Vertical** option (up becomes down, and vice versa). Alternatively, activate **Rotate by Angle** and then choose an angle option.

➤ **Invert the cutout colors**   Select **Image**, **Invert Colors** (or tap **Ctrl+I**). This technique tells Paint to change black to white and white to black, and the other colors to change to their complementary colors.

➤ **Stretch the cutout**   To scale the cutout to either a smaller or larger size, use the **Image**, **Stretch/Skew** command (or press **Ctrl+W**). Paint displays the Stretch and Skew dialog box. In the **Stretch** group, use the **Horizontal** and **Vertical** text boxes to enter the percentage value that you want to use to stretch the cutout. Values over 100% get you a larger image, whereas values less than 100% get you a smaller image.

➤ **Skew the cutout**   To tilt the cutout at an angle, run the **Stretch/Skew** command to display the Stretch and Skew dialog box. In the **Skew** group, use the **Horizontal** and **Vertical** text boxes to enter the number of degrees by which you want the cutout tilted. Enter values between –89 and 89.

The Paint window shown in the following figure demonstrates a few of these cutout techniques.

Paint offers lots of special effects for playing around with cutouts.

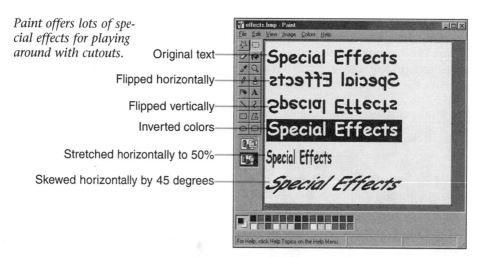

Original text

Flipped horizontally

Flipped vertically

Inverted colors

Stretched horizontally to 50%

Skewed horizontally by 45 degrees

Big, Bigger, Biggest: Seeing More of Your Drawing

The Magnifier tool zooms in to give you a detailed view of a small chunk of the drawing. However, what Paint users often clamor for is a view that shows them *more* of the drawing. Here are three ways to get it:

➤ To temporarily chuck all the Paint paraphernalia (the menu, Toolbox, Color Box, and so on) and enlarge the window so that it usurps the whole screen, select **View**, **View Bitmap** (or poke **Ctrl+F**). To return to your regular view, click the mouse or press any key.

➤ To hide only certain Paint knickknacks, pull down the **View** menu and deactivate some or all of the following commands: **Tool Box** (you can also press **Ctrl+T** here), **Color Box** (or hit **Ctrl+L**), and **Status Bar**.

➤ Removing the Tool Box and Color Box is a bit drastic, but it's possible to leave them visible and still gain some extra elbow room. Move the mouse pointer into the thin gray area beside the tools or above and below the colors, and then drag the mouse into the drawing area. When you release the mouse button, the boxes morph into "floating" toolbars that rest on top of your drawing.

Setting the Image Attributes

If you find yourself running out of room in the drawing area, you can expand the canvas by increasing the size of the drawing. The size of the image as well as a few other options are part of the image attributes. To work with these attributes, follow these steps:

1. Select the **Image**, **Attributes** command (or press **Ctrl+E**). Paint fires up the Attributes dialog box shown in the next figure.

2. Use the options in the **Units** group to select the measurement unit you want to work with.

3. Use the **Width** and **Height** text boxes to enter the new dimensions of the image.

4. While you're here, you might also need to convert the image between black-and-white and colors. You'll use the **Colors** option most of the time, but you should choose **Black and White** if your image uses only black, white, and shades of gray. This means your image will take up far less disk space.

5. When you're done, click **OK**.

The Attributes dialog box lets you change the size of a picture and switch between black-and-white and colors.

Taking a "Picture" of the Screen

Those us who were born without an artistic bone in our bodies are constantly on the lookout for ways to avoid creating a drawing from scratch. If you have something on your screen that you'd like to include in a drawing (it might be an icon or an image contained in a program), you can "capture" the screen image and then pluck out the detail you want. Windows 2000 gives you two ways to make this happen:

Screen Shot

A copy of the current screen image.

➤ If you want to grab the entire screen, lock, stock, and taskbar, press your keyboard's **Print Screen** key. (Depending on your keyboard, this key may be labeled "Print Scrn" or even "Prt Sc.")

➤ If you'd prefer to capture only the active window, press **Alt+Print Screen**, instead.

In both cases, the *screen shot* (as it's called) ends up on the Windows 2000 Clipboard. To get the image into Paint for processing, start Paint and select its **Edit**, **Paste** command. If Paint moans about the image being too large, click **Yes** to enlarge your drawing to fit the screen shot.

Another Use: Capturing Error Messages

Capturing the screen is also useful if want to report an error or problem to a tech support department. Capture the screen image while the error is displayed, paste the resulting image into Paint, and save it to a file. You can then email the file to the tech support department.

Being Digital: Using Scanners and Digital Cameras

Capturing a screen image might save you some artistic elbow grease, but its usefulness is limited. These days, the best way to get an image without having to expend a lot of creative energy is to grab it from either one of the following sources:

➤ **A document scanner** This contraption acts much like a photocopier in that it creates an image of a flat surface, such as a photograph or a sheet of paper. The difference is that the scanner saves the image to a graphics file on your hard disk instead of on paper.

➤ **A digital camera** This gadget acts much like a regular camera in that it captures and stores an image of the outside world. The difference is that the digital camera stores the image internally in its memory instead of on exposed film. It's then possible to connect the digital camera to your computer and save the image as a graphics file on your hard disk.

Windows 2000 comes with support for a variety of scanners and cameras, so getting your digital images from out here to in there has never been easier.

Installing a Scanner or Digital Camera

Windows 2000 offers a number of options for installing scanners and digital cameras:

> **Rely on Plug and Play.** Many of today's crop of scanners are Plug-and-Play compatible, so all you have to do is connect the scanner, turn it on, and then restart Windows 2000.

Administrators Only!

Only someone logged on as an Administrator can add devices using the Scanners and Cameras icon method.

> **Use the Scanners and Cameras icon.** Select **Start**, **Settings**, **Control Panel** and launch the **Scanners and Cameras** icon. When the Scanners and Cameras Properties dialog box shows up, click **Add** and then click **Next**. Windows 2000 takes a few moments to collect its thoughts, and then displays a list of scanner and digital camera manufacturers and models. Find your camera or scanner in this list, click **Next**, and follow the instructions on the screen. (You'll likely need your Windows 2000 CD at some point.)

> **Install the device software.** Any scanner or digital camera worth its salt will come with software for setting up the device. If the first two options don't work, try installing the software.

Capturing Digital Images

If you installed the scanner or digital camera software, your best bet is to use that software to capture the images.

Otherwise, because Windows 2000's Imaging program is conversant with many popular scanner and digital camera formats, you can use it as one-stop digital-imaging shop. This section shows you how to do just that.

Here are the steps to follow to use the Imaging program to capture an image:

1. Select **Start**, **Programs**, **Accessories**, **Imaging**, and eventually you'll see the Imaging window shown in the following figure.

Use the Imaging program to grab images from a scanner or digital camera.

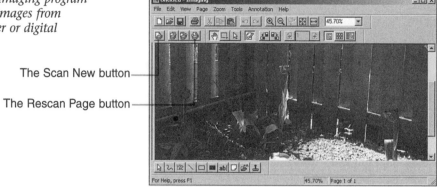

The Scan New button

The Rescan Page button

2. If you have multiple scanning devices, choose the **File**, **Select Device** command to open the Select Scanner dialog box. Highlight the device you want to use and then click **OK**.

3. Select **File**, **Acquire Image**, or click the **Scan New** toolbar button. Again, Windows 2000 loads the image capture window for the selected device. As before, the window you see depends on the device. The following figure shows the window that appears if you have a Hewlett-Packard scanner.

This is the window that appears for some Hewlett-Packard scanners.

4. Use the window to scan the image or download the image from the camera.

5. Select **File**, **Save** to save the image as a file on your hard disk.

Running a Rescan

If you're using a scanner, you might decide that your first pass was subpar and that you want to rescan the image. You might be tempted to run the Acquire Image command again, but that's a bit of a pain because it creates a whole new file. A better method is to run the **Page**, **Reacquire** command (or click the **Rescan Page** toolbar button). This tells the scanning software to replace the existing image with a newly scanned one.

What Happened

This chapter showed you how to make good use of Windows 2000's graphics features. You learned how to use Paint and its decent collection of tools and techniques, how to install a document scanner or digital camera, and how to use Imaging to get images from device to disk.

Crib Notes

➤ **The basic Paint method**   Click a tool, select a style (if applicable), choose the foreground and background colors, and then draw the shape. Most Paint tools operate by clicking and dragging within the drawing area.

➤ **Shift for accuracy**   Holding down **Shift** gets you a horizontal, vertical, or 45-degree angle line with the Line tool, a square with the Rectangle tool, or a circle with the Ellipse tool.

➤ **Grabbing screen shots**   Press **Print Screen** to capture an image of the full screen, or **Alt+Print Screen** to capture an image of just the active window.

➤ **Grabbing digital images**   In Imaging, select **File, Acquire**.

Chapter 8

The Sights and Sounds of Windows 2000 Multimedia

In This Chapter

➤ Coaxing Windows 2000 into playing animations, sounds, audio CDs, and DVD movies

➤ Turning the volume up or down

➤ Assigning sounds to Windows 2000 events

➤ Making voice recordings

➤ Everything you need to know to get Windows 2000 to tickle your eyes and ears

Multimedia can be roughly defined as using a computer to play, edit, and record sounds, animations, and movies so as to cause maximum annoyance to nearby colleagues or family members. Computers that reside in corporate offices or home offices are supposed to be serious machines, so multimedia is usually ignored. And, yes, it's true that multimedia can be used for frivolous purposes. (My own personal favorite is to record complex-sounding but ultimately meaningless pronouncements using a Henry Kissinger voice.) However, multimedia does have a more sober side. For example, there are companies distributing computer training in the form of movie files, and it's becoming common for people to record voice notes for inclusion in a presentation or an email message.

Multimedia

Using a computer to play, edit, and record sounds, animations, and movies.

Whatever your multimedia needs are, you'll be pleased to hear that Windows 2000 offers a number of tools for doing everything from playing multimedia files to recording sounds from a microphone or some other input source. This chapter shows you how to get in on the fun (uh, I mean, work).

Sound Hardware Is Required

For all the audio-related sections of this chapter, I've boldly assumed that your computer is already set up with the requisite hardware. Typically, this means that your machine has a *sound card* implanted within its innards and that there are speakers attached to the sound card. If you're not sure, look for a speaker icon in the system tray in the lower-right corner of the screen. If you see one, you're in business. If not, then you'll need to cajole a nearby geek to install the card and speakers for you. If you're purchasing a sound card, be sure that it's on the Windows 2000 Hardware Compatibility List, as described in Chapter 18, "Installing Software and Hardware."

We Are Merely Players: Playing Multimedia Files

Most of the multimedia your eyes and ears will see and hear will reside in files on your hard disk, on a CD-ROM or DVD disc, or on the Internet. Just to keep us all thoroughly confused, the world's multimedia mavens have invented dozens of different file formats, each of which has its own incomprehensible two- or three-letter acronym. To help you make some sense of all this, I've grouped all the various formats into a mere five categories for easier consumption:

➤ **Sound files**   These are files that contain sounds or music only. The two main types are audio files (also known as wave files) and MIDI files. (There's also a third type called MP3 that's used to play songs with near-CD quality. MP3 is an extremely popular format on the Internet.)

➤ **Animation files**   These are files that contain animated movies or shorts, and they might include sound. The three most popular formats are Video files (also called AVI files), MPEG files, and QuickTime files.

➤ **Movie files**   These are files that contain live action movies or shorts, and they usually have a soundtrack. These files use the same formats as animation files.

➤ **Audio CD tracks**   Windows 2000 treats the individual tracks on an audio CD as files, although you'll rarely deal with them that way yourself. Instead, you can have Windows 2000 play some or all of a CD's tracks from your CD-ROM or DVD-ROM drive.

➤ **DVD movies**   These are files that contain high-quality versions of feature films, documentaries, and other big-screen entertainment. Again, you never have to deal with these files directly.

Wave File

A standard Windows 2000 sound file.

MIDI File

MIDI stands for Musical Instrument Digital Interface. It's a sound file that plays music generated by electronic synthesizers.

Windows 2000 has a program to play all these types of files. The next three sections look at Windows 2000's three players: Media Player, CD Player, and DVD Player.

Using Media Player to Play Movie and Sound Files

Windows 2000's all-purpose multimedia player goes by the spectacularly uninspiring name of Media Player. But what it lacks in cachet, it more than makes up for in competence because Media Player can handle just about any sound, animation, or movie format you can throw at it.

To try Media Player, you have two ways to proceed:

➤ Select **Start**, **Programs**, **Accessories**, **Entertainment**, **Windows Media Player**.

➤ Find a media file to play and then double-click the file. If you don't have any media samples kicking around, open My Computer, open the WINNT folder (which is usually on drive C), and then open the Media folder. Here you should find a few dozen sound files for your listening pleasure. Double-click any file and Media Player launches, cues up the file, and then starts playing.

115

A Quick Click for Playing Media

An even easier way to play a media file is to click it within My Computer. Windows 2000 goes ahead and plays the file for you. In fact, the information panel on the left side of the window suddenly sprouts a mini "player" that you can use to control the playback.

The following figure shows the Media Player window that shows up. (If you opened a sound file, you'll see a smaller version of the window.)

This is the window you see when you launch Media Player.

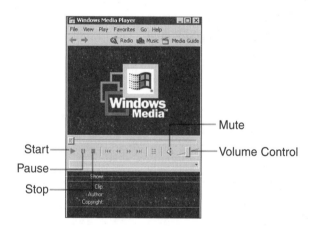

To open a media file, use the **File**, **Open** command (or press **Ctrl+O**). To control the playback, Media Player offers the following buttons:

➤ **Play**   Starts the media file.

➤ **Pause**   Pauses the media file. To resume playing, click the **Play** button.

➤ **Stop**   Stops the media file and returns to the beginning of the file.

➤ **Mute**   Turns off the sound playback.

➤ **Volume Control**   Controls the playback volume. Drag the slider to the left to reduce the volume, or to the right to increase the volume.

Media Player Keyboard Shortcuts

Here are a few useful shortcuts for playing files in Media Player:

Spacebar	Toggles Media Player between Pause and Play
. (period)	Stops the playback
Ctrl+M	Toggles the playback mute on and off
Up arrow	Turns the volume up
Down arrow	Turns the volume down

There also are four other controls—Skip Back, Rewind, Fast Forward, and Skip Forward—but they're activated only when you have a *show* open. (A show is a media file that contains multiple clips, much like an audio CD contains multiple tracks.)

Using CD Player to Play Audio CDs

If you like to listen to music while you use your computer (I find it helps to mask all the grumbling and cursing that I send my machine's way), the typical MIDI file isn't likely to set your toes a-tapping. No, if it's *real* music you're after, you need to convince Windows 2000 to play an audio CD.

An audio CD? On my computer?

Sure. Audio CDs use the same dimensions as CD-ROM discs, so any audio CD will fit snugly inside your CD-ROM drive (or your DVD-ROM drive, if you have one). From there, you use Windows 2000's CD Player program to play the CD's tracks.

To give CD Player a spin, insert the audio CD into the CD-ROM drive and the program should load automatically after a few seconds. (If CD Player remains in the wings, you can push it onstage by selecting **Start**, **Programs**, **Accessories**, **Entertainment**, **CD Player**.)

If you used previous versions of Windows, you'll be happy to know that the Windows 2000 version of CD Player is a big improvement. For one thing, CD Player can connect to the Internet and grab data (such as the title, artist, and track info) about the current CD (which CD Player rather quaintly calls an "album"). That's why, when CD Player first loads (and each time you insert a new CD), it displays a dialog box asking whether you want to download the disc's data from the Internet. This is a great feature, but let's hold off on it for a bit. Click **Cancel** to get rid of the dialog box.

117

Audio CDs with Programs

Some audio CDs do double–duty as data CDs and come with programs you can run. In some cases, the program will run automatically when you insert the CD. So be forewarned that after you insert an audio CD, you might see something other than (or in addition to) CD Player on the screen.

With that dialog box banished, you can now get a clear view of the slick-looking CD Player window. The idea is that the CD Player is supposed to look like a real CD player, and I think they've come pretty close (ignoring the Options and Internet buttons, which you aren't likely to find on a real-world player). The following figure points out some of the highlights.

Some useful features of the CD Player window.

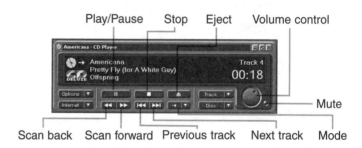

Not only does CD Player look like a regular CD Player, but it also works like one. For example, you click **Play** to crank up the music, click **Scan Back** and **Scan Forward** to zip backward and forward through the current track, click **Previous Track** and **Next Track** to leap from track to track, and click **Stop** to get some quiet time.

To adjust the volume, CD Player gives you two options:

➤ **Volume control**   Drag this control clockwise to increase the volume, or counterclockwise to decrease the volume.

➤ **Mute**   Click this button to toggle the sound on and off.

Other features include the Track drop-down list, which lets you choose a particular track to play; the Disc drop-down list, which lets you select a CD to play (you need to have more than one CD-ROM drive for this to be of much use); the Eject button which spits out the CD; and the Mode drop-down list, which gives you the following choices:

118

➤ **Standard**   Plays all the tracks once in their predefined order.

➤ **Random**   Plays the tracks willy-nilly (that is, in random order).

➤ **Repeat Track**   Repeats the current track over and over.

➤ **Repeat All**   Repeats the entire disc over and over.

➤ **Preview**   Plays only the first five seconds of each track.

No Sound?

If you don't hear anything when CD Player is playing, the problem might be that your CD-ROM drive isn't connected to your system's sound card. There's a small cable that supposed to run from the back of your CD-ROM drive to a special port attached to the sound card. Without that cable, your CD-ROM will remain mute.

If you have Internet access, then you've probably been dying to try out CD Player's spiffy Internet features. (I show you how to get wired in Chapter 11, "Getting on the Internet.") Okay, okay. Go ahead and connect to the Internet. After that's done, pull down the Internet list and select one of the following commands:

➤ **Download track names**   Click this command to download data about the disc from the Internet, including the disc title, the artist, and the names of all the tracks.

➤ **Internet music sites**   Click this command to reveal a submenu that contains links to music-related Web sites.

After CD Player has grabbed the disc's vital statistics, the Internet menu immediately sprouts a bunch of new commands. Here are the most important ones:

➤ **Search the Net**   This command throws open a submenu that contains various search options for the current artist and CD.

➤ **More about artist**   This command visits a Web page that offers background info and articles about the current artist.

➤ **More about this album**   This command launches your Web browser and takes you to a Web site that gives you info about the current disc.

Advanced CD Player Options

The CD Player is simple to use, but it does have some annoying quirks. Fortunately, you can change or eliminate many of these quirks by pulling down the Options menu and clicking Preferences. The Preferences dialog box offers Player-related items in the Player Options tab (such as the ability to control the preview length) and disc-related items in the Album Options tab (such as telling CD Player not to pester you to download disc data at startup). You can use the Playlist tab to set up the CD to play only certain songs in a certain order.

Using DVD Player to Play DVD Movies

Windows 2000 comes with built-in support for the new DVD drives that are all the rage (with some people, anyway). DVD stands for, well, nobody's really sure! Depending on whom you talk to, it either means Digital Versatile Disc or Digital Video Disc. (I suggest Dumb, Very Dumb or, depending on the kind of movie you're watching, Digital Viagra Dose.)

Acronymic quibbles aside, DVD is exciting news because it means that full-length feature films can now fit on a CD-size platter. Not only that, but thanks to the inclusion of the DVD Player in the Windows 2000 box, you can watch those films from the comfort (?) of your own PC.

To take advantage of DVD Player, you need two things:

➤ **A DVD drive**   That's pretty obvious, I guess.

➤ **A DVD decoder**   This is an extra chunk of hardware that enables your computer to process the video and audio torrent that the DVD drive sends its way. Note that there are also software-based decoders.

Assuming that your DVD hardware is up to snuff and installed, you're ready for the show to begin.

If You Installed the DVD Stuff Yourself

If you went the do-it-yourself route on the DVD hardware, Windows 2000 will recognize the new gadgets the next time you start your computer and will take a minute or two to load the necessary software bits. You'll eventually see a dialog box named Welcome to DVD that claims you have to set up the DVD decoder and your "VGA adapter." (The latter is the internal component that generates what you see on your screen.) In this case, click **Setup** to continue. Your screen now goes spastic for a few seconds, which is normal. When the video contortions are over, you'll be returned to the Welcome to DVD dialog box. Click **Done** to wind up this portion of the show.

At this point, all you have to do is plop a DVD movie disc into the DVD drive and then close the drive. Windows 2000 will detect the disc's presence automatically, launch the DVD Player in response, and start playing the movie. (If none of this happens for some reason, or if the disc was already in the drive when you started the computer, you can cue up the DVD Player by hand by selecting **Start**, **Programs**, **Accessories**, **Entertainment**, **DVD Player**.) You end up with not one but *two* DVD Player windows: There's a large one that displays the movie, and a smaller one that offers various controls, as shown in the following figure. (If you don't see this window, it just means that it's minimized, so you need to click its taskbar button.)

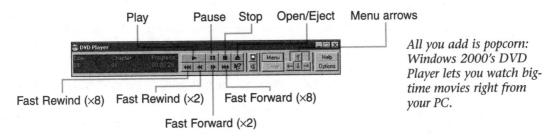

All you add is popcorn: Windows 2000's DVD Player lets you watch big-time movies right from your PC.

As pointed out in the figure, DVD Player has the standard controls for starting, stopping, rewinding, and fast forwarding. Here's a quick summary of some techniques that are unique to DVD Player:

➤ **Playing the movie full-screen**   Click the **Full Screen Mode** button, or right-click the **Progress** display and then click **Full Screen** in the shortcut menu. To get out of full-screen mode, press **Esc**.

➤ **Adjusting the volume** Click the **Volume** button. This displays Windows 2000's Volume Control, which I discuss a bit later in this chapter (see "Getting the Volume Just Right").

➤ **Working with the DVD's menu** Many DVD movies come with a menu of selections. To access that menu, click the **Menu** button. After the menu is displayed, you can either work with it directly, or else use the DVD Player's menu arrow buttons to move through the menu choices. When you get to the menu item you want, click the **Enter** button to select it.

➤ **Moving through the disc's chapters** Most DVD discs are organized into *chapters*. You can skip forward and backward through the chapters by right-clicking the **Progress** display, clicking **Go to** in the shortcut menu, and then clicking either **Previous Chapter** or **Next Chapter**.

➤ **Skipping ahead to a specific time in a title or chapter** Right-click either the **Title** display or the **Chapter** display. In the shortcut menu that pops up, click either **Search Title** or **Search Chapter**. In the dialog box that appears, use the **Hour**, **Minute**, and **Second** spin boxes to select a start time, and then click **OK**.

➤ **Show subtitles** Click **Options** and then click **SubTitles**.

➤ **Setting parental controls** This enables you to specify which users of the computer are able to watch movies with what ratings. Click **Options** and then click **Set Ratings**. The first time you do this, DVD Player prompts you to enter an administrator password. Click **OK** to get to the Administrator Logon dialog box, type your password in the two text boxes, and then click **OK**. When you get to the Set Ratings dialog box, enter a **User Name**, choose the maximum **Rating** for that person, enter a **Password**, and then click **Save**.

Getting the Volume Just Right

The Media Player and the CD Player both come with built-in volume controls. However, rather than fiddling with these individual volume doohickeys, Windows 2000 offers a single place to make all your auditory adjustments. It's called the Volume Control, and I show you how it works in this section.

The easiest way to use the Volume Control is via the taskbar's Volume icon. As shown in the following figure, clicking this icon pops up the Volume box, which enables you to do two things (which apply to all the sounds on your system):

➤ Drag the slider up (to pump up the volume) or down (to quiet things down a bit).

➤ Activate the **Mute** button to turn off the sound altogether.

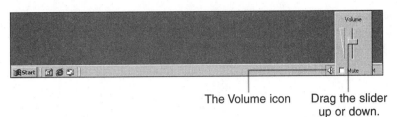

*Click the **Volume** icon to display this box and adjust the volume for all sound sources on your machine.*

The Volume icon   Drag the slider up or down.

Ixnay the Volume Icon

If you think you'll be using the Volume Control only rarely, you can reduce the taskbar clutter by removing the Volume icon. To do this, select **Start**, **Settings**, **Control Panel**, and then launch Control Panel's **Sounds and Multimedia** icon. In the Sound and Multimedia Properties dialog box, deactivate the **Show Volume Control on the Taskbar** check box. You can still get to the Volume Control via the Start menu.

Volume Control also comes in a beefier version that enables you to control the volume for individual sound sources. To see this version, you have two choices:

➤ Double-click the taskbar's **Volume** icon.

➤ Select **Start**, **Programs**, **Accessories**, **Entertainment**, **Volume Control**.

Either way, the Volume Control window steps up to the mike, as shown here.

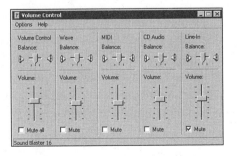

Use the Volume Control to set the volume and speaker balance for the various sound sources available on your machine.

123

The layout of the Volume Control window depends on how sound is structured in your computer, but the five sections shown in the figure are typical:

➤ **Volume Control**   This is the Big Cheese section that controls the sound for all your sound devices.

➤ **Wave**   This section controls the sound for regular sound files (those wave file doodads I mentioned earlier).

➤ **MIDI**   This section governs MIDI files.

➤ **CD Audio**   This section controls the sound for audio CDs and DVD movies.

➤ **Line-In**   This section controls the sound for devices that are attached to the back of your sound card. Examples include an external CD-ROM drive and a TV tuner card.

In all cases, you have three ways to mess with the sound output. Use the **Balance** slider to adjust the balance between your speakers; use the **Volume** slider to turn the volume up or down; use the **Mute** check box to toggle sound on and off.

Note that all these settings go into effect right away. When you're done, select **Options**, **Exit** to make everything permanent.

Assigning Sounds to Things Windows 2000 Does

As you work with Windows 2000, you'll hear various beeps and boops in response to certain events, such as when some dialog boxes appear and when a new email message arrives. Although you might think all these sounds are set in stone, it turns out that you can control not only which sounds play in response to which events, but whether Windows 2000 plays *any* sounds at all.

To change the sound that plays for a Windows event, follow these steps:

1. Select **Start**, **Settings**, **Control Panel**, and then launch Control Panel's **Sounds and Multimedia** icon. You eventually end up at the Sound and Multimedia Properties dialog box, shown here.

Use this dialog box to muck about with Windows 2000's sound events.

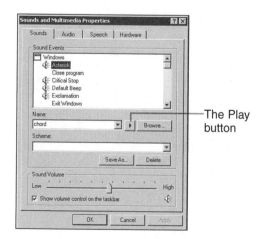

The Play button

2. Use the **Sound Events** list to highlight the event you want to work with. (If an event has a volume icon beside it, it means a sound is associated with that event.)

3. Use the **Name** list to select the sound you want played when the event occurs. If you'd prefer blissful silence, select **(None)**. If the sound you want doesn't appear in the list, click **Browse** to pick out the sound file using a dialog box.

Sound Previews

Not sure what a particular sound sounds like? No problem: Just click the **Play** button and Windows 2000 will give you a preview of the sound.

Besides changing the sounds for individual events, you can also work with entire *sound schemes* that control many events at once. Windows 2000 offers two methods for dealing with sound schemes:

➤ **To select a predefined sound scheme**   Use the **Scheme** list. If you want to put a gag on Windows 2000, select the **No Sounds** scheme.

➤ **To create your own custom sound scheme**   Begin by associating sounds to the various events you want to hear. After that's done, click **Save As**, enter a catchy name for the new scheme, and then click **OK**.

When you've completed your sound labors, click **OK** to make it so.

On the Air: Recording Your Own Sound Files

Most modern sound cards are capable not only of playing sounds, but also of recording them. If you have a microphone attached to your sound card, you can record voice messages and attach them to email messages, business documents, or a Web page. Windows 2000 is also happy to record anything that's currently on the go in Media Player or CD Player. So, if you need simple recording for presentations or posterity, Windows 2000 can do it.

The tool of choice here is called Sound Recorder, and you bring it into the studio by selecting **Start**, **Programs**, **Accessories**, **Entertainment**, **Sound Recorder**. The following figure shows the window that appears.

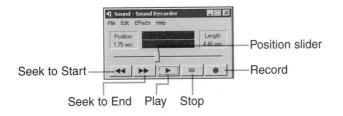

Use Sound Recorder to record voice messages or something from one of Windows 2000's media players.

The first thing you have to decide is the level of quality you want for your recording. Here's what you do:

1. Select the **File**, **Properties** command. Sound Recorder gives up the Properties for Sound dialog box.

2. Click **Convert Now** to jump over to the Sound Selection dialog box.

3. Use the **Name** list to choose one of the following quality levels:

   ➤ **CD Quality**   This level gives you high-quality sound in *stereo*, no less. The downside is that it eats disk space for breakfast, and it has a *big* appetite: a mind-boggling 172 kilobytes per *second*! Needless to say, you should work with this level only for very short sound clips and only if you require the best sound possible. (Having a huge hard disk with lots of free space would help, as well.)

   ➤ **Radio Quality**   This level uses a much lower quality (although it's still acceptable for most business needs), and records only in mono. The good news is that it chews up disk space at the rate of only about 21 kilobytes per second.

   ➤ **Telephone Quality**   This level offers the lowest-quality sound (also in mono), and it takes up a mere 10 kilobytes for each second of recording. Use this level when you're just learning Sound Recorder and when you just need quick-and-dirty recordings.

4. Click **OK** to get back to the Properties for Sound dialog box.

5. Click **OK** to return to Sound Recorder.

With that done, you're ready to record. Here goes:

1. If you're making a voice recording, grab your microphone. If you're recording from a multimedia file, open the appropriate program (such as CD Player) and cue up the file.

2. Click the **Record** button.

3. If you're making a voice recording, clear your throat and then speak (scream, sigh, whatever) into the microphone. If you're recording a multimedia file, play the file.

4. When the recording is complete, click the **Stop** button.

5. To hear your audio masterpiece, click the **Play** button.

6. If everything sounds good to your ears, save the recording by selecting **File**, **Save**, entering a name for the file in the Save As dialog box, and then clicking **Save**.

Recording to the Max

The amount of recording time you have depends on the recording level you choose. The maximum is 60 seconds.

Rolling your own sounds is fine, but Sound Recorder boasts quite a few options for cranking up the fun meter a notch or two. Check these out:

➤ **To adjust the volume of the recording**   Pull down the **Effects** menu and select either **Increase Volume (by 25%)** or **Decrease Volume**.

➤ **To change the playback speed**   Pull down the **Effects** menu and choose either **Increase Speed (by 100%)** (the Alvin and the Chipmunks on speed effect) or **Decrease Speed** (the Darth Vader on Valium effect).

➤ **To add an echo...echo...echo**   Pull down the **Effects** menu and select the **Add Echo** command. This creates a nifty echo effect that makes your recording sound like it's being played in a cave.

➤ **To reverse a sound**   Pull down the **Effects** menu and select **Reverse**. This plays the recording backward so you can hear those hidden satanic messages.

➤ **To mix in another sound file**   First, use the position slider to set the spot where you want the other file to start playing. Then select **Edit**, **Mix with File**, highlight the other sound file in the Mix With File dialog box, and then click **Open**. The result is two files that play at the same time, which is a handy way to add some nice background music to a narrative recording.

When you've finished playing around with recordings (don't forget to eat!), select **File**, **Exit** to get out of there.

What Happened

This chapter took you on a tour of Windows 2000's multimedia marvels. I began by showing you how to operate the three media file player programs: Media Player, CD Player, and DVD Player. You also learned how to use the Volume Control to adjust Windows 2000's noise level, how to assign sounds to (or remove sounds from) system events, and how to record your own sounds for presentations or posterity.

Crib Notes

➤ **Multiple multimedia formats**   Multimedia files come in five generic flavors: sound files (such as wave, MIDI, and MP3), animation files, movie files, audio CD tracks, and DVD movies.

➤ **Media Player is the workhorse**   The Media Player program can handle most kinds of multimedia files. To use it, double-click a file.

➤ **Automatic CD playing**   In most cases, your audio CDs will start playing automatically after you insert the disc.

➤ **Quick volume change**   The fastest way to adjust the volume is to click the **Volume** icon in the system tray, and then use the slider that pops up to set the noise level.

➤ **Recording other media**   The Sound Recorder can record whatever is currently running in the Media Player, CD Player, or DVD Player.

Part 3

Getting Connected I: The Web, Email, and More

For many years, lots of purse-lipped parents, uptight teachers, and pontificating pundits frowned upon computers because they saw them as noninteractive machines that served only to encourage antisocial behavior. Boy, did they ever get that wrong! As proof, you need look no further than the tens of millions of people who are on the Internet, and the hundreds of millions of people who want to be on the Internet. Believe me, these people aren't clamoring to listen to cheesy MIDI music. No, they want to connect. They want to read what other people have written; they want to exchange email epistles; they want to participate in newsgroups; they want to make "phone calls" through their modems; they want to chinwag in chat rooms. In other words, the opposite has happened: Computers have become interactive machines that encourage socializing. Who'd a thunk it? If you want to get in on all this fun, the half dozen chapters here in Part 3 will tell you everything you need to know.

Chapter 9

Modem Operandi: Setting Up Your Modem

In This Chapter

➤ A modicum of modem theory, designed for the squeamish

➤ Telling Windows 2000 about your modem

➤ Making some strategic modem adjustments

➤ Setting up dialing locations for calling card and long distance calls

➤ Everything you need to know to keep your thoroughly modern modem squeaking and squawking

To most normal people, everything about a modem seems, well, *unlikely*. It begins with the connection: The modem dials a phone number and then proceeds to make a racket that sounds like a battle between bloodthirsty banshees. After the connection is established (and, the battle ended, blissful silence reigns once again), we then send a command or data. This somehow goes through the modem (with the lights on external models flickering spastically), and then out to the phone line, a medium normally used to transmit voice. We're somehow supposed to believe that the data actually reaches the other end intact, where another modem proceeds to grab the data and return a response. I don't know—the whole process seems downright preposterous.

But, hey, it works, as you'll see in this chapter. I'll show you how to get your modem set up in Windows 2000, how to adjust its settings, and how to check that it works properly. You'll also learn how to configure Windows 2000 to handle calls that go through a long distance provider or a calling card. I'll begin by running through some important modem concepts that, I hope, will make the modem's inner workings seem a little less absurd.

Lines and Transfers and Bits, Oh My!

Fortunately, the incomprehensibility of the modem isn't a barrier to actually *using* one of the darn things. However, you'll sometimes have to make a few adjustments in order to connect to a remote system. Similarly, if you have problems with a connection, you'll need to know what settings to tweak. And, finally, there's a certain amount of jargon that just seems to come with the territory and that you'll trip over no matter what. For all these reasons, a bit of background will not only shed some light on the modem's mysteries, but will also help keep your online sessions running smoothly.

To that end, here's a list of communications words and phrases that takes you through all the basic concepts you need to know, in the order that you need to know them.

Modem   An electronic device that somehow manages to transmit and receive computer data over telephone lines. The word *modem* was coined by taking the "mo" of *modulation* (defined a bit later) and stitching it together with the "dem" of *demodulation* (ditto). Modems come in three flavors:

➤ **External**   A box that sits on your computer or on your desk. You attach it to your computer by running a *modem cable* from the back of the modem to a *serial port* (or possibly a USB port) in the back of the computer.

➤ **Internal**   A circuit board that attaches to your computer's innards.

➤ **PC Card**   This kind comes in the shape of a PC Card wafer, and is used almost exclusively with notebook computers that have PC Card sockets.

External Versus Internal

If you're in the market for a modem to use with a desktop computer, should you choose an external model or an internal one? Each type has its advantages. For the external variety, you can switch the modem from one computer to another, they're easy to install, and they have a panel of lights that at least tell you whether the modem is working. For the internal type, they don't take up any desk space, they don't need a big, fat power supply, they don't use up a serial port, you don't have to remember to turn them on, and they tend to be less expensive.

Bit   Short for "binary digit," and it represents the most basic unit of computer information. Within your computer, data is stored using tiny electronic devices called *gates*, each of which holds a single bit. These gates can be either on (which means electricity flows through the gate) or off (no electricity flows through the gate). For the likes of you and me, the number 1 represents a gate that's on, and the number 0 represents a gate that's off.

Byte   Eight *bits* strung together, which represents a single character of data. For example, the letter "X" is represented by the following byte: 1011000. Weird, I know. Further, the mathematicians tell us that a byte can have 256 possible combinations of ones and zeros (prove it for yourself by raising 2 to the power of 8), and those combinations represent all possible characters: lowercase letters, uppercase letters, numbers, symbols, and so on.

Waves   How sounds are transmitted through a telephone line. When you talk, you create a sound wave that vibrates a diaphragm in the phone's mouthpiece. The vibration converts the sound wave into an equivalent electromagnetic wave, which is then sent along the phone line. At the other end, the wave vibrates a diaphragm in the earpiece, which reproduces the original sound wave, and your voice is heard loud and clear.

> **Check This Out**
>
> **Come On, Feel the Noise**
>
> You hear the modem's racket only during the connection process, but the yowling goes on for the duration of the connection. Fortunately, most modems are merciful enough to shut off the racket after the connection is established.

Modulation   The process that the modem uses to get computer data ready for transmission along a phone line. That is, the digital commands and data—in the form of *bits*—are converted into tones that the phone system understands. Those tones are the caterwauling and wailing that you hear when the modems first try to connect.

Demodulation   As you might expect, this is the opposite of *modulation*. That is, it's the process that the modem uses to convert the incoming tones back into the original digital data.

Bps   Stands for bits per second, and it's used to measure the speed at which the modem spews data through a phone line.

Data transfer rate   The maximum (theoretical) speed at which a modem can send data, and it's measured in *bps*. Most modern modems support one of the following data transfer rates: 28,800bps, 33,600bps, or 56,000bps. If you're looking to buy a modem, get one that supports 56,000bps (which is sometimes called V.90, for reasons too geeky to go into here).

Kbps   Kilobits per second, or thousands of bits per second. *Data transfer rates* are often measured this way, so the three main rates are also written as 28.8Kbps, 33.6Kbps, and 56Kbps.

Serial port   A plug in the back of your computer into which you insert the *modem cable*. If you have an internal modem, the serial port is built into the modem's circuit board, so you never have to worry about it and there's no cable to run. On most computers, the serial port is named COM1.

Modem cable   A special data cable that connects an external modem to a PC. The cable attaches to a port in the back of the modem on one end, and to a *serial port* in the back of the computer on the other end.

Female   A port or plug that has holes. (Hey, I don't make this stuff up. The world of modem geeks was predominantly male until recently, so a bit of sexism is inevitable.)

Male   A port or plug that has pins.

Cable connection   Your external modem is useless until you connect it to your PC. Connecting the modem cable is straightforward (as far as these things go, anyway) if you remember one thing: There's usually only one possible place for each end of the cable to plug into. On the modem side, the port is wide and has 25 holes arranged in two rows, and the modem cable has a plug that has a similar shape with 25 pins arranged in two rows. On the computer side, the serial port is narrower with only nine pins arranged in two rows, and the corresponding modem cable plug has the same shape with nine holes arranged in two rows.

Cable Connection Conundra

Some older computers might throw you for a loop with nonstandard port arrangements. For example, your computer might have *two* identical 9-pin serial ports. In this case, see whether the ports are labeled (usually as COM1 and COM2). If so, make a note of the one you use; if not, you'll have to guess (you can always switch ports later if things don't work). Another unusual arrangement is to have both a 9-pin serial port *and* a 25-pin serial port. If that's the case and the 9-pin port is being used (say, by your mouse), then you'll need a modem cable that has a computer-side plug with 25 holes. (Alternatively, you can buy an adapter that enables a 9-hole cable to plug into a 25-pin port.)

Flow control　A procedure that enables the modem and the computer to interact so that incoming data is received properly if the computer is ready, or is put off temporarily if the computer is busy with some other chore. Note that although there are two varieties of flow control—software and hardware—the majority of systems prefer the taste of the latter. Therefore, if you're having communications problems, be sure your modem is set up for hardware flow control. (I'll show you how to adjust this and the other settings mentioned in this section a bit later. See "Modem Modifications: Some Settings You Hopefully Won't Need to Set.")

Connection settings　A collection of communications settings that both your modem and the remote modem must have in common to establish a successful connection. There are three connection settings to consider:

➤ **Data bits**　The number of *bits* in a character, as defined by the remote system. Yes, I know I said earlier that a *byte* represents a character and that there are 8 bits in a byte. However, that applies only to PCs. If the remote modem is attached to a non-PC (such as a big mainframe job), the number of bits in a character might be different (7 is common).

➤ **Parity**　An extra *bit* that tags along for the ride if the remote system uses fewer than 8 *data bits*. This extra bit is used for error checking to see whether the data the modem just received was corrupted on its journey.

➤ **Stop bit**　Yet another extra *bit* that's sent. This one goes at the end of the *data bits*, and it marks the end of the character.

Standard Settings

These connection settings might seem awfully esoteric and, you're right, they are. In fact, there's a good chance you'll never have to worry about them. If you do, however, the good news is that there are only two combos that are used in the majority of connections:

➤ 7 data bits, even parity, 1 stop bit (often abbreviated to 7-E-1). You usually see these settings associated with large online services that use mainframe computers (such as CompuServe).

➤ 8 data bits, no parity, 1 stop bit (8-N-1). You usually see these settings associated with bulletin board systems and PC-to-PC connections.

Protocol   A standard method by which your modem and the remote modem exchange data. Just as following the correct protocol is crucial in human diplomatic circles, so is agreeing to use the same electronic protocol in modem diplomacy.

Error correction   A standard *protocol* that enables the two modems to determine whether incoming data contains errors and should be re-sent. If you find the remote system is terminating the connection unexpectedly, try disabling error correction.

Compression   A standard *protocol* where the sending modem squeezes data into a smaller size, and the receiving modem restores the data to its normal size. Because the data being sent is smaller, this improves data transfer times.

Download   To receive data from a remote computer.

Upload   To send data to a remote computer.

File transfer protocol   A *protocol* that enables two computers to properly coordinate file *downloads* and *uploads*.

Getting Your Modem Ready for Action

Like any chunk of hardware, Windows 2000 has to know your modem exists before you can use it. Fortunately, Windows 2000 is pretty good at detecting modems, so there's a good chance that during the installation it figured out what kind of modem you have all by itself. Not sure? Here's how to check:

1. Select **Start**, **Settings**, **Control Panel**, and then fire up the **Phone and Modem Options** icon.

2. At this point, there's a slight chance that you'll see a dialog box named Location Information. If not, jump down to step 3; otherwise, you have to enter four bits of info (click **OK** when you're done):

   ➤ **What country/region are you in now?**   Use this list to select your country.

   ➤ **What area code (or city code) are you in now?**   Use this text box to type in your current area code.

   ➤ **If you dial a number to access an outside line, what is it?**   Use this text box to type in the digits required to access an outside line (such as 9 or 8), if any.

   ➤ **The phone system at this location uses**   Activate either **Tone Dialing** or **Pulse Dialing**.

3. In the Phone And Modem Options dialog box that comes up, display the **Modems** tab.

4. If you see your modem listed, as shown in the following figure, then you're in luck because it means that Windows 2000 is modem-ready, so you can click **Cancel** to bail out. If you don't see any modem, then you need to install it, as described in the next section.

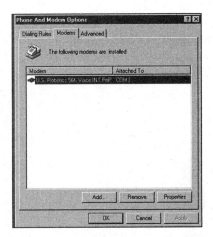

If you see your modem listed, say "woo hoo" because you don't have to bother with the modem installation rigmarole.

Installing the Modem

Here are the steps to follow to tell Windows 2000 about your modem:

1. If you have an external modem, be sure that it's attached properly to your computer and that it's turned on.

2. Open the **Phone And Modem Options** dialog box and display the **Modems** tab, as described in the previous section.

3. Click **Add**. The Install New Modem wizard appears.

4. Click **Next**. Windows 2000 probes your computer's serial ports for the telltale signs of a lurking modem.

5. If Windows 2000 finds your modem, it will display it in the **Detected Modems** list. Click **Next**. (If your modem wasn't found, I'll explain what to do after these steps.) Windows 2000 installs the necessary software to make your modem work properly, and then tells you the operation was a success.

6. Click **Finish**.

Can't Click Add?

If Windows 2000 refuses to budge when you click **Add**, it probably means that you don't have sufficient privileges to install new hardware on your machine. You need to log on with administrative privileges, or find someone who can do it for you.

137

What happens if Windows 2000 fails to find your modem? This is highly unusual, so you should first check that your modem is attached properly and turned on. If something was amiss, click **Back** and then click **Next** to try again. If nothing was wrong with the modem, or if Windows 2000 *still* can't find it, curse your luck and then follow these steps to install the modem by hand:

1. In the dialog box where Windows 2000 tells you it didn't find your modem, click **Next**. Windows 2000 ruminates for a few seconds, and then displays a list of modems.

2. Use the **Manufacturers** list to highlight your modem's maker.

3. Use the **Models** list to highlight your modem.

Don't See Your Modem?

If your modem is nowhere in sight, or if you're not sure which one to choose, highlight **(Standard Modem Types)** in the **Manufacturers** list, and then highlight your modem's speed in the **Models** list. For example, if you have a 28,800bps modem, highlight **Standard 28800 bps Modem**. Alternatively, if your modem came with a disk, insert the disk, and then click the **Have Disk** button to install the appropriate software.

4. Click **Next**. Windows 2000 wonders which port your modem is using.

5. Highlight the correct port (usually **COM1**) and then click **Next**. Windows 2000 installs the necessary files and tells you when the setup is done.

6. Click **Finish**.

Modems and Phone Cables

The last bit of fiddling that's necessary to make your modem happy is to attach the telephone cable. If you're like most people, your telephone and modem will probably share the same line. In this case, you don't have to switch the cable between the phone and the modem all the time. Instead, it's possible to get a permanent, no-hassle setup that'll make everyone happy. The secret is that all modems have two telephone cable jacks in the back:

➤ **Line jack**   This one is usually labeled "Line" or "Telco," or it has a picture of a wall jack.

➤ **Telephone jack**   This one is usually labeled "Phone" or it has a picture of a telephone.

Follow these directions to set things up:

1. Run a phone cable from the wall jack to the modem's line jack.
2. Run a second phone cable from the telephone to the modem's telephone jack.

This setup lets you use the phone whenever you need it—the signal goes right through the modem (when you're not using it, of course)—and lets you use the modem whenever you need it. You're welcome.

A Checkup: Running the Modem Diagnostics

Before jumping on the modem communications bandwagon, you should take a second to ensure your modem is healthy and ready for the ordeal to come. Windows 2000 has a diagnostics test you can run by following these steps:

1. Display the **Modems** tab of the Phone And Modems Options dialog box (as described earlier).
2. If you happen to have multiple modems installed, click the one you want to work with.
3. Click **Properties** to display the modem's Properties dialog box.
4. Display the **Diagnostics** tab.
5. Click **Query Modem**. Windows 2000 attempts to start up a conversation with the modem.
6. If everything goes well, the dialog box will fill up with all sorts of gibberish. If something's amiss, an Error dialog box will pop up to let you know the bad news. If that happens, check your connections and modem, and be sure you installed the correct modem type. Click **OK** until you're back in the Phone And Modem Options dialog box.

Modem Modifications: Some Settings You Hopefully Won't Need to Set

If your sanity is still relatively intact after making it through my description of how modems do their thing, then you'll be well aware of just what a complex piece of work it all is. You also won't be surprised to hear that modem communications is a finicky, fussy, business where connections seem to give up the ghost at the merest provocation. If that happens, your best bet is to get on the horn with the remote

139

system's tech support geeks to see whether they know what went wrong. Alternatively, the brave (or perhaps the foolhardy) can try a little troubleshooting on their own. This section runs through a few modem settings that you can tweak. (Before going any further, I should warn you that not all modems support all of the settings I discuss in this section.)

Begin by displaying the **Modems** tab of the Phone And Modems Options dialog box (as described earlier). If you have multiple modems set up, click the one you want to work with, and then click **Properties** to display the dialog box shown here.

The General tab offers the following things to play with:

The Administrator Thing Again

The Properties button is clickable only if you're logged in to Windows 2000 with Administrator-level privileges.

➤ **Speaker Volume**   This slider governs the volume of the modem's cacophonous connections. If you can't stand all that noise, drag the slider to the **Off** position for some peace and quiet. If you're having connection troubles, it helps to know whether the modem is getting as far as the noisy connection part, so you should leave the volume turned up.

➤ **Maximum Port Speed**   This is the speed at which your computer fires data at the modem. You shouldn't ever have to change this, but trying a lower speed can solve some rare communications problems. You might also need to move to a slower speed if you have an older (read: slowpoke) computer.

➤ **Wait for Dial Tone Before Dialing**   When this check box is activated, it tells the modem to hold its communications horses until it has detected a dial tone. This is a good thing, so you should leave this option turned on. If, however, your modem just can't seem to recognize the dial tone (which can happen in some countries), or if you need to dial the call manually, deactivate this option.

The next stop on your journey is the Advanced tab. Fortunately, you can safely ignore the Extra Initialization Commands text box. Instead, click **Change Default Preferences** to display a dialog box like the one shown in the following figure. (I'll bet you didn't know your modem *had* preferences!)

This dialog box is the starting point for your modem machinations.

Speed Dialing

Actually, there *is* one little thing you can add to the **Extra Initialization Commands** text box that will make your modem dial faster:

    ATS11=60

This sets the time between each dialed number to 60 milliseconds. Try lowering this number gradually until the modem no longer dials properly, and then return the setting to the lowest one that worked. (You might be able to get down to 40 or 45, depending on your modem.)

Here's what you get:

➤ **Disconnect a Call If Idle for More Than *x* Mins** Activating this check box orders the modem to hang up from the remote system if nothing's happened for the number of minutes specified in the text box (which is set to 30, initially). This is a good idea if you occasionally find yourself leaving a connection open accidentally (particularly if you're calling long distance or if your Internet service provider charges by the minute).

Use this dialog box to change the default preferences for your modem.

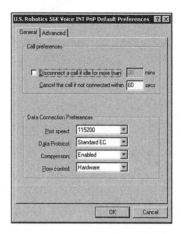

➤ **Cancel the Call If Not Connected Within *x* Secs**   This tells the modem not to bother with the call if it can't connect to the remote system within the number of seconds specified in the text box.

➤ **Port Speed**   This is the same as the Maximum Port Speed option you saw earlier. Beats me why there are two of 'em!

➤ **Data Protocol**   This is the error correction protocol that I talked about earlier. **Standard EC** is fine in most cases. If the remote system tells you that you must use something called V.42, then change this to **Forced EC**. If you're having data transmission problems, you can sometimes correct them by selecting **Disabled** (although I don't recommend this).

➤ **Compression**   This is the compression protocol that I mumbled something about earlier. In most cases, you can leave this as **Enabled**.

➤ **Flow Control**   This list contains the flow control options. Hardware is by far the most commonly used today. If the remote system tells you that you must use either "software" flow control or "XON/XOFF" flow control, select the **Xon/Xoff** option.

The final collection of preferences can be found on the **Advanced** tab, shown here. As you can see, this tab controls the values of the three connection settings that I foisted upon your poor brain earlier: **Data Bits**, **Parity**, and **Stop Bits**. (There's also a **Modulation** list that can be ignored.) Click **OK** to return to the Modem Properties dialog box, and then click **OK** again to return to the Phone And Modem Options dialog box.

Use the Advanced tab to specify the connection settings.

Where You're At: Setting Up Dialing Locations

If you're like most people, you probably always use your modem from the same place (such as at the office or at home). In that case, you just dial the modem the same way every time. However, what if your location changes and you need to deal with different dialing options? (I'm assuming here that you're using a notebook computer that can come along for the ride.) Here are some fer instances:

➤ You travel to another area code, so the call becomes long distance.

➤ You're out of town on business and you need to place all calls through a long distance provider or a calling card.

➤ You want to connect from some remote location that requires you to first dial 9 to get an outside line.

➤ You bring your computer home and have to disable call waiting before making the connection.

For all these and many similar situations, Windows 2000 lets you set up separate *dialing locations* in which you change one or more of the dialing options. To get started, open the **Phone And Modems Options** dialog box (as described earlier) and display the **Dialing Rules** tab. You should see an existing location, which was set up during the Windows 2000 installation. Click **New** to drag the New Location dialog box in by the scruff of the neck (see the following figure).

The General tab contains the basic options for the new location:

➤ **Location name** Enter a name for the new location (such as "Calls from the Coast" or "Call Waiting's Outta There!").

➤ **Country/region** Use this list to specify the country you'll be in when you're dialing.

➤ **Area code** Use this text box to specify the area code you'll be in when you're dialing.

143

➤ **To access an outside line for local calls, dial**   Use this text box to type in the number (or numbers) that must be dialed to get an outside line for local calls (such as 9).

➤ **To access an outside line for long distance calls, dial**   Use this text box to type in the number (or numbers) that must be dialed to get an outside line for long distance calls (such as 8).

➤ **To disable call waiting, dial**   Activate this check box to disable call waiting before initiating the call. Note, too, that you also have to use the list to specify the proper code that the phone system requires to disable call waiting. (If you're not sure about the proper code, ask your phone company. If the code they give you isn't in the list, type it in by hand.)

Use the New Location dialog box to create a new dialing location.

What's So Bad About Call Waiting?

Remember earlier when I told you that the modem spends much of its time converting computer data into tones that can be sent across phone lines? Well, call waiting also uses tones to signal an incoming call. If the modem hears those tones, it will probably get *very* confused and you could lose your connection.

➤ **Dial using**   Activate the appropriate option for your phone dialing: **Tone** or **Pulse**.

144

Area Code Rules, Dude!

Area codes are getting increasingly confusing. There are two main things that are causing the weirdness:

➤ **Calling the same area code** In this situation, you don't usually have to bother with the area code. However, some phone systems insist that you include the area code even if the other number is in the same area code. In some cases, these are long distance calls, so you even have to dial a 1 (or some other number) to start the call.

➤ **Calling a different area code** This situation normally requires that you dial a 1, followed by the area code, followed by the number. However, in some larger cities, the phone company has actually run out of numbers in the main area code, so they've created a whole new area code for the city. These aren't usually long distance calls, however, so even though you have to include the area code, you don't usually have to dial a 1 (or whatever) to get started.

Note that in both cases, the area code applies only to certain phone number prefixes. (The prefix is the first three digits of the seven-digit number.)

If you have to make any calls in these situations, you need to define a new *area code rule* to handle it. Here's how it's done:

1. In the New Location dialog box, display the **Area Code Rules** tab.

2. Click **New** to display the New Area Code Rule dialog box shown here.

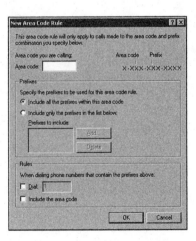

Use this dialog box to create a new area code rule.

3. Use the **Area Code** text box to enter the area code you'll be calling.

4. If the rule will apply only to certain phone number prefixes, activate the **Include Only the Prefixes in the List Below** option. Then click **Add**, enter the prefix (or prefixes), and click **OK**.

5. If you need to dial a country code (such as 1) before the area code, activate the **Dial** check box and use the text box to enter the number.

6. To force Windows 2000 to dial this area code, activate the **Include the Area Code** check box.

7. Click **OK**.

Using Long Distance and Calling Card Dialing

When you're on the road, you'll often find yourself having to make calls that cost money. For example, if you're in a hotel that charges for calls, you might want the charge to go through your calling card. Similarly, if you're out of town and forced to make a long distance call, you might want to route the call through a long distance carrier.

For these types of situations, Windows 2000 lets you specify either calling card data or a long distance access number. To get started, display the **Calling Card** tab in the New Location dialog box (see the next figure).

Use the Calling Card tab to set up your calling card or long distance carrier.

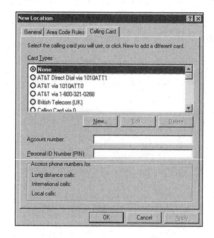

Here's the simplest route to take:

1. In the **Card Types** list, highlight the type of calling card or long distance carrier you have.

2. Enter your **Account number**.

3. Enter your **Personal ID Number (PIN)**.

If your calling card or long distance carrier isn't in the list, click **New** to get to the New Calling Card dialog box, shown next. Alternatively, if your card or carrier is listed, you might need to adjust its settings. In that case, highlight the card or carrier and then click **Edit** to get the Edit Calling Card dialog box (which is identical to the New Calling Card dialog box).

146

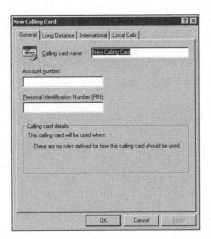

Use this dialog box to define a new calling card or long distance carrier.

This dialog box has four tabs, so let's see what each one holds.

The **General** tab is as good a place as any to start. Here you need to enter three things: the **Calling Card Name** (this will appear in the Card Types list), your **Account Number**, and your **Personal Identification Number (PIN)**.

You use the **Long Distance** tab to specify the steps that must be followed to make a long distance call. The first thing to do is specify your card's **Access Number for Long Distance Calls**. After that's done, you define the steps by clicking the buttons below the **Calling Card Dialing Steps** box. There are six buttons for your clicking finger to tickle:

➤ **Access Number**   Click this button to add the long distance access number to the steps.

➤ **PIN**   Click this button to add your PIN to the steps.

➤ **Wait for Prompt**   Click this button to display a dialog box with various things that the system must wait for before continuing the dialing. You can have the system wait for a dial tone, a completed voice message, or a specified number of seconds.

➤ **Account Number**   Click this button to add your account number to the steps.

➤ **Destination Number**   Click this button to add the number you're calling to the steps. You also get a dialog box in which you can tell Windows 2000 to also dial the country code and area code.

➤ **Specify Digits**   Click this button to add one or more digits (as well as * and #) to the steps.

The idea is that you click these buttons in the order that they must appear in the card's calling sequence. If you make a mistake, use the **Move Up** and **Move Down** buttons to shuffle things around.

If your card requires different sequences for international and local calls, follow the same steps using the **International** and **Local Calls** tabs.

When you're done, click **OK** to return to the New Location dialog box. Then click **OK** to return to the Phone And Modem Options dialog box.

What Happened

This chapter showed you how to get your modem moving. I began by running through a list of modem and communications concepts. From there, you learned how to tell Windows 2000 about your modem, run diagnostics on the new modem, and how to set various properties, most of which were useful only for troubleshooting. I closed by showing you how to create a new dialing location, and how to set up that location to use a calling card or long distance carrier.

Crib Notes

➤ **Modem speed**   Modems measure their data transfer rate in bits per second (bps). The highest speed currently available in 56,000bps, which is what I recommend that you buy if it won't break your budget.

➤ **Installing a modem**   Open the Control Panel's **Phone And Modem Options** icon, display the **Modems** tab, and then click **New**.

➤ **Your phone and your modem**   To have both your phone and your modem available for use, run a phone cable from the wall jack to the modem's line port, and run a second cable from the phone to the modem's telephone jack.

➤ **Turn off call waiting**   If you're using your modem on a line that has call waiting, be sure you tell Windows 2000 to turn off call waiting before dialing for data dollars.

Chapter 10

Using Your Modem for Faxing and Phone Dialing

In This Chapter

➤ Getting your modem to dial your phone for you

➤ Sending a fax message

➤ Using and creating fax cover pages

➤ Receiving incoming faxes

➤ Annotating received faxes

➤ Interesting ways to put your modem to good use

Now that your modem is ready to motor, it's time to take it for a spin. (Don't worry: There are no "information superhighway" metaphors anywhere in this book.) This chapter helps you do just that by focusing on a couple of modem-related functions. You'll begin by learning how to convince your modem to dial your phone for you. From there, you'll turn to something *really* useful: faxing. I'll show you how to use your modem to send faxes, including how to create custom cover pages to go along for the ride. I'll also show you how to receive incoming faxes, including how to annotate those faxes.

Bear in mind that this chapter assumes you have a modem attached to your machine and that Windows 2000 knows about the modem. (If you'll be doing some faxing, then you must have a fax modem installed.) If that's not the case, head back to Chapter 9, "Modem Operandi: Setting Up Your Modem," to trudge through the installation process.

Cross Reference

For all this to work, you have to have your phone attached to your modem, as described in Chapter 9's "Modems and Phone Cables" section on p. 138.

Stop the Presses! Modem Dials Phone!

If you don't have one of those fancy-schmancy speed-dial phones on your desk, Windows 2000 can provide you with the next best thing: Phone Dialer. This is a simple program whose only mission in life is to accept a phone number from you and then use your modem to dial the number for you automatically. You then pick up the handset and proceed with the call normally. (If you think this sounds like a for-lazy-people-only feature, then, well, you might be right. However, remember that the PC is *supposed* to be a labor-saving device, so you shouldn't feel guilty.)

You get into Phone Dialer by selecting **Start**, **Programs**, **Accessories**, **Communications**, **Phone Dialer**. You'll see a window that looks suspiciously like the one shown in the following figure.

The Phone Dialer is only too happy to do your dialing dirty work.

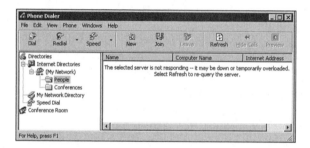

If Phone Dialer displays a message about the "selected server" not responding, nod your head knowingly and ignore the whole thing. To dial a number, follow these steps:

Cross Reference

To learn how to place Internet calls, see Chapter 14's "Using Phone Dialer to Make Phone Calls over the Internet" section, p. 220.

1. Select **Phone**, **Dial**, or click the **Dial** button in the toolbar. The Dial dialog box reports for duty.

2. Type the phone number in the text box. If you're dialing an extension, precede the number with an **x**. (This box moonlights as a list. After you've dialed one or more numbers, they'll appear in the list so you can select them from there.)

3. Be sure the **Phone Call** option is activated.

Phone Dialer and Directories

Phone Dialer comes with a list of folders on the left side, and this list includes Directories (the main folder), Internet Directories, and My Network Directory. What's with all the directories? Well, a directory is really just a database of names and phone numbers. It runs on a server computer, which can be located on the Internet or on your network. Any network-based directory should have been set up automatically by your network administrator. If you know of an Internet directory, you can add it by selecting **Edit**, **Add Directory**.

4. If you want this number to appear in Phone Dialer's Speed Dial list (more on this a bit later), activate the **Add Number to Speed Dial List** check box.

5. Click **Place Call**. After a couple of seconds, you'll hear (through your modem's speaker) the number being dialed.

6. Pick up the receiver and proceed with the call as usual.

The following figure shows the extra windows that appear while a call is in progress. The Phone Call window offers three icons you might find useful:

➤ **Touchtone Keypad**   Click this icon to display an extra window with buttons that represent the keys on a telephone's keypad. If you need to enter any numbers during the call, click the appropriate buttons in the Touchtone Keypad window.

➤ **Add to Speed Dial**   Click this icon to add the current number to the Speed Dial list.

➤ **Disconnect**   Click this icon to end the call.

To redial a call, you have the following choices:

➤ Select **Phone**, **Dial** and then use the list to select a recently dialed number.

➤ Select **Phone**, **Redial** and then select a number from the submenu that appears.

➤ Pull down the toolbar's **Redial** list and click the number you want to dial.

These extra windows show up when Phone Dialer initiates a call.

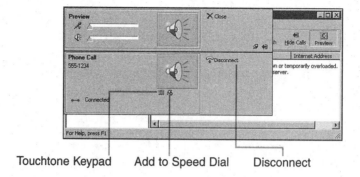

Touchtone Keypad   Add to Speed Dial   Disconnect

Phone Dialer is certainly handy, but it becomes downright useful when you take advantage of its speed-dialing feature. You can program all kinds of frequently called numbers, which are then easily accessed via the Speed Dial folder or toolbar list.

To program a speed dial button, try these steps:

1. Select **Edit**, **Add to Speed Dial List**. The Speed Dial dialog box leaps into the fray.
2. Use the **Display Name** text box to enter a name for this entry.
3. Use the **Number or Address** text box to enter the phone number.
4. Be sure the **Phone Call** option is activated.
5. Click **OK** to save the info.

With all that done, you can launch any of your speed dial entries by using any of the following methods:

➤ Select **Phone**, **Speed Dial** and then select the entry you want to dial from the submenu that appears. (You can also select **Speed Dial List** to make changes to your speed dial entries.)

➤ Pull down the toolbar's **Speed** list and click the entry. (You can also click **Edit Speed Dial List** to make changes to your speed dial entries.)

➤ Select the **Speed Dial** folder and then double-click the entry.

You also can work with Phone Dialer without the window cluttering your desktop. Select the **File**, **Hide Phone Dialer Window** command, and the window will make itself scarce. To place calls, click the Phone Dialer icon in the taskbar's system tray. This displays the **Dial**, **Redial**, and **Speed Dial** commands. To bring the Phone Dialer window back, click **Open**.

When you're done with Phone Dialer, select **File**, **Exit Phone Dialer**, and then click **Yes** when the program wonders whether you know what the heck you're doing.

How to Turn Your PC into a Fax Machine

With the email revolution upon us, the idea of communicating via fax has begun to seem downright quaint. However, that's not to say that faxing doesn't still have a role to play in the modern business world. After all, not everyone is on email (as hard as that is to believe sometimes), and the fax remains the fastest way to transmit, say, an order form or nontext tidbits such as maps and diagrams.

So, having now fully justified the effort I spent writing this section, let's see how you go about getting into the fax fast lane.

The first thing you need to do is fill in some information about yourself. Windows 2000 uses this data to fill in some fields on your cover pages automatically. Here are the steps to follow:

1. Select **Start**, **Settings**, **Control Panel** to open the Control Panel window.

2. Launch the **Fax** icon. The Fax Properties dialog box surfaces.

3. Fill in the fields in the **User Information** tab, shown in the following figure.

4. When you're done, click **OK**.

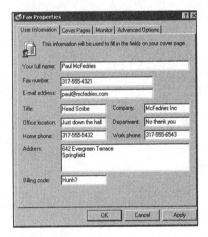

Before you send a fax, fill in the fields in the User Information tab.

Shipping Out a Fax

To fire off a fax, Windows 2000 gives you two ways to proceed:

➤ You can fax a simple note by sending just a cover page.

➤ You can fax a more complex document by sending it to Windows 2000's fax "printer."

Let's start with the simple cover page route:

1. Select **Start**, **Programs**, **Accessories**, **Communications**, **Fax**, **Send Cover Page Fax**. The Send Fax Wizard arrives on the scene.

2. The initial dialog box isn't much use, so just click **Next** to get on with it.

3. The first time you run this wizard, a dialog box shows up and asks whether you want to edit your user information. You've done that already, so say "Hah!", activate the **Keep the Current User Information** option, and click **OK**. The Send Fax Wizard finally does something sensible by displaying the Recipient and Dialing Information dialog box, as shown in the following figure.

The Send Fax Wizard takes you through the steps necessary to send a simple cover page fax.

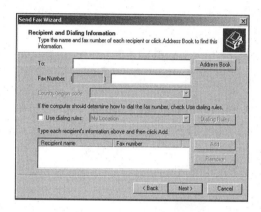

4. Fill in the following fields:

   ➤ **To:**   Enter the name of the fax recipient.

   ➤ **Fax Number:**   Use these two text boxes to enter the area code (if necessary) and phone number for the fax recipient.

   ➤ **Country/Region Code:**   Select the country code for the fax recipient's phone number.

5. Click **Add**.

6. If you want to send the fax to several people, repeat steps 4 and 5 as necessary.

7. When you're ready to move on, click **Next**. The next Send Fax Wizard dialog box muscles its way onto the screen.

8. Fill in the following fields:

   ➤ **Cover Page Template**   Select the cover page you want to use. (See "Creating a Fax Cover Page," later in this chapter, to find out about these predefined cover pages.)

   ➤ **Subject Line**   Enter the subject of the fax.

   ➤ **Note**   Enter your message.

9. Click **Next**.

10. If you have a scanner installed on your system, the Send Fax Wizard will ask whether you want to scan a document to go along with the fax. If you do, click **Scan** to launch the scanner software. When you're done, click **Next**.

11. The wizard now pesters you for the time you want the fax sent (click **Next** when you're done):

    ➤ **Now** Sends the fax ASAP.

    ➤ **When Discount Rates Apply** Sends the fax between 8:00 p.m. and 7:00 a.m. I'll show you how to change these times a bit later (see "A Few Fax Options").

    ➤ **Specific Time in the Next 24 Hours** Sends the fax at the specified time. (This is a spin box with a time value. To change the value, click the hour or the minute and then either type the value you want or click the arrows.)

12. In the final wizard dialog box, click **Finish**. The Fax Monitor window replaces the wizard so that you can see what's happening with the fax.

What's in a Fax Name?

Windows 2000 assigns a name to your fax machine. This is known in the trade as the TSID: Transmitting Station Identifier. When the other person receives your fax, your TSID is displayed at the top of each page. If the other person is receiving on a computer, the TSID appears in the "From" line and possibly even the "Subject" line. Unfortunately, the default TSID is "Fax," which redefines the word "uninspiring." To fix this, first select **Start, Programs, Accessories, Communications, Fax, Fax Service Management**. In the Fax Service Management window that lays claim to the desktop, click **Devices**, click your modem to highlight it, and then select **Action, Properties**. In the dialog box that appears, edit the **TSID** text box. (For example, it's common to change it to your company name, your department name, or your own name.) Click **OK** and then click the **Close** button to exit the window.

Simple notes on a cover page are fine, but if you want to go beyond this, you have to take a different tack. Specifically, you have to use WordPad or some other program to create a document, and you then fax that document to the recipient. Here's how it works:

1. Create the document that you want to ship.

155

2. Select the program's **File**, **Print** command to get to the Print dialog box, select **Fax** as the printer (see the next figure), and then click **Print**. Our old friend the Fax Send Wizard reappears.

To fax from a program, select Fax as the printer.

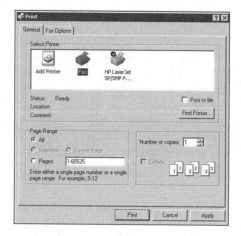

3. Follow the previously outlined steps to set the fax options. (Note that with this method you don't have to bother with a cover page. When you get to the Preparing the Cover Page dialog box, deactivate the **Include a Cover Page** check box.)

4. In the final wizard dialog box, click **Finish** to send the fax.

Creating a Fax Cover Page

You saw earlier that the Send Fax Wizard offers four prefab cover pages that you can use. If you're not exactly thrilled with these default pages, you can modify them to suit your style, or you can create new pages from scratch.

To edit and create fax cover pages, Windows 2000 offers the Fax Cover Page Editor. To launch this program, you have a couple of ways to proceed:

➤ **If you want to create a new cover page** Select **Start**, **Settings Control Panel** and then launch the **Fax** icon. In the Fax Properties dialog box, display the **Cover Pages** tab and click **New**.

➤ **If you want to modify a prefab cover page** This is quite a bit harder to do. First open **My Computer** and click the **Search** button to display the Search bar. In the **Search for Files or Folder Named** text box, enter ***.cov**, and then click **Search Now**. After a second or two, the Search Results window shows the cover page files: **confdent**, **fyi**, **generic**, and **urgent**. Double-click the file you want.

The following figure shows the Cover Page Editor with the "generic" cover page ready for editing.

Style toolbar   Drawing toolbar   Text button

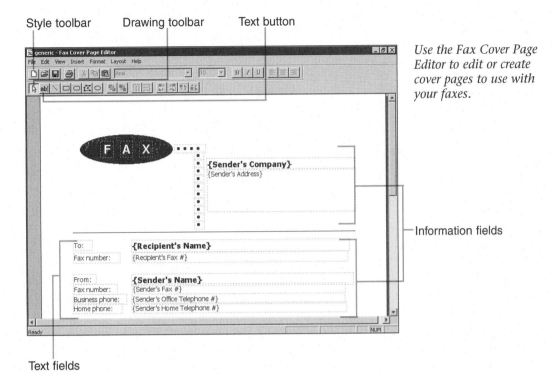

Use the Fax Cover Page Editor to edit or create cover pages to use with your faxes.

Information fields

Text fields

You work with the Cover Page Editor by doing three things:

➤ Inserting information fields

➤ Inserting text fields

➤ Inserting graphics fields

Information fields hold data. For example, the **{Sender's Company}** field (these fields always show up surrounded by braces) tells Windows 2000 to insert the name of the sender's company each time you use this cover page when you send a fax. With the Cover Page Editor, you can insert fields for recipient, sender, and message data:

➤ **Recipient fields** These are fields related to the recipient of the fax. Select **Insert Recipient** and then select either **Name** or **Fax Number**.

➤ **Sender fields** These are the fields you filled in earlier. Select **Insert**, **Sender** to get a submenu with a whack of choices, including **Name**, **Fax Number**, and **Company**.

➤ **Message fields** These are fields related to the fax message. Select **Insert**, **Message**, and then select one of the following: **Note**, **Subject**, **Date/Time Sent**, or **Number of Pages**.

Cross Reference

To refresh your skills with the Paint drawing tools, head back to Chapter 7, and see the section "Tool Time: How to Use the Paint Tools," p. 99.

Selecting Stuff

To select a field, give it a click. If you need to select multiple fields, hold down **Ctrl** and click each field.

When you select a field command, the editor plops the field onto the cover page. You then use your mouse to drag the field to the position on the page that you want. You also can format a field by using the buttons on the Style toolbar or by selecting the **Format**, **Font** or **Format**, **Align Text** commands.

Text fields are basically just text boxes. They're used to provide captions for the information fields or to jazz up the cover page with titles, subtitles, and headings. Here are some techniques you can use with text fields:

➤ **To insert a text field** Click the **Text** button on the Drawing toolbar. Now drag the mouse inside the cover page to create a box for the field, and then type in your text.

➤ **To change the text in an existing field** Double-click the field and then edit the text.

➤ **To format a text field** Use the **Style** toolbar or the **Format** menu commands.

Graphics fields hold images that you can use for logos, separators, or just to add some style to the cover page. The Cover Page Editor's Drawing toolbar sports several buttons for drawing objects. All these tools work the same way as the corresponding tools in Paint. Here's a rundown:

Click This...	To Create This...
＼	A straight line.
▢	A rectangle. (If you hold down the **Shift** key while dragging, you get a square.)
▢	A rectangle with rounded corners.
▨	A polygon.
⬭	An ellipse. (If you hold down the **Shift** key while dragging, you get a circle.)

The Cover Page Editor also contains quite a few options for mucking around with the layout of the fields. Here's a rundown of the buttons and commands that are available:

Click This...	To Do This...
	Move the selected field in front of any fields that overlap it. You also can select **Layout**, **Bring to Front**, or press **Ctrl+F**.
	Move the selected field behind any fields that overlap it. Alternatively, select **Layout**, **Send to Back**, or tap **Ctrl+B**.
	Space the selected fields evenly across the page. The other way to go about it to select **Layout**, **Space Evenly**, **Across**.
	Space the selected fields evenly down the page. For some variety, select **Layout**, **Space Evenly**, **Down**.
	Align the selected fields along their left edges. The other way to go is to select **Layout**, **Align Objects**, **Left**.
	Align the selected fields along their right edges. You also can choose the **Layout**, **Align Objects**, **Right** command.
	Align the selected fields along their top edges. Selecting **Layout**, **Align Objects**, **Top** also works.
	Align the selected fields along their bottom edges. As you've probably guessed by now, you can also select **Layout**, **Align Objects**, **Bottom**.

When you're finished with a cover page, save it in the **Personal Coverpages** folder. Select **File**, **Save As** and, in the Save As dialog box, open **My Documents**, then **Fax**, and then **Personal Coverpages**.

Receiving a Fax

The ability to broadcast a fax to the far corners of the planet right from your computer is handy, to say the least. However, my favorite part of computer-based faxing is the opposite chore: receiving incoming faxes. Why? Let me count the ways:

➤ **No more slimy, curly, fax paper** When you receive a fax on your computer, it's stored as a file which you can keep electronically or later print on *real* paper.

➤ **No more wasted paper** If a junk fax comes in, you can delete it from existence without having to ever print it.

➤ **Easier storage** Because received faxes are digital files, you don't need to print them and then file them. Instead, you can organize the fax feature's folders to hold related messages.

➤ **Easier annotation** As you'll see a bit later, Windows 2000 comes with a program that lets you "write" on a received fax.

Strangely, Windows 2000 isn't set up to receive faxes automatically. Instead, you have to poke it in the eye and tell it to grab incoming faxes. Here's how:

1. Select **Start**, **Programs**, **Accessories**, **Communications**, **Fax**, **Fax Service Management**. The Fax Service Management window hops to it.

2. Click **Devices**, click your modem to highlight it, and then select **Action**, **Properties**. You'll see a dialog box similar to the one shown in the following figure.

Use this dialog box to activate fax receiving.

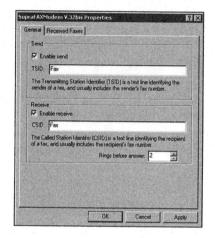

3. Activate the **Enable Receive** check box.

4. Judiciously ignore the **CSID** text box.

5. Use the **Rings Before Answer** spin box to enter the number of rings you want Windows 2000 to wait for before answering the darn phone.

6. While you're here, you might as well display the **Received Faxes** tab, which offers three choices for handling faxes that come your way:

   ➤ **Print On**   Activate this check box to have Windows 2000 foist the fax on whatever printer you choose in the accompanying list.

   ➤ **Save in Folder**   Activate this check box to have Windows 2000 park the fax in whatever folder is specified in the text box to the right.

   ➤ **Send to Local E-mail Inbox**   Activate this check box to have Windows 2000 ship the fax to the inbox of your email program.

7. Click **OK** to get back to the Fax Service Management window.

8. Click the **Close** button to shut down the window.

You're now ready to receive. When a fax call comes in, the Fax Monitor dialog box elbows its way to the fore and shows you the progress of receiving it. When it's done, the fax is handled according to whatever options you activated in the **Received Faxes** tab.

MAPI Mumblings

Having incoming faxes sent to your email account is a handy way of keeping all your messages in one place where you can keep an eye on them. Unfortunately, Outlook Express isn't quite smart enough to handle this. Instead, you need to have a special kind of email program—one that's "MAPI enabled," whatever that means. Programs that qualify include Microsoft Outlook and Microsoft Exchange.

Sharing Voice and Fax Calls on the Same Line

By default, Windows 2000 is set up to automatically answer incoming calls after a certain number of rings. That's great if you have a dedicated fax line, but what if you share voice and fax calls on the *same* line? In this case, you'll want to have some control over when Windows 2000 answers the phone. To do this, select **Start**, **Settings**, **Control Panel** and then launch the **Fax** icon. In the Fax Properties dialog box, display the **Answer Monitor** tab, activate the **Enable Manual Status for the First Device** check box, and then click **OK**. The next time the phone rings, Windows 2000 displays an **Answer This Call?** message. To have Windows 2000 answer the phone, click **Yes**.

If you're storing the faxes in the default folder, you can get there using the following techniques:

➤ Select **Start**, **Programs**, **Accessories**, **Communications**, **Fax**, **My Faxes**.

➤ Double-click the **Fax** icon in the taskbar's system tray area.

After you get to the My Faxes window, open the **Received Faxes** folder and then double-click the fax file. This launches a program called Imaging Preview (shown in the next figure), which then displays your fax.

Double-clicking a fax file displays the fax in the Imaging Preview window.

Open image for editing

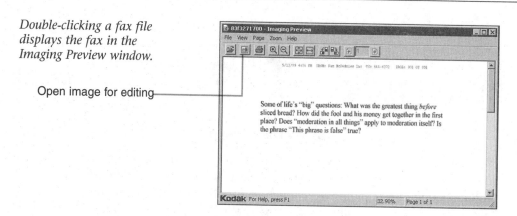

The Page and Zoom menus contain the commands you'll use most often, so let's see what they offer. I'll begin with the Zoom menu:

Select This...	Or Click This...	To Do This...
Zoom, Zoom In		Zoom in on the fax. Alternatively, tap **Ctrl+Up arrow**.
Zoom, Zoom Out		Zoom out from the fax. The other way to go about it is to press **Ctrl+Down arrow**.
Zoom, Fit to Height		Adjust the fax magnification so that the height of the fax matches the height of the window.
Zoom, Fit to Width		Adjust the fax magnification so that the width of the fax matches the width of the window.
Zoom, Best Fit		Adjust the magnification of the fax so that whitespace is minimized.
Zoom, Actual Size		Adjust the fax magnification so that the fax appears lifesized.
Zoom, 25% etc.		Adjust the fax magnification to the specified percentage.

Here are the commands on the Page menu:

Select This...	Or Click This...	To Do This...
Page, Previous	⬅	Return to the previous page, if you're viewing a multipage fax. Pressing **Ctrl+Page Up** also works.
Page, Next	➡	Move forward to the next page. To be different, press **Ctrl+Page Down**.
Page, First		Move to the first page.
Page, Last		Move to the last page.
Page, Go To		Move to a specific page number.
Page, Rotate Page, Right		Rotate the page to the right by 90 degrees.
Page, Rotate Page, Left		Rotate the page to the left by 90 degrees.

When you're done, select **File**, **Exit** to close the fax.

Using Imaging to Annotate a Fax

The Imaging Preview program just lets you take a gander at the fax. If you'd like to edit the fax by adding highlights, "rubber stamps," comments, or other annotations, this section shows you how it's done.

The first thing you need to do is open the fax in the full-blown version of the Imaging program. To do that, first open the fax in the Imaging Preview window, as described in the previous section. Now either select **File**, **Open Image for Editing**, or click the **Open Image for Editing** toolbar button. You'll now see a dialog box wondering whether you want to open "images" (it means faxes) for edit by default. In other words, it wants to know whether you'd like to open your faxes in the full-blown version of Imaging right away. This avoids having to select the Open Image for Editing command, so if you'll be doing a lot of fax annotating, click **Yes**. If you think you'll be annotating faxes only occasionally, click **No**.

With all that malarkey out of the way, your fax opens in the Imaging window, shown in the following figure.

Annotate

To add comments, graphics, highlights, or "rubber stamps" to a received fax.

Use the Imaging program to add snarky comments and other annotations to a received fax.

Annotation toolbar——

Here's a rundown of the commands on the Annotation menu:

Select This...	Or Click This...	To Do This...
Show Annotations		Toggle the annotations on and off.
Make Annotations Permanent		Make the annotations a permanent part of the fax file. (This prevents other people from editing your text.) After you've done this, you can no longer select the annotations.
Select Annotations		Enable the **Annotation Selection** tool. Use this tool to select an annotation by clicking it.
Freehand Line		Draw a freehand line on the fax.
Highlighter		Draw a yellow highlight on the fax.
Straight Line		Draw a straight line on the fax.
Hollow Rectangle		Draw a border-only rectangle on the fax.
Filled Rectangle		Draw a filled rectangle on the fax.
Typed Text		Draw a text box on the fax. You can then type a note in the text box.
Attach-a-Note		Draw a "sticky note" on the fax. You can then add text to the note.
Text from File		Insert text from a text file on the fax.

Select This...	Or Click This...	To Do This...
Rubber Stamps	🔲	"Stamp" the fax with a message. There are four default messages: Approved, DRAFT, Received, and Rejected, although you can also create your own if you select the command from the menu.

After you've annotated the fax, be sure to select **File**, **Save** to keep your changes. When you're done, select **File**, **Exit** to close the program.

A Few Fax Options

I'll close this chapter with a look at a few semiuseful options for customizing your Windows 2000 faxing experience. To get to these options, select **Start**, **Programs**, **Accessories**, **Communications**, **Fax**, **Fax Service Management** to get the Fax Service Management window onboard. Be sure that **Fax Service on Local Computer** is highlighted, and then select **Action**, **Properties**. In the dialog box that wends its way to you, here's a rundown of what you get to mess with on the **General** tab (click **OK** when you're done):

➤ **Number of Retries**   Specifies the number of times Windows 2000 attempts to send a fax.

➤ **Minutes Between Retries**   Specifies how many minutes Windows 2000 waits before it tries to send a fax again.

➤ **Days Unsent Fax Is Kept**   Specifies the number of days the fax is kept in the fax queue if Windows 2000 can't get it to go through.

➤ **Print Banner on Top of Each Sent Page**   Deactivate this check box to tell Windows 2000 not to include the banner at the top of each page you fire off. The banner includes the date, your TSID, the receiving fax number, and the number of pages.

➤ **Use the Sending Device TSID**   Deactivate this check box to tell Windows 2000 not to include your fax modem's Transmitting Station Identifier in the banner. Instead, Windows 2000 uses your fax number.

➤ **Don't Allow Personal Cover Pages**   Activate this check box to disallow the use of personal cover pages. You can still create them, but they won't appear in the Send Fax Wizard's list of cover pages.

➤ **Archive Outgoing Faxes In**   Use this text box to specify the storage location for the faxes that you send.

➤ **Discount Period Starts**   Use this spin box to set the starting time for the telephone discount period in your area. Also, use the **ends** spin box to set the ending time for the discount rate.

What Happened

This chapter showed you how to put your modem to good use. You began by learning how to get your modem to dial voice calls for you. The rest of the chapter was spent figuring out how to turn your computer into a reasonably powerful fax machine.

Crib Notes

➤ **Sending a simple fax**   To fax a simple note on a cover page, select **Start**, **Programs**, **Accessories**, **Communications**, **Fax**, **Send Cover Page**, and then follow the Send Fax Wizard's lead.

➤ **Faxing a document**   To fax a document from a program, select **File**, **Print**, choose the Fax "printer," and then click **Print**.

➤ **Setting up fax reception**   Select **Start, Programs, Accessories, Communications, Fax, Fax Service Management**, click **Devices**, click your modem, select **Action, Properties**, and then activate **Enable Receive**.

➤ **Viewing a received fax**   The quickest method is to double-click the system tray's **Fax** icon.

➤ **Annotating a fax**   In the Imaging Preview window, select **Edit, Open Image for Editing**.

Chapter 11

Getting on the Internet

In This Chapter

➤ Setting up a spanking new Internet account

➤ Transferring the details of an existing account into Windows 2000

➤ Specifying the details of an existing account yourself

➤ Getting connected to the Internet

➤ A review of Windows 2000's Internet tools

➤ Everything you need to know to get from your place to cyberspace

I wrote the very first edition of *The Complete Idiot's Guide to Windows* way back in 1993. You can scour that book with a magnifying glass and as fine-toothed a comb that you can lay your hands on, and you won't find the word "Internet" anywhere. Those were the Good Old Days when your social standing didn't depend on having both an email address and a Web page, when "http://" was just a meaningless collection of letters and symbols to most people, and when Bill Gates' billions could be counted using just your fingers.

Nowadays, the Internet's tentacles have insinuated themselves into every nook and cranny of modern life. Businesses from corner-hugging Mom 'n Pop shops to continent-straddling corporations are online; Web pages are now counted in the hundreds of millions; and people send more email messages than postal messages.

It truly is a wired (which, remember, is just "weird" spelled sideways) world, and if you feel like you're the only person left who isn't online, this chapter will help. I'll tell you exactly what you need to make it happen, and then I'll take you through the connection process, step-by-finicky-step.

Windows 2000 offers no fewer than three different routes to Internet connection glory. Whichever avenue you pursue, you start things up the same way: by launching the desktop's **Connect to the Internet** icon. (If you don't see that icon anywhere, don't sweat it because you can still get things started by selecting **Start**, **Programs**, **Accessories**, **Communications**, **Internet Connection Wizard**.) The Internet Connection Wizard fades in and offers you options for the three routes right off the bat. Here's a summary of the three options along with pointers to the relevant sections of this chapter:

➤ **I want to sign up for a new Internet account** This is the path to take if you don't currently have an Internet account and you want to sign up for one through Windows 2000. In this case, see the section titled "Interstate I1: Setting Up a New Account."

➤ **I want to transfer my existing Internet account to this computer** If you already have an Internet account, you can (in some cases, anyway) get Windows 2000 to transfer the account settings to your computer. This route is covered in the section titled "Interstate I2: Transferring an Existing Account."

➤ **I want to set up my Internet account manually, or I want to connect through a local area network (LAN)** If you already have an existing account but Windows 2000 can't transfer it, then you need to take a walk on the wired side and set up the account yourself. For modem connections, see "Interstate I3: Setting Up an Existing Account Manually."

Cross Reference

For network connections, head for Chapter 21, "Using Windows 2000 to Set Up a Small Network," and see "The Connection Point: The Network Interface Card," p. 325.

Make your choice and then click **Next**.

As a final note before you begin, this chapter assumes that you already have your modem installed and ready for the rigors of the Internet. If you haven't proceeded that far yet, head back to Chapter 9, "Modem Operandi: Setting Up Your Modem."

Interstate I1: Setting Up a New Account

If you activated the **I Want to Sign Up for a New Internet Account** option, Windows 2000 will walk you through the process of choosing and setting up the new account. Here's what happens:

1. The Internet Connection Wizard makes your modem dial a number. When connected, the wizard downloads a list of Internet service providers (ISPs) in your area. The wizard then displays a list of these ISPs, as shown here.

2. Use the **Internet Service Providers** list to select the provider you want.

3. After you've chosen a provider, click **Next**.

4. In the next wizard dialog box, enter your vital statistics (name, address, and so on). The provider will need all this before you can sign up with them. When you're done, click **Next**.

Internet Service Provider (ISP)

A company that takes your money in exchange for an Internet account, which is what you need to get online.

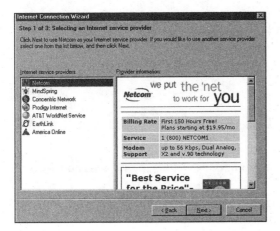

Conveniently, the Internet Connection Wizard displays a list of ISPs in your area.

5. The rest of the steps vary from provider to provider, but you'll likely be asked for some or all of the following:

   ➤ Credit card information

   ➤ The access plan you want to use

   ➤ A username and password for your account

6. The final wizard dialog box will likely show you the particulars of your account (such as your email address). Make a note of this info in case you need it later on. Click **Finish** to complete the wizard.

Rates and Stuff

Each time you select a provider, the **Provider Information** box gives you the goods on the provider's rates and special offers.

Interstate 12: Transferring an Existing Account

If you activated the **I Want to Transfer My Existing Internet Account to This Computer** option, Windows 2000 will attempt to grab your account data from your existing ISP. This option works almost exactly like the new account setup covered in the previous section:

1. The wizard dials the modem and retrieves a list of providers in your area.
2. If your provider is listed, highlight it and click **Next**. The wizard connects to the provider and then prompts you for some account data, as shown here.

The Internet Connection Wizard prompts you to enter your username, password, and other account data.

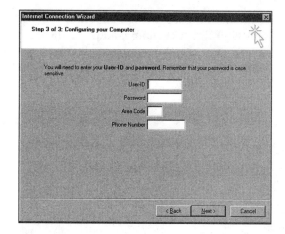

3. Enter your **User-ID** and **Password**, as well as the ISP's **Area Code** and **Phone Number**.
4. Click **Next**. The wizard logs in to your account, retrieves your settings, and then sets up your Internet connection in Windows 2000. You eventually see a wizard dialog box with your account data.
5. Click **Next**.
6. In the final wizard dialog box, click **Finish**.

Interstate 13: Setting Up an Existing Account Manually

If your existing Internet account can't be transferred, then you'll need to build the connection with your bare hands. This section runs through the data you need and takes you through the rest of the Internet Connection Wizard's steps.

What You Need to Know Before Getting Started

To successfully set up a connection to your Internet account, you need to have the proper bits of information from your ISP. Here are the basic tidbits you need:

➤ The phone number you have to dial to connect to the ISP.

➤ The username (which might also be called your logon name) and password that you use to log on to the ISP.

➤ The username and password for your email account. (These are almost always the same as your logon name and password.)

➤ The type of server the ISP uses for incoming email: POP3, IMAP, or HTTP.

➤ The Internet name used by the ISP's incoming mail server (this often takes the form mail.provider.com).

➤ The Internet name used by the ISP's outgoing mail server (this is almost always the same as the incoming email server).

Some ISPs also require some or all of the following advanced settings:

➤ The type of connection the ISP requires. This is usually PPP, but SLIP and C-SLIP are also sometimes used.

➤ Whether you need to log on to the ISP manually.

➤ Whether your ISP provides you with a "script" for automating the logon procedure.

➤ Whether your ISP assigns you a permanent IP address. If so, you need to know the address.

➤ Whether your ISP provides you with IP addresses for their Domain Name Servers (DNS). If so, you need to know the addresses for the primary and alternate servers.

Log On

To provide your ISP with your username and password, and so gain access to the wonder that is the Internet.

Mail Server

A computer that your ISP uses to store and send your email messages.

IP Address

A crazy-looking series of numbers and dots (such as 123.234.56.78) that serves as your computer's address when you're connected to the Internet.

Didn't I tell you this was finicky stuff? Don't worry if you find all this gobbledygook to be completely meaningless. You need hold it in your brain only for as long as it takes to set up your connection, and then it can be discarded for all time (or at least until you get your next computer and have to start everything from scratch once again; doh!).

What You Need to Do After Getting Started

With all that info at your side, you're now ready to set up the account. Here are the rest of the steps to trudge through:

1. The next wizard dialog box presents you with your first choice. I'm assuming in this chapter that you're going online using your trusty modem, so be sure the **I Connect Through a Phone Line and a Modem** option is selected and then click **Next**.

2. The wizard now asks you for the phone number of your ISP. Enter the **Area Code**, **Telephone Number**, and **Country/Region Name and Code**. If the call doesn't require the country code or area code, deactivate the **Use Area Code and Dialing Rules** check box.

3. Now you come to a fork in the wizard's road: whether you need to enter advanced settings to set up the connection. These advanced settings include the following: the connection type (PPP or SLIP), whether you need to log on manually, your IP address, and your ISP's DNS server addresses. If you don't need to enter these settings, click **Next** and skip to step 7. Otherwise, click **Advanced** to display the Advanced Connection Properties dialog box (see the next figure) and proceed to step 4.

*Click **Advanced** to get to this dialog box. Note that most ISPs don't require you to set any of these options.*

4. On the **Connection** tab, you have two groups to deal with:

   ➤ **Connection Type**   Activate the appropriate connection type option: **PPP**, **SLIP**, or **C-SLIP**.

   ➤ **Logon Procedure**   Activate **None** if you don't have to log on to your ISP; if you have to type some information to log on, activate **Log On Manually**; if your ISP provided you with a "script" that automates the logon, activate **Use Logon Script** and then enter the location of the script (click the **Browse** button to use the Open dialog box to select the script file).

5. On the **Addresses** tab, you have another couple of groups to overcome:

   ➤ **IP Address**   If your ISP assigns you an IP address automatically, activate **Internet Service Provider Automatically Provides One**. Otherwise, activate **Always Use the Following** and then enter your IP address in the **IP Address** text box.

   ➤ **DNS Server Address**   If your ISP assigns DNS addresses automatically, activate **My ISP Automatically Provides a Domain Name Server (DNS) Address**. Otherwise, activate **Always Use the Following** and then enter the DNS server addresses in the **Primary DNS Server** and **Alternate DNS Server** text boxes.

6. Click **OK** to return to the Internet Connection Wizard, and then click **Next**.

7. In the next wizard dialog box, enter your **User Name** and **Password** (the latter appears only as asterisks, for security), and then click **Next**.

8. The wizard now asks you to name your new connection. It suggests something excruciatingly dull such as **Connection to 555-1234**, but you don't have to stand for that. Enter your own creative name, and then click **Next**.

Not Done Yet: Setting Up Your Internet Email Account

The next stage of the process involves setting up your Internet email account. Here's what happens:

1. When the Internet Connection Wizard asks whether you want to set up your Internet mail account, be sure **Yes** is activated, and then click **Next**.

2. The wizard asks for your display name, which is the name other folks see when you send them a message. Enter the name you want to use in the **Display Name** text box (most people just use their real name), and click **Next**.

3. Now the wizard pesters you for your email address. Enter your address in the **E-mail Address** text box, and click **Next**.

173

4. Next on the wizard's to-do list is gathering info about your ISP's email server. You have three things to fill in (as usual, click **Next** when you're done):

   ➤ **My Incoming Mail Server Is A**   Use this list to specify the type of email server your ISP uses. Most are POP3.

   ➤ **Incoming Mail (POP3, IMAP, or HTTP) Server**   Enter the name of the server that your ISP uses for incoming mail.

   ➤ **Outgoing Mail (SMTP) Server**   Enter the name of the server that your ISP uses for outgoing mail.

5. The next items on the agenda are your account details: your **Account name** and your **Password**. If you don't want to be pestered for your password each time you connect, leave the **Remember password** check box activated. Click **Next** after that's finished.

6. Don't look now, but you're done! In the final wizard dialog box, you can connect to the Internet right away by leaving the **To Connect to the Internet Immediately...** check box activated. (See the next section for the details on connecting.) Click **Finish** to get outta there.

Making the Connection

Now that you have your account details down pat, it's time to put that account to good use by connecting to the Internet. The easiest way to get the connection going is to crank up any of the Internet programs mentioned later in this chapter (see "Now What? Windows 2000's Internet Features"). For example, you can launch the Internet Explorer Web browser. Windows 2000, ever eager to please, offers tons of ways to do this, but the following three are the most common:

➤ Launch the desktop's **Internet Explorer** icon.

➤ Click the **Launch Internet Explorer Browser** icon in the taskbar's Quick Launch section.

➤ Select **Start**, **Programs**, **Internet Explorer**.

At this point, Windows 2000 might mumble something about **The Web Page You Requested Is Not Available Offline**. Say "Well, duh!" and click **Connect**. This gets you to the Dial-Up Connection dialog box, shown in the following figure.

This dialog box offers the following toys:

➤ **Connect to**   This list should show the name of the connection you made earlier. If you happen to have multiple connections, use this list to select the one you want.

➤ **User name**   This is the username you use to log on to your ISP.

➤ **Password**   This is the password you use to log on to your ISP.

174

➤ **Save password**   When this check box is activated, Windows 2000 is kind enough to enter your password automatically. If you're worried about somebody else monkeying around with your account, you'll sleep better at night if you deactivate this option.

➤ **Connect automatically**   If you activate this option, Windows 2000 bypasses the Dial-up Connection dialog box entirely. Instead, it just leaps right into the connection. This is a real timesaver if you never have to change any of the data in this dialog box.

➤ **Connect**   Click this button to get the connection process going.

➤ **Settings**   Click this button to adjust your connection settings.

➤ **Work Offline**   Click this button if you change your mind about connecting.

This dialog box is the launch pad for your Internet forays.

Adjust the data as necessary and, when you're ready, click **Connect**. Windows 2000 taps your modem on the shoulder, passes it the phone number, and the connection process begins in the usually noisy modem fashion. If your ISP requires you to log on manually, a screen will appear and the ISP's prompts (such as "User Name" and "Password") will appear. Type in whatever information you're asked for (press **Enter** after you've entered each item).

After a few more seconds of navel-gazing, Windows 2000 finally lets you know that you're now up and online by displaying the Connection Complete dialog box and by adding a connection icon to the system tray.

When you've stood just about all you can stand of the Internet's wiles, you can log off by right-clicking the connection icon in the taskbar's system tray, and then clicking **Disconnect** (see the following figure). When Windows 2000 asks you to confirm the disconnect, click **Yes**.

*Right-click the **Connection** icon to disconnect from the Internet.*

This icon appears while you're on the Internet.

175

Now What? Windows 2000's Internet Features

Okay, so you've managed to get your Internet connection up and surfing. Where do you go from here? Ah, you'll be happy to know that the Net is your oyster because Windows 2000 offers just about everything you need to make things happen online. Here's a quick review of all the Windows 2000 features, and where to find out more about them:

➤ **Internet Explorer**   As I said, this is Windows 2000's World Wide Web browser. The Web is a vast storehouse of information presented in *pages* located on computers all over the world. These pages are created by individuals, corporations, and agencies, and they usually contain *links* that, when clicked, take you directly to other pages. See Chapter 12, "Weaving Your Way Through the World Wide Web."

➤ **Outlook Express email**   This is Windows 2000's Internet email program. Email is a system that enables you to exchange electronic messages with other email users, whether they're across town or across the ocean. See Chapter 13, "Everybody's Doing It: Sending and Receiving Email Messages."

➤ **Outlook Express newsgroups**   Outlook Express also doubles as Windows 2000's newsgroup reader. A newsgroup is a kind of electronic message board devoted to a particular topic. People "post" questions and comments to the newsgroup (there are thousands to choose from), other folks respond to those posts, and still others respond to the responses. It will all become clear in Chapter 14, "More Online Conversations: Newsgroups and Internet Phone Calls."

➤ **NetMeeting and Phone Dialer**   You use both of these programs to place "telephone calls" over the Internet. NetMeeting also can be used to "chat" (exchange typed messages in real time), collaborate with other people on a program, and more. Again, Chapter 14 is the place to go to learn how all this is done.

What Happened

This chapter showed you how to go from tired to wired by getting Windows 2000 connected to the Internet. I first ran through the two easiest connection routes: setting up a new account and transferring an existing account. The bulk of the chapter was spent on the third route: setting up an existing account with the sweat of your own brow. After all that, I showed you how to make the connection and then went through a summary of Windows 2000's Net tools.

Crib Notes

➤ **Running the Internet Connection Wizard** After you create your account, the desktop's Internet Connection Wizard disappears in an invisible cloud of smoke. If you need to run this wizard again, select **Start, Programs, Accessories, Communications, Internet Connection Wizard**.

➤ **Manual connection tidbits** If you'll be setting up your connection by hand, your ISP should provide you with the settings and data you need: the access phone number, your username and password, the type of mail server, the address of the mail server, and so on.

➤ **Getting connected** Making the leap to the Internet is as easy as starting any Internet program, such as Internet Explorer. When the Dial-Up Connection dialog box wanders in, click **Connect**.

➤ **Getting disconnected** To return to the real world, right-click the **Connection** icon in the taskbar's system tray, and then click **Disconnect**.

Chapter 12

Weaving Your Way Through the World Wide Web

In This Chapter

➤ Using Internet Explorer to navigate Web pages

➤ Saving Web pages to your Favorites list

➤ Working with Web pages offline

➤ Searching for the information you need

➤ How to use Netscape instead of Internet Explorer

➤ Tips and techniques to help you get the most out of your online surfin' safaris

Whether you're 19 or 90, a world traveler or a channel surfer, I don't think I'm going out on a limb when I say that you've probably never seen anything quite like the World Wide Web. We're talking here about an improbably vast conglomeration of the world's wit, wisdom, and weirdness. Arranged in separate *pages* of information, the Web is home to just about every conceivable topic under the sun. If someone's thought of it, chances are someone else has a Web page about it.

The great thing about the Web is that it's not just a bunch of corporate marketing hoo-ha (although there's plenty of that, to be sure). No, *anyone* can publish a page, so the Web reflects the different interests, idiosyncrasies, and eccentricities of the general population.

If the Web has a downside, it's that it's *too* big (there's no "index," per se, so finding the info you need can be hard) and that it's *too* easy to publish a page (with no editors in sight, there's no guarantee that the info you find is accurate or even true).

Page

A document on the Web that contains text, images, and usually a few links.

Still, there are ways to search for data, and you can usually corroborate something by looking for other pages that have the same data.

So, the Web is definitely worth a look or three. This chapter helps you get those looks by showing you how to use Windows 2000's Internet Explorer program, which is designed to surf (to use the proper Web verb) Web sites. You'll learn all the standard page navigation techniques, and you'll learn all the features that Internet Explorer offers for making your online journeys more efficient and pleasant.

Exploring Internet Explorer

The easiest way to get Internet Explorer off the ground is to click the **Launch Internet Explorer Browser** icon in the taskbar's Quick Launch section. (If you prefer more of a workout, you can either double-click the desktop's **Internet Explorer** icon or select **Start**, **Programs**, **Internet Explorer**.) If you're using a modem, Windows 2000 prompts you to connect to the Internet. After you've done that, Internet Explorer loads, as shown in the following figure. (Note that the initial Web page you see might be different from the one shown here.)

When you launch Internet Explorer, you'll see a window that looks suspiciously like this one.

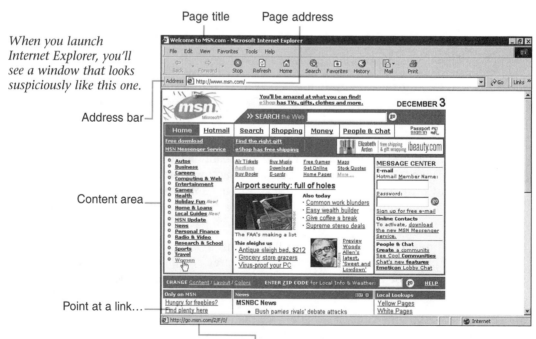

180

What you're seeing here is a *Web page*, and it has all sorts of goodies, including lots of text, a few images, places where you can type stuff, and more.

Before learning how to get around the Web, take a second to get your bearings in the Internet Explorer window. Here are a few features you should be comfy with:

➤ **Page title** The left side of the title bar always displays the title of the current page.

➤ **Address bar** This toolbar contains a long text box that displays the Web address of the current page. You also can use the Address bar to enter the address of another page you want to view (more on this a bit later).

➤ **Content area** This is the large expanse below the Address bar and the Links toolbar, and it's where the page content appears.

Basic Web Navigation Techniques

With that brief introduction out of the way, it's time to start wandering the Web. This section runs through a few techniques for getting from one page to another.

The most straightforward method is to click any *link* that strikes your fancy. Click the link and you're immediately (depending on the speed of your Internet connection) whisked to the other page.

How can I tell what's a link and what isn't?

That, unfortunately, is not as easy as it used to be. Originally, link text appeared underlined and in a different color. That's still the usual case for a link these days, but you can also get nonunderlined links, as well as

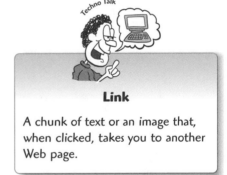

Techno Talk

Link

A chunk of text or an image that, when clicked, takes you to another Web page.

images that are links. The only real way to be sure is to park your mouse pointer over some likely-looking text or an image, and then watch what happens to the pointer. If it changes into a hand with a pointing finger, then you know for sure that you've got a link on your hands.

What if I know the address of the page I want to peruse?

Easy money. Here's what you do:

➤ Click inside the Address bar, delete the existing address, type in the address you want to check out, and then either press **Enter** or click **Go**.

Internet Explorer's Address Suggestions

After you've used Internet Explorer for a while, it will often "suggest" an address after you've type in a few characters. If you see the address you want in the list that appears, use the down arrow key to highlight the address, and then press **Enter** (or click **Go**).

➤ If the address is one that you've visited recently, use the Address bar's drop-down list to select it.

Why the heck are Web addresses so, well, weird!

Probably because they were created by geeks who never imagined they'd be used by normal people. Still, they're not so bad after you figure out what's going on. Here's a summary of the various bits and pieces of a typical Web address (or *URL*, which is short for Uniform Resource Locator, another geekism):

`http://www.mcfedries.com/books/cigwin2000/index.html`

`http://` This strange combination of letters and symbols tells the browser that you're entering a Web address. Note that the browser assumes *every* address is a Web address, so you don't need to include this part if you don't want to.

`www.mcfedries.com` This is what's known as the *domain name* of the server computer that hosts the Web page (`www.mcfedries.com` is my Web server).

`/books/cigwin2000/` This is the Web server directory in which the Web page makes its home.

`index.html` This is the Web page's filename.

Ugh. Is there any easier way to get somewhere?

If you're not sure where you want to go, the default start page—it's called MSN.com—has lots of choices. For example, click any of the categories on the left to see lots of links related to that topic.

What if I jump to one page and then decide I want to double back to where I was?

That's a pretty common scenario. In fact, you'll often find that you need to leap back several pages, and then leap forward again. Fortunately, Internet Explorer makes this easy thanks to its Back and Forward toolbar buttons. Here's what you can do with them:

➤ Click **Back** to return to the previous page.
➤ Click **Forward** to move ahead to the next page.

➤ To go back several pages at once, drop down the **Back** button's list and click the page you want.

➤ To go forward several pages, drop down the **Forward** button's list and click the page you want.

Changing the Start Page

If you don't like Internet Explorer's default start page, it's easy to change it. First, surf to the page that you want to use as the new start page. Then select the **Tools, Internet Options** command to lure the Internet Options dialog box out into the open. In the **General** tab, click **Use Current**. If you decide later on that you prefer Internet Explorer's default home page, click **Use Default**. If you'd rather not see any page at startup, click **Use Blank**.

Techniques for Efficient Web Gallivanting

The paradox of the Web is that even though it doesn't really exist anywhere (after all, where is the amorphous never-never land of cyberspace?), it's still one of the biggest earthly things you can imagine. There aren't hundreds of thousands of pages, or even millions of them for that matter. No, there are *hundreds of millions* of Web pages. (Of course, if you ignore all the pages that are devoted to Pamela Anderson Lee then, yes, there *are* only a few hundred thousand pages.)

To have even a faint hope of managing just a tiny fraction of such an inconceivably vast array of data and bad MIDI music, you need to hone your Web browsing skills with a few useful techniques. Fortunately, as you'll see in the next few sections, Internet Explorer has all kinds of features that can help.

Saving Sites for Subsequent Surfs: Managing Your Favorites

One of the most common experiences that folks new to Web browsing go through is to stumble upon a really great site, and then not be able to find it again later. They try to retrace their steps, but usually just end up clicking links furiously and winding up in strange Net neighborhoods.

If this has happened to you, the solution is to get Internet Explorer to do all the grunt work of remembering sites for you. This is the job of the Favorites feature, which holds "shortcuts" to Web pages and even lets you organize those shortcuts into separate folders.

Here's how you tell Internet Explorer to remember a Web page as a favorite:

1. Use Internet Explorer to display the page.

2. Select **Favorites**, **Add to Favorites** to get the Add Favorite dialog box onscreen. (I'm going to ignore the **Make Available Offline** check box for now. I'll tackle it later on in the section titled "The Unwired Surfer: Reading Pages Offline.")

3. The **Name** text box shows the name of the page, which is what you'll select from a menu later on when you want to view this page again. If you can think of a better name, don't hesitate to edit this text.

4. Most people end up with dozens or even hundreds of favorites, so it's a good idea to organize them into folders. To save this favorite in a folder, click **Create In**. (If you don't want to bother with this, skip to step 7.)

5. The Favorites feature has only two folders at the start: Links and Media, neither of which you should use for this. Instead, click **New Folder**, enter a name for the new folder in the dialog box that comes up, and then click **OK**.

6. Click the folder in which you want to store your favorite.

7. Click **OK** to finish.

After you have some pages lined up a favorites, you can return to any one of them at any time by pulling down the **Favorites** menu and clicking the page title. (If the favorite is stored in a folder, click that folder to open its submenu, and then click the page.)

Another Way to Get to Your Favorites

If you find yourself constantly pulling down the Favorites menu to get at your favorite pages, you might prefer to have the Favorites list displayed full-time. You can do that by clicking the **Favorites** button in the toolbar. Internet Explorer then sets aside a chunk of real estate on the left side of the window to display the Favorites list.

If you need to make changes to your favorites, you can do a couple of things right from the Favorites menu. Pull down the menu and then right-click the item you want to work with. In the shortcut menu that slinks in, click **Rename** to change the item's name, or click **Delete** to blow it away.

For more heavy-duty adjustments, select the **Favorites**, **Organize Favorites** command. Not surprisingly, this pushes the Organize Favorites dialog box into view, as shown in the following figure. You get four buttons to play with:

➤ **Create Folder**   Click this button to create a new folder. (Tip: If you click an existing folder and then click this button, Internet Explorer creates a subfolder.) Internet Explorer adds the folder and displays **New Folder** inside a text box. Edit to taste, and then press **Enter**.

➤ **Move to Folder**   Click this button to move the currently highlighted favorite into another folder. In the Browse for Folder dialog box that saunters by, highlight the destination folder, and then click **OK**.

➤ **Rename**   Click this button to rename the currently highlighted favorite. Edit the name accordingly, and then press **Enter**.

➤ **Delete**   Click this button to nuke the currently highlighted favorite. When Windows 2000 asks whether you're sure about this, click **Yes**.

When you're done, click **Close** to return to Internet Explorer.

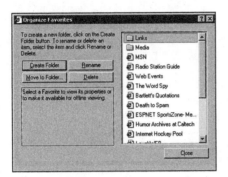

Use the Organize Favorites dialog box to put your favorites in apple-pie order.

Order Out of Chaos: Searching for Sites

Serendipitous surfing—clicking willy-nilly in the hope of finding something interesting—can be fun if you've got a few hours to kill. But if you need a specific tidbit of information *now*, then a click click here and click click there just won't cut the research mustard. To save time, you need to knock the Web down to a more manageable size, and Internet Explorer's Search feature can help you do just that.

The idea is straightforward: You supply a search "engine" (as they're called) with a word or two that describes the topic you want to find. The search engine then scours the Web for pages that contain those words, and presents you with a list of matches. Does it work? Well, it depends on which search engine you use. There are quite a few available, and some are better than others at certain kinds of searches. The biggest problem is that, depending on the topic you're looking for, the search engine might still return thousands of matching sites! You can usually get a more targeted search by adding more search terms and by avoiding common words.

Here's the basic procedure to follow to use the Search feature:

1. Click the **Search** button in the toolbar. Internet Explorer responds by shoehorning the Search bar into the left side of the content area, as shown in the following figure.

Use the Search feature to have Internet Explorer rifle through the Web's contents for a specific topic.

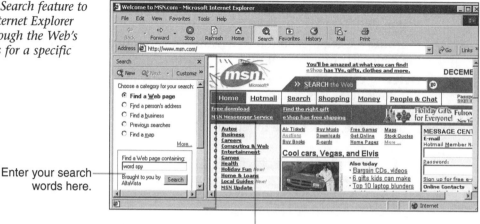

Enter your search words here.

The Search bar

2. Be sure the **Find a Web Page** option is activated.

3. Use the **Find a Web Page Containing** text box to enter the word or phrase you want to find.

4. Click **Search**. Internet Explorer runs the search and then displays the results a few seconds later. As you can see in the next figure, you get a series of links in the Search bar. (Generally speaking, the higher the link is in the list, the better the page it points to matches your search text.) Clicking a link displays the page in the rest of the content area.

After the search is done, the Search bar displays a list of links to matching pages.

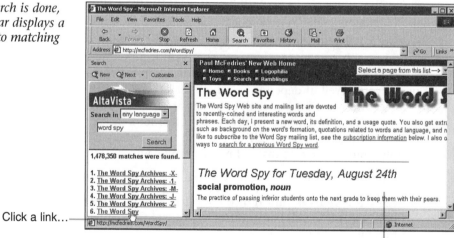

Click a link...

...to display the page here.

5. To get to more links, scroll down to the bottom of the Search bar. Here you'll see a **Next >>** link, which displays the next 10 matches.

6. When you've finished searching, click the **Search** toolbar button again to close the Search bar.

Here are a few notes to bear in mind when using the Search bar:

➤ **Running the same search on another engine** As I said, the Web has quite a few search engines. To try your search in another engine, click the **Next** button near the top of the Search bar. Each time you do this, Internet Explorer runs the search in a different engine. You can also click the **Next** button's downward-pointing arrow to select a search engine from a menu.

➤ **Changing the search engine order** If you find that you prefer some search engines to others for the kinds of searches you do, you can change the order to put those engines near the top of the list. To do that, click the Search bar's **Customize** button to get to the Customize Search Settings window (shown here). In the **Find a Web Page** section, use the upward- and downward-pointing arrows to change the order of the items in the search engine list.

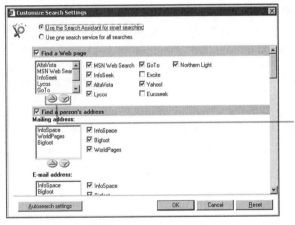

Use this window to customize Internet Explorer's Search feature.

Click the buttons to change the search engine order.

➤ **Changing the available search engines** While you're in the Customize Search Settings window, use the check boxes in the **Find a Web Page** section to choose which search engines Internet Explorer uses. (A deactivated check box means that search engine doesn't show up in the Search bar.)

Address Bar Searching

If you don't like the Search bar usurping a big chunk of the Internet Explorer window, you can also run searches from the Address bar. Just type in a word or phrase and press **Enter**. Note that Internet Explorer always uses the same engine for these quickie searches. To specify a different search engine, display the Search bar, click **Customize** to get to the Customize Search Settings dialog box, and then click **Autosearch Settings**. In the Customize Autosearch Settings dialog box that falls in, use the **Choose a Search Provider for Address Bar Searches** list to choose the search engine you want, and then click **OK**.

Bread Crumbs in Cyberspace: Using the History List

You've seen so far how Internet Explorer keeps track of your "clickstream": the pages you've visited in the current session. You can then use the Back and Forward buttons for to-and-fro surfing. That works well for the sites you've seen in the current Internet Explorer session, but what if you want to go back to a nonfavorite site you saw yesterday or even last week? That might seem like a tall order, but it turns out that Internet Explorer has a tall memory. In fact, the program offers a History feature that remembers pretty much everywhere you've gone for the past 20 days! Here's how it works:

1. Click the **History** button in the toolbar. By this time, you won't be surprised to see a History bar show up on the left side of the window, as shown in the following figure.

2. You now do one of the following:
    - ➤ If the date you want to work with was this week, click the day (such as **Monday**).
    - ➤ If the date you want is in a previous week, click the week (such as **2 Weeks Ago**) and then click the day.

3. Internet Explorer displays a list of the sites you visited on that day. Click the site you want. This gives you a list of the pages you visited on that site.

4. Click the page you want to see. Internet Explorer displays the page in the rest of the content area.

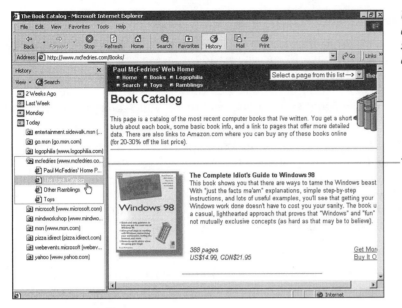

Use the History bar to see a list of the places you've seen over the past 20 days.

The History bar

Internet Explorer also offers a couple of methods for dealing with the History bar's links:

➤ **Sorting the list**   Click the History bar's **View** button and then click a sort option (such as **By Most Visited**).

➤ **Searching the list**   If you do a lot of surfing, your History bar will be crammed to the gills with links. To find the one you want, click the History bar's **Search** button, enter a word or phrase in the **Search For** text box, and then click **Search Now**.

When you're done with the History bar, you can hide it by clicking the **History** toolbar button once again.

Check This Out

Altering History

Internet Explorer stores 20 days' worth of page addresses in the History bar, but there's no problem changing that. First, select **Tools, Internet Options** to awaken the Internet Options dialog box. In the **General** tab, use the **Days to Keep Pages in History** spin box to specify the number of days you'd prefer Internet Explorer to use. If you'd like to start from scratch, click **Clear History**. Click **OK** to put the new settings into effect.

The Unwired Surfer: Reading Pages Offline

Many Web fans have a few pages that they check out regularly because the content is always changing. Let's say you have 10 such pages and it takes you an average of five minutes to read each one. That's 50 minutes of online time you've used up. Wouldn't it be better if Internet Explorer could somehow grab those pages while you weren't around (at night, for example), and then let you read them while you're not connected?

Well, *sure* it would be! That's probably why the Windows 2000 programmers added the Synchronize feature to Internet Explorer. This feature lets you designate Web pages to be available offline (that is, when you're not connected to the Internet). You then download the latest version of those pages by running the Synchronize command whenever you like. Internet Explorer also is happy to set up an automatic synchronization that can be scheduled any time you prefer.

To make a page available offline, begin by using either of the following techniques:

➤ **If the page is set up as a favorite** Pull down the **Favorites** menu and display the shortcut for the page. Then right-click that shortcut and click **Make Available Offline**.

➤ **If the page isn't yet set up as a favorite** Display the page and then select **Favorites**, **Add to Favorites** to meet up with the Add Favorite dialog box. Activate the **Make Available Offline** check box and then click **Customize**.

Whichever route you take, you'll end up with the Offline Favorite Wizard staring you in the face. Here's how it works:

1. The first wizard dialog box just offers an introduction, so click **Next**.

2. The next wizard dialog box wonders whether you want any pages that are linked to the favorite to be downloaded, as well. If you don't care about the linked pages, activate **No**; otherwise, activate **Yes** and then use the **Download Pages *x* Links Deep from This Page** spin box to specify how many levels of links you want grabbed. Click **Next** when you're ready to proceed.

3. The wizard now would like to know how you want the page synchronized:

   ➤ **Only When I Choose Synchronize from the Tools Menu** Select this option if you want to control when the synchronization occurs. If you choose this option, click **Next** and then skip to step 5.

   ➤ **I Would Like to Create a New Schedule** Activate this option if you want Internet Explorer to perform the synchronization automatically on a preset schedule. If you select this option, click **Next** and then proceed to step 4.

Don't Go Too Deep!

If you elect to download pages that are linked to the favorite page, you can choose to go 1, 2, or 3 levels deep. Going 1 level deep means just the pages linked to the favorite page are downloaded. Going 2 levels deep means that you also get any pages that are linked to the pages that are linked to the favorite page. For example, if the favorite page has 10 links, and each of those linked pages also has 10 links, you'll end up downloading 100 pages! Obviously, you want to exercise some caution here because you could end up with a massive download on your hands.

4. If you elected to set up a synchronization schedule, you'll see a dialog box with scheduling options. Here's a rundown of the controls you get to mess with (click **Next** when you're ready to move on):

   ➤ **Every *x* Days**   Specify the number of days between synchronizations.

   ➤ **At**   Specify the time you want the synchronization to happen.

   ➤ **Name**   Enter a name for this synchronization schedule.

   ➤ **If My Computer Is Not Connected...**   Activate this check box to have Internet Explorer connect your computer to the Internet to download the page (or pages). Note that this option works only if you don't have to log on manually to your ISP.

Synchronize

To download a copy of a Web page so that the version you have stored on your computer is the same as (that is, is synchronized with) the version on the Web.

5. The final wizard dialog box wants to know whether the Web page requires you to log on. If not, activate **No**; if so, activate **Yes** and then fill in your **User Name** and **Password** (twice). Click **Finish** to complete the synchronization setup.

6. If you're adding a new favorite, you'll end up back in the Add Favorite dialog box. Select a folder for the favorite (if necessary) and then click **OK**.

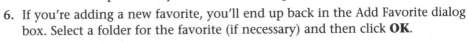

If you elected to go the manual synchronization route, you can download the pages for offline perusing at any time by selecting the **Tools**, **Synchronize** command. In the Items to Synchronize dialog box, deactivate the check boxes for any items you don't want to synchronize, and then click **Synchronize**.

The Items to Synchronize dialog box also enables you to make some adjustments to your items and to the Synchronize feature:

➤ **To adjust the settings for a synchronized item**   Highlight the item in the Items to Synchronize dialog box, and then click **Properties**. The dialog box that claws its way onto the screen has three tabs for you:

Web Document   Deactivate the **Make This Page Available Offline** check box to stop synchronizing this page.

Schedule   Use this tab to change the synchronization schedule for the page.

Download   Use this tab to change the number of link levels you want downloaded. A very handy feature on this tab is the **When This Page Changes, Send E-Mail To** check box. If you activate this and then fill in your **E-Mail Address** and **Mail Server (SMTP)** (the Internet name of your ISP's outgoing mail computer), Internet Explorer will send you an email to let you know that the page has changed.

➤ **To adjust the settings for the Synchronize feature as a whole**   Click **Setup** to project the Synchronization Settings dialog box onto the screen. Once again, you have three tabs to play with:

Logon/Logoff   Use this tab to set up a synchronization every time you log on and log off Windows 2000.

On Idle   Use this tab to set up a synchronization when your computer hasn't been used for a while. To control when this synchronization happens, click the **Advanced** button.

Scheduled   Use this tab to adjust the synchronization schedules that you've defined so far.

"What If I Want to Use Netscape?"

Internet Explorer comes free with Windows 2000, and it's built right into the fabric of the operating system. However, that doesn't mean you can't use an alternative Web browser such as Netscape Navigator. Just download the browser from Netscape (go to `http://home.netscape.com/`) and then install it.

You should note, however, that Netscape will probably set itself up to be Windows 2000's default browser. (Some versions of Netscape are polite enough to ask you whether this is what you want.) This means that if you launch a shortcut to a Web page, it's Netscape that displays the page, not Internet Explorer.

What do you do if you'd prefer to use Internet Explorer as the default browser? This isn't a problem, but you first have to tell Internet Explorer to check to see whether it's the default. You do this by following these steps:

1. Select **Tools**, **Internet Options** to open the Internet Options dialog box.
2. Display the **Programs** tab.
3. Activate the **Internet Explorer Should Check to See Whether It Is the Default** check box.
4. Click **OK**.

Now shut down Internet Explorer and then start it back up again. This time, you'll see the dialog box shown here. If you want to restore Internet Explorer's position as the default browser, click **Yes**; otherwise, click **No**.

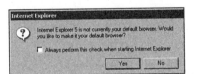

If Netscape takes over as Windows 2000's default browser, Internet Explorer will seek to regain its lost crown.

Sharing Favorites and Bookmarks

If you use both Internet Explorer and Netscape, a big problem you'll run into is that they don't share a common list of favorites—which are called **bookmarks** in the Netscape world. However, Internet Explorer is happy to either export the Favorites look to Netscape's bookmarks list or import the bookmarks as favorites. Select the **File**, **Import and Export** command.

What Happened

This chapter showed you how to use Internet Explorer to ply the electronic highways and byways of the World Wide Web. I gave you a quick tour of the Internet Explorer screen, and then ran through a bunch of basic Web navigation techniques. You then learned four ways to make your surfing more efficient: Favorites, Search, History, and Synchronization. I closed with a quick look at using Netscape Navigator in Windows 2000.

Crib Notes

➤ **Going Internet Exploring** To start Internet Explorer, click the **Launch Internet Explorer Browser** icon in the taskbar's Quick Launch section. (Alternatively, you can either double-click the desktop's **Internet Explorer** icon or select **Start, Programs, Internet Explorer**.)

➤ **Navigation for novices** To light out for another page, either click a link or type a URL in the Address bar and then press **Enter**. Use the toolbar's **Back** button to return to the previous page, and use the **Forward** button to head the other way.

➤ **Playing favorites** Run the **Favorites, Add Favorites** command to save a page on the Favorites menu.

➤ **Site searching** To scour the Web for a particular topic, click the **Search** button to get the Search bar onscreen, enter a word or two, and then click **Search**.

➤ **Offline surfing** To get Internet Explorer to download a page for leisurely offline reading, select **Favorites, Add Favorites** and activate the **Make Available Offline** check box.

Chapter 13

Everybody's Doing It: Sending and Receiving Email Messages

In This Chapter

➤ Composing and sending a message

➤ Adding potential recipients to the Windows 2000 Address Book

➤ Working with signatures and attachments

➤ Getting and reading incoming messages

➤ Filtering and blocking incoming missives

➤ Everything you need to know to get yourself a seat on the email bandwagon

---

With all those lush graphics, animated images, and clickable links, the Web is clearly the sexy side of the Internet. (Of course, the Web is also home to humungous image files that take forever to download, execrable MIDI music, and links that don't work, so the Web also qualifies as the ditzy side of the Internet.) That's one reason why the Internet has become so popular over the last few years. But I think an even bigger reason is the emergence of email as the second most popular form of communication in the developed world (behind only the telephone). Just when the pursed-lip-and-furrowed-brow crowd thought letter writing was doomed to die out as an art form, along comes email to show that millions of people really do like to exchange notes—they just hate licking envelopes and stamps.

It also helps that shipping out an email message is a simple and quick operation, so complete email idiocy is a state that no one stays in for long. This chapter will prove just that by running through the admirable email capabilities of Windows 2000's Outlook Express program.

Internet Email Primer

If you're new to the Internet email game, you might want to dip a toe or two into the waters before diving in. To that end, I have an Internet email primer available on my Web site. Check it out at the following address:

```
http://www.mcfedries.com/Ramblings/email-primer.html
```

Getting Started with Outlook Express

Windows 2000 gives you an easy way and a hard way to launch Outlook Express:

➤ **The easy way**   Click the **Launch Outlook Express** icon in the taskbar's Quick Launch area.

➤ **The hard way**   Select **Start**, **Programs**, **Outlook Express**.

Cross Reference

To revisit configuring your Internet connection, see Chapter 11's "Interstate 13: Setting Up an Existing Account Manually" section on page 170.

If when you were configuring your Internet connection back in Chapter 11 you were negligent in your email account setup duties, Outlook Express will ask the Internet Connection Wizard to step in for a moment to run through the necessary steps.

At this point, your computer might beep testily at you and Outlook Express might display a message asking whether you want to "go online." We'll save that for later, so just click **No** for now to get on with things.

At long last, the Outlook Express window shows itself, and it looks much like the one in the following figure.

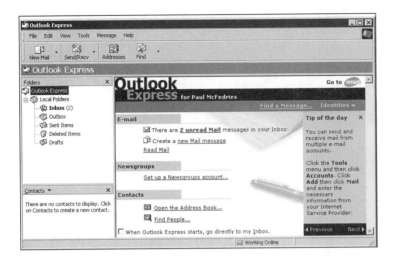

Use Outlook Express to ship and receive Internet email messages.

A More Sensible Startup

The default Outlook Express startup screen shows a collection of common chores (such as **Create a New Mail Message**). Most people don't find this screen particularly useful, so they just click the **Inbox** folder (which is where all your incoming messages first get stored). If you'd like Outlook Express to open the **Inbox** folder automatically at startup, activate the **When Outlook Express Starts, Go Directly to My Inbox** check box.

Using Outlook Express to Send an Email Message

Let's begin the Outlook Express tour with a look at how to foist your e-prose on unsuspecting colleagues, friends, or members of your family. This section shows you the basic technique to use, and then gets a bit fancier in discussing the Address Book, signatures, and other Outlook Express sending features.

Composing the Message

Without further ado (not that there's been much ado to this point, mind you), here are the basic steps to follow to fire off an email message to some lucky recipient:

1. Click the **New Mail** button in the toolbar, or select **Message**, **New Message**. (Keyboard fans will be pleased to note that pressing **Ctrl+N** also works.) You end up with the New Message window onscreen, as shown here.

197

The New Message window is where you cobble together an email message.

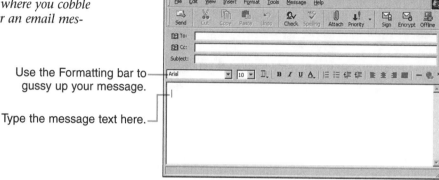

Use the Formatting bar to gussy up your message.

Type the message text here.

2. In the **To** text box, type in the email address of the recipient. (It's perfectly acceptable to enter multiple addresses in this text box. Use a semicolon (;) or a comma (,) to separate each address.)

3. If you want to send a copy of the message to a different recipient, enter their email address in the **Cc** text box. (Again, you can enter multiple addresses, if you're so inclined.)

Cc and Its Bcc Cousin

"Cc" stands for either *courtesy copy* or *carbon copy*; nobody really knows for sure. There's also an email creature called the *blind courtesy* (or *carbon*) *copy* (Bcc), which also delivers a copy of the message to a specified recipient. However, none of the other recipients see that person's address anywhere. To enter a Bcc address, activate the **View, All Headers** command to add a **Bcc** field to the New Message window.

4. Use the **Subject** line to enter a subject for the message. (The subject acts as a kind of title for your message. It's the first thing the recipient sees, so it should accurately reflect the content of your message, and it shouldn't be too long. Think *pithy*.)

5. Decide what type of message you want to send. You have two choices, both of which are commands on the **Format** menu:

➤ **Rich Text (HTML)**   Choose this command to include formatting in your message. This enables you to make your message look its best. However, if your recipient's email program doesn't support this formatting, then she might have problems. (Just so you know, HTML stands for Hypertext Markup Language. It's a series of codes used to format characters and things, and it's what's used to create Web pages.)

➤ **Plain Text**   Choose this command to send out the message without any formatting. This makes life easier for your recipient if she doesn't have an email program that supports formatting. If you're not sure what your recipient is using, choose this command anyway.

6. Use the large, empty, area below the Subject line to type in the message text (also known as the *message body*).

7. If you chose the Rich Text (HTML) format, after you're inside the message text area, you'll notice that the buttons on the Formatting bar suddenly become available, as do more of the Format menu commands. Use these buttons and commands to change the font, format paragraphs, add a background image, apply stationery, and more. (*Stationery* is a prefab set of formatting options.)

No Spell Check?

You might be intrigued that Outlook Express has a **Spelling** command on the **Tools** menu (as well as a **Spelling** toolbar button). However, you might also be bummed that you can't select it. That's because Outlook Express doesn't actually have its own spell checker. Instead, it just rides the spell checking coattails of other programs, such as Microsoft Word. So, you can run the Spelling command only if you have a spell-check-ready program installed.

8. When your message is fit for human consumption, you have two sending choices:

➤ **If you're working online**   Click the **Send** toolbar button or select **File**, **Send Message** (or try **Alt+S** on for size). Outlook Express sends the message, no questions asked.

➤ **If you're working offline**   Click the **Send** toolbar button or select **File**, **Send Message** (or press **Alt+S**). In this case, Outlook Express coughs up a dialog box that tells you the message will bunk down in the Outbox folder until you're ready to send it. This is good because it means you can compose a few messages before connecting to the Internet. When you're ready to actually ship the messages, select the **Tools**, **Send and Receive**, **Send All** command in Outlook Express. (You also can drop down the **Send/Recv** toolbar button, and then click **Send All**.)

Note that after your message is Net-bound, Outlook Express also is kind enough to save a copy of the message in the Sent Items folder. This is handy because it gives you a record of all the missives you launch into cyberspace.

Populating the Address Book

If you find yourself with a bunch of recipients to whom you send stuff regularly (and it's a rare emailer who doesn't), you'll soon grow awfully tired of entering their addresses by hand. The solution is to toss those regulars into the Windows 2000 Address Book. That way, you can fire them into the To or Cc lines with just a few mouse clicks.

Here's how you add someone to the Address Book:

1. Click the **Addresses** button or select the **Tools**, **Address Book** command. (Keyboard diehards can get their kicks by pressing **Ctrl+Shift+B**. Note, too, that you also can work on your Address Book when Outlook Express isn't running. In this case, select **Start**, **Programs**, **Accessories**, **Address Book**.)

2. Click the **New** toolbar button and then click **New Contact**, or else select **File**, **New Contact** (you can also slam **Ctrl+N**). The Address Book conjures up the Properties dialog box shown here.

Use this dialog box to spell out the particulars of the new recipient.

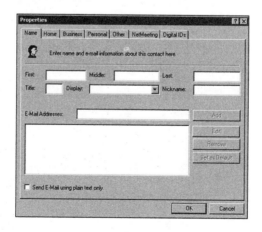

3. In the **Name** tab, enter at least the person's **First** and **Last** names.

4. Use the **E-Mail Addresses** text box to enter the recipient's address, and then click **Add**.

5. If you want this person to receive only plain text messages, activate the **Send E-Mail Using Plain Text Only** check box.

6. Fill in the fields in the other tabs, if you feel like it.

7. When you're done, click **OK** to add the new recipient.

After you have a contact in your Address Book, Outlook Express gives you a ton of ways to get them a message. Here are my two favorite methods:

➤ In the New Message window, click **To** or **Cc** to get the Select Recipients dialog box. Click the contact name and then click **To** (or **Cc** or **Bcc**).

➤ The Outlook Express window has a Contacts area that lists everyone in the Address Book. Use this area to double-click the name of the recipient you want to use.

One final note. If you set up the recipient to receive only plain text messages, when you send the message, you'll see a dialog box asking what format you want to use. In this case, you'd click **Send Plain Text**.

Group Email Gropes

One of the Internet's most enduring pastimes is to send out jokes and trivia to a select group of friends and colleagues. (Some folks find this annoying, but most see it as all in good fun.) The best way to do this is to organize those recipients into a *group*. That way, you can send a message to all of them just by specifying the group name in the To line. To create a group, select the Address Book's **File**, **New Group** command (or press **Ctrl+G**). Enter a **Group Name** and then click **Select Members** to add recipients to the group.

Creating Signatures

In email lingo, a *signature* is a chunk of text that appears at the bottom of all your messages. Most people use their signature to give contact information, and you'll often see sigs (that's the hip short form) adorned with witty quotations or sayings. Outlook Express even lets you create multiple signatures, so you can tailor them to various audiences.

Here are the steps to plow through to create a signature or two:

1. Select the **Tools**, **Options** command.

2. In the Options dialog box that climbs into the ring, display the **Signatures** tab.

3. Click **New**. Outlook Express adds a new item to the **Signatures** list.

4. Use the **Text** box to enter the signature.

5. Annoyingly, Outlook Express gives each signature a boring name such as Signature #1. You'll want to give them more meaningful names, so click the signature in the **Signatures** list, click **Rename**, enter a snappier name, and then press **Enter**.

6. Repeat steps 3–5 to create more signatures.

7. If you want Outlook Express to tack on the default signature to all your messages, activate the **Add Signatures to All Outgoing Messages** check box. If you'd rather not have the signature show up when you reply to a message or forward a message to someone, leave the **Don't Add Signatures to Replies or Forwards** check box activated.

8. When you're done, click **OK** to return to Outlook Express.

The Default Signature

The "default signature" is the first signature you create. To set up some other signature as the default, display the Signatures tab again, highlight the signature, and then click **Set As Default**.

Attachment

A file that latches on to a message and is sent to the recipient.

If you elected not to add your signature automatically, it's easy enough to toss it into a message that you're composing. In the New Message window, move the cursor to where you want the text to appear, and then select **Insert**, **Signature**. (If you have multiple signatures defined, a submenu with a list of the sigs will slide out. Select the one you want to use.)

Inserting Attachments and Other Hangers-On

Most of your missives will be text-only creations (with possibly a bit of formatting tossed in to keep things interesting). However, it's also possible to send entire files along for the ride. Such files are called, naturally enough, *attachments*. They're very common in the business world, and it's useful to know how they work. Here goes:

1. In the New Message window, either click the **Attach** toolbar button or select **Insert**, **File Attachment**. The Insert Attachment dialog box rears its head.

2. Find the file you want to attach and then highlight it.

3. Click **Attach**. Outlook Express returns you to the New Message window where you'll see a new **Attach** box that includes the name of the file.

Some Useful Sending Options

Let's complete our look at the sending side of Outlook Express by running through a few options related to sending messages. To see these options, select the **Tools**, **Options** command and then display the **Send** tab, shown in the following figure. Here's a once-over of what's available (click **OK** when you're done):

➤ **Save Copy of Sent Messages in the 'Sent Items' Folder**   Deactivate this check box to tell Outlook Express not to bother putting copies of your messages in Sent Items. I don't recommend doing this because you'll probably refer to previously sent notes on many an occasion.

➤ **Send Messages Immediately**   When this option is activated and you're working online, Outlook Express will transmit your messages as soon as you send them (unless, of course, you select the Send Later command). If you'd rather that Outlook Express hold its sending horses, deactivate this check box.

➤ **Automatically Put People I Reply to in My Address Book**   This option is on by default, which is downright silly because it means that every last person to whom you send a reply will get stuffed into your Address Book. That's dumb, so you might consider deactivating this one.

➤ **Automatically Complete E-Mail Addresses When Composing**   After you have some names in your Address Book, you can start typing a name and Outlook Express will "guess" the rest of the name based on the Address Book entries. If you don't like this feature, deactivate this check box to turn it off.

➤ **Include Message in Reply**   When this option is activated and you reply to a message (I'll show you how to do that a bit later), Outlook Express adds the original message to your reply message. This is a good idea because it reminds the recipient of what they said, so you should leave this option on.

➤ **Reply to Messages Using the Format in Which They Were Sent**   When this check box is activated, Outlook Express sets up your replies using the same format that the sender used. For example, if you get a plain text message and you reply to it, the reply will automatically be set up as plain text, as well. Again, I recommend leaving this one on.

➤ **Mail Sending Format**   These options determine the default format that Outlook Express uses for your messages. Select either **HTML** or **Plain Text**.

The Send tab is loaded with ways to customize sending messages in Outlook Express.

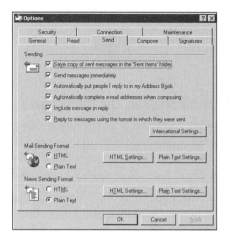

Using Outlook Express to Get and Read Email

Some people like to think of email as a return to the days of *belles-lettres* and *billets-doux* (these people tend to be a bit pretentious). Yes, it's true that email has people writing again, but this isn't like the letter writing of old. The major difference is that email's turnaround time is usually much quicker. Instead of waiting weeks or even months to get a return letter, a return email might take as little as a few minutes or a few hours.

So, if you send out a missive with a question or comment, chances are you'll get a reply coming right back at you before too long. Any messages sent to your email address are stored in your account at your ISP. Your job is to use Outlook Express to access your account and grab any waiting messages. This section shows you how to do that and shows you what to do with those messages after you've got them safely stowed on your computer.

Mailing Lists

Another good way to be sure your email Inbox stays populated is to subscribe to a *mailing list*. This is an email-based forum that discusses a particular topic. For example, in my Word Spy mailing list, I send out a new or recently coined word and its definition each day (see http://www.logophilia.com/WordSpy/). There's a directory of mailing lists available at http://www.liszt.com/.

Receiving Incoming Messages

Here are the steps to stride through to get your email messages:

1. Outlook Express offers two different postal routes:

   ➤ **To only receive messages** Either drop down the **Send/Recv** toolbar button and then click **Receive All**, or select **Tools**, **Send and Receive**, **Receive All**.

   ➤ **To send and receive messages** If you have outgoing messages waiting in your Outbox folder, either drop down the **Send/Recv** toolbar button and then click **Send and Receive All**, or select **Tools**, **Send and Receive**, **Send and Receive All**. (Keyboardists can just press **Ctrl+M**.)

2. If you're currently working offline, Outlook Express asks whether you want to go online. Say "Obviously!" and click **Yes**.

3. Outlook Express connects to your mail account, absconds with any waiting messages, and then stuffs them into your Inbox folder. If you were working offline previously, disconnect from the Internet if you no longer need the connection.

4. If it's not already displayed, click the **Inbox** folder so you can see what the e-postman delivered.

Reading Your Messages

The following figure shows the Inbox folder with a few messages. The first thing to notice is that Outlook Express uses a bold font for all messages that you haven't read yet. You also get info about each message organized with the following half-dozen columns:

➤ **Priority** This column tells you whether the sender set up the message with a priority ranking. If you see a red exclamation mark, it means the missive was sent with high priority (this is the "handle this pronto, buster!" symbol); if you see a blue, downward-pointing arrow, it means the note was sent with low priority (this is the "handle this whenever, man" symbol).

➤ **Attachment** If you see a paper clip icon in this column, it means the message was accompanied by a file attachment. See "Dealing with Attachments," later in this chapter.

➤ **Flag** If you want to remind yourself to deal with a message, you can "flag" it for a future follow-up (a sort of digital string-tied-to-the-finger thing). You do this by highlighting the message and then selecting the **Message**, **Flag Message** command. This adds a flag icon in this column.

➤ **From** This column tells you the name (or occasionally, just the email address) of the person or company that sent you the message.

➤ **Subject** This column shows you the subject line of the message which will, hopefully, give you a brief description of the contents of the message.

➤ **Received** This column tells you the date and time the message was received.

After you've pilfered your incoming messages from your ISP, they get stored in your Inbox folder.

Priority ——————

Attachment ——————

Flag ——————

Unread messages are shown in bold type.

Outlook Express offers two methods for seeing what a message has to say:

➤ Highlight the message in the Inbox folder. Outlook Express displays the text of the note in the Preview pane. After about five seconds, Outlook Express removes the bolding from the message to indicate that it has been read.

➤ Highlight the message in the Inbox folder and then select **File, Open**. (For the heck of it, you also can press **Ctrl+O** or just **Enter**.) This method opens the message in its own window.

To read other messages, either repeat these procedures or use any of the following Outlook Express techniques:

➤ **To read the previous message in the list**   Select **View, Previous Message**. (**Ctrl+<** works, as well; if you have the message window open, click the **Previous** toolbar button.)

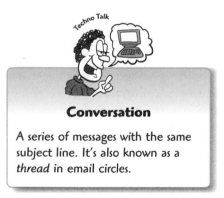

Techno Talk

Conversation

A series of messages with the same subject line. It's also known as a *thread* in email circles.

➤ **To read the next message in the list** Select **View, Next, Next Message**. (**Ctrl+>** also does the job; if you have the message window open, click the **Next** toolbar button.)

➤ **To read the next *unread* message**   Select **View, Next, Next Unread Message** (you can also press **Ctrl+U**).

➤ **To read the next unread conversation** Select **View, Next, Next Unread Conversation** (or press **Ctrl+Shift+U**).

Dealing with Attachments

As I mentioned earlier, if you get a message that has one or more files tied to it, you see a paper clip icon in the Inbox folder's Attachment column. You also see a larger paper clip icon in the upper-right corner of the preview pane. Outlook Express gives you a few ways to handle any attachments in the current message:

Check This Out

Grouping Messages by Conversation

Before you can use the Next Unread Conversation command, you have to group all the messages from the same conversation. To do that, activate the **View**, **Current View**, **Group Messages by Conversation** command.

➤ **Save the file** Select **File**, **Save Attachments** to convince the Save Attachments dialog box to drop by. If there are multiple files, use the **Attachments to Be Saved** list to highlight the ones you want to save. Use the **Save To** text box to specify where you want the files to be stored (click **Browse** to choose the folder from a dialog box). Then click **Save** to dump the file (or files) onto your hard disk.

➤ **Save the file from the preview pane** Click the paper clip icon in the upper-right corner of the preview pane to see a list that includes the filename of the attachment. Click **Save Attachments** and follow the steps I just took you through.

➤ **Open the file** If you just want to see what's in the file, you can open it. To do that, click the paper clip icon in the upper-right corner of the preview pane, and then click the file name. This gets you to the Open Attachment Warning dialog box. From here, be sure the **Open It** option is activated, and then click **OK**.

What to Do with a Message After You've Read It

This section gives you a rundown of all the things you can do with a message after you've read it. In each case, you either need to have a message highlighted in the Inbox folder, or you need to have the message open. Here's the list:

➤ **Ship out a reply** If you think of a witty retort, you can email it back to the sender either by selecting **Message**, **Reply to Sender**, or by clicking the **Reply** toolbar button. (The keyboard route is to poke **Ctrl+R**.)

➤ **Ship out a reply to every recipient** If the note was foisted on several people, you might prefer to send your response to everyone who received the original. To do that, either select **Message**, **Reply to All**, or click the **Reply All** button. (The keyboard shortcut is **Ctrl+Shift+R**.)

➤ **Forward the message to someone else** To have someone else take a gander at a message you received, you can forward it to them either by selecting **Message**, **Forward**, or by clicking the **Forward** button. (Keyboard dudes and dudettes can press **Ctrl+F**.)

Forwarding an Exact Copy of the Message

A forwarded message contains the original message text, which is preceded by an "Original Message" header and some of the message particulars (who sent it, when they sent it, and so on). If you'd rather have your recipient see the message exactly as you got it, use the **Message, Forward As Attachment** command, instead.

➤ **Move the message to some other folder**   If you find your Inbox folder is getting seriously overcrowded, you should think about moving some messages to other folders. To move a message, select **Edit, Move to Folder** (or press **Ctrl+Shift+V**). In the Move dialog box that shows up, highlight the destination folder and then click **OK**. (You can create a new folder by clicking the **New Folder** button, entering a name for the folder in the New Folder dialog box, and then clicking **OK**.)

➤ **Delete the message**   If you don't think you'll have cause to read a message again, you might as well delete it to keep the Inbox clutter to a minimum. To delete a message, either select **Edit, Delete**, or click the **Delete** button. (A message also can be vaporized by pressing **Ctrl+D**).

Retrieving Deleted Messages

Note that Outlook Express doesn't get rid of a deleted message completely. Instead, it just dumps it in the **Deleted Items** folder. This way, if you find that you deleted the message accidentally, you can head for Deleted Items and then move it back into the Inbox.

Using Rules to Filter Out Boneheads and Bores

It's an unfortunate fact of online life that the email system is the source of many unwanted messages. Whether it's the scourge of unsolicited commercial email (also known whimsically as *spam*), or someone you've had a falling out with, you'll inevitably end up getting some messages that you instantly delete.

You can save yourself the bother by setting up Outlook Express to delete these annoyances for you. You can also go beyond this by having Outlook Express look for certain messages and then automatically move them to another folder, send out a reply, flag the messages, and much more.

Let's begin with the most straightforward case: blocking incoming messages from a particular email address. *Blocking* means that any message that comes in from that address is automatically relegated to the Deleted Items folder, so you never see the message. There are two ways to set up the block:

➤ **Block the sender of a message**   If you already have a message from the address that you want to block, highlight the message and then select **Message, Block Sender**. Outlook Express displays a dialog box that tells you the address has been added to the "blocked senders list." It also asks whether you want to expunge any other messages from this address that are in the current folder (click **Yes** if you do).

➤ **Block a specified email address**   If you don't have an email specimen from the address you want to block, select **Tools, Message Rules, Blocked Senders List**. This displays the Message Rules window with the **Blocked Senders** tab displayed. Click **Add**, enter the **Address** you want to block, and then click **OK**.

If you have a change of heart down the road, you can remove the block by selecting **Tools, Message Rules, Blocked Senders List**, highlighting the address in the **Blocked Senders** tab, and then clicking **Remove**. (Click **Yes** when Outlook Express asks you to confirm.)

If you need to filter messages based on conditions other than (or in addition to) the email address, or if you want to do something other than just delete a message, then you need to set up *message rules*. These rules tell Outlook Express exactly what to look for (such as specific words in the Subject line or message body) and exactly what to do with any messages that meet those conditions (move them to a folder, forward them, and so on).

Here are the steps to follow to set up a message rule:

1. Select the **Tools, Message Rules, Mail** command. Outlook Express relinquishes the New Mail Rule dialog box.

2. In the **Select the Conditions for Your Rule** list, activate the check box beside a condition that you want to use to single out an incoming message. Outlook Express adds the condition to the Rule Description box.

209

3. In most cases, the Rule Description text includes underlined text. For example, if you activate the **Where the Subject Line Contains Specific Words** condition, the "contains specific words" portion will be underlined, as shown in the following figure. The idea here is that you click the underlined text to specify the exact condition (in this case, a word or two that specifies which Subject lines are to be filtered).

Most conditions require you to add specific words or addresses.

Click the underlined text to edit the condition.

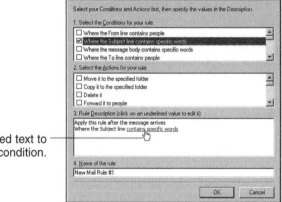

4. Repeat steps 2 and 3 to set up other conditions, if necessary.

5. In the **Select the Actions for Your Rule** list, activate the check box beside an action you want Outlook Express to perform on the selected messages. Again, Outlook Express adds the action to the Rule Description box.

6. Many actions also have the underlined text, so be sure to click the text to enter a specific value.

7. Repeat steps 5 and 6 to set up other actions, if necessary.

8. Use the **Name of the Rule** text box to enter a descriptive name for the rule.

9. Click **OK**. Outlook Express displays the Message Rules dialog box with your new rule shown in the **Mail Rules** tab.

What Happened

This chapter showed you how to use Outlook Express to work with Internet email. You spent the first half of the chapter learning about sending messages. I showed you the basic steps for composing and sending a message, how to use the Address Book, how to create a signature, and how to insert a file as an attachment. The rest of the chapter concentrated on receiving notes. You learned how to connect to your ISP and get your waiting messages, how to read messages, how to deal with attachments, and what to do with a message after you've read it. I closed with a look at some techniques for filtering incoming messages.

Quick Address-Based Rules

If you're creating a rule based on the address of an existing message, you can save yourself a bit of time by highlighting the message and then selecting **Message**, **Create Rule from Message**. This displays the New Mail Rule dialog box with the **Where the From Line Contains People** condition activated and filled in with the address of the sender.

Crib Notes

➤ **Outlook Express takeoff**   Either click the **Launch Outlook Express** icon in the Quick Launch area, or select **Start**, **Programs**, **Outlook Express**.

➤ **Go to the Inbox**   It's best to launch Outlook Express and go directly to the Inbox folder. To do that, activate the **When Outlook Express Starts**, **Go Directly to My Inbox Folder** check box.

➤ **Composing a message**   Click the **New Mail** button (or select **Message**, **New Message**), enter the address and a Subject line, fill in the message body, and then click **Send**.

➤ **Receiving messages**   Click the **Send/Recv** button and then click **Receive All** (or select **Tools**, **Send and Receive**, **Receive All**).

➤ **Filtering messages**   To automatically delete mail from some bozo, highlight the message and then select **Message**, **Block Sender**. For more sophisticated filtering, create a rule by selecting **Tools**, **Message Rules**, **Blocked Senders List**.

Chapter 14

More Online Conversations: Newsgroups and Internet Phone Calls

In This Chapter

➤ Using Outlook Express to work with newsgroups

➤ Using Phone Dialer to make Internet-based phone calls

➤ Making phone calls over the Net using NetMeeting

➤ Using NetMeeting for transferring files, chatting, and sharing programs

➤ A few more ways to get in your two-cents' worth online

All my email ramblings in Chapter 13 served to introduce you to the Internet's most popular form of communication. However, communication is really what the Internet is all about, so you can bet dollars to doughnuts that there are other ways to confab. There are, in fact, dozens of ways to get a Net conversation started.

This chapter shows you a few of those ways. Most of the chapter focuses on two technologies: newsgroups and Internet phone calls. However, you'll also learn about chatting, collaborating on programs, and more.

Using Outlook Express to Participate in Newsgroups

If you enjoy the thrust-and-parry of a good conversation, then you'll likely get a kick out of newsgroups. To understand what they're all about, think of a newspaper's Letters to the Editor section. The newspaper publishes an article or an editorial, and then someone writes to the editor to convey just how shocked and appalled they are. Yet another reader might write to rebut that letter, others might rebut the rebutter, and so on.

Newsgroup

An online discussion forum devoted to a particular topic.

Signal-to-Noise Ratio

In newsgroup lingo, the *signal-to-noise ratio* is a measure of how many good posts there are (signal) compared to how many bad posts there are (noise). Unfortunately, most newsgroups feature a relatively low signal-to-noise ratio.

That's pretty much a newsgroup in a nutshell. Each one is devoted to a particular topic. People send messages to the newsgroup (this is called *posting* to the group), other people respond to those messages with posts of their own, and so on.

That's not to say, however, that a newsgroup is just one big argument. There's plenty of debating that goes on, to be sure, but a newsgroup also is about sharing information, asking and answering questions, and generally just yakking about whatever topic interests you. And there are *thousands* of these newsgroup things, so there's bound to be *something* that interests you.

It should be said at this point that, unlike a Letters to the Editor section, there's usually no newsgroup "editor" to ensure messages pass muster. As a result, many newsgroups are a chaotic mass of spam (unsolicited commercial messages), flames (vitriolic and insulting posts), and off-topic messages.

Setting Up a News Account

All the newsgroup fun and games happen within Outlook Express, so your first order of business is to start the program. (Remember that the quickest route is to click the Launch Outlook Express icon in the Quick Launch toolbar.) After you've done that, follow these steps to set up the news account supplied by your Internet service provider:

1. Select **Tools**, **Accounts**. Outlook Express slips the Internet Accounts dialog box under the door.

2. Display the **News** tab. If you already see an account listed here, pump your fist and say "Yes!" because it looks like your ISP set one up for you automatically. You have my permission to skip the rest of these steps.

214

3. Click **Add** and then click **News**. Outlook Express asks the Internet Connection Wizard to make a return engagement. The first wizard dialog box asks you for your display name.

4. Enter your name (you don't have to use your real name if you don't want to), and then click **Next**. The wizard asks for your email address.

5. Enter your address (again, this is optional) and click **Next**. The wizard mumbles something about an "NNTP" server. This is the name of the computer that your ISP uses to handle newsgroup traffic.

Spam? No Thanks, I'm Not Hungry

If I might be so bold, I'd like to suggest that you *not* enter your real email address. The most popular method that companies use to gather email addresses for spam purposes is to grab them from newsgroup posts. If you still want to give folks the capability to respond to you directly, "mung" your address by adding "NOSPAM" or some other text (for example, `biff@provider.com-NOSPAM`).

6. Enter the name of the server in the **News (NNTP) Server** text box. If you have to sign in to the server, activate the **My News Server Requires Me to Log On** check box. Click **Next**.

7. If you told the wizard that you have to log on, use the next dialog box to enter your **Account Name** and **Password**, then click **Next**.

8. In the final wizard dialog box, click **Finish** to return to the Internet Accounts dialog box.

9. Click **Close** to return to Outlook Express. You're now asked whether you want to download a list of the account's newsgroups.

10. Click **Yes** to connect to the Internet and download the newsgroups from the server. Note that, because there are so many groups, this might take quite a while.

When the newsgroup download is done, you're dropped off at the Newsgroup Subscriptions dialog box. You'll learn more about this dialog box a bit later, so click **Cancel** for now. After you're back in Outlook Express, notice that the Folders list has grown a new branch, the name of which will be the name of your ISP's news server. Click that "folder" to highlight it. If Outlook Express asks whether you want to view a list of newsgroups, click **No** (you'll get there is a sec).

Understanding Newsgroup Nomenclature

When most people encounter newsgroups for the first time, they're thrown for a loop by the weird names used by the groups. Before moving on, let's take a second and see whether we can pound some sense into those names.

Techno Talk

What's All This About Usenet?

Usenet is the official Net name for the news system. It's not a particularly descriptive or euphonious name, so Microsoft just sticks with the simpler "news."

All newsgroup names use the following general format:

```
category.topic
```

Here, *category* is the general classification to which the group belongs, and *topic* is the subject discussed in the newsgroup. For example, consider the following newsgroup name:

```
rec.pets
```

This group is part of the rec category, which contains groups related to recreational activities. The pets part tells you that this group's topic is general discussions about pets. (News aficionados would pronounce this name as "reck dot pets.")

Note, however, that most newsgroup names are quite a bit longer because newsgroups usually cover specific topics. This means that a group's name often has one or more subtopics. Here's an example:

```
rec.pets.dogs.breeds
```

For the category part of the name, you'll mostly see the following seven:

comp	Computer hardware and software topics
misc	Miscellaneous topics
news	Topics related to Usenet news and newsgroups
rec	Recreational topics: entertainment, hobbies, sports, and so on
sci	Science and technology topics
soc	Social topics: sex, culture, religion, politics, and so on
talk	Topics used for debates about controversial political and cultural ideas

You'll also see tons of newsgroups in the alt (alternative) hierarchy. As the name implies, these newsgroups cover nonmainstream topics.

For further discussion of newsgroup names and other news tidbits, please see the following page on my Web site:

```
http://www.mcfedries.com/Ramblings/usenet-primer.html
```

Subscribing to a Newsgroup

The first thing you need to do is subscribe to a newsgroup or two. *Subscribing* means that the newsgroup shows up in the Outlook Express Folders list as a subfolder of the news account.

To subscribe, you need to get the Newsgroup Subscriptions dialog box back onscreen by selecting the **Tools, Newsgroups** command, or by clicking the **Newsgroups** toolbar button. (Pressing **Ctrl+W** also works.) Either way, you end up at the dialog box shown in the following figure.

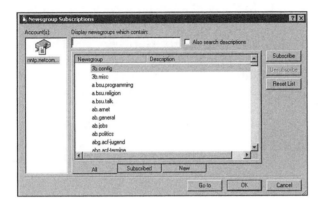

You use this dialog box to subscribe to newsgroups.

Follow these steps to subscribe to a newsgroup:

1. Click the name of the newsgroup you want to subscribe to. Alternatively, use the **Display Newsgroups Which Contain** text box to enter part of the newsgroup name. In this case, Outlook Express filters the list to show only those groups that contain the text you entered.

2. With the newsgroup highlighted, you now have two ways to proceed:

   ➤ **Go To** Click this button if you just want to have a gander at the newsgroup without committing to a subscription. When you click this button, Outlook Express closes the dialog box.

   ➤ **Subscribe** Click this button to subscribe to the newsgroup. Outlook Express adds an icon beside the newsgroup name to remind you that you're subscribed.

3. To continue subscribing, repeat step 2 ad nauseum.

4. When you're done, click **OK** to get back to Outlook Express.

Newsgroup Icon Guide

When you're slaving away in the Newsgroup Subscriptions dialog box, you'll notice two different icons that show up beside the newsgroups. A newspaper icon indicates a subscribed group, whereas an asterisk icon appears beside groups that are new since you last connected. (You can also see the new groups by displaying the New tab.)

Downloading Newsgroup Messages

As I mentioned earlier, subscribing to a newsgroup means the group's name appears as a subfolder of the news account in the Outlook Express Folders list. What you have to do now is download a list of the messages that have been posted to the newsgroup. Here's how:

1. In the Outlook Express Folders list, click the name of the newsgroup you want to work with.

2. Select the **Tools**, **Get Next 300 Headers** command. Outlook Express connects to the Internet (if necessary) and then runs off with the first 300 headers from the newsgroup. (A header contains only the name of the person who sent the post, the Subject line, the date the post was sent, and the size of the post.) The following figure show the Outlook Express window with some downloaded headers.

Click a plus sign (+) to open a thread.

Outlook Express with a few newsgroup headers downloaded.

The total number of messages in the newsgroup.

The total number of headers yet to be downloaded.

3. If there are more headers to download, repeat step 2 as often as necessary.

At this point, the newsgroup becomes more or less like the Inbox folder. This means you can read any message just by highlighting it and viewing the text in the preview pane. (You also can double-click the message to open it.) The only difference is that Outlook Express must be connected to the Internet to download the message text.

One of the crucial concepts you need to understand about newsgroups is the idea of a *thread*. As I mentioned earlier, newsgroups operate by people sending in messages, other people responding to those messages, and still others responding to the responses. A group of messages under the same Subject line (ignoring the Re: that's added to the responses) is a thread. Happily, Outlook Express organizes all the newsgroup messages by thread. That's why you see some messages with plus signs (+) beside them. Clicking the plus sign "opens" the thread so that you can see the other messages.

Please, Sir, Can I Have Some More Headers?

You can control the number of headers that Outlook Express downloads at one time. Select **Tools, Options** and display the **Read** tab. Use the **Get x Headers at a Time** spin box to enter the number of headers you want downloaded each time. (The maximum number is 1,000.)

Posting a Message to a Newsgroup

In newsgroup lingo, a *lurker* is someone who just views the group's messages without sending any messages of their own. Lurking is a good idea at first because it lets you get a feel for the types of discussions featured in the group. When you think you're ready to post something yourself, Outlook Express gives you a few ways to do it:

➤ **Send a response to the newsgroup**   Click the original message to highlight it, and then either select **Message, Reply to Group** or click the **Reply Group** toolbar button. (Keyboard connoisseurs might prefer to press **Ctrl+G**.)

➤ **Send a response to the message author only**   If you prefer that your response go only to the author of a message, click the message and then either select **Message, Reply to Sender** or click the **Reply** button. (**Ctrl+R** is the way to go from the keyboard.) Remember that many people monkey with their email address to avoid spam, so double-check the address before sending your response.

➤ **Send a response to the newsgroup and the author**   Click the message and then select **Message, Reply to All**. (Pressing **Ctrl+Shift+R** will also get the job done.)

➤ **Send a new message**   Either select **Message, New Message** or click the **New Post** button. (You also can slam **Ctrl+N**.)

Using Phone Dialer to Make Phone Calls over the Internet

It's not at all surprising that you can use the Internet to send data back and forth in the form of Web pages, email messages, and newsgroup posts. What *is* surprising, however, is that you can use the Internet to have voice conversations with other users, even if they're halfway across the Earth! What's even more surprising is that these "phone calls" cost nothing more than the cost of your Internet connection time.

The wonder of such an amazing technological turn was clearly not lost on the Windows 2000 developers. That's because Windows 2000 comes with not one, but *two*, programs that enable you to make such calls. This section shows you how to use Phone Dialer, which is the simpler of the two. In the next section, I'll show you how to do it using NetMeeting.

Cross Reference

You first learned about Phone Dialer back in Chapter 10, "Using Your Modem for Faxing and Phone Dialing." If you need to refresh your memory, jump back to see "Stop the Presses! Modem Dials Phone!," p. 150.

Before proceeding, be sure that both you and the person you're calling have the following hardware and software:

➤ A sound card.

➤ A microphone for the sound card.

➤ The Phone Dialer program (it must be the Windows 2000 version; the one that comes with Windows 95 and Windows 98 doesn't support Internet calls). Note that the other person must have this program running or the NetMeeting program (which must be running).

If you're the one doing the calling, you also need to know the *IP address* of the callee. This acts like a phone number for the other person.

Some ISPs supply each of their users with a permanent IP address. However, most ISPs supply each user with a temporary IP address each time they log on. To find out the current IP address in Windows 2000, follow these steps:

1. Connect to the Internet.

2. Double-click the connection icon that appears in the taskbar's system tray.

3. Display the **Details** tab. Your IP address is the number displayed beside **Client IP address** (see the following figure).

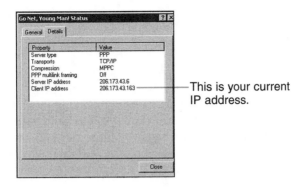

Use this dialog box to figure out your current IP address.

This is your current IP address.

That's fine if the person I'm calling is running Windows 2000. What if they're using NetMeeting on Windows 95 or Windows 98? Can they find out their IP address?

Sure, no problem. What they have to do is connect to the Internet, select **Start**, **Run** to get to the Run dialog box, type `winipcfg`, and click **OK**. In the IP Configuration dialog box, the **IP Address** box tells what they need to know.

With all that rot out of the way, here are the steps to follow to place an Internet call using Phone Dialer:

Techno Talk

Domain Dialing

If your ISP assigned you a permanent IP address, then it's likely they also gave you a corresponding *domain name*. If so, then other people also can use your domain name to initiate calls to you.

1. Connect to the Internet, if you aren't online already. (Note, too, that the person you're calling must also be connected to the Internet.)
2. Launch Phone Dialer by selecting **Start**, **Programs**, **Accessories**, **Communications**, **Phone Dialer**.
3. Select **Phone**, **Dial** or click the **Dial** button. Phone Dialer summons the Dial dialog box.
4. Type in the other person's IP address or domain name.
5. Be sure the **Internet Call** option is activated.
6. Click **Place Call**. Phone Dialer reaches out over the Internet and contacts the remote user.
7. The remote user's Phone Dialer program rings and displays two options: Take Call and Reject Call. They must click **Take Call** to establish the connection. (If they're using NetMeeting, instead, they have to click **Accept**.)
8. Use your sound card microphone to talk to the other person.

Using NetMeeting to Make Phone Calls over the Internet

I mentioned at the beginning of this section that Windows 2000 boasts *two* programs that let you speak for free to other people over the Internet, no matter how far-flung those folks might be. The second program that accomplishes this mini-miracle is called NetMeeting. It does everything that Phone Dialer can do, but it goes well beyond that with lots of other high-tech goodies. These include the capability to transfer files, chat (type text messages), share a running program, and more.

Some Relatively Painless Configuration Chores

As you can imagine, NetMeeting is a much more complex beast than the relatively simple Phone Dialer. So, it will come as no surprise that you have to trudge through a rather lengthy setup procedure before NetMeeting will do anything useful. Still, you have to go through this only once, so it's not so bad. Here we go:

1. Select **Start**, **Programs**, **Accessories**, **Communications**, **NetMeeting**. When you do this for the first time, the Microsoft NetMeeting wizard materializes.

2. The initial dialog box merely summarizes what NetMeeting can do, so click **Next** to get to something more useful.

3. The next wizard dialog box pesters you for a few vital statistics. At the very least, you have to provide your **First Name**, **Last Name**, and **E-Mail Address**. (The other fields are optional.) Click **Next** to move on.

4. Now the wizard blathers on about a "directory server." The deal here is that Microsoft and other companies run computers that maintain lists of people who are using NetMeeting. This makes it easy to find other users, but it also might mean you get a crank call or two. If you don't need such a service (if you know whom you want to call, for example), deactivate the **Log On to a Directory Server When NetMeeting Starts** check box. Click **Next** when you're ready to continue.

5. Now the wizard wonders about the speed of your Internet connection. This is important because NetMeeting will tailor the data that comes your way to match the speed of your connection. Activate the appropriate option and click **Next**.

Going Incognito

If you're shy, don't worry about using your real name and email address. NetMeeting works just fine if you use a pseudonym and a false address. The only time the latter might be a problem is when someone tries to email you from the directory server. If that's something you'd like other people to be able to do, then use your real email address.

If you want to log on to a directory server, but you don't want your name listed, it's possible to hide your listing. To do this, once you get into NetMeeting, select **Tools**, **Options**, display the **General** tab, and then activate the **Do Not List My Name in the Directory** check box.

6. The next stage of the setup involves the Audio Tuning Wizard. This wizard's mission is to set up your sound card to handle the rigors of Net-based calling. The first dialog box is just an intro, so click **Next**.

7. If you happen to have multiple **Recording** or **Playback** devices on your system, the wizard will first ask which one you want to use. Be sure you choose your sound card in both cases, and then click **Next**.

8. The Audio Tuning Wizard's next chore is to ensure that the audio playback level is acceptable. Click **Test** to get the wizard to start playing a very annoying sound. Adjust the **Volume** slider to taste, and then click **Stop** when the noise level feels right. Click **Next** to head for another dialog box.

9. Now the Audio Tuning Wizard wants to ensure that your voice won't be distorted. To do that, you get the dialog box shown in the following figure. The

idea is that you speak into the microphone using your normal chatting-on-the-phone voice. As you do, the wizard adjusts the **Recording Volume** level accordingly. When the level has stabilized, click **Next**.

Speak into the microphone to help the Audio Tuning Wizard tune your system to your voice.

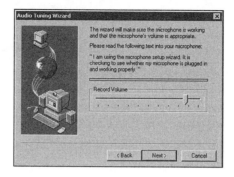

10. Click **Finish** in the final Audio Tuning Wizard dialog box.

With that procedure thankfully done, NetMeeting finally shows up, as shown in the next figure. (If you chose not to log on automatically, you can do so at any time by selecting **Call**, **Log On to Microsoft Internet Directory**. Note that NetMeeting won't prompt you to start your Internet connection. Therefore, you should always connect to the Net by hand before attempting to log on to any directory server.)

The NetMeeting window.

Placing a Call

NetMeeting is most often used to place calls over the Internet, so let's see how that works:

1. Select **Call, New Call**, or click the **Place Call** button. (Keyboard mavens can press **Ctrl+N**.) The Place a Call dialog box butts in, as shown in the following figure.

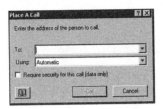

Use this dialog box to get a NetMeeting call off the ground.

2. Use the **To** list to specify the person you want to call. You have four choices:

   ➤ If you're both logged on to the same directory server, enter the person's email address.

   ➤ If you're logged on to different servers, enter the server name, a slash (/), and the person's email address (for example: ils.microsoft.com/bill@bubba.com).

   ➤ Enter the other person's IP address, if you know it.

   ➤ If you're doing the NetMeeting thing over a network, enter the network name of the other person's computer.

3. Select **Automatic** in the **Using** list.

4. Click **Call**. (If NetMeeting detects that the other person is using a different version of NetMeeting, it will display a dialog box to let you know. In this case, click **OK**.)

5. On the other end, the person hears a telephonelike ring, and then sees a window like the one shown here. They have two choices:

   ➤ **Accept**   They click this button to answer the call.

   ➤ **Ignore**   They click this button to reject the call. If the ingrate clicks this button, NetMeeting will let know that you've been rejected and will ask whether you want to send the person a message. If you do, click **Yes**.

This window pops up when someone tries to call you.

Automatic Accept and Ignore

If you're feeling particularly extroverted, you can tell NetMeeting to answer every incoming call automatically. To set this up, activate the **Call, Automatically Accept Calls** command.

On the other hand, if you're feeling introverted, you might not want to answer *any* incoming calls. That's no problem, either. Just pull down the **Call** menu and activate the **Do Not Disturb** command.

If the other person accepts your call, NetMeeting displays the people who are participating in the "meeting." Now, just speak into your microphone and have yourself a good old-fashioned chinwag.

When you're done, you can end the call by selecting the **Call, Hang Up** command or by clicking the **Hang Up** button.

NetMeeting SpeedDialing

If you have friends, family, or colleagues whom you call regularly, you should consider putting them on NetMeeting's SpeedDial list for easier access.

To create a SpeedDial entry, you have two choices:

➤ **If you're already in a call with that person**   Right-click their name and then click **Add to SpeedDial List**.

➤ **If you're not in a call**   Select **Call, Create SpeedDial**. Enter the person's **Address**, select **Automatic** in the **Call Using** list, and be sure that **Add to SpeedDial List** is activated. Click **OK**.

To call someone using their SpeedDial entry, select **Call**, **Directory** and then choose **SpeedDial** in the Select a Directory list. Highlight the person's address and click **Call**.

Other Things You Can Do After You're Connected

If Internet phone calls were the only tricks up NetMeeting's sleeve, then you'd probably be better off just using Phone Dialer. However, NetMeeting's sleeves are quite huge, meaning it has lots of other features you can play with. Here's a summary of some other NetMeeting techniques you can use while you're in a call:

➤ **File transferring**   You can send the other person a file by selecting the **Tools**, **File Transfer** command (or by poking **Ctrl+F**). In the dialog box that bubbles up to the surface, select **File**, **Add Files**, highlight the file, and then click **Add**. Now select **File**, **Send All**. The other person sees a window that displays the progress of the transfer. They can click **Delete** if they don't want to accept the file. If they do accept the file, they can select **Tools**, **File Transfer** and then **File**, **Open Received Files Folder** to see where it went.

➤ **Chat conversing**   If you don't have a sound card or microphone, or if you don't want other people to hear your conversation, NetMeeting's Chat feature might be the way to go. This feature enables you to type messages to the other person. To get into the Chat feature, either select **Tools**, **Chat** or click the **Chat** button. (Pressing **Ctrl+T** also is a possibility.) A Chat window appears on both computers. To send some text, type it in the **Message** box, and then press **Enter**.

➤ **Whiteboard collaborating**   NetMeeting's Whiteboard feature is really just a version of Paint that's been suitably modified. The idea is that you use the Paint tools to draw shapes and type text. Everything you do is reflected on the other person's Whiteboard, so you can collaborate on a project or idea. To get to the Whiteboard, select **Tools**, **Whiteboard** or click the **Whiteboard** toolbar button. (To give the mouse a breather, press **Ctrl+W**, instead.)

➤ **Program sharing**   If you want to demonstrate a technique to the other person, or if you want to be able to collaborate on a document beyond what the Whiteboard can do, then you need to use NetMeeting's application sharing. This enables you to run a program on one machine, and have the other user see exactly what you're doing. It's even possible for the other person to assume control of the program and run its commands, enter text, and so on. To use this feature, start the program that you want to share. Then either select **Tools**,

Sharing or click the **Share Program** button. This gives you a list of the running programs, so click the program you want to work with and then click **Share**. If you'd like the other person to be able to manipulate the program, click the **Allow Control** button.

What Happened

This chapter closed out your look at Windows 2000's Internet features by showing you three more ways to exchange pleasantries online. You began by learning how to use Outlook Express to get in on newsgroup discussions. From there, you learned how to use Phone Dialer to place "phone calls" over the Internet. I finished the chapter by showing you how to use NetMeeting to not only make Net-based calls, but also how to transfer files, chat, use a whiteboard, and share programs.

Crib Notes

➤ **Creating a news account**   In Outlook Express, select **Tools**, **Accounts**, display the **News** tab, and then click **Add**, **News**.

➤ **Newsgroup names**   Newsgroups have monikers that use the form `category.topic`, where `category` is the general classification for the group (such as "rec" for recreation) and `topic` is the subject of the group (such as "pets").

➤ **Subscribing to a newsgroup**   Select **Tools**, **Newsgroups** (or click the **Newsgroups** button), highlight the group, and then click **Subscribe**.

➤ **Requirements for Net-based calls**   You need a sound card, a microphone attached to the card, and either Phone Dialer or NetMeeting on both ends.

➤ **Net calls via Phone Dialer**   Select **Phone**, **Dial**, enter the remote person's IP address, and then click **Place Call**.

➤ **Net calls via NetMeeting**   Select **Call**, **New Call**, enter the remote person's address, and click **Call**.

Part 4

Tailoring Windows 2000 to Suit Your Style

*In these media-saturated times, quoting media guru Marshall McCluhan has become the ulti-
mate badge of the so-hip-it-hurts set. Always happy to jump on a passing bandwagon, I
hereby offer this book's token McLuhanism: "The mark of our time is its revulsion against
imposed patterns." This shameless name- and quote-dropping is meant not to impress, but to
introduce the theme of Part 4: customizing Windows 2000. The out-of-the-shrink-wrap look
and feel of Windows 2000 certainly qualifies as an "imposed pattern," and it was designed by
Microsoft to be suitable for the person it considers to be a typical user. However, if the notion
of being "typical" fills you with fear and loathing, then you've come to the right place because
the four chapters coming up will show you how to refurbish Windows 2000 to suit your tastes
and the way you work.*

Chapter 15

Redoing the Desktop

In This Chapter

➤ Messing with desktop wallpaper and patterns

➤ Redoing the desktop colors and fonts

➤ Adding stuff to the Active Desktop

➤ Monkeying around with the display's screen area and colors

➤ A cornucopia of desktop decoration treats

For most of its history, the PC has maintained a staid, nay, *dull* exterior. Fortunately, the Nuthin'-But-Beige school has given way in recent years to some almost-stylish machines cavorting in gunmetal gray or shiny black exteriors. And with the Apple iMac now available in several different psychedelic shades, it's likely that colorful machines will become the norm before too long.

That's a good thing because lots of people don't like the same old same old. These rugged individualists want to express themselves and that's hard to do with beige. The same goes for the Windows 2000 desktop. Sure, that standard slate blue background is pleasant enough, but maybe you're more into reds or yellows. If so, Windows 2000 offers plenty of ways to make your mark with a custom desktop color or background.

Yo, Geek Boy! Changing the desktop sounds great and everything, but most of the time I can't even see it. Isn't all this just a waste of time?

Hey, who're you calling a geek? It's actually not a waste of time because many of the changes you make to the desktop apply to Windows 2000 as a whole. For example, you can change the colors of window titles and borders, alter the font used in the taskbar, and change the overall size of the screen area. You'll learn all about these and many more customization options in this chapter.

Every last one of these customizations take place within the friendly confines of the Display Properties dialog box, shown in the following figure. To get this dialog box on the desktop, use either of the following techniques:

➤ Right-click an empty section of the desktop and then click **Properties** in the shortcut menu.

➤ Select **Start**, **Settings**, **Control Panel** and then launch the **Display** icon.

You'll be running all of this chapter's desktop tweaks from this dialog box.

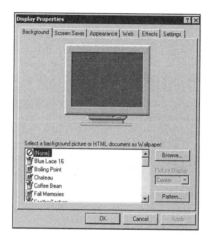

Background Check: Changing the Desktop Background

It's true that the desktop is usually hidden, particularly if, like me, you prefer to run your programs maximized. Still, there are plenty of times when the desktop is visible, such as at startup and when you close your programs. And the desktop also is only a mouse click away thanks to the Show Desktop icon on the taskbar's Quick Launch area. If that's enough of an excuse for you to tweak the look of the desktop, then you'll enjoy this section where I tell you about two kinds of desktop customizations: wallpaper and patterns.

Wallpapering the Desktop

Wallpaper is an image or design that replaces the desktop's default solid color background. (Before you ask, no, I'm not sure why Microsoft calls it "wallpaper" when you're supposed to be thinking that your screen is like the top of a desk. It's either a mixed metaphor or the Microsoft offices have a *very* strange interior designer.) You can choose one of the prefab wallpapers that come with Windows 2000, or you can easily create your own. Let's start with the simplest case of picking out one of the predefined wallpapers:

1. In the Display Properties dialog box, open the **Background** tab (shown in the previous figure).

2. Use the **Select a Background Picture...** list to click one of the wallpaper names. Keep one eye peeled on the fake monitor above the list. This gives you a preview of what the wallpaper will look like. (Some of the images take a second or two to show up, so patience is required.)

3. Use the **Picture Display** list to select one of the following values:

    ➤ **Center**   Displays a single copy of the wallpaper in the center of the screen. This is a good choice for large wallpapers.

    ➤ **Tile**   Displays multiple copies of the wallpaper repeated so they fill the entire desktop. Choose this option for small wallpapers.

    ➤ **Stretch**   Displays a single copy of the wallpaper extended on all sides so it fills the entire desktop. This is the one to use if the wallpaper image almost fills the desktop.

4. Click **OK** to put the wallpaper into effect. (You also can click **Apply** if you'd prefer to leave the Display Properties dialog box open and ready for action.)

Choosing Another Image As Your Wallpaper

Windows 2000's list of approved images isn't the only wallpaper game in town. There's no problem using some other image if that's what you'd prefer. To do this, click the **Browse** button to promote the Browse dialog box, find and highlight the image file, and then click **Open**.

Creating Your Own Wallpaper

The images listed in the Background tab are a decent start, but what if you prefer the homegrown approach? In other words, what if you have an image you've created yourself and you'd like to use it as your wallpaper? If the image is already saved as a file, consider the following two possibilities:

➤ If you copy or move the file into either the WINNT folder or the WINNT\Web\Wallpaper folder, the filename will automatically appear in the list of wallpapers.

➤ In the Background tab, use the **Browse** button to pick out your file.

If you've just created the image in Paint, you have another couple of choices on Paint's **File** menu that transform the current image into wallpaper:

➤ **Set As Wallpaper (Tiled)**   Select this command to tile the image to fill the entire desktop.

➤ **Set As Wallpaper (Centered)**   Select this command to center the image on the desktop.

Something a Little Different: A Desktop Pattern

A variation on the wallpaper theme is a *pattern*: a simple black design that covers the desktop. Many people prefer this to the more ornate (some might say garish) wallpaper images. Here's how to select a pattern:

1. In the Display Properties dialog box, open the **Background** tab.

2. In the list of wallpapers, select **(None)**.

3. Click **Pattern**. Windows 2000 offers up the Pattern dialog box, shown here.

Windows 2000 offers a nice collection of patterns for the discriminating desktop designer.

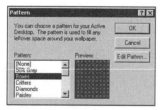

4. Use the **Pattern** list to choose a pattern. Check out the **Preview** box to see what will happen to your desktop if you choose the selected pattern.

5. When you've made your choice, click **OK** to return to the Display Properties dialog box.

6. Click **OK** to exit the Display Properties box or **Apply** if you want to make more changes.

If you're feeling creative, you might want to try your hand at creating your own pattern. It's quite easy, as the following steps show:

1. Get the Pattern dialog box back on the screen, as described in the preceding steps.

2. Use the **Pattern** list to choose the pattern you want to use as your starting point.

3. Click **Edit Pattern**. The Pattern Editor puts in an appearance, as shown in the following figure.

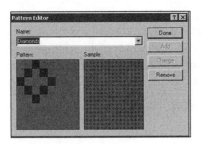

Use the Pattern Editor to put together your own personal pattern.

4. Change the pattern **Name** (this lets you preserve the original pattern).

5. Modify the pattern as follows:

   ➤ To add a black square (a pixel), click an empty part of the pattern. You also can drag your mouse to add a line of black squares.

   ➤ To remove a black square, click it.

6. To save your work, click **Change**.

7. To add your handiwork to the list of patterns, click **Add**. (If you later decide that your creation isn't worthy, you can expunge it from the list by clicking **Remove**.)

8. When you're done, click **Done** (duh).

While You're Here: Setting Up a Screen Saver

A *screen saver* is a moving pattern that appears on your screen after your computer has been idle for a while. Its purpose is to prevent images from burning into your screen, but most folks just like to look at the wild effects. To set a screen saver, open the **Screen Saver** tab in the Display Properties dialog box, and use the **Screen Saver** drop-down list to pick one out. Use the **Wait** spin box to set the number of minutes of idle time it takes before the screen saver kicks in.

Makeover Time: Changing the Desktop Colors and Fonts

Wallpapers and patterns affect only the desktop background. However, it's possible to redo much more of the Windows 2000 interface (as the geeks like to call the stuff you see on your screen). Among many other things, you can change the font, color, and size of icon titles; the color of window title bars, scrollbars, and backgrounds; and the fonts and colors used in dialog boxes. This section shows you how to do it.

It all happens in the **Appearance** tab of the Display Properties dialog box, shown here.

The Appearance tab lets you change the font, color, and size of tons of Windows 2000 bits and pieces.

Watch these phony windows to see what kind of mess each scheme will make.

The easiest way to change things is to select one of the ready-made appearance schemes from the **Schemes** list. Each time you select a scheme, take a gander at the fake windows above the list to get a preview of the havoc the new scheme will wreak on your system. If you find one that's you, click **OK** or **Apply** to put it into effect.

If you're feeling a bit more ambitious, you can create your own appearance scheme by plowing through these steps:

1. Use the **Item** list to choose which element of the screen you want to play with.

2. Use the following techniques to customize the selected element:

   ➤ If it's possible to change the size of the item, the **Size** spin box beside the Item list will be enabled. Use this spin box to adjust the size to taste.

   ➤ If it's possible to change the color of the item, the **Color** button (the one beside the Item list) will be enabled. The idea here is that you click the downward-pointing arrow to drop down a color *palette*, and then click the color you want. To pick out a custom color, drop down the palette, click **Other**, and use the **Color** dialog box to create a shade you like.

➤ Some screen elements (such as the Active Title Bar item) can display a color *gradient*, where one color fades into another. In this case, you use the **Color** button (again, the one beside the Item list) to pick the first color, and the **Color 2** button to pick the second color. (To get a color gradient, your display must be set up to use more than 256 colors. See "Changing the Screen Area and Color Depth," later in this chapter.)

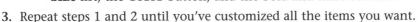

Sights for Sore Eyes

If you find you have trouble reading the text on your screen, Windows 2000 has schemes that can help. Look for scheme names that include either **(large)** or **(extra large)**.

➤ If the item has text, use the **Font** list to change the typeface. You also can adjust the font using the **Size** list, the **Color** button, and the bold and italic buttons.

3. Repeat steps 1 and 2 until you've customized all the items you want.

4. Click **Save As**, enter a name in the Save Scheme dialog box, and click **OK** to return to the Display Properties dialog box.

5. Click **OK** or **Apply** to put your new scheme into production use.

The Active Desktop: Your Desktop As a Web Page

The standard desktop backgrounds—wallpapers, patterns, and colors— are fine as far as they go, but they lack that element of interactivity that folks exposed to the World Wide Web have come to expect. If you're one of those folks, then I'm sure you'll get a kick out of Windows 2000's new *Active Desktop*. This variation on the desktop theme enables you to populate your desktop with stuff normally seen in Web pages or even with an entire Web page.

To try this out, get to the Display Properties dialog box and open the **Web** tab. Activate the **Show Web Content on My Active Desktop** check box. This enables whatever items are in the list of Web content. At first, you have only **My Current Home Page**, which is the home page defined in Internet Explorer. As you can see in the following figure, when you click **Apply**, the desktop suddenly turns into an actual Web page with live links and everything. Note, however, that you can't really "surf" the desktop because the links go only one level deep. That is, clicking any link will change the desktop page accordingly, but clicking subsequent links will open Internet Explorer in order to fetch the page.

You can turn your desktop into an honest-to-goodness Web page.

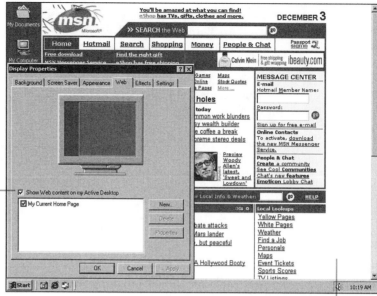

Activating this check box...

...displays your Internet Explorer home page on the desktop.

That's pretty slick, but you also can talk Windows 2000 into displaying a different Web page or other Web page content. Here's how:

1. In the **Web** tab, click **New**. Windows 2000 coughs up the New Active Desktop Item dialog box, shown here.

Use this dialog box to add more Web knick-knacks to the Active Desktop.

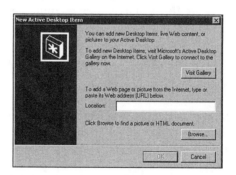

2. There are two paths you can take from here:

   ➤ **Visit Gallery**   Click this button to launch Internet Explorer and head for Microsoft's Active Desktop Gallery. This is a Web page that offers quite a few *Active Desktop items* that you can add to your system. The **Gallery Index** offers several categories to click (such as News, Sports, and

Entertainment). This gives you a list of items. Click an item to see a description. From there, click the **Add to Active Desktop** button. When Internet Explorer asks whether you're sure about all this, click **Yes**.

➤ **Location**   Use this text box to enter the address of a Web page. This can be the full URL of a page on the Web, or the location of an HTML file on your hard disk or your network. (If you're not sure about the location of a non-Web item, click **Browse** to use the Browse dialog box to find it.)

3. Whichever method you use, you eventually end up at the Add item to Active Desktop dialog box. Click **OK**. Windows 2000 downloads the content and adds the item to the desktop.

4. If you went the Location route, you'll be dropped back in the Web tab. Click **OK** or **Apply**.

The nice thing about Active Desktop items is that they can be moved and sized as required. Here's a review of the techniques to use:

➤ **To move an item**   First move the mouse pointer over the item. This gets you a border around the item. Now drag any border.

➤ **To resize an item**   Move the mouse pointer over the top border. After a couple of seconds, you get a larger bar across the top of the item, as shown in the following figure. Drag this bar to move the item.

➤ **To maximize an item**   Click the **Cover Desktop** button.

➤ **To maximize an item without affecting the desktop icons**   Click the **Split Desktop with Icons** button.

➤ **To close an item**   Click the **Close** button.

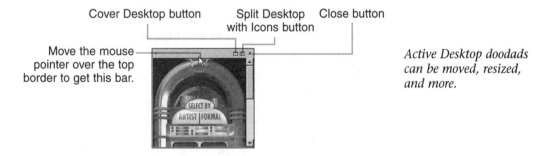

Cover Desktop button   Split Desktop   Close button
with Icons button

Move the mouse pointer over the top border to get this bar.

Active Desktop doodads can be moved, resized, and more.

"Effectations": Changing Desktop Icons and Visual Effects

Continuing our tour of the Display Properties dialog box, we come to the **Effects** tab, shown in the following figure. The top part of this tab—the **Desktop Icons** group—controls the icon images used by a few of the standard desktop icons. To change an icon, highlight it, click **Change Icon**, highlight an icon in the Change Icon dialog box, and click **OK**.

239

More Icons

The Change Icon dialog box shows only a few icons. For more variety, click **Browse**, open the **system32** folder, and highlight one of the following files: **moricons.dll**, **progman.exe**, or **shell32.dll**. Click **Open** to view all the icons within the file.

Use the Effects tab to set various options for desktop icons and visual effects.

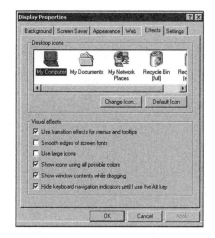

The rest of the dialog box is taken up by the **Visual Effects** group, which offers the following check boxes:

> ➤ **Use Transition Effects for Menus and Tooltips**   With this check box activated, menus fade in and fade out, and ToolTips scroll in and scroll out. (Again, you get these effects only if you're running Windows 2000 with more than 256 colors. See the next section.) If these effects bug you for some reason, deactivate this check box to turn them off.

➤ **Smooth Edges of Screen Fonts**   Activating this check box tells Windows 2000 to smooth the jagged edges (*jaggies*, in the vernacular) that appear when you use large fonts. Don't bother with this if you never use large fonts or aren't bothered by jaggies.

➤ **Use Large Icons**   If you crank up this option, Windows 2000 inflates the size of the desktop icons.

➤ **Show Icons Using All Possible Colors**   Windows 2000 boasts some nice-looking icons, and they look that way because they use all the colors of your system.

Possible Problems with All Possible Colors

When it's activated, the **Show Icons Using All Possible Colors** option will on rare occasions cause some systems to take too long to redraw the desktop each time you display it. If that happens to you, deactivate this check box.

➤ **Show Window Contents While Dragging**   When you move a window, the entire contents of the window remain visible. If your system takes a long time to display the new window position as you move it, your moves will go much faster if you deactivate this check box. If you do this, then you'll see only the outline of a window as you move it.

➤ **Hide Keyboard Navigation Indicators Until I Use the Alt Key** When I told you how to use menus in Chapter 2, "A Field Guide to Windows 2000 for the Uninitiated," I told you that you can use the keyboard to pull down a menu by holding down Alt and pressing the underlined letter in the menu name. Unfortunately, Windows 2000 shows only the underlined letters after you hold down Alt. If you'd prefer that Windows 2000 show the underlined letters full-time, deactivate this check box.

Arranging Desktop Icons

Speaking of desktop icons, you should know that Windows 2000 also enables you to move and sort the icons. You move them by dragging them with your mouse. After you've done that, you can get the icons nice and neat by right-clicking the desktop and then clicking **Line Up Icons** in the shortcut menu. To sort the icons, right-click the desktop, click **Arrange Icons**, and then click a sort order: **by Name**, **by Type**, **by Size**, or **by Date**. Felix Unger types can keep things in apple-pie order all the time by activating the **Auto Arrange** command.

Changing the Screen Area and Color Depth

The last bit of desktop decoration I'll put you through in this chapter relates to various display settings. Again, these are options that apply not just to the desktop, but to everything you see on your screen. You'll find these settings in the **Settings** tab of the Display Properties dialog box, shown next.

The Settings tab lets you muck around with your display.

The name of your monitor ——

—— The name of your video adapter

Techno Talk

Video Adapter

An internal circuit board that gets instructions about what to display from the processor, and then tells the monitor what to show on the screen. Also known as the *video card* or *graphics card*.

Let's begin with the **Display** area. This line shows you two things:

➤ **The name of your monitor**   This tells you what type of monitor you have.

➤ **The name of your video adapter**   This tells you what type of video adapter resides inside your system.

These two chunks of hardware determine the values you can select in the **Settings** tab's other two groups: Colors and Screen area.

The **Colors** group consists of a single list. The items in this list specify how many colors Windows 2000 can use to display stuff. This is called the *color depth*. Here are some notes:

➤ In general, the more colors you use, the sharper your screen images will appear.

➤ If you're working with graphics, you'll want to use as many colors as possible.

➤ On the other hand, if you find that your screen display is sluggish, then you should consider reducing the number of colors.

Colors? Bits? What's Going On?

The Colors list is confusing because it has one value in colors—256 Colors—and the rest uses bits—such as High Color (16-bit). This is actually consistent, but you'd never know it. You see, Windows 2000 uses a specified number of bits (on/off values) for each screen pixel (see my discussion of the Screen area setting, that follows). The lowest number of bits is 8, and because 2 to the power of 8 is 256, that's the minimum number of colors you can choose. Other typical bit values are 15 (32,268 colors), 16 (65,536 colors), and 24 (16,777,216 colors). There's also 32-bit color, but that's the same as 24-bit (the extra 8 bits are used by some applications for "masking" existing colors so that they appear transparent).

The **Screen Area** slider determines the number of pixels used to display stuff on the screen. I've mentioned pixels before, but it's worth repeating myself here: A *pixel* is an individual pinpoint of light. All the colors you see are the result of thousands of these pixels getting turned on and set to display a specific hue.

The lowest screen area value is 640 by 480. This means that Windows 2000 uses pixels arranged in a grid that has 640 columns and 480 rows. That's over 300,000 pixels for your viewing pleasure! The number of higher screen area values you can pick depends on your monitor and on your video adapter. Here are some notes:

➤ The more pixels you use (that is, the higher you go on the Screen area slider), the smaller things will look on the screen.

➤ You might be able to go to a higher screen area value only by using a smaller number of colors. Video adapters have only a certain amount of memory, so you'll often have to trade off one value with the other.

➤ In general, you should tailor the screen area value with the size of your monitor. If you have a tiny monitor (13 inches or less), use 640 by 480; if you have a standard 14- or 15-inch monitor, try 800 by 600; for 17- or 19-inch monitors, head up to 1,024 by 768; if you're lucky enough to have a 21-inch behemoth, go for 1,600 by 1,200 (if your video adapter will let you).

When you've made your changes, click **OK** or **Apply**. Windows 2000 displays a dialog box letting you know that it's about to apply the new settings. Say "Tell me something I don't know, Electron Boy" and click **OK**. Windows 2000, true to its word, changes the settings and then asks whether you want to keep them. Click **Yes**. If things don't look right for some reason, click **No** to return to your normally sched-uled display settings.

Wonky Display? Don't Touch Anything!

If your display goes haywire when Windows 2000 applies the new settings, it prob-ably means that you tried some combo that was beyond the capabilities of your adapter/monitor team. Your screen likely will be unreadable, but don't panic. Windows 2000 will automatically reset the display after 15 seconds.

What Happened

This chapter showed you a number of ways to redo the desktop. You learned how to select a wallpaper and create your own wallpaper, specify a pattern, modify the desk-top colors and fonts, and change a few visual effects. I also showed you how to take advantage of Windows 2000's new Active Desktop. I closed by giving you the goods on two display settings: the color depth and the number of pixels used in the screen area.

Crib Notes

➤ **Displaying the Display Properties** Either right-click the desktop and then click **Properties**, or select **Start**, **Settings**, **Control Panel** and then launch the **Display** icon.

➤ **Wallpaper options** Most wallpaper images are small, so you need to use the **Tile** option to get the fill effect. For larger images, use either **Center** or **Stretch**.

➤ **Raise your colors** To get the most out of Windows 2000's visual effects, set up your system to use more than 256 colors.

➤ **Tailor your pixels** Try to use a screen area value that matches your moni-tor. For most monitors, 800 by 600 is ideal.

Chapter 16

Revamping the Start Menu and Taskbar

In This Chapter

➤ Changing Start menu settings

➤ Adding your own shortcuts to the Start menu

➤ Quick taskbar tweaks

➤ Creating custom taskbar toolbars

➤ Useful strategies for taking control of the bottom part of your screen

---

Ever have one of those days where it just feels like time is flying by much too quickly for you to get all your work done? What's that? *Every* day is like that? Tell me about it. What's a time-starved body to do? Well, other than, say, quitting your job, there's not much you can do to free up big chunks of time. A better approach is to work on small slivers of time. That is, you find something you do a hundred times a day and figure out a way to save 10 seconds each time you do it. Voilà! You've just freed up over 15 minutes for more productive pursuits.

A good candidate for this kind of small-time timesaver is your computer. For example, you probably deal with the Start menu and taskbar dozens of times a day, so you can save yourself lots of time by using these items as efficiently as you can. That's the focus of this chapter as I show you all kinds of ways to customize the Start menu and taskbar.

A Smart Start: Reconstructing the Start Menu

The Start menu is your royal road to Windows 2000's riches, as well as to the programs installed on your machine. Because you use this road a lot during the course of a day, you'll probably want to make this road as short and as straight as possible. Fortunately, Windows 2000 gives you lots of ways to customize the Start menu to do this and to suit the way you work.

What's with These Crazy New Menus?

Before getting to the customizing stuff, let's talk about the Start menu customizing that Windows 2000 does on its own. After you've used Windows 2000 for a while, one day you'll suddenly notice that a bunch of commands have disappeared from the Start menus. In their place, you see only a mysterious double arrow at the bottom of each menu, as shown in the following figure.

One day, you'll wake up to find that many of the Start menu items appear to have been kidnapped.

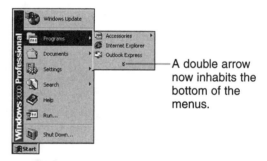

A double arrow now inhabits the bottom of the menus.

What gives? The missing items aren't gone, they're merely in hiding. You see, Windows 2000 has been spying on you. Each time you select something from the Start menu (not counting the main Start menu, which isn't affected by any of this), Windows 2000 makes a note. After a while, it consults its notes and then decides to display only those Start menu items that you've used most often. The rest are hidden away under the assumption that you won't miss them much because you don't use them. Theoretically, this makes it easier to choose stuff from the Start menu because you have fewer items to wade through. This new feature is called *Personalized Menus.*

It's kinda creepy, but I guess it makes sense. What if I want to select one of those hidden commands?

In that case, things get a little less efficient. What you have to do is click the double arrow at the bottom of the menu. This rescues the other items from Start menu purgatory, and you proceed normally. (Note that the hidden items appear sunken into the menu.)

It's all a bit tough to get used to, but don't worry if you don't like it. Later in this chapter, I'll show you how to turn off the Personalized Menus feature.

Toggling Some Start Menu Settings On and Off

Windows 2000's Start menu boasts a number of new settings that you can turn on and off. These settings enable you, among other things, to add the Favorites list as a submenu, display the Control Panel icons as a submenu, turn off the Personalized Menus, and more.

To get to these settings, you have a couple of ways to go:

➤ Select **Start**, **Settings**, **Taskbar & Start Menu**.

➤ Right-click an empty section of the taskbar and then click **Properties**.

Either way, the Taskbar and Start Menu Properties dialog box comes off the bench. Now display the **Advanced** tab, which is shown in the following figure.

Use the Advanced tab to rejig the Start menu.

What you're dealing with here is the list of check boxes in the **Start Menu Settings** group. Each one toggles a particular Start menu feature on and off. Here's a quick summary of the features:

➤ **Display Administrative Tools**   Activating this check box adds a new submenu: Start, Programs, Administrative Tools. (To get to these tools previously, you had to open Control Panel's **Administrative Tools** icon.) This new menu contains advanced tools used by system administrators, so it's unlikely you need to worry about it.

➤ **Display Favorites**   Activating this check box tosses the Favorites submenu onto the main Start menu.

Cross Reference

Remember your Favorites? If you don't, jump back to Chapter 12, "Weaving Your Way Through the World Wide Web," and look under "Saving Sites for Subsequent Surfs: Managing Your Favorites," p. 183.

➤ **Display Logoff**   Activating this setting forces Windows 2000 to put a Log Off *User* command on the main Start menu (where *User* is the name of the user who's currently logged on). This is easier than selecting **Start**, **Shut Down** and then choosing **Log Off *User*** in the Shut Down Windows dialog box.

➤ **Expand Control Panel**   Turning on this option tells Windows 2000 to display all the Control Panel icons in a submenu when you select **Start**, **Settings**, **Control Panel**. If you use Control Panel frequently, you'll find the submenu route is faster than opening the Control Panel window and then launching an icon.

➤ **Expand My Documents**   If you activate this check box, Windows 2000 displays a submenu containing your My Documents files when you select **Start**, **Documents**, **My Documents**.

➤ **Expand Network and Dial-Up Connections**   When this setting is activated, Windows 2000 displays a submenu listing your connection icons when you select **Start**, **Settings**, **Network and Dial-up Connections**.

➤ **Expand Printers**   I think you know the drill by now. Activating this check box displays a menu of your installed printers when you select **Start**, **Settings**, **Printers**.

Getting to the Windows

Bypassing windows such as Control Panel and Printers is a faster way to work, but what if you need to see those windows in the future? That's no problem. What you need to do is right–click the command (such as **Start**, **Settings**, **Control Panel**) and then click **Open** in the shortcut menu.

➤ **Scroll the Programs Menu**   This setting determines what Windows 2000 does if the Programs menu contains so many items that the entire menu can't fit into the height of the screen. When this setting is off, Windows 2000 displays Programs as a two-column menu. When this setting is on, Windows 2000 displays Programs as a single menu with up and down arrows on the top and bottom, respectively. You click these arrows to scroll through the menu.

You'll find another couple of Start menu settings to play with on the **General** tab, shown in the next figure:

> ➤ **Show Small Icons in Start Menu**   If you light up this option, the Start menu goes on a diet: It loses the "Windows 2000" banner along the side and it uses smaller versions of its icons. This is useful if you find that some Start menus are too big for the screen.

> ➤ **Use Personalized Menus**   This setting controls the new Personalized Menus feature. If you don't like this feature, you can turn it off by deactivating this check box.

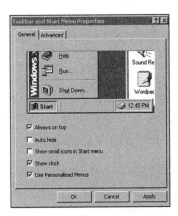

The General tab includes a couple of Start menu settings.

To put the new settings into effect, click **OK** or **Apply**. (You'll be working with the Advanced tab a bit more in the next section, so you might want to click **Apply** to leave the dialog box onscreen.)

Adding Your Own Start Menu Items (and Removing Them, Too)

Most new Windows 2000 users just assume the arrangement of icons on the Start menu is set in stone. They're right, to a certain extent. Everything on the main Start menu from Shut Down to Programs is fixed and can't be messed with by anyone. However, you saw in the previous section that it's possible to plunk the Log Off and Favorites commands onto the main Start menu, so this section isn't totally off-limits.

What *is* a bit surprising is that the rest of the Start menu is completely open for business. You can add icons, move them around, rename them, delete them, and more. I show you how to do all of this in the next three sections.

Let's begin with the simplest case: adding an icon to the Start menu. You usually don't have to worry about this when you install an application. That's because most of today's programs are hip to the Start menu, so they'll add an icon or three during their installation procedure. However, there are two cases when you'll need to add an icon yourself:

249

➤ If you want easy access to a particular document that you use often.

➤ If you installed an older program that isn't Start-menu savvy.

To make this easy for you, Windows 2000 provides the Create Shortcut Wizard. As an example, let's see how you add a Start menu icon for Windows 2000's Welcome program, which displays the Getting Started with Windows 2000 window. Here's what you do:

1. Select **Start**, **Settings**, **Taskbar & Start Menu** to get to the Taskbar and Start Menu Properties dialog box (if it isn't still onscreen from the previous section).

2. In the **Advanced** tab, click **Add**. The Create Shortcut Wizard makes an entrance.

3. Use the text box to enter the location of the document or the file that launches the program. Be sure you include the disk drive, folder, and filename. Alternatively, click **Browse** and use the dialog box to pick out the file. For our example, click **Browse**, open drive C (assuming that's where Windows 2000 was installed), open the **WINNT** folder, highlight **welcome** (the one with the Windows logo beside it), and click **OK**. The following figure shows the initial dialog box with the location filled in.

The Create Shortcut Wizard takes you step-by-step through the process of adding an icon to the Start menu.

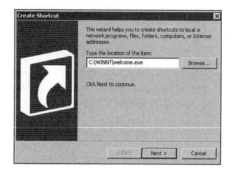

4. Click **Next**. The wizard wonders which Start menu folder you want to use, as shown here.

Choose a Start menu home for the new icon.

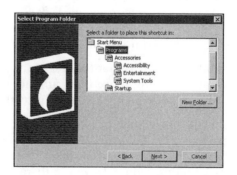

5. You have two choices:

   ➤ If you want to use one of the existing folders, click it to highlight it.

   ➤ If you'd prefer a fresh folder, first highlight the folder in which you want the new folder created. Now click **New Folder**, enter the folder name, and press **Tab**.

6. Click **Next**. The final wizard dialog box suggests a name for the new icon.

7. Adjust the name, if necessary, and then click **Finish**.

What about the opposite procedure, when you need to get rid of something on the Start menu? I'm glad you asked:

1. Select **Start**, **Settings**, **Taskbar & Start Menu** to open the Taskbar and Start Menu Properties dialog box.

2. In the **Advanced** tab, click **Remove**. The Remove Shortcuts/Folders dialog box sprints onto the screen.

3. Highlight the icon or folder you want to rub out.

4. Click **Remove**. Windows 2000 asks whether you're sure.

5. Click **Yes**. Windows 2000 deletes the item and returns you to the Remove Shortcuts/Folders dialog box.

6. Click **Close**.

Why a Folder?

If you're creating a Start menu icon, what's all this about a folder? Well, you'll see in the next section that each submenu (Programs, Accessories, and so on) on the Start menu is actually a folder on your hard disk.

It's Okay to Delete Shortcuts

Remember that the icons you delete are only shortcuts that point to the original program file or document. You're not deleting the originals.

The "Advanced" Route (Not!): The Start Menu Folder

I briefly mentioned a page or two ago that the Start menu submenus are actually folders on your hard disk. In fact, the entire Start menu structure (with the exception of the set-in-stone items on the main Start menu) can be found within the following folder (where *User* is your Windows 2000 username):

```
C:\Documents and Settings\User\Start Menu\
```

251

What good does it do you to know this? Simply that it means you can use all the basic file and folder techniques from Chapter 3, "Using My Computer to Work with Files and Folders," to add, rename, and delete items, and to make the overall Start menu structure more efficient. For example, suppose you use the Send Cover Page Fax command quite a bit. Launching this command is normally a six-click ordeal (**Start**, **Programs**, **Accessories**, **Communications**, **Fax**, **Send Cover Page Fax**). If you were to move this command onto the main Start menu, you'd cut down the launch effort to a mere two clicks.

To get to the Start Menu folder collection, you can use My Computer to get there on your own. However, Windows 2000 offers two potentially faster methods:

➤ Right-click the **Start** button and then click **Explore**.

➤ In the **Advanced** tab, click **Advanced**.

The following figure shows the Start Menu folder with the Programs folder high-lighted. For the most part, you use the exact same techniques for moving, renaming, and deleting files and folders as you learned in Chapter 3. To create new Start menu items, please keep the following two points in mind:

➤ To add icons to any Start menu, be sure you always create a shortcut. Never move a document or program file into the Start Menu folders. To ensure that you always create a shortcut, right-drag the document or program file, drop it inside the Start Menu folder you want to use, and then click **Create Shortcut(s) Here**.

➤ If you create a folder within the Start Menu folder, it becomes a submenu on the Start menu.

For maximum flexibility, use the Start Menu folder to work with the Start menu icons and sub-menus.

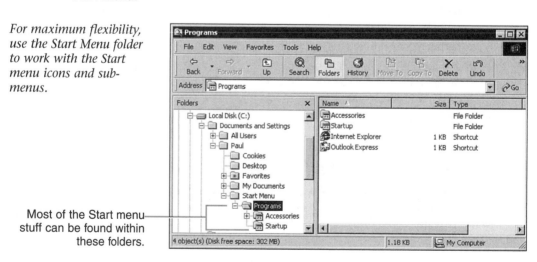

Most of the Start menu stuff can be found within these folders.

Even Easier Ways to Mess with the Start Menu

To close out your look at customizing the Start menu, here are a few tips and techniques that can make this part of your life even easier:

➤ **Right-click convenience**   You can perform many maintenance chores right from the Start menu itself. Right-click a start menu shortcut or submenu and you'll get a menu with all kinds of useful commands, including Cut, Copy, Delete, and Rename.

➤ **Quick Start menu shortcuts**   If you want a shortcut on the main Start menu, drag it from My Computer and drop it on the **Start** button.

➤ **Drag-and-drop rearranging**   Speaking of dragging and dropping, you can also display the Start menu and then use your mouse to drag the commands directly. You can drop them higher or lower on the same menu or even drop them onto another menu altogether.

➤ **Sorting an out-of-sorts menu**   If you've been dragging Start menu items hither and yon, you might end up with menus that are no longer in alphabetical order. If that offends your inner neat freak, it's easy enough to fix. Just right-click the offending menu and then click **Sort by Name**. To get all the menus back in shape, return to the **Advanced** tab and click the **Re-sort** button.

➤ **Wiping out the Documents menu**   As you probably know, the Documents menu (**Start**, **Documents**) contains a list of the last 15 documents you worked on. If you don't want anyone else to see this list, you can scrub it clean by returning to the **Advanced** tab once again and clicking the **Clear** button.

Renovating the Taskbar

Like the Start menu, the taskbar also seems to be an unmalleable feature of the Windows 2000 landscape. If that were true, however, then this chapter would end right about here. The fact that you still have a few pages left to slog through tells you that, indeed, the taskbar is readily malleable. Not only that, but most of the taskbar customizations you'll see over the next few sections are practical timesavers and not just mere "Hey, Ma, look what I can do!" tricks.

Shifting the Taskbar Around

The taskbar, recumbent on the bottom of the screen, seems quite comfy. However, that position might not be comfy for *you*, depending on the ergonomics of your desk and chair. Similarly, you might have a program where you need to maximize the available vertical screen space, so you might not appreciate having the taskbar usurp space at the bottom of the screen. These are mere molehills that can be easily leapt by moving the taskbar to a new location:

1. Point the mouse at an empty section of the taskbar.

2. Hold down the left mouse button and move the pointer toward the edge of the screen where you'd rather see the taskbar situated. As you approach an edge, the taskbar suddenly snaps into place.

3. When the taskbar is on the edge you want, release the mouse button.

What if you're not so much interested in moving the taskbar as in resizing it? For example, if you're feeling particularly frisky, you might end up with a whack of programs on the go. However, each of those programs claims a bit of taskbar turf. The more programs you have running, the tinier the taskbar buttons become. Eventually, as you can see in the following figure, the text on the buttons becomes indecipherable.

Who can tell what each of these taskbar buttons represents?

The way you fix that is by expanding the taskbar from its single-row setup to a setup that has two or more rows. Here's how:

1. Move the mouse pointer so that it rests on the top edge of the taskbar. The pointer changes into a vertical two-headed arrow.

2. Drag the edge of the taskbar up slightly. After you travel a short distance, a second taskbar row springs into view. Unfortunately, you now have the Quick Launch toolbar on one row and the taskbar on another.

3. To fix that, move the mouse pointer so that it rests on the vertical bar near the left edge of the taskbar. This time, the pointer morphs into a horizontal two-headed arrow.

4. Drag the taskbar up and drop it just to the right of the icons in the Quick Launch toolbar. You should now see an arrangement similar to the one in the following figure.

To see the button text, stretch the taskbar into this two-row configuration.

Some Useful Taskbar Options

The next round of taskbar touchups involves a small but useful set of properties, which can be displayed by using either of the following techniques:

➤ Select **Start**, **Settings**, **Taskbar & Start Menu**.

➤ Right-click an empty section of the taskbar and then click **Properties**.

This reunites you with your old friend the Taskbar and Start Menu Properties dialog box. This time, however, you'll be dealing with the three of the check boxes on the **General** tab (shown earlier in this chapter):

Bringing the Taskbar Up for Air

It's still possible to get to the taskbar with **Always on Top** turned off. Either minimize the window, or else press **Ctrl+Esc** (or the 🪟 key, if you have one) and then press **Esc**.

➤ **Always on Top**   When this option is activated, the taskbar remains in view even if you maximize a window. That's usually a good thing. However, if you really need that extra bit of screen room, deactivate this check box. This means that a maximized window takes up the entire screen.

➤ **Auto Hide**   If you activate this check box, Windows 2000 shrinks the taskbar to a teensy gray strip that's barely visible along the bottom of the screen. This gives a maximized window more room to stretch its legs. When you need the taskbar for something, just move the mouse pointer to the bottom of the screen. Lo and behold, the full taskbar slides into view. When you move the mouse above the taskbar, the taskbar sinks back whence it came.

➤ **Show Clock**   Deactivating this check box hides the clock that normally resides in the taskbar's system tray.

Refurbishing the Quick Launch Toolbar

The Quick Launch toolbar is a great innovation because it's handy (it's always visible) and easy (single-click the icons to launch them). Unfortunately, Windows 2000 deposits a mere trio of icons in this section, which seems like a waste of a precious resource. Forget that. As you'll soon see, it's not that hard to add as many icons as you like to the Quick Launch area.

The secret is that the Quick Launch icons are really just files (two of them are shortcuts) in a folder named Quick Launch. Therefore, if you add your own shortcuts to the Quick Launch folder, the icons will show up in the Quick Launch toolbar and you'll be set.

There are two methods you can use to add shortcuts to the Quick Launch folder:

➤ **The easy method**   Open **My Computer**, drag the program file you want to add, and drop it inside the Quick Launch toolbar. (You can also drag an icon from any Start menu and drop it inside the Quick Launch toolbar.)

➤ **The hard method**   Right-click an empty section of the Quick Launch toolbar (this is a bit hard to do because there's not that much empty space) and then click **Open** to open the Quick Launch folder window. Click the **Folders** button to get the Folder list, and then drag shortcuts into the Quick Launch folder.

Displaying and Tweaking Taskbar Toolbars

I've used the phrase "Quick Launch toolbar" a few times so far in this book. What's all this about a *toolbar*? It's no big secret. In the same way that some programs have toolbars to give you one-click access to features, so does the taskbar have its own collection of toolbars for one-click wonderment. Quick Launch is one such taskbar toolbar, but there are others. To view them, first right-click an empty spot on the taskbar. In the shortcut menu that unfurls, click **Toolbars** to get a submenu with four choices (I'm ignoring the New Toolbar command for now; see the next section for more info on it):

➤ **Address**   This command toggles the Address toolbar on and off. This toolbar is a version of the Address bar that appears in Internet Explorer (as well as Windows 2000's folder windows). You can use it to type in Web addresses. When you press **Enter**, Internet Explorer fires up and loads the specified page.

➤ **Links**   This command toggles the Links toolbar on and off. This toolbar is the same as the Links bar in Internet Explorer.

➤ **Desktop**   This command toggles the Desktop toolbar on and off. This toolbar contains the same icons as the ones on the Windows 2000 desktop. This is useful if you normally run your programs maximized and so rarely see the desktop.

➤ **Quick Launch**   This command toggles the Quick Launch toolbar on and off.

If you activate any of these extra toolbars, you'll probably need to increase the number of taskbar rows (as explained earlier) to accommodate everything comfortably.

Each of these toolbars also boasts a few customization options that can help reduce the clutter on the taskbar. To see these options, right-click an empty section of the toolbar you want to work with. The resulting shortcut menu contains a bunch of commands, but we care only about the following three:

➤ **View**   This command displays a submenu with two options: **Large** and **Small**. These options determine the relative size of the toolbar icons.

➤ **Show Text**   This command toggles the icon captions on and off. If you think you can recognize an icon from its image alone, then turning off the text will enable you to fit many more icons on a given chunk of toolbar real estate.

➤ **Show Title**   This command toggles the toolbar title (which appears on the left side of the toolbar) on and off. Again, you can give your toolbar icons a bit more elbow room by turning off the title.

Move Those Toolbars

You can move any of these toolbars by using the same technique that I showed you earlier for the taskbar. On my own system, I have the Address toolbar and the taskbar along the bottom of the screen, the Quick Launch toolbar along the right side of the screen, and the Links toolbar along the left side of the screen. It's busy, but boy, is it efficient!

Creating Your Own Toolbars

The taskbar's collection of four companion toolbars is a good start. However, it turns out that it's possible to display the contents of *any* folder as a taskbar toolbar. Here's how:

1. Right-click an empty section of the taskbar, and then click **Toolbars**, **New**, **Toolbar**. Windows 2000 offers up the New Toolbar dialog box, shown here.

Use this dialog box to pick out which folder you want to double as a taskbar toolbar.

2. Use the tree to find and highlight the folder you want to moonlight as a toolbar.

3. Click **OK**. Windows 2000 displays the folder as a toolbar.

4. Adjust the new toolbar's options, as needed.

What Happened

This chapter showed you how to customize both the Start menu and the taskbar. For the Start menu, you first learned about Windows 2000's new Personalized Menus.

257

From there, I showed you how to toggle some options on and off (including those Personalized Menus), how to create your own Start menu shortcuts, and how to work with Start menu items directly from the Start menu.

For the taskbar, I began by showing you how to move and resize it. From there, you learned about some taskbar options, how to customize the Quick Launch toolbar, how to display and customize other taskbar toolbars, and how to create your own toolbars from folders.

Crib Notes

➤ **Start menu and taskbar options**   These are available by selecting **Start**, **Settings**, **Taskbar & Start Menu**, or by right-clicking an empty stretch of the taskbar and then clicking **Properties**.

➤ **Adding Start menu stuff**   Display the **Advanced** tab and click **Add**.

➤ **Direct Start menu modifications**   Display the **Start** menu and then right-click any command.

➤ **Moving and sizing the taskbar**   Drag an empty section of the taskbar to move it; drag the top edge of the taskbar to size it.

➤ **Quick Quick Launch customizing**   The easiest way to add icons to the Quick Launch toolbar is to drag program files and drop them onto the toolbar.

Chapter 17

Making My Computer Your Own

In This Chapter

➤ Messing with the My Computer window

➤ Changing the file and folder view

➤ Sorting files and folders

➤ Creating custom Web views for folders

➤ All kinds of useful options and settings that will help you emphasize the "My" in My Computer

After the mostly aesthetic redecorating you did back in Chapter 15, "Redoing the Desktop," things turned decidedly more practical with the customizations outlined in Chapter 16, "Revamping the Start Menu and Taskbar." You'll stay on that practical path in this chapter as I show you a few ways to reconstruct My Computer. You'll learn how to rearrange the My Computer window, change how files and folders are displayed, and sort files and folders. On a slightly more frivolous note, you'll also learn how to create custom folder backgrounds and perform other Web view tweaks.

Points of View: Changing the My Computer View

Let's begin the My Computer renovations with a few methods for changing the view. I'll divide this into four areas: changing the layout of the My Computer window, customizing the toolbar, switching how file and folders are displayed in the content area, and sorting files and folders.

Bar-Gains: Toggling My Computer's Bars On and Off

My Computer is awash in bars. There are the menu bar, the toolbar, the Address bar, and the status bar. And those are just the ones you see by default. There are plenty of other bars lurking beneath the surface. So, to start things off on an easy note, this section shows you how to display the various My Computer bars, as well as how to hide those that you don't use.

The commands you need are on the **View** menu. Let's start with the **Toolbars** command, which shoves out a submenu that has four commands that correspond to My Computer's four available toolbars. (I talk about the Customize command in the next section.) In each case, you display a toolbar by activating its command (so that it has a check mark beside it), and you hide a toolbar by deactivating its command. Here's a summary of the four toolbars:

➤ **Standard Buttons**   This toolbar is displayed by default and it's the one that you see under the menu bar. See the next section, "Customizing the Standard Buttons Toolbar," to learn how to control the look of this all-important toolbar.

➤ **Address Bar**   This toolbar is displayed by default and it appears under the Standard Buttons toolbar. It displays the name of the current folder and you can use it to navigate to other folders (or even to Web page addresses).

➤ **Links**   This is the Links bar that you normally see only in Internet Explorer. If you display it here, clicking any button in the Links bar will display the corresponding Web page within the My Computer window.

➤ **Radio**   This is a toolbar that enables you to listen to a radio station piped in over the Web. This is useful only if you have a fast connection to the Internet and if you have that connection established while you work within My Computer.

Speedy Toolbar Toggling

You also can toggle a toolbar on and off by right-clicking any displayed toolbar and then clicking the toolbar name in the shortcut menu that shows up.

Next up on the View menu is the Status Bar command. This command toggles the status bar at the bottom of the window on and off. I recommend that you leave the status bar as is because it offers some semiuseful info:

➤ If you highlight a menu command, a short description of the command appears in the status bar.

➤ Each time you open a folder, the status bar tells you how many files and subfolders ("objects") are in the folder and how much hard disk space the files take up.

➤ If you select one or more files, the status bar tells you how many files you selected and what their total size is.

The View menu's Explorer Bar command also spits out a submenu. In this case, the submenu offers a number of commands that toggle various bars on and off within the Explorer bar. There are five in all:

➤ **Search** This toggles the Search bar on and off. You use the Search bar to find files on your hard disk.

➤ **Favorites** This toggles the Favorites bar on and off. You use the Favorites bar to display your list of favorites. These are normally Web sites, but you also can define a folder as a favorite.

➤ **History** This toggles the History bar on and off. The History bar displays a list of the folders that you've visited each day for the past 20 days. It works the same as the History bar used by Internet Explorer.

➤ **Folders** Toggles the Folders bar on and off. The Folders bar gives you a bird's-eye view of your computer's disks and folders, which makes it much easier to navigate your system (see the following figure). I highly recommend turning on this Explorer bar and leaving it on full-time.

➤ **Tip of the Day** This command toggles the Tip of the Day bar on and off. As its name implies, this bar displays a brief Windows 2000 tip each day. This bar is a bit different in that it appears along the bottom of the My Computer window.

Customizing the Standard Buttons Toolbar

Techno Talk

Explorer Bar

A pane that shows up on the left side of the My Computer window, and that's used to display bars (such as the handy Folders bar).

Cross Reference

I covered searching back in Chapter 3, "Using My Computer to Work with Files and Folders." Go to "Searching for Long-Lost Files," p. 52, for the details.

Cross Reference

The details on favorites can be found in Chapter 12, "Weaving Your Way Through the World Wide Web." See the section "Saving Sites for Subsequent Surfs: Managing Your Favorites," p. 183.

The Standard Buttons toolbar (which I'll just call "the toolbar" from now on) is a bit of an odd duck. Some buttons have text (such as the Back button) and some don't (such as the Forward button). Also, it doesn't include buttons for three commonly used commands: Cut, Copy, and Paste. You can fix this idiosyncratic behavior by tweaking the toolbar.

261

Cross Reference

For the goods on the History bar, see Chapter 12's "Bread Crumbs in Cyberspace: Using the History List" section, p. 188.

To begin, select **View**, **Toolbars**, **Customize**. (You also can right-click the toolbar and then click **Customize** in the shortcut menu.) My Computer lobs the Customize Toolbar dialog box your way, as shown here.

For easier navigation, always display the Folders bar in My Computer.

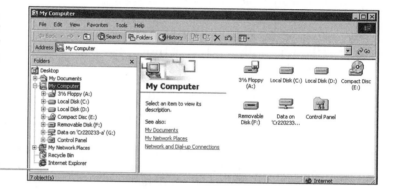

The Folders bar⎯

Explorer Bar Shortcuts

Three of the Explorer bars offer shortcut methods for toggling themselves on and off:

➤ **Search**   Click **Search** in the Standard Buttons toolbar, or press **Ctrl+E**.

➤ **Favorites**   Click **Favorites** in the Standard Buttons toolbar, or press **Ctrl+I**.

➤ **History**   Click **History** in the Standard Buttons toolbar, or press **Ctrl+H**.

The extra toolbar buttons
that you can display

The toolbar buttons that
are currently displayed

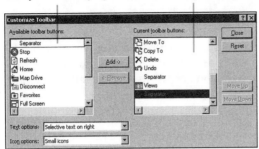

*Use this dialog box to
knock some sense into My
Computer's main toolbar.*

Here's a summary of the techniques you can use:

Adding an extra button to the toolbar   Highlight it in the **Available Toolbar Buttons** list and then click **Add**. Use the **Separator** item to add a vertical bar to the toolbar. This is used to separate groups of related buttons.

Removing a button from the toolbar   Highlight it in the **Current Toolbar Buttons** list and then click **Remove**.

Separator

In a toolbar, a vertical bar that separates groups of related buttons.

Changing the order of the buttons Highlight any button in the **Current Toolbar Buttons** list and click **Move Up** or **Move Down**.

Controlling the button text   Use the **Text Options** list:

➤ **Show text labels**   This option adds text to every button. This makes the buttons much easier to figure out, so I recommend going with this option.

➤ **Selective text on right**   This is the default option, and it displays text on only some buttons. As I've mentioned, this is a pretty dumb way of doing things.

➤ **No text labels**   This option displays every button using just its icon. If you already know what each icon represents, selecting this option will give you a bit more room because the toolbar will be at its narrowest.

Controlling the size of the icons   Use the items in the **Icon Options** list. Select either **Small Icons** (this is the default) or **Large Icons**.

Click **Close** to put your new settings into effect.

Views You Can Use: Changing How Folders and Files Are Displayed

In the standard My Computer view, each file and folder is displayed using a big, fat icon. However, there are also several other views you can try on for size. You access these views either by pulling down the **View** menu or by clicking the **Views** button in the toolbar. There are five possibilities:

➤ **Large Icons** This is the default honkin' icon view.

➤ **Small Icons** This view displays files and folders using smaller, cuter versions of the icons.

➤ **List** This view also displays the files and folders using small icons, but everything is arrayed in multiple columns, as shown here.

My Computer in List view.

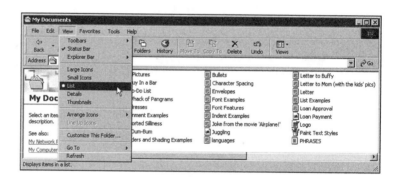

➤ **Details** This view displays the files and folders using a four-column list, as shown in the following figure. For each file and folder, you see its Name, its Size, its Type (such as WordPad Document), and the date and time it was last Modified. However, these aren't the only columns available. There's actually a truckload of them, and you can see the complete list by selecting **View**, **Choose Columns**. (This command is around only when you're in Details view.) In the Column Settings dialog box, use the check boxes to toggle columns on and off.

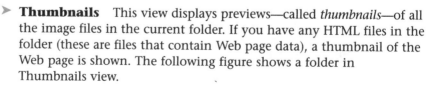

➤ **Thumbnails** This view displays previews—called *thumbnails*—of all the image files in the current folder. If you have any HTML files in the folder (these are files that contain Web page data), a thumbnail of the Web page is shown. The following figure shows a folder in Thumbnails view.

Click these column headings to sort the folder contents.

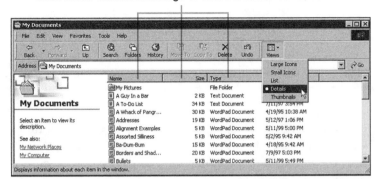

*My Computer in
Details view.*

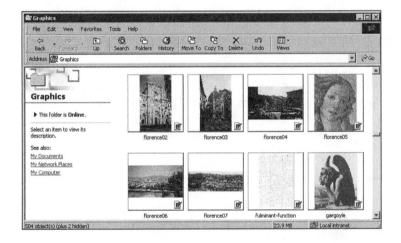

*My Computer in
Thumbnails view.*

Ordering My Computer Around: Sorting Files

To complete your reading of My Computer's views news, let's see how you sort the files and subfolders in the current folder. By default, file and subfolders are sorted alphabetically by name, with the subfolders displayed first, and then the files. You can change this by selecting the **View**, **Arrange Icons** command, which reveals a submenu with five choices:

➤ **By Name** This is the default sort order.

➤ **By Type** This command sorts the folder alphabetically by the type of document.

➤ **By Size** This command sorts the folder numerically by the size of each file.

➤ **By Date** This command sorts the folder according to the date and time when each item was last modified.

➤ **Auto Arrange** Selecting this command toggles the Auto Arrange feature on and off. When it's on, My Computer automatically re-sorts the folder (using the current sort choice) whenever you add, rename, or delete a file or folder.

265

Savvy Sorting

If you're in Details view, you can sort a folder by clicking the column headers (as pointed out in the Details view figure, shown earlier). For example, clicking the **Size** column header sorts the folder by size. Clicking the header again switches the sort between ascending and descending.

Start Spreading the Views: Applying a View to All Folders

The view options—specifically, the icon view (Large Icons, Small Icons, and so on) and the sort order—you set for one folder are immediately jettisoned when you leap to another folder. If you'd like to use one set of options for *all* your folders, you can tell Windows 2000 to make it so. Here are the steps to follow:

1. Set up a folder just the way you like it.
2. Select **Tools**, **Folder Options**. The Folder Options dialog box skids into the screen.
3. Display the **View** tab.
4. Click **Like Current Folder**. Windows 2000 asks you to confirm.
5. Click **Yes** to get back to the Folder Options dialog box.
6. Click **OK**.

If you grow tired of these view options and you want to go back to the original look and feel, display the **View** tab once again and click **Reset All Folders**.

A Folder Face-Lift: Customizing a Folder

Besides changing how subfolders and files are displayed within a folder, My Computer also offers a few other folder customizations: adjusting the background and text, adding a comment, and changing the Web view options. The next three sections fill you in on the gory details.

Refurbishing the Folder Background and Text

Back in Chapter 3, I told you a bit about this newfangled Web integration business, and I showed you what havoc it wreaks on the My Computer window. This includes displaying each folder as though it were a Web page.

One of the things that a Web designer can do to a page is change the background on which the page text is displayed, and to change the color of the text to match that background. You can do the same things with your folders. So, if you're tired of the plain white background and boring black text you get in the standard view, follow these steps to try something with a little more oomph:

Cross Reference

For a refresher course on Web integration, see "How Web Integration Changes My Computer," p. 55.

1. In My Computer, display the folder that you want to customize.

2. Select **View**, **Customize This Folder**. The Customize This Folder Wizard parachutes into the fray.

3. The first dialog box doesn't have anything interesting to say, so click **Next** to get to a more useful dialog box named Customize This Folder.

4. Be sure the **Modify Background Picture and Filename Appearance** check box is the only check box that's activated, and then click **Next**. The wizard changes shirts to show you the dialog box in the following figure.

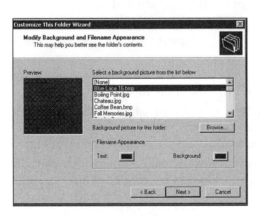

Use this dialog box to revamp the current folder's background and text.

5. Use the **Select a Background Picture from the List Below** list to choose the background image you want to use. (If you have some other image that you'd rather use, click **Browse** to pick out the file by using a dialog box.)

6. To change the color of the text used to display file and folder names, click the **Text** button. Use the color palette that pops up to click the color you want to live with.

7. To change the color of the background used by file and folder names, click the **Background** button to pick out the color you want from the palette that appears.

8. Click **Next**. The wizard customizes the folder and then displays the last of its dialog boxes.

9. Click **Finish**.

Adding a Folder Comment

You've seen how a folder's Web view displays an information area to the left of the folder contents. This area displays the title of the folder, info on whatever file is currently selected, and messages from the Windows 2000 powers-that-be. Interestingly, you also can add your own two cents' worth by inserting a *comment* that gets displayed in the information area when no file or folder is selected. Here's how:

1. Use My Computer to display the folder that you want to customize.

2. Select **View**, **Customize This Folder** to get the Customize This Folder Wizard going, and then click **Next**.

3. Activate the **Add Folder Comment** check box. (Also, be sure to deactivate the other check boxes.) Click **Next** when you're ready for more action. The Add folder comment dialog box appears.

4. Use the large text box to enter the text you want to display. The following figure is a composite image that shows some text I entered and how that text looks in the information area. Here are some notes to bear in mind:

   ➤ If you know HTML, feel free to augment your text with any tags that strike your fancy.

   ➤ This brain-dead text box doesn't give you any way to start a new line. Instead, you need to add the
 (line break) tag, as shown in the figure.

   ➤ If you have Internet access, you can add links to Web pages. The general format to use is <A HREF="*address*">*Link text*</A>. Here, *address* is the full address of the page, and *Link text* is the text you'll click.

   ➤ If you don't have Internet access (or even if you do, for that matter), you can create links that point to folders on your hard disk. You use the same format, except you use the folder location as the address. Here's an example: <A HREF="C:\My Documents">Go to My Documents</A>.

These words and tags...

Use this wizard dialog box to add text and HTML tags to display in the information area.

...are displayed as shown here.

5. Click **Next** to get to the last wizard dialog box.

6. Click **Finish**.

Changing the Web View Folder Template

The layout of a folder when it's in Web view is determined by something called a *folder template*. This is a file that tells Windows 2000 "Okay, put the contents here and the information area there, and then add in these other doodads." Windows 2000 actually ships with four different templates, so you can play around with them and pick one you like. Here's what you do:

1. Use My Computer to display the folder that you want to customize.

2. Select **View**, **Customize This Folder** to start up the Customize This Folder Wizard, and then click **Next**.

3. Activate the **Choose or Edit an HTML Template for This Folder** check box.

HTML Know-How

If you wouldn't know HTML from H.G. Wells, you might want to take a peek at my book *The Complete Idiot's Guide to Creating a Web Page*. It will tell you everything you need to know about HTML (and then some).

269

(Be sure to deactivate any other check boxes that are active.) Click **Next** and the wizard's Change Folder Template dialog box bursts through the door, as shown here.

Use this wizard dialog box to select a folder template.

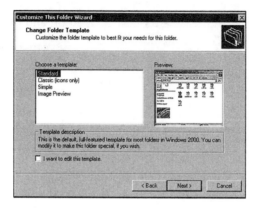

4. Use the **Choose a Template** list to, well, choose a template. The **Preview** box gives you some idea of what the selected template does, and then **Template Description** box tells you a bit more about the template.

5. If you know HTML and you're feeling your oats, you might want to take a stab at customizing the template by hand. If so, activate the **I Want to Edit This Template** check box. Otherwise, leave this check box deactivated.

6. Click **Next**.

7. If you elected to monkey with the template, Windows 2000 opens it up in Notepad. Make your changes, save them, and then exit Notepad.

8. Click **Finish**.

What Happened

This chapter gave you the goods on customizing various aspects of My Computer. You learned how to change the view, including toggling Explorer bars on and off, customizing the toolbar, changing the icons, and sorting stuff. You also learned how to customize a folder, including changing the background and text, inserting a folder comment, and changing the Web view template.

Crib Notes

➤ **Toggling toolbars** Select **View**, **Toolbars** (or right-click a displayed toolbar) to see a list of toolbars that can be toggled on and off.

➤ **Displaying the Folders bar** Activate the **View**, **Explorer Bar**, **Folders** command, or activate the **Folders** button in the toolbar.

➤ **Customizing the toolbar** Select **View**, **Toolbars**, **Customize** (or right-click the toolbar and then click **Customize**).

➤ **Changing the icon view** Choose one of the following commands on the **View** menu (or the toolbar's **Views** button): **Large Icons**, **Small Icons**, **List**, **Details**, or **Thumbnails**.

➤ **Sorting files and folders** Select **View**, **Arrange Icons** and then select a sort order. You also can sort in Details view by clicking the column headings.

➤ **Getting a global view** Set up a folder the way you want it, select **Tools**, **Options**, display the **View** tab, and click **Like Current Folder**.

➤ **Customizing a folder** Select **View**, **Customize This Folder**, click **Next**, and then select a customization option.

CHUNKA
CHUNKA

Chapter 18

Installing Software and Hardware

In This Chapter

➤ Installing a program on your computer

➤ Kicking a program off your computer

➤ Adding devices to your computer

➤ Letting Windows 2000 know about a new device

➤ Step-by-step instructions for movin' 'em in and movin' 'em out

---

One of the (few) things I like about computers is that you're never stuck with the out-of-the-box configuration. If you have a TV set, by contrast, pretty much the only way to improve on it is to buy a better set. With a computer, though, improving your lot is often just a matter of installing some software or plugging in a peripheral.

If you're looking to take your computer to the next level, this chapter can help. In it, you'll learn how to install software, attach devices, and let Windows 2000 know about a new device. You'll also learn how to rid your computer of software and hardware add-ons that have worn out their welcome.

From There to Here: Installing a Program

I've spent most of my time in this book showing you how to operate one Windows 2000 program or another. You've seen so far that Windows 2000 comes stocked with a decent collection of software that does the job as long as your needs aren't too lofty. However, what if your needs *are* lofty, or if you're looking to fill in a software niche that Windows 2000 doesn't cover (such as a spreadsheet program, a database, or an action game)? In that case, you need to go outside the box and purchase the appropriate program.

After you've got the program, your next chore is to install it. This means that you run a "setup" routine that makes the program ready for use on your computer. Most setup procedures perform the following tasks:

➤ Create a new folder for the program.

➤ Copy to the new folder and to other strategic folders on your hard disk any files that the program needs to run.

➤ Adjust Windows 2000 as needed to ensure that the program runs properly.

How you launch this setup routine depends on how the program is distributed:

AutoRun

A feature that automatically launches a program's setup routine after you insert its CD-ROM or DVD-ROM disc.

➤ **If the program is on a CD** In this case, you might not have to do much of anything. Most computer CDs support a feature called *AutoRun*. This means that when you insert the disc into your CD-ROM (or DVD-ROM) drive for the first time, the setup routine gets launched automatically.

➤ **If you downloaded the program from the Internet** In this case, you'll end up with the downloaded file on your hard disk. Be sure this file resides in an otherwise-empty folder and then double-click the file. This will either launch the setup routine or it will "extract" a bunch of files into the folder. If the latter happens, look for an application file named **Setup** (or, more rarely, **Install**), and then double-click that file.

For all other cases—a CD-based program that doesn't start automatically or a program distributed on floppy disks—your best bet is to get Windows 2000 to launch the setup routine for you. Here's how:

1. Select **Start**, **Settings**, **Control Panel** to fire up the Control Panel window.

2. Launch the **Add/Remove Programs** icon. Windows 2000 introduces you to the Add/Remove Programs window.

3. Click the **Add New Programs** icon.

4. Click the **CD or Floppy** button. Windows 2000 prompts you to insert the CD or floppy disk. (For the latter, if you have multiple disks, be sure you plop in the first disk, which will be labeled "Disk 1" or "Setup Disk" or some variation on that theme.)

5. Insert the disc and click **Next**. Windows 2000 roots around in your CD-ROM drive and floppy disk drive to see whether it can find a setup routine. At this point, one of two things will happen:

➤ **Windows 2000 finds a setup file**   In this case, you'll see a dialog box such as the one shown in the following figure.

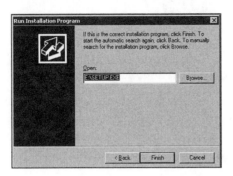

If Windows 2000 success-fully locates a setup file, it displays the name and location of the file here.

➤ **Windows 2000 doesn't find a setup file**   In this case, you still see the referenced dialog box, but the text box will be blank. You can either fill in the drive, folder, and filename yourself, or you can click **Browse** to find it using another dialog box.

6. Click **Finish** to get the installation underway.

From here, follow the instructions and prompts that the setup routine sends your way. (This procedure varies from program to program.)

From Here to Nowhere: Uninstalling a Program

Most programs seem like good ideas at the time you install them. Unless you're an out-right pessimist, you probably figured that a program you installed was going to help you work harder, be more efficient, or have more fun. Sadly, lots of programs don't live up to expectations. The good news is that you don't have to put up with a loser program after you realize it's not up to snuff. You can *uninstall* it so it doesn't clutter up your Start menu, desktop, hard disk, or any other location where it might have inserted itself.

Uninstall

To completely remove a program from your computer.

The even better news is that, most of the time, Windows 2000 can take care of the uninstall dirty work for you automatically. Let's see how it works:

1. Select **Start**, **Settings**, **Control Panel** and crank up the **Add/Remove Programs** icon once again.

275

Uninstallation Privileges

If a program was installed by someone who has higher privileges than you (such as your network's system administrator), Windows 2000 won't let you uninstall the program. Only someone with equal or higher privileges can run the uninstall.

2. In the Add/Remove Programs window, click the **Change or Remove Programs** icon. (This icon is clicked by default when you first open this window.) As you can see in the following figure, the window lists the programs that Windows 2000 thinks are installed on your system. When you highlight a program, the list also tells you the size of the program, how often you used it, and when you last used it.

This window displays a list of the programs installed on your machine.

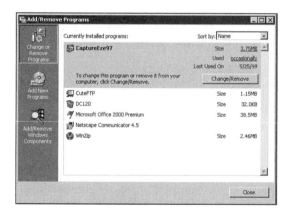

3. You now have two choices:

   ➤ **If you see your program in the list** Click the program to highlight it, and then click **Change/Remove**. (In some cases, you just click the **Remove** button.) Windows 2000 loads a program that will uninstall the application.

   ➤ **If you don't see your program** Click **Close** and skip the rest of these steps to see how to uninstall a program by hand.

4. The uninstall program usually asks you to confirm that you want to go through with this. Click **Yes** (or whatever) to proceed. Other programs might give you the opportunity to change the application's settings or to remove the application. In this case, be sure you choose the latter.

5. When the uninstall is complete, you usually see a dialog box letting you know. Click **OK** to wipe your hands of the program.

Plenty of programs aren't smart enough to be able to uninstall themselves automatically. For these dim-witted brutes, you need to roll up your sleeves and perform the removal by hand. Here's a checklist to run through:

Shut Down the Program!

Before running through this checklist, be sure the program you're wiping out isn't running. To be extra safe, exit and then restart Windows 2000 to ensure that the program doesn't have any open files hunkered down in memory.

➤ **Find the folder** Most programs park themselves into their own folder during installation. Use My Computer to find that folder.

➤ **Save data files** If you used the program to create any documents, I'd suggest saving those documents just in case you need them at a later date. (For example, you might have a change of heart and decide to install the program again.) To save the data files, create a new folder (make it a subfolder of My Documents) and move the files into that folder.

➤ **Fry the folder** With your data files safe and sound, you can now delete the program's folder.

➤ **Sweep the Start menu** If the program put any icons or submenus on the Start menu, open the Start menu and, for each of the offending items, right-click it and then click **Delete** to expunge it.

➤ **Clean the Quick Launch toolbar** Some programs also like to add an icon or two to the handy Quick Launch toolbar (who can blame them?). To get rid of any such icon, right-click it and then click **Delete**.

➤ **Dust the desktop** If the program added any icons to the desktop, drag them into the **Recycle Bin**.

Adding On: Installing a Hardware Device

Software installation is usually a painless operation that often requires just a few mouse clicks on your part. Hardware, however, is another kettle of electronic fish altogether. Not only must you attach the device to your machine (which might even require that you remove the cover to get inside the computer), but you also have to hope that two devices don't conflict with each other.

The latter is less of a problem thanks to Windows 2000's new support for something called *Plug and Play*. This enables Windows 2000 to immediately recognize a new device and to configure that device automatically. It's a kind of hardware nirvana that makes it easy for average Joes and Josephines to upgrade the physical side of their computers. To make it work, however, you need two things:

➤ **Devices that support Plug and Play**   Most new hardware doodads are Plug and Play-friendly. However, to be safe, check the box to be sure it says "Plug and Play" before buying anything.

➤ **Devices that are compatible with Windows 2000**   Windows 2000, finicky beast that it is, won't work with just any old device. Again, before buying a device, check the box to see whether it says anything about being compatible with Windows 2000. Also, your Windows 2000 package should have come with a Hardware Compatibility List, which lists the devices that have been tested with Windows 2000.

The Hardware Compatibility List Online

If you have Web access, you can check out the Hardware Compatibility List using the following page on Microsoft's site:

> http://www.microsoft.com/hwtest/hcl/

Understanding Hardware Types

Although there are thousands of devices available, and dozens of device categories, I like to organize devices according to how you attach them to the computer. From this point of view, there are four types to worry about:

➤ **External plug-in devices**   These are devices that use some kind of cable to plug into a *port* in the back of the PC. These devices include keyboards, mice, joysticks, modems, printers, speakers, and monitors. These kinds of devices are easy to install if you remember one thing: The computer's ports each have a unique shape, and the cable's plug has a shape that matches one of those ports. So, there's usually only one possible place into which any cable can plug.

➤ **PC Card (PCMCIA) devices**   These types of devices are the easiest to install because they simply slip into any one of the computer's PC Card slots (or *sockets*, as they're called). Note, however, that these slots are almost always found only on notebook computers.

➤ **Internal disk drives**   These are the toughest devices to install not only because you have to get inside your computer, but also because there are lots of steps involved. Here's the basic procedure:

1. Shut down your computer (using **Start**, **Shut Down**), unplug the power cable, and then remove the front cover. (Note that you also might need to remove the computer's main cover to do this.)

2. Use screws (usually provided with the drive) to attach the "rails" to the sides of the disk drive. (These are usually long, skinny bits of plastic with several holes in them.)

3. The front of your computer should have several *drive bays* open. Insert the disk drive into one of these bays, and use screws to attach the rails to the chassis of the computer.

Two Identical Ports?

The exception to this is if the back of the computer has two ports with identical configurations. In most cases, that just means your machine offers two of the same port type, so you can plug your device into either one.

4. Attach a power supply cable to the back of the disk drive. (The power supply cable is a multicolored collection of thin cables that runs into a single plug. Most computers have a number of such plugs available.)

5. Attach a data cable to the back of the drive. The data cable should have been supplied with the disk drive. You then attach the other end of the cable to the appropriate port inside the computer. (You'll need to read your device documentation to find out the correct way to go about this.)

6. If you're inserting a CD-ROM or DVD-ROM drive, you'll probably also need to run an audio cable (supplied with the drive) from the back of the drive to your sound card.

Makin' It Fit

If the front cover won't quite fit, then you need to adjust the position of the drive within the bay. Try different screw positions to shift the drive up or down. If that doesn't work, try adjusting the position of the rails on the side of the drive.

7. Put the front cover back on the computer (and the main cover, if you took that off, as well). Before doing this, you'll probably need to remove the plate that previously blocked the drive bay you used.

8. Plug the power cable back in and then turn the computer on.

➤ **Internal circuit boards**   These are cards that plug into slots inside your computer. There are circuit boards for all kinds of things, including sound cards, graphics cards, network cards (see the following figure), and video decoder cards (which usually come with DVD-ROM drives nowadays). These kinds of devices have always seemed intimidating to nongeeks, but anyone with a minimum of coordination can install them. Here are the basic steps:

1. Shut down your computer (using **Start**, **Shut Down**), unplug the power cable, and then remove the main cover.

2. Find an empty slot for your circuit board and remove the backplate (the metal plate beside the slot on the back of the computer).

Which Slot Do You Use?

Inside the machine, you'll see a series of long, thin, slots. On most modern PCs, there are two types of slots: PCI slots—which are shorter and are usually white or beige—and ISA slots—which are usually longer and black. So, what you need to do is find an empty slot that fits the plug part of your circuit board (see the following figure).

3. Orient the circuit board so that the plug part is lined up with the slot inside the computer, and the board's backplate is toward the back of the computer.

4. Using gentle but consistent pressure, maneuver the board's plug into the slot. Be sure you insert the board as far as it will go. (Tip: The easiest way to tell whether the board is inserted all the way is to look at the board's backplate. If the part where you insert the screw is flush with the screw hole, then the board is inserted fully.)

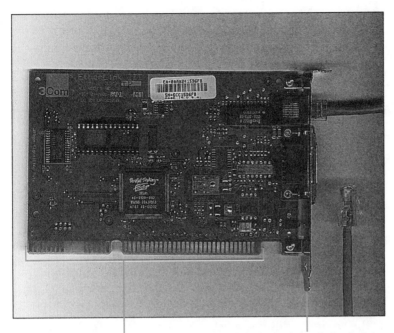

A typical ISA circuit board that slips inside a computer.

This is the part that plugs into the slot.   This is the board's backplate.

5. Screw the board's backplate to the computer chassis.

6. If the board requires any internal cables (see the board's documentation), plug them in.

7. Put the computer cover back on.

8. Plug the power cable back in and turn the computer on.

Running the Add/Remove Hardware Wizard

Your device and your computer are now shacked up, but they're not married yet. To get a full relationship going, Windows 2000 has to install a tiny bit of software called a *device driver*. This miniprogram has the code that operates (drives) the device, so it acts as a kind of middleman between the device and Windows 2000.

In the best of all possible worlds, after you've attached the device (and, if necessary, restarted your computer), Windows 2000 will recognize the new limb and will display the New Hardware Found dialog box. (This is my favorite dialog box because it means I have little if any work to do from here. An under-your-breath "Yes!" is the appropriate reaction to seeing this dialog box.) Windows 2000 then proceeds to install the device driver and any other software required to make the device go. This is automatic, for the most part, but you'll occasionally be asked a few simple questions to complete the setup. In particular, you might see the Found New Hardware Wizard, which will lead you through the installation of a device driver. (The process is similar to upgrading a driver, so see "Upgrading a Device Driver," later in this chapter.)

281

This Wizard Talks Only to Administrators

Only users with Administrator privileges can run the Add/Remove Hardware Wizard.

If, for some reason, Windows 2000 doesn't automatically recognize your new device, all is not lost. That's because Windows 2000 comes with a hardware helper called the Add/Remove Hardware Wizard, which will scour every nook and cranny of your system to look for new stuff. Here's how it works:

1. Select **Start, Settings, Control Panel** to crack open the Control Panel window.

2. Launch the **Add/Remove Hardware** icon. The Add/Remove Hardware Wizard wipes the grease from its hands and comes out to meet you.

3. The initial dialog box just tells you some things you already know, so click **Next**.

4. In the next wizard dialog box, be sure the **Add/Troubleshoot a Device** option is activated, and then click **Next**. The wizard starts looking for Plug-and-Play devices.

5. When that's done, the wizard hands you a list of all the devices installed on your machine. Click **Add a New Device** at the top of the list, and then click **Next**.

6. When the wizard asks whether you want Windows 2000 to search for devices, be sure the **Yes, Search for New Hardware** option is activated, and then click **Next**.

7. The wizard now runs through a lengthy detection process. When it's done, it displays a list of the new devices that it found, as shown here. (If no new devices were found, the wizard will let you know the bad news. In this case, see the instructions following these steps to learn how to install the device by hand.) If, for some reason, you don't want a device installed, deactivate its check box.

8. Click **Next**. The wizard installs the device drivers and then lets you know when everything's done.

9. In the final wizard dialog box, click **Finish**.

If the wizard failed in its quest to find your device, you can stick Windows 2000's nose in it, so to speak, by specifying exactly which device you added. To get started, you have two choices:

➤ If you're starting the Add/Remove Hardware Wizard from scratch, follow the preceding steps 1–5. Then, in step 6, be sure you activate the **No, I Want to Select the Hardware from a List** option, and click **Next**.

➤ If you're still in the wizard at the dialog box that tells you Windows didn't find any new devices, click **Next**.

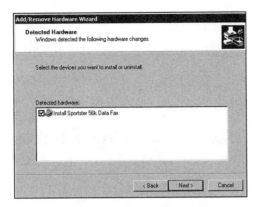

If the wizard successfully hunted down your device, it will show up in this dialog box.

Either way, you now follow these steps:

1. The wizard displays a whack of device categories in the **Hardware Types** list. Highlight the category that applies to your device, and then click **Next**.

2. The wizard takes a few seconds to gather its thoughts, and then it displays a list of device manufacturers and devices. For example, the following figure shows the dialog box that appears for the Network adapters category. You have two ways to proceed from here:

   ➤ Highlight the device maker in the **Manufacturers** list, and then highlight the name of your device in the other list.

   ➤ If your device is nowhere to be found, it's likely that you received a disk inside the device package. Insert the disk and then click **Have Disk**. In the Install from Disk dialog box, enter the location of the disk (type the drive letter followed by a colon (:) and a slash (\), such as **A:**) and click **OK**. (If Windows 2000 complains about not being able to find anything on the disk, click **Browse** and look for a subfolder on the disk.) You'll eventually see a list of models that can be installed. Highlight your model.

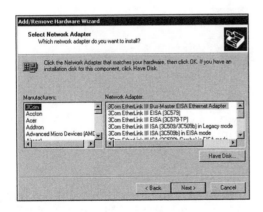

Use this dialog box to pick out the device manufacturer and model.

283

3. Click **Next**. The wizard tells you that it will now install the drivers for the device.

4. Click **Next**. The wizard, true to its word, installs the device drivers. Note that you might need to insert your Windows 2000 CD at this point.

5. When all is said and done, click **Finish** to close the wizard.

Getting Fresh Drivers

There's a good chance the troubleshooter that shows up will want to load a different device driver using the Upgrade Device Driver Wizard. See the next section to learn how this wizard works.

Troubleshooting a Device

If you have a device that doesn't work within Windows 2000, the first thing you should check is that the device is installed properly and turned on. If that doesn't get you anywhere, run the Add/Remove Hardware Wizard once again and be sure the **Add/Troubleshoot a Device** option is activated. When you get to the list of hardware on your system, find your device and see whether it has a yellow icon superimposed on it, as shown in the next figure. If so, highlight the device, click **Next**, and then click **Finish**. This starts one of Windows 2000's troubleshooters, which will help you solve the problem.

If Windows 2000 and a device aren't getting along, you'll see a yellow icon.

Here's the yellow icon. ——

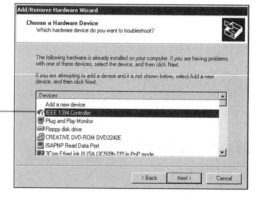

Upgrading a Device Driver

If a device isn't working properly, there's a good chance that its driver has become corrupted, or the driver used during installation was an incorrect version, so you need to replace the driver. You can go about this using either of the following methods:

➤ Follow the troubleshooting steps from the previous section.

➤ Select **Start**, **Settings**, **Control Panel**, and then launch the **System** icon. Display the **Hardware** tab and then click **Device Manager**, which shows a list of all your hardware. Double-click the device, display the **Driver** tab, and then click **Update Driver**.

Either way, you eventually end up at the Upgrade Device Driver Wizard. Here what you do now:

1. Click **Next** to get to a more useful dialog box.
2. Be sure the **Search for a Suitable Driver for My Device** option is activated, and then click **Next**. The wizard displays the dialog box shown here.

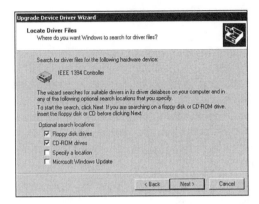

Use this dialog box to tell the wizard where to go.

3. Use the four check boxes to let the wizard know where it should search for the new driver:

   ➤ **Floppy disk drives**   Activate this check box to search your floppy drive for a driver. This is the way to go if you have a floppy disk that came with the device.

   ➤ **CD-ROM drives**   Activate this check box to search your CD-ROM drive for a driver. This is the check box of choice if you have a CD that came with the device, or if you want the wizard to search the Windows 2000 CD.

   ➤ **Specify a location**   Activate this check box to search a specific folder on your hard disk or network for a driver. If you downloaded an updated driver from the manufacturer's Web site, use this option to specify the folder in which you saved the file.

   ➤ **Microsoft Windows Update**   Activate this check box to have the wizard contact the Windows Update Web site for a driver.

Getting Drivers from the Web

The manufacturer's Web site is an excellent place to get the latest and greatest drivers for a device. Look for a link named "Technical Support" or "Device Drivers" or "Downloads."

4. When you've made your choice (or choices), click **Next**. The wizard starts looking for an appropriate driver for the device.

5. If the wizard finds a new driver, it will let you know. Click **Next** to install it. (If no updated driver was found, click **Back** twice, activate the **Display a List of the Known Drivers for This Device...** option, and click **Next**. Now, follow the instructions given earlier for picking out a device driver by hand.)

6. In the final wizard dialog box, click **Finish**.

Removing a Device

If a device suddenly becomes tiresome and boring, or if you get a better device for your birthday, you need to remove the old device from your computer and then let Windows 2000 know that it's gone. The exception to this is if the device supports Plug and Play. If it does, then Windows 2000 will recognize that the device is gone and it will adjust itself accordingly. Otherwise, you need to get the Add/Remove Hardware Wizard on the case again:

1. Select **Start**, **Settings**, **Control Panel**, run the **Add/Remove Hardware** icon, and click **Next** in the first dialog box.

2. Activate the **Uninstall/Unplug a Device** option and then click **Next**.

3. If your device is gone for good, activate **Uninstall a Device**. If you've just unplugged a device only temporarily, activate **Unplug/Eject a Device**. Click **Next**. The wizard displays the list of devices on your system.

4. Activate the device and then click **Next**. The wizard asks whether you're sure about this.

5. Activate **Yes** and click **Next**. The wizard removes all traces of the device.

6. In the last wizard dialog box, click **Finish**.

What Happened

This chapter showed you how to welcome new guests to your computer, and how to kick them out after the party's over. On the software side, you learned how to install programs and how to uninstall them (both automatically and by hand). On the hardware side, you learned how to install the various device types and how to run the Add/Remove Hardware Wizard to let Windows 2000 know about the device. You also learned how to troubleshoot a device, upgrade a device driver, and remove a device.

Crib Notes

➤ **Automatic CDs**   Most computer CD-ROM (and DVD-ROM) discs support AutoRun, so the installation program will run automatically after you insert the disc.

➤ **Installing and uninstalling made easy**   Use Control Panel's **Add/Remove Programs** icon to help you install and uninstall programs.

➤ **Best hardware bets**   To ensure the easiest hardware configuration, buy only devices that are both Plug and Play-compatible and Windows 2000-compatible.

➤ **Peruse the ports**   When installing an external device, remember that its cable can plug into only a single, complementary port on the back of the computer.

➤ **Hardware helper**   If Plug and Play doesn't work, use Control Panel's **Add/Remove Hardware** icon to help you install and uninstall devices.

➤ **Get drivers from the Web**   Remember that most manufacturers offer device drivers for download from their Web site.

Part 5

Taking Care of Your System

Taking care is all the rage these days. When we leave, people are always telling us to "Take care." TV commercials in ad nauseum numbers nag us to take better care of ourselves. It's like we've become a nation of caretakers, eager to grab care wherever we can find it and stuff it into mental pockets for later use.

This mindset serves you well here in Part 5. It's only a couple of chapters long, but they're important chapters if you care at all about taking care of your computer. Chapter 19 shows you how to back up your precious data so that you can recover it just in case something untoward should befall your machine. Chapter 20 takes you through a list of preventative measures and system maintenance techniques for giving your system a healthy glow. Take care!

Chapter 19

Backing Up Your Data (The Better-Safe-Than-Sorry Department)

In This Chapter

➤ Notes on performing real-world backups

➤ Putting together a backup job

➤ Scheduling automatic backups

➤ Recovering backed-up files

➤ Preparing for emergencies

➤ Backup tips and techniques that will help you sleep better at night

Back in Chapter 2, "A Field Guide to Windows 2000 for the Uninitiated," I told you why it was so important to save your documents as often as possible while you work. The reason was that opened documents are held in memory, which is wiped clean when you shut down your computer. To preserve your work, you need to run the Save command to record your changes to the relatively safe confines of your hard disk.

Note the use of the word "relatively" in the previous sentence. Yes, hard disks keep your data intact when you switch off your machine. However, hard disks are also mechanical devices that simply wear out over time. Not only that, but a hard disk can succumb to all kinds of other maladies: computer viruses, power surges (not uncommon during lightning storms), program crashes, hard knocks, and more.

In other words, your data is at risk *right now*. Not months or years from now. *Now*. To help prevent the gray hairs, ulcers, and fists through the monitor that would result from losing all your precious documents, you need to start backing up your system regularly. The good news is that Windows 2000 comes with a backup program that makes it easy to make backup copies of your stuff. You can even set up a backup schedule so that everything happens automatically. This chapter tells you everything you need to know.

Back Up Your Files? Hallelujah!

If I sound like a bit of a backup evangelist, that's probably because I *am* one. You see, I had a hard disk crash on me a couple of years ago. I had been lazy about backing up, which meant that hundreds of my documents and files were lost for good. So, like a reformed smoker who preaches about the evils of tobacco, I'm a reformed non-backer-upper who preaches about the evils of putting off backups.

Backing Up: Some Things to Consider

Other than a few people who insist on living in It-Can't-Happen-to-Me Land, I think most folks get the "why" part of backing up. They just don't get the "how" part. That is, they'd like to run backups, but it's such a time-consuming pain in the you-know-what, so it just doesn't seem worth the hassle. "Sorry, I'd like to do a backup, but I have to call the IRS to schedule an audit."

If backing up seems like too much of a bother, there are plenty of things you can do to make it easier:

Forget floppies   Unlike previous versions (when it went by the NT moniker), you can back up files to floppy disks in Windows 2000. However, that's a bad way to go because it requires about 17 floppies to back up just 100MB. If you're like most people, you probably have hundreds of megabytes to protect, so backing up to dozens of floppy disks is no one's idea of fun, I'm sure.

Use better backup destinations   For easiest backups, use a medium that has a relatively large capacity. That way, you won't spend your time shuffling disks in and out. Windows 2000 supports all kinds of backup and storage devices, but here are a few to bear in mind:

➤ **Zip disks**   These hold 100MB (the latest ones hold 250MB), which is a heckuva lot better than a floppy disk.

➤ **Jaz disks**   These come in 1GB and 2GB flavors, so they have plenty of capacity.

➤ **Tape drives**   These typically come in multigigabyte capacities and are pretty cheap, so they're the most common choice used by backup aficionados.

➤ **Hard disks**   This is a great choice if you happen to have a second hard disk in your system. (Be sure it's a second disk, and not just a single disk that's been divided in two.)

➤ **Network locales**   If you have a small network at home or in a small office, you might consider turning one machine's large hard disk into a backup destination. On larger networks, see whether your system administrator has set aside space for you on a server.

Cross Reference

Before purchasing any device, be sure to consult the Windows 2000 Hardware Compatibility List that I mentioned in the previous chapter. See "Adding On: Installing a Hardware Device," p. 277.

Back up your documents first   The only things on your system that are truly irreplaceable are the documents that you've created with the sweat of your own brow. So, if backup space is at a premium, just include your documents in the backup job. You can always install your programs again later, if need be.

Organize your documents   If you're going to go the documents-only route, you'll make your life immeasurably easier if you store everything in subfolders that all reside within a single folder (such as My Documents). That way, when you're telling Windows 2000 which files to back up, you need only select the main folder. Another plus for this approach is that any files you add to this folder will be included automatically the next time you run the backup.

Back up your downloaded programs   If you've downloaded programs and files from the Internet, it can be a lot of trouble to get new copies of that stuff if your system goes down for the count. So, you should include downloaded files as part of your backup job.

Take advantage of backup types After you've decided on all the files that should be part of the backup, don't waste time by backing up every single one of those files each time you do a backup. Instead, it's possible to use *backup types* to tell Windows 2000 to back up only those files that have changed. Windows 2000 supports no fewer than five backup types:

➤ **Normal** Backs up each and every file, each and every time. (Note that by "each and every file," I mean "each and every file in the backup job.") All files are marked to indicate they've been backed up.

➤ **Incremental** Backs up only those files that have changed since the most recent Normal or Incremental backup. This is the fastest type because it includes only the minimum number of files. Again, the files are marked to indicate they've been backed up.

➤ **Differential** Backs up only those files that have changed since the most recent non-Differential backup. That is, the files are *not* marked to indicate they've been backed up. So, if you run this type of backup again, the same files get backed up (plus any others that have changed in the meantime).

Archive Flags and Other Backup Trivia

How does the Backup program mark files that have been backed up? Well, each file has what's known in the trade as an *archive flag* (sometimes called an archive bit or an archive attribute). When you make changes to a file, that flag gets raised. This is the file's way of saying "Yo, Backup Boy! I need backing up!" When you include a file in a Normal or an Incremental backup, the flag is lowered to indicate that the file has been backed up. Note, however, that a Differential backup does *not* lower the flag.

➤ **Daily** Backs up only those files that were modified on the day you run the backup.

➤ **Copy** Makes copies of the selected files. This type of backup does not mark the files as having been backed up. This means you can use it for quick backups without interfering with your backup strategy (discussed next).

Create a backup strategy Finally, you should come up with a backup strategy that makes sense for you, and then you should stick to that strategy no matter what. A typical strategy might go something like this:

➤ Run a Daily backup each day.

➤ Run an Incremental backup once a week. Delete the previous week's Daily and Incremental backups.

➤ Run a Normal backup once a month. When done, delete the previous month's Incremental and Normal backups.

Creating and Running a Backup Job

Now that we've knocked the whole backup process down to size, let's whip out the brass tacks and get down to business. To get started, select **Start**, **Programs**, **Accessories**, **System Tools**, **Backup**. After a second or two, the Backup window jumps onto the desktop, as shown here. The next two sections take you through the two procedures for backing up: the Backup Wizard and creating a backup job by hand.

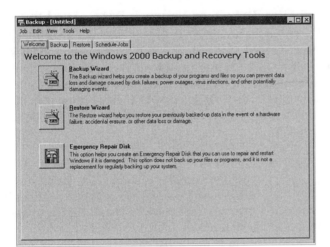

This is the initial screen you see when you crank up the Backup program.

Techno Talk

What's a Backup Job?

I've been using the term *backup job* with abandon so far in this chapter, so let's define it before moving on. A backup job is a file that specifies a few particulars about your backup. These particulars include the files you want backed up, the location where the files will be backed up, and any backup options you specify along the way.

Using the Backup Wizard

The Backup Wizard's step-by-step approach makes it easy to create and launch a backup job. Here's what happens:

1. Click the **Backup Wizard** button, or select **Tools, Backup Wizard**. The Backup Wizard pulls itself out of a hat.

2. As is usually the case, the first Backup Wizard dialog box is completely useless, so click **Next**.

3. The next wizard dialog box gives you three choices (click **Next** when you're done):

   ➤ **Back Up Everything on My Computer**   Select this option to back up absolutely every last thing on your system. This is really practical only if you have a small hard disk or if you have a backup destination with tons of free space. If you choose this route, skip to step 5.

   ➤ **Back Up Selected Files, Drives, or Network Data**   Select this option to pick out exactly which files to back up. This is your best backup bet.

   ➤ **Back Up Only the System State Data**   Select this option to back up just the files that Windows 2000 uses to store its configuration. These are absolutely crucial files, and you'll be able to recover your system much faster if you back them up. However, it's easy to include these files in any backup, so you don't really need to select this option. If you decide to run it anyway, skip to step 5.

One Click Is All It Takes

Now you see why I suggested you include all your documents in sub-folders within My Documents. To back up all your data files, all you have to do is activate the **My Documents** check box. One click and you're done. What could be easier?

4. If you elected to back up only selected files, you'll see the Items to Back Up dialog box shown next. The idea here is that you use the items in the **What to Back Up** list to choose which drives, folders, or files you want to include in the backup. You do this by activating the check box beside each item you want to back up. (To include that "System State" stuff, open the **My Computer** branch and activate the **System State** check box.) When you're ready, click **Next**.

5. Now the wizard wants to know the backup destination. Use the **Backup Media Type** list to choose the type of backup media (such as a file or a tape device) you want to use. Use the **Backup Media or File Name** text box to specify the location of the backup. (You can click **Browse** to choose the location from a dialog box.) Click **Next** to proceed.

6. The wizard displays a summary of the backup job settings. Say "Hold on a minute there, buster!" and click **Advanced**. You'll then run through a series of dialog boxes. Here's a quick summary (click **Next** after each one):

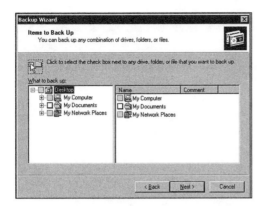

If you decided to select the backup job files yourself, you'll get this dialog box coming at you.

➤ **Type of Backup** Use the **Select the Type of Backup Operation to Perform** to choose a backup type (Normal, Incremental, and so on).

➤ **How to Back Up** If you have ultra-important data and you don't want anything to go wrong, activate the **Verify Data After Backup** check box. This ensures that your data was backed up without mishap, but it basically doubles the total backup time.

➤ **Media Options** You can either append this backup to an existing backup job (this is your best choice in most situations) or have this backup replace an existing backup job.

➤ **Backup Label** Use the text boxes to label the backup job and the backup media. You can leave the suggested text as is.

➤ **When to Back Up** Choose **Now** to start the backup immediately. Alternatively, select **Later** and click **Set Schedule** to run the backup at a future time. See "Staying Regular: Scheduling Backup Jobs," later in this chapter.

7. Click **Finish**. Backup gathers the files and then starts backing them up. If the backup media gets full, you'll be prompted to insert another one. When the backup job is complete, you'll see a report.

8. Click **Close**.

From here, you might want to save your backup job for future use. I'll show you how to do that later on (see "Saving and Reusing Backup Jobs").

Creating a Backup Job with Your Bare Hands

The Backup Wizard ensures that you don't forget anything, but it's a bit of a long haul to get from A to Backup. You can usually speed up the entire process by creating a backup job by hand. To give this a whirl, display the **Backup** tab to get the window shown here.

Use the Backup tab to define a backup job yourself.

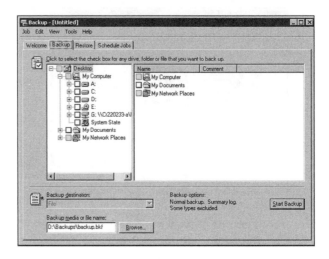

System State Safety

If you want to include Windows 2000's configuration data in your backup (which is a darn good idea), be sure to activate the **System State** check box.

To create the backup job, use the following controls:

➤ **Click to select the check box for any drive, folder, or file that you want to back up** As with the Backup Wizard, you activate the check boxes beside the items you want to include in the backup.

➤ **Backup Destination** Use this list to select the type of backup media you're using.

➤ **Backup Media or File Name** Use this text box to enter the backup location (or click **Browse**).

To choose the backup type, follow these quick steps:

1. Select **Tools**, **Options** to ask the Options dialog box to come out and play.
2. Display the **Backup Type** tab.
3. Use the **Default Backup Type** list to choose the backup type.
4. Click **OK**.

To launch the backup, click the **Start Backup** button. Again, Backup gathers the files and then performs the backup. When you see the report, click **Close**.

Saving and Reusing Backup Jobs

Because you'll be backing up regularly, you'll almost certainly run the same backup job again in the future. To avoid reinventing the backup job wheel, you should save your settings for later use. To do this, be sure the **Backup** tab is displayed and then select **Job**, **Save Selections**. In the Save Selections dialog box, enter a **File Name** for the job, and then click **Save**.

298

To reuse a backup job down the road, display the **Backup** tab and select **Job**, **Load Selections**. If Backup asks whether you want to clear your current sections, click **Yes**. Use the Open dialog box to highlight your backup job, and then click **Open**.

Staying Regular: Scheduling Backup Jobs

Combining my backup tips with the Backup program's ease of use, you see that backing up doesn't have to be drudgery that you avoid at all costs. That's a good thing, to be sure, but it's all for naught if you don't get into the habit of backing up your stuff regularly. We're all busy, I know, so although you might be convinced that backing up is as important as breathing, *remembering* to do it (backing up, that is) can be a problem.

To help out, Backup lets you set up one or more schedules that make everything happen automatically. There are two ways to go about this:

➤ Create a backup job and set up a schedule for it. As described earlier, click **Advanced** in the final wizard dialog box, and then set up the schedule after you see the When to Back Up dialog box. I describe the scheduling details in this section.

➤ Display the **Schedule Jobs** tab, as shown in the following figure. Either double-click the date when you first want to run the backup, or highlight the date and click **Add Job**. This launches the Backup Wizard. Follow the wizard's dialog boxes until you get to the When to Back Up dialog box. At this point, Backup may ask you to enter a password for the schedule. If so, enter the password you want to use in the two text boxes (this isn't an important step, so I usually just leave them blank), and click **OK**.

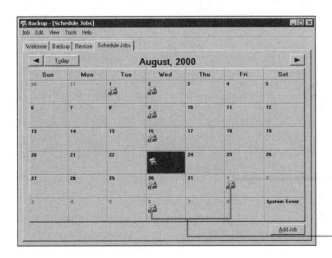

Use the Schedule Jobs tab to view and create scheduled backup jobs.

These icons indicate scheduled backup jobs.

299

Let's run through the specifics of creating a schedule:

1. In the When to Back Up dialog box, enter the name of the backup job in the **Job Name** text box.

2. Click **Set Schedule**. The Schedule Job dialog box appears, right on schedule, as shown here.

Use this dialog box to set up a schedule for the backup job.

3. Use the following controls to set the schedule:

   ➤ **Schedule Task**   Specifies the frequency of the schedule (Daily, Weekly, and so on).

   ➤ **Start time**   Specifies when the backup job begins. If the backup job doesn't require you to swap any disks in and out (in other words, if you can run the backup without being there), then it's best to choose a time when you won't be using your computer (such as the wee hours of the morning).

   ➤ **Advanced**   Click this button to set an **End Date** for the schedule (that is, the date after which the schedule is no longer in effect) and whether you want to **Repeat Task**.

   ➤ **Schedule Task *Whenever***   The group below these options (the name of which depends on what you choose in the Schedule Task list; for example, Schedule Task Once) sets the specifics of the backup frequency. For example, if you selected Weekly in the Schedule Task list, you use this group to specify which day of the week you want the backup to run.

4. The **Settings** tab is chock-full of options for controlling the scheduled backup job. For example, you can have Backup stop the job if it runs beyond a specific length of time, you can have the job run only if your computer has been idle for a while, and much more.

5. When you're done, click **OK**.

Preparing for the Worst: System Recovery Options

If a system goes kaput, one of the most common reasons is a corrupted system file that Windows 2000 requires to get itself out of bed in the morning. Therefore, you can often resurrect a seemingly dead system by repairing those mucked-up files. This sounds like it would be hard, but the Backup program has a feature that makes it relatively easy: the Emergency Repair Disk. This disk contains information about your system that Windows 2000 can use to repair a broken computer.

Creating an Emergency Repair Disk

Here are the steps to follow to create your very own Emergency Repair Disk:

1. In the **Welcome** tab, click the **Emergency Repair Disk** button. Alternatively, select **Tools**, **Create an Emergency Repair Disk**. Backup requests that you insert a blank, formatted disk in drive A.

2. Insert the disk and then click **OK**. Backup tosses the repair info onto the disk and then lets you know when it's done.

3. Click **OK**.

At this point, it would be a good idea to label the disk (use "Emergency Repair Disk" or something equally as dull) and put it in a safe place.

Recovering Your System

Here's the basic procedure to follow if your system has fallen and it can't get up:

1. Insert the first of the Windows 2000 Setup floppy disks in your floppy drive and then restart your computer. (If your system can boot from the CD-ROM drive, put in the Windows 2000 CD, instead.)

2. Run through the first part of the Setup program.

3. Setup eventually asks whether you want to install a fresh copy of Windows 2000 or repair an existing installation of Windows 2000:

   ➤ If you still have access to your hard disk, choose the repair option. When Setup asks how you want to repair your system, be sure you select the fast repair option. Follow the instructions onscreen. This includes inserting the Emergency Repair Disk and your Windows 2000 CD.

   ➤ If your hard disk has been replaced or wiped out, you need to install a fresh copy of Windows 2000.

4. When the repair or installation is complete, restart your computer.

Recovering Files from a Backup Job

When disaster strikes (notice I didn't say *if* disaster strikes), you need to first get your system back on its digital feet as described in the previous section. After that's done, you can then restore your files from your backup job (or jobs). Again, you do this either by using a wizard or by hand.

Using the Restore Wizard

Begin by selecting **Start**, **Programs**, **Accessories**, **System Tools**, **Backup** to launch the Backup program. Here's what happens if you enlist the Restore Wizard to do the job:

1. Either click the **Welcome** tab's **Restore Wizard** button, or select **Tools**, **Restore Wizard**.

2. As usual, click **Next** to get past the Wizard's annoying introductory dialog box. The What to Restore dialog box takes its place.

3. In the **What to Restore** list, open the branch to expose the folders you backed up. Activate the check boxes beside the drives, folders, and files you want to restore (see the next figure) and then click **Next**.

Activate the check boxes for the items you want to restore.

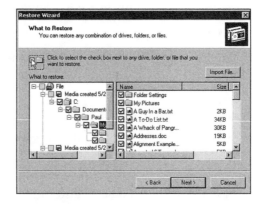

4. Click **Advanced** to run through the following dialog boxes:

   ➤ **Where to Restore**   Choose where you want Backup to place the restored files. You'll usually select **Original Location** for this. You also can choose **Alternate Location** to put the files and folders somewhere else (to avoid overwriting newer versions of the files, for example), or **Single Folder** to put all the files into one folder. (In both these cases, a text box appears so that you can enter the new location.)

   ➤ **How to Restore**   Choose whether Backup should replace existing files that have the same name.

   ➤ **Advanced Restore Options**   You can ignore this dialog box.

5. Click **Finish**. Backup recovers the files and displays a report.

6. Click **Close**.

Restoring Files by Hand

As with backing up, restoring files is a bit faster if you do everything manually. To get started, display the **Restore** tab. Now use the following controls to set up the restore:

➤ **Click to Select the Check Box for any Drive, Folder, or File That You Want to Restore**   Use this list to open the backup job you want to use, and then to activate the check boxes beside the drives, folders, and files you want to restore (see the following figure).

➤ **Restore Files To**   Use this list to specify where you want the files restored.

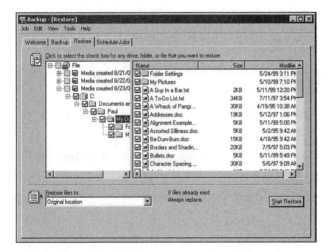

Use the Restore tab to restore your backed-up files by hand.

To determine whether Backup should replace existing files, follow these steps:

1. Select **Tools**, **Options** to get to the Options dialog box.

2. Display the **Restore** tab.

3. Choose the option you want.

4. Click **OK**.

To get the restore operation underway, click the **Start Restore** button. When Backup says something about advanced options, ignore it and click **OK**. In the **Enter Backup File Name** dialog box, be sure the correct backup file is shown, and then click **OK**. Backup restores the files and then displays a report. Click **Close**.

303

What Happened

This chapter gave you one less thing to worry about by showing you how to use Windows 2000's Backup program to make backups of your precious files. I began by running through a few suggestions for making the whole backup process easier and faster. From there, you learned how to back up both with the Backup Wizard and by hand. Should a problem arise, you also learned how to recover backed-up files and create and use an Emergency Repair Disk.

Crib Notes

➤ **One last bit of proselytizing**   Your hard disk is an accident waiting for a place to happen, so start backing up your files right away.

➤ **Easier backups**   To make backups something to look forward to, avoid floppy disks, use a destination with lots of space, keep all your documents in one spot, and use backup types.

➤ **Follow a backup strategy**   Run a Daily backup each day, an Incremental backup each week, and a Normal backup each month.

➤ **Stay on schedule**   For best results, create a backup schedule so that your backups happen automatically.

➤ **Recovering backed-up files**   In the **Welcome** tab, click **Restore**; in the **Restore** tab, use the controls to determine the specifics of the restoration.

Chapter 20

Painless System Maintenance Chores

MOP
MOP

In This Chapter

➤ Expunging unneeded files from your system

➤ Using Check Disk to check your hard drive for errors

➤ Speeding up your hard disk using Disk Defragmenter

➤ Setting up a system maintenance schedule

➤ Using the Windows Update Web site to stay ahead of the curve

➤ Five easy Windows 2000 pieces that will help keep your system in the pink

---

Chapter 19, "Backing Up Your Data (The Better-Safe-Than-Sorry Department),"
showed you how to back up your system and then recover everything when the
inevitable crash occurs. After you've backed up your files, however, that doesn't
mean you should just sit around and wait for your computer to start sucking mud.
("Sucking mud" is a colorful phrase used by programmers to refer to a crashed
machine. Legend has it that the phrase comes from the oilfield lament "Shut 'er
down, Ma, she's a-suckin' mud!") No, what you *should* be doing is a little proactive
system maintenance to help prolong your machine's life and to help propel your
system to new heights of efficiency and speed. This chapter takes you through five
two-word tools that will help you do just that: Disk Cleanup, Check Disk, Disk
Defragmenter, Task Scheduler, and Windows Update.

Cleaning House: Using Disk Cleanup to Delete Junk Files

Ever wonder how much free space you have left on your hard disk? It's easy enough to find out. Just fire up My Computer and highlight your hard disk. As you can see in the following figure, the information area shows you how much free space you have left to work with.

Highlight your hard disk in My Computer to see how much disk real estate is left to be developed.

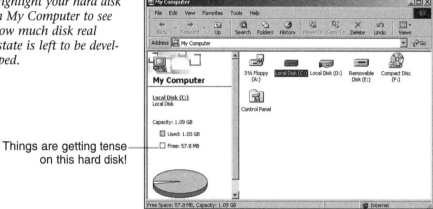

Things are getting tense on this hard disk!

If you find that you're running out of room, Windows 2000 can help. It has a program called Disk Cleanup that can rid your system of all kinds of unnecessary files, including the following:

Check This Out

Running Out of Room

How do you know when your hard disk is getting low on disk space? The answer depends on the disk. If it's the disk where Windows 2000 is stored, then you should never let that disk get much below 100MB of free space. If it's some other disk that you use to store programs and files, then you should start getting worried when the free space drops to around 25MB or 50MB.

➤ **Downloaded program files**   These are miniprograms used by some World Wide Web pages and that are downloaded onto your hard disk when you view such pages. After that, they just sit around doing nothing, so they can be safely deleted.

➤ **Temporary Internet files**   These are copies of Web pages that Internet Explorer keeps on hand so that the pages view faster the next time you visit them. Saying goodbye to these files will slow down some of your surfing slightly, but it will also rescue lots of disk space.

➤ **Offline Web Pages**   These are Web pages that you've set up as favorites and for which you've activated the "Make available offline" feature. This means that Internet Explorer stores updated copies of these pages on your computer for offline surfing. Deleting them means that you'll have to go online to view them.

Cross Reference

For more on using network files even when you're not connected to the network, go to Chapter 22, "Using Windows 2000's Networking Features," and read "You *Can* Take It with You: Working with Offline Files," p. 354.

➤ **Recycle Bin**   These are the files that you've deleted recently. Windows 2000 stores them in the Recycle Bin for a while just in case you delete a file accidentally. If you're sure you don't need to recover a file, you can clean out the Recycle Bin and recover the disk space.

➤ **Temporary files**   These are "scratch pad" files that some programs use to doodle on while they're up and running. Most programs are courteous enough to toss out these files, but a program or computer crash could prevent that from happening. You can delete these files at will.

➤ **Temporary offline files**   These are copies of network files that Windows 2000 saves on your hard disk temporarily. It's pretty safe to delete these files.

➤ **Offline files**   These are permanent copies of network files that reside on your hard disk. Having these files enables you to work with them even when you're not connected to the net-

Cross Reference

I talk about offline Web pages in Chapter 12, "Weaving Your Way Through the World Wide Web." See the section titled "The Unwired Surfer: Reading Pages Offline." p. 190

work. If you no longer need these files, delete them to clear some room on your hard disk.

➤ **Catalog files for the Content Indexer**   These are files that have been left behind by the Windows 2000 Indexing Service. You don't need these files, so you can delete them with abandon.

Cross Reference

In Chapter 3, "Using My Computer to Work with Files and Folders," I discussed the indexing service under "Searching for Long-Lost Files," p. 52.

Follow these steps to use Disk Cleanup to trash any or all of these kinds of files:

1. Windows 2000 offers you two different routes to get started:

   ➤ Select **Start**, **Programs**, **Accessories**, **System Tools**, **Disk Cleanup**. If you have multiple hard disks, the Select Drive dialog box will ask you which one you want to work with. Use the **Drives** list to pick out the drive, and then click **OK**.

   ➤ In My Computer, highlight the hard disk and select **File**, **Properties**. (Alternatively, right-click the hard disk and then click **Properties**.) In the dialog box that beams up, click the **Disk Cleanup** button.

2. Either way, you end up at the Disk Cleanup window shown here. Activate the check box beside each type of file you want to blow to kingdom come.

Use Disk Cleanup to obliterate all kinds of more-or-less useless files from your hard disk.

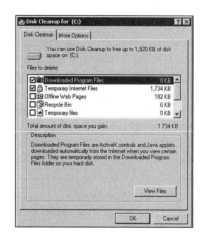

3. Click **OK**. Disk Cleanup asks whether you're sure.
4. Click **Yes**.

Keeping Your Hard Disk Humming with Check Disk

I mentioned in the previous chapter that you should back up your files frequently because all hard disks eventually go to the Great Computer in the Sky. However, it's

possible to avoid a premature hard disk death (as well as lost files and otherwise-inexplicable system crashes) by regularly checking your disk for errors. (By "regularly," I mean about once a week or so.) Here's how you do it:

1. Log on to Windows 2000 with Administrator-level privileges.

2. Shut down any programs that are on the loose.

3. In My Computer, highlight your hard disk and select **File**, **Properties**. (For the heck of it, you also can try right-clicking the hard disk and then clicking **Properties**.)

4. In the dialog box that clears customs, display the **Tools** tab, as shown here.

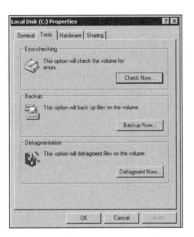

The Tools tab gives you access to a few hard disk tools.

5. Click the **Check Now** button. This gets you an appointment with the Check Disk dialog box.

6. Check Disk offers two checking options:

   ➤ **Automatically Fix File System Errors** Activate this check box to have Windows 2000 handle the dirty work of fixing any file problems that it finds. This gives you one less thing to fret about, so activating this option is a good idea.

   ➤ **Scan for and Attempt Recovery of Bad Sectors** Activate this option to have Check Disk examine the physical surface of the disk for corruption. This is a good idea because a lot of bad sectors means not only that you might not be able to store files reliably, but also that your hard disk might be heading

Sector

A storage location on a hard disk. A "bad" sector is one in which no information can be stored.

for a crash. Note, however, that this slows down the check considerably, so you should probably use this option only once a month or so.

7. Click **Start** to get the Check Disk show on the road.

8. If any errors are found (and you didn't activate the **Automatically Fix File System Errors** option), you'll see a dialog box alerting you to the bad news. Follow the instructions provided.

9. When the check is done, a dialog box lets you know. Click **OK**.

Tidying Up Your Hard Disk with Disk Defragmenter

With its 3D-ish icons and slate blue desktop, Windows 2000 surely presents a polished surface to the world. However, when it's just kicking around at home, Windows 2000 is a bit of a slob. I'm thinking, in particular, about how Windows 2000 stores files on your hard disk. It's actually remarkably casual about the whole thing, and tosses bits and pieces of each file wherever it can find room. This doesn't matter much at first, but after a while you end up with files that are scattered willy-nilly all over your hard disk. This is a problem because it means that to open a file, Windows 2000 has to make lots of little, time-consuming trips to the far corners of the hard disk in order to gather up all those disparate chunks.

Some Stuff About Sectors

Why does Windows 2000 break up files into separate chunks in the first place?

The reason has to do with those sector things I mentioned earlier. The size of each sector varies, but 16KB and 32KB are common. If a file is larger than that, Windows 2000 has no choice but to divide up the file into sector-sized slabs.

Okay, but why are these file nuggets scattered around the disk?

That's because when you delete a file, its sectors become available for other files to use. Windows 2000 is a bit lazy, so when it saves a file, it just uses the first empty sectors that it comes across.

This is why computers that feel nice and zippy when you first take them out of the box seem to get more sluggish over time. In geek terms, the problem is that the files on your hard disk have become *fragmented*. The solution is to run the Windows 2000 Disk Defragmenter program, which will rearrange the contents of your hard disk so that each file's hunks are arranged consecutively (or *contiguously*, as the geeks like to say). Don't worry, though: Your documents and programs don't get changed in any way and your disk contents will look exactly the same when you view them in My Computer.

Defragmenting Other Disk Types

It's worth keeping in mind that Disk Defragmenter also works with zip disks and Jaz disks.

Before getting to the Disk Defragmenter details, here's a bit of prep work you need to do:

➤ Log on to Windows 2000 with Administrator-level privileges.

➤ Shut down all running programs.

➤ Run the Check Disk program to be sure there are no errors on your hard disk. In particular, be sure you activate the **Scan for and Attempt Recovery of Bad Sectors** check box.

➤ Run Disk Cleanup and get rid of any files you don't need.

Here's how Disk Defragmenter works:

1. You can get underway by using either of the following techniques:

   ➤ Select **Start**, **Programs**, **Accessories**, **System Tools**, **Disk Defragmenter**.

   ➤ In **My Computer**, highlight your hard disk and select **File**, **Properties**. (Or right-click the hard disk and then click **Properties**.) In the dialog box that gets piped in, display the **Tools** tab and click the **Defragment Now** button.

2. The following figure shows the Disk Defragmenter window that results. If you have multiple disk drives, click the one you want to work with.

Use Disk Defragmenter to put your hard disk affairs in order.

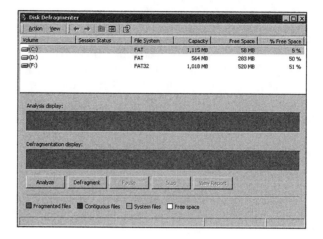

3. Click the **Analyze** button. This tells Disk Defragmenter to have a gander at the chosen disk and see just how defragmented it is.

4. After a few seconds, you'll see the Analysis Complete dialog box, which will display one of the following messages:

   ➤ **This Volume Does Not Need Defragmenting** This is the "Woo hoo!" message because it means your disk isn't fragmented too much and you can bypass the defragment for now. Click **Close** and exit Disk Defragmenter.

   ➤ **It Is Recommended That You Defragment This Volume** Disk Defragmenter tends to be a bit reluctant to call for a defragment, so if you see this message, then you *know* that your system needs to be straightened up. In this case, you should click **Defragment** (although you also can click **Close** and start the defragment from the Disk Defragmenter window).

5. If you're back in the Disk Defragmenter window and you want to run the defragment from there, click **Defragment**. Disk Defragmenter reanalyzes the disk and then gets down to work. While this happens, compare the **Analysis Display** with the **Defragmentation Display**. Over time, you'll start to see more blue (contiguous files) and less red (fragmented files).

This Might Take a While

The defragmenting process might take some time, depending on the size of your disk and how severely fragmented it is. Because it's not unusual for a defragment job to take a couple of hours or more, consider running Disk Defragment just before you leave the office or go to bed.

6. When the job is complete, Disk Defragmenter displays a dialog box to let you know. Click **Close**.

7. If you want to defragment another disk, repeat steps 2–6.

8. To exit Disk Defragmenter, click the **Close** button in the upper-right corner.

Defrag Frequency

How often you use Disk Defragmenter depends on how much you use your computer. If you give your machine a real workout on most days, run the analysis portion of Disk Defragmenter about once a week. If your computer gets only light use, crank up Disk Defragmenter about once a month.

Setting Up a System Maintenance Schedule

As with backing up, performing system maintenance doesn't do you much good if you get around to it only once in a while. If you want to keep your system firing on all cylinders, then you need to perform regular maintenance. In these hectic times, however,

Cross Reference

For the nitty-gritty on scheduling backup jobs, head for the section in Chapter 19 titled "Staying Regular: Scheduling Backup Jobs," p. 299.

it's hard to remember even to eat, much less to run Disk Cleanup once a week. The solution is the Task Scheduler, which is really a special folder called Scheduled Tasks. Its job is to enable you to set up a particular program to run at a specified time, or to run multiple times on a schedule (such as once a week).

Use the Scheduled Tasks folder to keep your main-tenance chores regular.

These tasks were added using the Backup program.

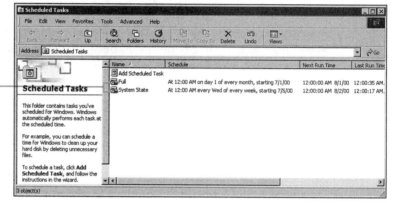

To get started, select **Start, Programs, Accessories, System Tools, Scheduled Tasks**. Windows 2000 donates the Scheduled Tasks folder, as shown here. You usually just see the Add Scheduled Task icon, but you might see other icons that were created by other programs. For example, the Full and System State icons shown in the figure were put there by the Windows 2000 Backup program, as described in Chapter 19.

Here are the steps to run through to create a new schedule for a program:

1. Launch the **Add Scheduled Task** icon. The Scheduled Task Wizard arrives in a flurry of electrons.

2. The first dialog box is as useless as all the other wizard openers, so click **Next**.

3. The next wizard dialog box provides you with a list of programs to schedule, as shown in the following figure. Click the program you want to schedule and then click **Next**. If you don't see the program, click **Browse**, use the Select Program to Schedule dialog box to highlight the program, and then click **Open**. Here are some pointers for the system maintenance tools:

   ➤ **Disk Cleanup**   If this program doesn't appear in the list, use the Select Program to Schedule dialog box to highlight C:\WINNT\system32\cleanmgr.

   ➤ **Check Disk**   Unfortunately, this program can't be scheduled. Bummer.

   ➤ **Disk Defragmenter**   If this program doesn't appear in the list, use the Select Program to Schedule dialog box to highlight C:\WINNT\system32\dfrg.

   ➤ **Backup**   Although it's possible to use the Select Program to Schedule dialog box to pick out this program (it's C:\WINNT\system32\ntbackup), I don't recommend it. Instead, you should use the Backup program's sched-uling feature, because it will set up the scheduled task correctly.

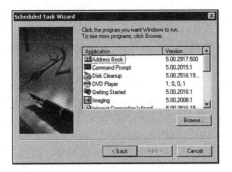

Use this dialog box to pick out the program you want to schedule.

4. The next wizard dialog box asks you to enter a name for the task. (The wizard suggests the name of the program or the name of its file, but you can use anything you want.)

5. You also use this dialog box to pick out the frequency with which you want the task to run: **Daily**, **Weekly**, and so on. When you've made your choice, click **Next**.

6. The layout of the dialog box that shows up next depends on the frequency you chose. For example, the following figure shows the dialog box that lands if you chose the Weekly schedule. Set up the specifics of the schedule, and then click **Next**.

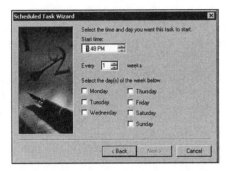

This is the dialog box that appears if you chose the Weekly schedule.

7. Now the wizard pesters you for the username and password of a user. The idea here is that the task will run as though that user were logged on. For example, if you're running Disk Defragmenter, you need to specify a user who has Administrator privileges. Click **Next** when you've entered the info.

8. In the final wizard dialog box, click **Finish**.

If you need to make changes to the scheduled task, highlight it and select **File**, **Properties**. (You also can double-click the task or right-click the task and then click **Properties**.) The dialog box that elbows its way onto the desktop has three tabs. Use

315

Running a Scheduled Task by Hand

You can run a scheduled task at any time by highlighting it in the Scheduled Tasks window and selecting **File**, **Run**. (It's also permissible to right-click the task and then click **Run**.)

the **Task** tab to change the program command and the user info; use the **Schedule** tab to change the program's schedule; and use the **Settings** tab (shown in the following figure) to adjust some scheduling options. Here's a quick look at these settings:

➤ **Delete the Task If It Is Not Scheduled to Run Again** If you set up your task to run only once, activate this check box to have Task Scheduler delete it for you when the task is complete.

➤ **Stop the Task If It Runs for *x* Hours *y* Minutes** Activate this check box to set the maximum number of hours and minutes that the task can take. This is a good idea because it shuts down any task that might be stuck.

➤ **Only Start the Task If the Computer Has Been Idle for at Least** Activating this check box tells Task Scheduler not to run the task if you're still playing with your computer. Use the spin box below it to specify the number of minutes your machine must be idle before the task starts.

➤ **If the Computer Has Not Been Idle That Long, Retry for up To** Use this spin box to specify the number of minutes that Task Scheduler should wait for the computer to become idle.

➤ **Stop the Task If the Computer Ceases to Be Idle** Activating this check box convinces Task Scheduler to bail out of the task if you start using your machine while the task is in progress.

➤ **Don't Start the Task If the Computer Is Running on Batteries** If you activate this check box, Task Scheduler won't bother with the task if it detects that your notebook is on battery power.

➤ **Stop the Task If Battery Mode Begins** Activating this check box orders Task Scheduler to shut down the task if you switch your notebook from AC to batteries.

Use the Settings tab to tweak how the scheduled task runs.

Keeping Up with the Windows Joneses: The Windows Update Web Site

Windows 2000 is a moving target. Oh, it might look stationary, but while you're busy learning where things are and how things work, the Microsoft programmers are busy fixing bugs, improving existing features, and adding new features. In previous versions, these changes would be packaged into massive *service packs* that you could download from the Web or get on CD. With Windows 2000, however, Microsoft is taking a different tack and is going to have individual fixes and improvements available on a special Web site called Windows Update. You just head for that site, pick out the new trinkets you want, and then download them. Everything gets installed automatically, so it's pretty much a no-brainer.

Assuming you have an Internet connection going, follow these steps to use Windows Update:

Cross Reference

For a refresher course on connecting to the Internet, see Chapter 11, "Getting on the Internet," p. 167.

1. Select **Start**, **Windows Update**. Internet Explorer arrives on the scene and loads the Windows Update home page, shown here. (This page will likely change over time, so what you see might be different that what's shown in the figure.)

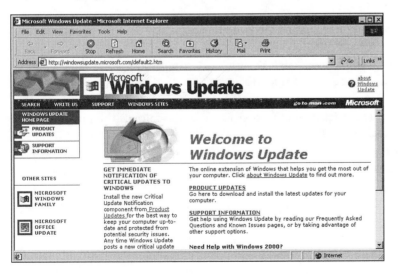

Use the Windows Update Web site to grab the latest and greatest Windows 2000 stuff.

2. Click the **Product Updates** link.

3. If you see a Security Warning dialog box at this point, it just means that Windows Update needs to install some software on your machine. Be sure to click **Yes**.

4. You'll now see a list of the available Windows 2000 updates. The following figure gives you an idea of what the page will look like. (The page you see will probably look a bit different.)

This page presents you with a list of the available updates.

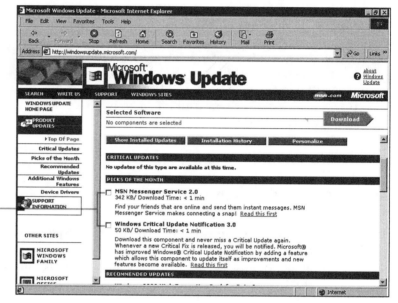

Activate one or more of these check boxes.

5. To download and install an update, activate its check box. Repeat as needed to select all the updates you want.

6. When you're ready to proceed, click **Download**. Internet Explorer takes you to a page that lists all your selected updates.

7. Click **Start Download**. (You'll probably see a License Agreement. If so, shudder at the legalese and click **Yes**.) Internet Explorer downloads the update and then installs it automatically.

8. If Windows 2000 asks you to restart your computer after the upgrade has been installed, click **Yes**.

What Happened

This chapter showed you how to keep your system running smoothly by using Windows 2000's system maintenance tools. You learned how to use Disk Cleanup to trash unnecessary files; how to use Check Disk to scope out hard disk errors; and how to use Disk Defragmenter to be sure your files hang together on your hard disk. I was also happy to show you how to use the Task Scheduler to set up a regular maintenance schedule. I closed by showing you how to use the Windows Update Web site to grab what's new and improved with Windows 2000.

Crib Notes

➤ **The Tools tab**   If you highlight a hard disk in **My Computer** and then select **File**, **Properties**, the resulting dialog box has a **Tools** tab with three buttons: **Check Now** (which runs Check Disk), **Backup Now** (which runs Backup), and **Defragment Now** (which runs Disk Defragmenter).

➤ **Administrator-only tools**   To run Check Disk and Disk Defragmenter, you need to log on to Windows 2000 with Administrator-level privileges.

➤ **Bad-sector check**   Bad hard disk sectors can cause all kinds of woes. Therefore, you should activate Check Disk's **Scan for and Attempt Recovery of Bad Sectors** check box about once a month or so.

➤ **What's the frequency, Kenneth?**   You should run Disk Cleanup every couple of weeks, Check Disk every week (and the bad-sector check every month), and Disk Defragmenter every week (every month if your machine gets only light use). You should check in with the Windows Update Web site once a month or so.

319

Part 6

Getting Connected II: Windows 2000 and Networking

Windows 2000 was born to network. In fact, the Setup program assumes your computer is going to be part of a network, and Windows 2000 almost seems to be disappointed if that turns out not to be the case. So, you'll make your operating system very happy indeed if you get your machine connected to a nearby network. Happily for you, the three chapters here in Part 6 show you how to do exactly that. You learn how to get connected to a network, how to make use of network resources (such as printers), how to let other network users access your computer's resources, and how to dial in to your network from a remote locale. You even learn how to set up your own small network! Just turn the page to begin...

Chapter 21

Using Windows 2000 to Set Up a Small Network

In This Chapter

➤ Getting the scoop on the hardware you need for your network

➤ Learning about the two easiest network structures to use

➤ Network configuration and the Windows 2000 Setup program

➤ Configuring a computer for network duty

➤ Everything you need to know to get your computers up and networking

Large, companywide networks have been around for many years, and until recently networking was an exclusive fiefdom ruled by the panjandrums in the IT department. Nobody minded this situation because a big network was (and is) hideously complex to set up and administer. But then people in small offices and home offices (the SOHO crowd) start noticing the numerous benefits of networking computers: easy file sharing, internal email, reduced hardware expenses (because all the computers can share, say, a single printer), and so on. However, they also worried about the costs associated with networking: paying a consultant thousands of dollars to set up the network, the extra time required to administer everything, the charges for technical support calls, and so on.

My goal in this chapter is to show you how to virtually eliminate those costs while still retaining all of the benefits that a network can bestow. Specifically, I'll show you how to take the computers in your small office or home office and turn them into a small network. You'll learn how to install the hardware, connect everything, and configure each machine. The key word here is *small*. Yes, *large* networks are only for those with a Ph.D. in electrical engineering, but a small network is well within the capabilities of most folks, and that includes *you*. Just follow my simple steps in this chapter and you'll have your network connected before you know it.

Basic Network Know-How

A *local area network* (LAN) is a group of computers that are relatively close together (for example, in the same office or in the same house) and that are connected via a cable that plugs in to special hardware inside each machine. (For variety, I'll use the terms *LAN* and *network* interchangeably in this chapter.) This cable connection enables the computers to share data with one another and access devices (such as printers and CD-ROM drives) on other machines.

Networks come in two basic flavors:

➤ **Client/server** In this type of network, one machine—called the *server*—acts as kind of "boss" to all the other machines—the *clients*. For example, the server usually won't let you and your client computer on the network unless you enter an approved username and password. For this to work, the server computer must use a special *network operating system* designed for servers. For example, you could use Windows 2000 Server, the big brother of Windows 2000 Professional. Note, however, that you *can't* use Windows 2000 Professional as a server operating system.

➤ **Peer-to-peer** In this type of network constitution, all the machines are created equal. That is, no one machine lords it over any of the others, and each computer has more or less equal access to the network. (I say "more or less" because access depends on the privilege level of the user and on which resources the other machines have shared with the network. I'll give you more details on this in Chapter 22, "Using Windows 2000's Networking Features.")

So, which one should you choose? Well, unfortunately, the operating systems required by a server are expensive and relatively difficult to administer. In the end, this means that a client/server setup is overkill for a small network. Conversely, peer-to-peer is a much simpler network style to set up and maintain. Therefore, it's the one I recommend you adopt and it's the one I discuss in this chapter and the next two.

Stuff You Need: Understanding Network Hardware

In a sense, setting up a network is all about setting up the appropriate hardware. This is particularly true of Windows 2000, which (as you'll see a bit later) does a great job of installing whatever networking software is required after it detects (or is told about) the presence of networking hardware. Therefore, it's no exaggeration to say that the key to getting your network configured with the least amount of fuss is to research and purchase the correct hardware bric-a-brac up front. The next few sections tell you everything you need to know.

324

The Connection Point: The Network Interface Card

Networking begins and ends (literally) with a component called the *network interface card*, or NIC, for short. (Depending on the geek you're talking to, a NIC can also be called a *network adapter* or a *network card*.) The network cable (see the next section) that connects all the computers actually plugs into the back of a NIC that resides in each machine. Therefore, the NIC is each machine's connection point to the network.

NICs come in three basic configurations:

➤ **Circuit board**   This is the most common type of NIC, and it plugs into a slot inside the computer. Prices vary widely, but you can get good boards between $80 and $130 (U.S.).

➤ **PC Card (PCMCIA)**   This type of NIC comes in the credit card-size PC Card format and it plugs into a PC Card socket on a notebook computer or a docking station. These are handy for notebook users, but they are slightly more expensive ($100 to $150 [U.S.]).

➤ **Universal Serial Bus (USB)**   This is a relatively new type of NIC, and it plugs into a USB connector in the back of the PC. (Most new PCs come with a couple of USB connectors.) This is, obviously, easier to install than the circuit board type, and they're reasonably priced ($90 to $130 [U.S.]).

Cross Reference

I gave you instructions for installing circuit boards back in Chapter 18, "Installing Software and Hardware." See "Understanding Hardware Types," p. 278.

After you've decided on the basic type (or types) of NIC you want, here's a checklist to run through to help you narrow your search a bit further:

➤ Be sure the NICs support something called *Ethernet*. (This is a type of network architecture, and it's the one used by the vast majority of networks.) There are two varieties: standard Ethernet (which boasts a network speed of 10Mbps and is less expensive) and Fast Ethernet (which runs at a speedy 100Mbps but is slightly more expensive). Note, too, that there are "10/100" NICs that support both types.

Cross Reference

As with all hardware, be sure the NIC you choose is listed on the Windows 2000 Hardware Compatibility List, described in Chapter 18. See "Adding On: Installing a Hardware Device," p. 277.

➤ Be sure the NICs have the appropriate cable ports. As you'll see in the next section, there are two basic types of cable, so you have to be sure that the NICs you choose have a port for the type of cable you decide to use. (Some NICs have ports for both types. Note, too, that a few NICs come with a third type of port—called an AUI port—that's rarely used.)

➤ For easiest installation, get NICs that support Plug and Play.

➤ For fastest performance in a circuit-board NIC, get the type that plugs into a PCI slot inside the computer.

Networking the Home

There have been a number of exciting new developments in the home networking field, including the capability to create a network at home by using your existing phone wiring. To keep up with the latest in this burgeoning area, watch the Home Networking News Web site:

```
http://www.homenetnews.com/
```

The Connection: The Network Cable

Although wireless networks are possible, they're slow and flaky. As a result, the majority of networks use cables to connect the various machines. As I mentioned earlier, your NICs and cables have to match because the cable connects to a port in the back of the NIC, so the port and cable jack must be compatible. Fortunately, although there are lots of different cable types, you need to consider only two when setting up your small LAN: twisted-pair and coaxial.

Twisted-pair cable is the most common type. (It's called twisted-pair because it consists of two copper wires twisted together.) It has on each end an *RJ-45 jack*, which is similar to (but a bit bigger than) the jacks used on telephone cables. The following figure points out the RJ-45 jack and shows a twisted-pair cable plugged into a NIC. Here are some other notes:

➤ This type of cable is most commonly used in the "star" network structure. See "The Star Structure," later in this chapter.

➤ Always ask for "category 5" twisted-pair cable. This is the highest quality and it's suitable for all types of Ethernet networks. It costs a bit more, but it's definitely worth it.

➤ Cables come in various lengths, so be sure you buy cables that are long enough to make the proper connections (but not so long that you waste your money on cable you don't use).

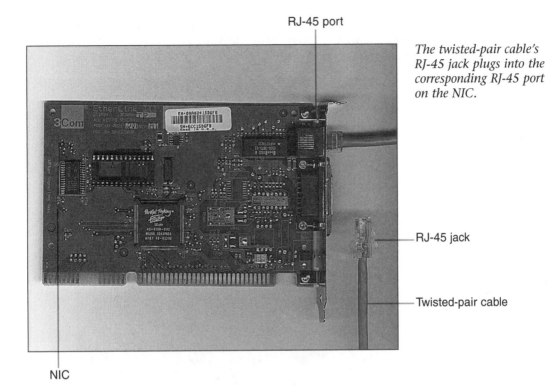

RJ-45 port

The twisted-pair cable's RJ-45 jack plugs into the corresponding RJ-45 port on the NIC.

RJ-45 jack

Twisted-pair cable

NIC

The other type of cable is *coaxial cable* (some network nerds refer to it as *thinnet cable*). It's somewhat reminiscent of the cables used with cable television connections, but network coaxial cable has "bayonet-style" connectors at each end. (They're called bayonet-style connectors because you plug them into the port and then give them a twist to lock them in place. This is similar, I suppose, to the way you connect a bayonet.) To use this type of cable, your NICs must have a corresponding BNC port in the back. The following figure shows an example of a coaxial cable, a NIC with a BNC port, and some other hardware you need.

Notice in the figure that the coaxial cable doesn't plug directly into the NIC. Instead, the cable plugs into a BNC port on the T-connector, and the T-connector plugs into the BNC port on the NIC. The idea is that you'd then plug another coaxial cable into the T-connector's other BNC port (for now, you can ignore the terminator shown in the figure), and then run that cable to another NIC on the network. Here are some notes:

➤ If you're not too clear about how to hook up your network using coaxial cable, I'll discuss this in more detail later on when I discuss the "bus" network structure. See "The Bus Structure," later in this chapter.

➤ Coaxial cable can't go any faster than 10MBps, so you can't use it with Fast Ethernet.

➤ Again, be sure you purchase cables that are the correct length.

If you're not sure which cable type to go with, don't sweat it just now. As I said, each type of cable is associated with a different network structure, so you should check out those structures before deciding on the cable.

The coaxial cable's bayonet-style connector plugs into a T-connector, which then plugs into the corresponding BNC port on the NIC.

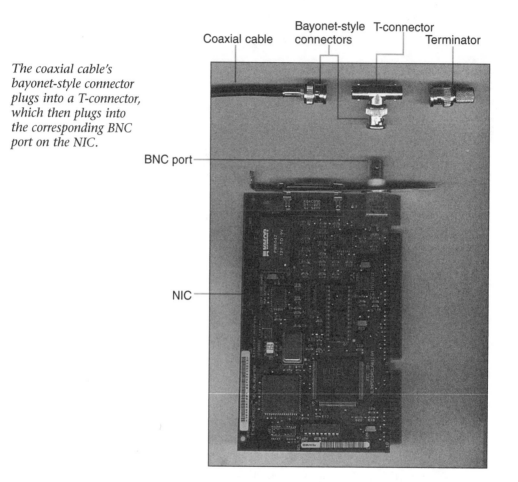

Deciding How to Structure Your Network

The last thing you have to consider before getting down to the short strokes is the overall network structure. The structure determines how each machine is connected to the network. (Networking jockeys use the highfalutin phrase *network topology*.) There are lots of possible structures, but luckily for you there are only two that are suitable for small LANs: star and bus.

The Star Structure

In the *star* structure, each NIC is connected to a *hub*, which serves as a central connection point for the entire network. A hub is a small box that has several (typically 4, 6, or 8) RJ-45 ports. Hubs vary widely in price from simple 10Mbps units that cost under $100 (U.S.) to massive machines costing in the thousands of dollars. For your small network, you shouldn't have to spend more than about $200 (U.S.).

For each computer, you run twisted-pair cable from the NIC to a port in the hub, as shown in the following diagram.

Get the Right Hub, Bub

Your hub must match the type of Ethernet you're using. For example, if you go with Fast Ethernet, then your hub must also support 100Mbps.

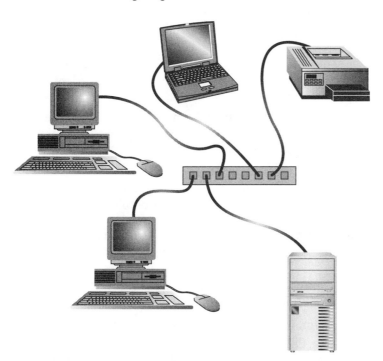

In the star structure, each machine is connected to the network by running twisted-pair cable from the NIC to the hub.

The Bus Structure

In the *bus* structure, each NIC is connected directly to another NIC using coaxial cables, T-connectors, BNC ports, and all that other stuff I mentioned earlier. The following diagram illustrates how this works. As you can see, you run the cable from one T-connector to the next. Note that you can't form a "circle" by attaching a cable from the last NIC to the first NIC. Instead, you have to put special connectors called *terminators* on the T-connectors of the first and last NICs.

Here's the basic bus structure where you connect NICs using coaxial cable. Note the terminators on the first and last NICs.

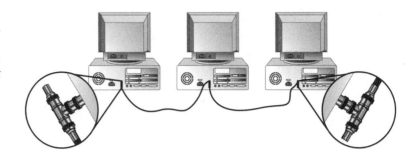

Decisions, Decisions: What Route Should You Take?

I've given you lots of choices to mull over so far, so there's a good chance your head is spinning a bit with all the permutations and combinations. Actually, though, you really have to consider only two configurations:

➤ NICs with RJ-45 ports arranged in a star structure that uses twisted-pair cable to connect each computer to a central hub. Here are the pros and cons of this configuration:

> **Pros** Easy to add and remove computers from the network (just plug them in and out of the hub; network isn't affected if one of the computers goes down; can be very speedy if you go with Fast Ethernet; the most common configuration, so you have a greater selection of NICs and hubs.

> **Cons** More expensive because it requires a hub; requires more cable because each cable must run from the NIC all the way to the hub.

➤ NICs with BNC ports arranged in a bus structure that uses coaxial cable to connect each computer directly. Some pros and cons to consider:

> **Pros** Least expensive; requires less cable because each connection has to reach only to the next computer.

> **Cons** Harder to add and remove computers from the network because each change requires changing the cabling on one or two other machines; entire network goes down if one machine goes down; limited to 10Mbps; lesser selection of NICs.

Of these two configurations, the former is the one I prefer, and it's the one I used to put together the test network that serves as an example throughout the chapters here in Part 6.

Getting a Machine Network-Ready

After you've made your decision about what network hardware to purchase, and after you've installed that hardware, your next task is to set up each machine for networking. The next three sections provide you with some different approaches to this.

Some Notes About Networking and the Windows 2000 Setup

If you're installing Windows 2000 on one or more of the would-be LAN computers, the Setup program takes you through a brief network setup. Here are some notes to bear in mind:

➤ Just prior to the network portion of the show, Setup asks you to enter a computer name. This is the name that other people on the LAN will see for the computer, so enter an appropriate (and unique) moniker. It can be as many as 63 characters long and it should use only letters, numbers, and hyphens. It's standard in small networks to use the first or last name of the person who'll be wrestling with the computer.

➤ If Setup asks whether you want to use a typical or custom network setup, be sure to choose the **Typical Settings** option.

➤ When Setup asks whether you want the computer to be a member of a domain, activate **No** and enter the name of your workgroup in the **Workgroup or Computer Domain** text box. This name can't be longer than 15 characters and can't include any of the following symbols:

  * = + \ | ; : " , < > ?

Workgroup Names Must Be Universal

For your LAN to work successfully (and simply), all the computers must use the same workgroup name. If you have a machine that uses a different name, I'll show you how to change it a bit later (see "Step 2: Identifying the Computer").

What's a Domain?

In case you're curious, a *domain* is a special type of workgroup that's monitored and controlled by a network server. They offer higher-level security and easier access to network resources. However, they're not suitable for your small network because you won't have the appropriate network server operating system.

"Look, Ma, No Hands!" Networking

If Windows 2000 knows anything, it's networking. In fact, as soon as Windows 2000 detects your NIC, it automatically busies itself behind-the-scenes by installing all the various software bits and pieces that are required to work with the network connection. In other words, you just attach the NIC (I'm assuming here that it's Plug and Play-compatible), fire up your machine, and within a few minutes of Windows 2000 starting, the computer will be network-ready.

How can you tell? The easiest way is to select **Start**, **Settings**, **Network and Dial-Up Connections**. When the Network and Dial-Up Connections window shows up, look for a **Local Area Connection** icon (see the following figure). If you see one, then your computer is connected to your LAN. Just like that!

There are a couple of things that might get in the way of this suspiciously easy process:

Wait for the Icon

It takes Windows 2000 a minute or two to install everything after it detects your NIC. So, if you don't see the Local Area Connection icon, give Windows 2000 a bit of time to get its act together.

➤ **Windows 2000 didn't recognize your NIC automatically** This can happen if the NIC isn't Plug and Play-friendly. In this case, see "Step 1: Telling Windows 2000 About Your Network Card" in the next section.

➤ **Windows 2000 doesn't have the right workgroup name** As I said, you enter the workgroup name during the Windows 2000 installation process. However, if you attached the NIC after the installation, Windows 2000 uses the generic name WORKGROUP. If this isn't right, or if you entered the incorrect name during Setup, you need to change it. See "Step 2: Identifying the Computer" in the next section.

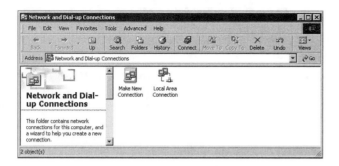

If you see the Local Area Connection icon, say, "Yippee!" because your computer is now a full-fledged member of the LAN.

The Five-Step Network Setup

If the automatic network setup didn't come to pass, all is not lost because you can still get things together by hand. This section presents a five-step program for configuring and tweaking the software side of a computer's network connection. However, there's a good chance you'll be able to get your computer on the network just by following Steps 1 and 2. How will you know when the network connection is successful? There are two things to look for:

➤ Select **Start**, **Settings**, **Network and Dial-Up Connections** and look for the **Local Area Connection** icon in the Network and Dial-Up Connections window. This tells you that your NIC is working fine and that Windows 2000 sees the network.

➤ Launch the desktop's **My Network Places** icon, and then launch the **Computers Near Me** icon. If all is well, then a window will appear that contains icons not only for your computer, but also for the other computers in your workgroup.

Step 1: Telling Windows 2000 About Your Network Card

Before we begin, note that everything in this section requires that you be logged in to Windows 2000 with Administrator-level privileges.

If your NIC doesn't support Plug and Play, Windows 2000 will likely walk right on by it during startup. In that case, you need to run the Add/Remove Hardware Wizard to give Windows 2000 a chance to detect the card. If the automatic detection doesn't sniff out the NIC, you should be able to pick out the NIC yourself. When you get to the list of hardware types, be sure to highlight **Network Adapters**.

Cross Reference

You learned about the Add/Remove Hardware Wizard in Chapter 18. For a reminder, check out "Running the Add/Remove Hardware Wizard," p. 281.

Step 2: Identifying the Computer

The network identity of your computer involves three things:

➤ **The computer name** This is a name that uniquely identifies the computer within the workgroup, and it's the name that you see when you open the Computers Near Me icon in My Network Places. You can use names as many as 63 characters long, and it's safest just to use letters, numbers, and hyphens. Most people enter the first or last name of the person who uses the computer.

➤ **The workgroup name** All the computers in your small network must enter the same workgroup name for them all to appear in the same workgroup. The name can be as many as 15 characters long, and it can't include any of the following symbols:

```
* = + \ | ; : " , < > ?
```

➤ **Whether the computer is part of a domain** A *domain* is a larger network grouping that is administered by a dedicated server. Your small network uses a workgroup, instead.

Here's how to change the network identity of a computer:

1. Windows 2000 offers a couple of routes to get things off the ground:

   ➤ Select **Start**, **Settings**, **Control Panel**, launch the **System** icon, and then display the **Network Identification** tab.

   ➤ Select **Start**, **Settings**, **Network and Dial-Up Connections** to get to the Network and Dial-Up Connections window. Select **Advanced**, **Network Identification**. This takes you to the System Properties dialog box with the Network Identification tab already selected.

2. Examine the **Full Computer Name** value and the **Member of Workgroup** value to see whether they're what you want.

3. If not, and you want to use a wizard to make your adjustments, click **Network ID** and follow the bouncing dialog boxes. However, I think it's easier and more direct to click **Properties** and end up in the Identification Changes dialog box, shown here.

Use this dialog box to change your computer's network ID.

4. Use the **Computer Name** text box to enter the computer name you want to use.

5. Activate the **Workgroup** option and then enter the workgroup name in the text box below it.

6. Click **OK**. A friendly dialog box drops by with a welcome message for the workgroups.

7. Click **OK** to return to the Network Identification tab.

8. Click **OK**.

9. When Windows 2000 asks whether you want to restart your computer, click **Yes**.

Step 3: Installing a Network Client

The rest of these network setup steps shouldn't be necessary. However, I'll take you through them just so you have a complete understanding of what's involved.

This section shows you how to install a *network client*. This is software that provides the basic networking functionality. The best client for our purposes is the Client for Microsoft Networks, which should be installed automatically. Here's how to check (and install it, if need be):

1. Select **Start**, **Settings**, **Network and Dial-Up Connections** to return once again to the Network and Dial-Up Connections window.

2. Highlight the **Local Area Connection** icon and then select **File**, **Properties**. (As usual, you also have the option of right-clicking the icon and then clicking **Properties**.) Windows 2000 sends in the Local Area Connection Properties dialog box, shown here.

3. If the **Client for Microsoft Networks** component is in the list, be sure its check box is activated. Click **OK** and skip the rest of these steps.

4. If you don't see it, click **Install** to bring up the Select Network Component Type dialog box.

5. Highlight **Client** and click **Add**. Windows 2000 displays a list of network clients.

6. Highlight **Client for Microsoft Networks** and click **OK**. Windows 2000 installs the client and then returns you to the Local Area Connection Properties dialog box.

This dialog box lists the various software components that comprise your network connection.

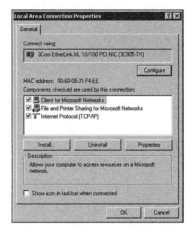

Step 4: Installing File and Printer Sharing

File and printer sharing is a crucial networking component because it enables your computer to give other network users access to certain of the machine's resources, such as a printer, a CD-ROM drive, a folder, and so on. This is called *sharing* those resources. Here's how to check for (and install, if necessary) file and printer sharing:

1. Select **Start**, **Settings**, **Network and Dial-Up Connections**, highlight the **Local Area Connection** icon and then select **File**, **Properties** to return to the Local Area Connection Properties dialog box.

2. If you see the **File and Printer Sharing for Microsoft Networks** component listed, be sure its check box is activated, click **OK**, and then bypass the rest of these steps.

3. If you don't see it, click **Install** to parlay with the Select Network Component Type dialog box.

4. Highlight **Service** and click **Add**. Windows 2000 hands you a list of available network services.

5. Highlight **File and Printer Sharing for Microsoft Networks** and click **OK**. Windows 2000 installs the service and runs you back to the Local Area Connection dialog box.

Step 5: Installing Network Protocols

The last component we'll deal with is the *network protocol*. This is a bit of software that determines how computers exchange information over the network. The key thing here isn't so much *which* protocol you use, but the fact that every computer in the workgroup must have *at least one* protocol in common. (A good analogy is to think of a group of people from different countries. They can communicate with one another only as long as they all have at least one language in common.)

In the typical Windows 2000 network setup, a protocol named *Internet Protocol (TCP/IP)* is installed. This should be all you need. Again, however, you can check that this protocol is installed, and possibly install TCP/IP or some extra protocols, by following these steps:

1. Select **Start**, **Settings**, **Network and Dial-Up Connections**, highlight the **Local Area Connection** icon and then select **File**, **Properties** to return to the Local Area Connection Properties dialog box.

2. If you see the **Internet Protocol (TCP/IP)** component listed, be sure its check box is activated, click **OK**, and then skip the rest of these steps.

3. To install a protocol, click **Install** to reunite with the Select Network Component Type dialog box.

4. Highlight **Protocol** and click **Add**. Windows 2000 digs up a list of available protocols.

5. Highlight the one you want—your best bets here are **Internet Protocol (TCP/IP)** and **NetBEUI Protocol**—and click **OK**. Windows 2000 installs the protocol and leaves you at the Local Area Connection dialog box.

6. Click **OK**.

What Happened

This chapter gave you the know-how you need to create a network suitable for a small office or home office. After a brief discussion of the benefits of a network, you learned why a peer-to-peer setup was best. From there, I took you on a tour of network hardware, including network interface cards and network cables, and then I showed you the two basic network structures: star and bus. The rest of the chapter looked at network setup both during and after the Windows 2000 installation.

Crib Notes

➤ **Peer-to-peer is peerless**   For a small network, use the peer-to-peer configuration because it's easier to maintain and much cheaper.

➤ **The nicest NICs**   Get NICs that support Ethernet (Fast Ethernet is best), are compatible with your network cable, and support Plug and Play.

➤ **The cable conundrum**   If you plan on using a star structure, you'll need twisted-pair cable (category 5 cable is highly recommended); if the bus structure is more your speed, go for coaxial cable.

➤ **Workgroup names**   Be sure that all the machines in your network use the same workgroup name.

➤ **The ideal network setup**   For foolproof networking, each machine's list of networking components should include Client for Microsoft Networks, File and Printer Sharing for Microsoft Networks, and Internet Protocol (TCP/IP).

Chapter 22

Using Windows 2000's Networking Features

In This Chapter

- ➤ Logging on to your network
- ➤ Getting to know the My Network Places folder
- ➤ Understanding users and permissions
- ➤ Graciously sharing your resources with the network
- ➤ Greedily accessing shared network resources
- ➤ Working with network files while not connected
- ➤ Lots of handy techniques that help you put all your hard (net)work to good use

With your network hardware gadgetry installed, the cables slung, and the workgroup computers configured for working in a group, your network is dressed to the nines and ready to party. Unfortunately, however, there isn't much partying that can be done at this stage. Think of a bunch of elegantly dressed people who've gone to a party and have been forced to stand in their own phone booths. (Yes, this *is* a seriously weird party.) They can see one another, and the technology is there to communicate with one another, but no one knows anyone else's phone number. That's pretty much the situation with the computers in your workgroup. They can see one another over the network, but that's about all they can do.

This chapter shows you how to get your workgroup party into high gear. I'll spend most of the chapter talking about *shared resources*: disk drives, folders, printers, and even Internet connections that have been set up so that people on the network can access and use them. You'll also learn a few other network techniques that will help you take advantage of this networked beast that you've built.

Startup Stuff: Logging On to Your Computer

Before getting to the juicy networking tidbits, let's take a second to talk about logging on to your computer. Even if you don't see any kind of log on prompt at startup, you're still logging on to the system. It's just that Windows 2000 is doing it behind the scenes. That's fine if you have a standalone computer (unless you're sharing the machine with other people), but it's not a good idea in a network environment. That's because, as you'll see later, logging in may give you automatic access to some network resources. Therefore, you don't want just anyone to be able to start up a machine and get into the network. Instead, for extra protection, you should give them a logon hurdle to jump at startup. Here's how:

1. Select **Start**, **Settings**, **Control Panel** and then launch the **Users** and **Passwords** icon.

2. This stuff requires Administrator-level privileges, so at this point you might see a dialog box asking for the username and password of an administrator. If so, enter the values and click **OK**. You end up at the Users and Passwords dialog box.

3. Be sure the **Users Must Enter a User Name and Password to Use This Computer** check box is activated.

Shared Resource

A local folder, disk drive, or printer that has been set up so that people on the network can use it.

4. For an extra level of security, you also can set up Windows 2000 to require a "secure boot." This just means that users have to press **Ctrl+Alt+Delete** at startup to get to the logon dialog box. This ensures that no one can break into your system and that no potentially harmful programs can run at startup. To set this up, display the **Advanced** tab and activate the **Require Users to Press Ctrl+Alt+Delete Before Logging On** check box.

5. Click **OK**.

6. If Windows 2000 asks whether you want to restart your computer, click **Yes**.

Your Starting Point: The My Network Places Folder

Most of your network travels will set sail from a special folder called My Network Places. Windows 2000 offers several ways to get there:

➤ Launch the desktop's **My Network Places** icon.

➤ Open **My Computer** and click the **My Network Places** link in the information panel on the left.

➤ Display My Computer's Folders bar and highlight **My Network Places** in the tree.

Whichever method you prefer, you end up with the My Network Places window staring back at you, as shown in the following figure.

The My Network Places folder is the starting point for your network meandering.

In its default guise, My Network Places offers you three icons:

➤ **Add Network Place** You use this icon to set up another computer's shared resource for use from your machine. See "Setting Up Network Places," later in this chapter.

➤ **Computers Near Me** This icon represents your workgroup. Launching this icon displays the Computers Near Me window, which will have one icon for each computer in the workgroup (see the next figure). From there, you launch an icon to open another window for the computer and see which resources they've shared. See "Playing with Other Folks' Shared Resources," later in this chapter.

➤ **Entire Network** This icon represents the network as a whole. On your small network, this is the same thing as your workgroup. In larger networks, however, opening this icon would display all the defined workgroups and domains. Because that's not the kind of network we're dealing with in this book, I'll ignore this icon.

The Computers Near Me window has an icon for each computer in your workgroup.

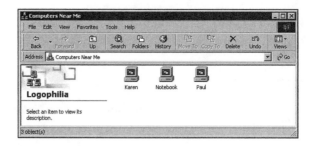

Workgroupies: Notes About Permissions and Users

As you'll see a bit later, when you share a folder or a printer so that it's available to the network, you must assign *permissions* to that shared resource. This just means that you specify who is allowed to access the resource. Windows 2000 gives you no fewer than four categories of permissions:

➤ **Everyone**   This catchall category gives everyone access to the resource, no questions asked.

➤ **Groups**   This category means that only those users who are members of a particular group (such as the Administrators group) can access the resource.

➤ **Computers**   This category assigns permissions to a computer name, which means that anyone who is logged on to that computer can access the resources.

➤ **Users**   This category assigns permissions to individual users.

Assigning permissions at the user level gives you the greatest flexibility to tailor who gets to mess with what on each machine. However, it does come with a couple of downsides:

➤ It takes the most work because each workgroup computer has to be told about each of the other users in the workgroup. And if you add a new user or remove a user, you have to make the adjustment on every machine.

➤ It represents a security risk because essentially you're giving every other user the capability to log on to every other machine using their own username and password.

For these reasons, I don't recommend going with user permissions. However, if you still want to try it, here are the steps to follow to configure a machine so that it knows about the users in a workgroup:

1. Select **Start**, **Settings**, **Control Panel** and then launch the **Users and Passwords** icon.

2. As before, enter an administrator's **User Name** and **Password**, if prompted. The following figure shows the Users and Passwords dialog box that eventually reaches you.

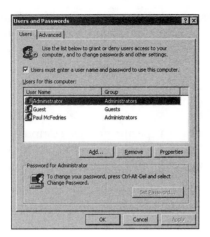

Use this dialog box to set up your workgroup's users on each machine.

3. Click **Add**. The Add New User wizard makes the scene.

4. Enter the **User Name** (the **Full Name** and **Description** are optional) and click **Next**.

5. Use the **Password** and **Confirm Password** text boxes to enter the user's password, and then click **Next**.

6. The wizard now asks you to assign an access level for the user. This doesn't affect the share permissions, so it's not that important. However, if you're worried about the user being able to log on to your computer, give them the lowest possible level: Activate **Other** and then highlight **Guests** in the list.

7. Click **Finish** to return to the Users and Passwords dialog box.

8. Repeat steps 3–7 to add other users, if necessary.

9. When you're done, click **OK** to exit the Users and Passwords dialog box.

Sharing Your Resources So Other Folks Can Play with Them

The lifeblood of any peer-to-peer network is the resources that have been shared by the various computers in the workgroup. To see why, just consider the variety of things that can be shared:

➤ **Folders**   You can set up common folders so that some or all of the network users can access files and documents.

➤ **Disk drives**   You can give users access to entire drives, including zip and Jaz drives.

➤ **CD-ROM drives**   You can set up a shared drive so that another user who doesn't have a CD-ROM drive can still run a program or access data. (Note that not all programs will run from a shared network CD-ROM.)

➤ **Printers**   By sharing a printer, you save either the expense of supplying each user with their own printer, or the hassle of moving a printer from one machine to another.

➤ **Internet connections**   You can set up an Internet connection on one machine and the other computers in the workgroup can then use that connection to access the Internet.

Not only can you share those resources with specific groups, computers, or users, as described earlier, but you also can tailor these permissions to give, for example, read-only access. The next couple of sections take you through the specifics of sharing resources.

Sharing Folders and Disks

The procedure for sharing a folder or a disk drive is the same. Here are the steps to follow:

1. In **My Computer**, display the folder or disk drive you want to share.
2. Highlight the folder or drive and then select **File**, **Sharing**. (Another approach is to right-click the folder or drive and then click **Sharing**.) The resource's Properties dialog box appears, and the Sharing tab is displayed.
3. Activate the **Share This Folder** option. (If this option is already activated, click **New Share**.)

Those Weird "Hidden" Shares

Windows 2000 creates a few so-called *hidden* shares during setup. For example, drive C has a hidden share named C$. (The $ at the end is what makes the share hidden.) These are for administrators so they can connect to any computer without having to worry about whether the user has shared a drive. This is why you'll sometimes go to share something and you'll see that it appears to already have been shared behind your back.

4. Enter a **Share Name** for the resource. The default here is the name of the folder or the letter of the drive, but feel free to use whatever you like.
5. Enter a **Comment** that describes the resource. The following figure shows an example of the Sharing tab filled in so far.

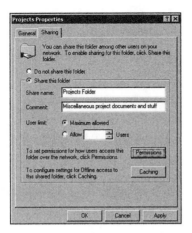

Use the Sharing tab to specify how you want a folder or disk drive shared with the network.

6. The **User Limit** options determine the maximum number of people who can access the resource at once. This isn't a concern on a small network, so just leave **Maximum Allowed** activated.

You come to a fork in the sharing road, at this point. If you want to give everyone on the network full access to the folder or drive, click **OK**. If, instead, you want to restrict access to the folder or drive, then you need to get into the whole permissions thing. That's the subject of the next section.

Sharing Adds an Icon to the Icon

After you share a resource, its icon gets tweaked a bit. Specifically, a hand with an open palm gets added underneath the icon, as though to "serve" the resource to the network.

The "In" Crowd: Setting Permissions

If the thought of just any network Tom, Dick, or Harriet being able to access your shared folder or drive gives you the willies, permissions will calm you down. Here's how to set them up:

1. In the **Sharing** tab, click **Permissions**. Windows 2000 sends out the Permissions for *x* dialog box, where *x* is the share name of the resource. The first time this happens, you should see **Everyone** in the **Name** list.

2. If you don't want to use the Everyone group, click **Remove**.

3. To get a new permission, click **Add**. The Select Users, Computers, or Groups dialog box is waved in.

4. Use the **Name** list to highlight who or what gets the permission:

➤ **Users**   These are the items that have an icon consisting of a single head. Be sure that the name of your computer is showing in the **Look In** list.

➤ **Groups**   These are the items that have an icon consisting of two heads in front of a computer. You have six choices: Administrators, Backup Operators, Guests, Power Users, Replicator, and Users. Again, you need to have the name of your computer displayed in the **Look In** list.

➤ **Computers**   These are the items that have an icon consisting of just a computer. To see these items, you have to select the name of your workgroup in the **Look In** list, as shown here.

Use this dialog box to choose the users, groups, or computers that get permission to access your shared resource.

To select a computer, choose your workgroup here...

...and then select the computer here.

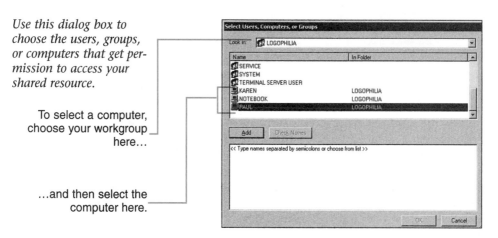

5. Click **Add**. The item gets plopped into the list.

6. Repeat steps 4 and 5 to add other items.

7. When you're done, click **OK**. This gets you back to the Permissions dialog box.

8. Now, for each item you added, you use the **Permissions** list to specify exactly what each one can do. Use the **Allow** and **Deny** check boxes to toggle the following permissions:

    ➤ **Read**   People can only view and open files and folders. They can't make any changes.

    ➤ **Change**   Same as Read, except users can also create new files and folders, rename and delete files and folders, and edit files.

➤ **Full Control** Same as Change. However, if you're using the NTFS file system, users can change file and folder permissions and take ownership of files and folders.

9. When you're finished, click **OK**.

What's All This About NTFS?

NTFS is a special file system supported by Windows 2000, and it gives you extra goodies such as the capability to assign permissions to specific files. To see whether a disk drive uses NTFS, highlight the drive in My Computer and select **File, Properties**. In the dialog box that pays a visit, look at the **File System** line and see whether it says **NTFS**.

Sharing a Printer

You'll be happy to hear that sharing a printer is a much simpler process than sharing a file or folder. In fact, sharing an existing printer takes just four steps:

1. Select **Start**, **Settings**, **Printers** to open the Printers folder for business.

2. Highlight the printer you want to share, and then select **File**, **Sharing**. (On the other hand, you might feel like right-clicking the printer and then clicking **Sharing**.) The printer's Properties dialog box appears, and the Sharing tab is conveniently picked out from the herd.

3. Activate the **Shared As** option and then enter a name for the share in the text box beside it (see the following figure).

4. Click **OK**.

Different Printer Strokes for Different Windows Folks

I'm assuming in these networking chapters that all your workgroup computers are running Windows 2000. However, it's no big whoop to include machines running other networkable flavors of Windows. If you do have a mixed bag of machines, you'll need to install the appropriate printer drivers for each Windows version you have. (There are drivers available for Windows 95 and 98, as well as Windows NT 3.1, 3.51, and 4.0.) To do that, click **Additional Drivers** to get a list of drivers, activate the check boxes beside each one you need, and then click **OK**.

Use the Sharing tab to share your printer with the network.

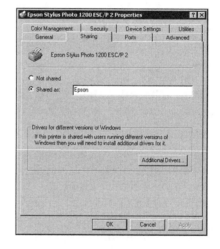

Cross Reference

Details on installing a new printer are in the "Got a New Printer? Tell Windows 2000 About It!" section, p. 72.

If you haven't installed your printer yet, you can set up sharing when you tell Windows 2000 about the printer. Just follow the steps that I outlined back in Chapter 5, "From Vapor to Paper: Printing Documents." When you get to the Add Printer Wizard's Printer Sharing dialog box, activate **Share As** and enter a name for the share.

Sharing an Internet Connection

Printers aren't the only things that can have their costs defrayed over multiple machines. Internet connections also can be spread among two or more computers, which saves you the expense of maintaining separate accounts. Assuming you have a working Internet connection on one computer, here's how to modify that connection to share it with the workgroup:

1. Open the **My Network Places** folder, as described earlier, and then click the **Network and Dial-Up Connections** to fire up the Network and Dial-Up Connections window.

2. Highlight the icon for the Internet connection, select **File**, **Properties**, and then display the **Sharing** tab, shown here.

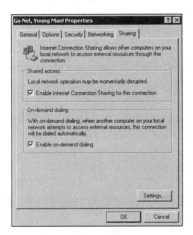

Use the Sharing tab to share access to the Internet.

3. Activate the **Enable Internet Connection Sharing for This Connection** check box.

4. I recommend leaving the **Enable On-Demand Dialing** check box activated. When this option is on, it means that Windows 2000 will automatically connect to the Internet when a workgroup computer tries to get to a Net site.

5. Click **OK**. Windows 2000 displays a long-winded message that talks about IP addresses and other gobbledygook. It eventually asks whether you're sure you want shared access.

6. Click **Yes**.

As far as the rest of the workgroup computers are concerned, you have to set them up to access the Internet through the network. Here's how:

1. Launch the Internet Connection Wizard.

2. Activate the **I Want to Set Up My Internet Connection Manually...** option and click **Next**.

Cross Reference

The full scoop on setting up an Internet connection can be found in the section titled "Interstate 13: Setting Up an Existing Account Manually," p. 170.

3. Activate **I Connect Through a Local Area Network (LAN)** and click **Next**.

4. Be sure the **Automatic Discovery of Proxy Server** option is activated, and click **Next**.

5. From here, follow the rest of the steps as outlined in Chapter 11, "Getting on the Internet."

Playing with Other Folks' Shared Resources

With your workgroup machines generously sharing their folders, drives, and printers, it's now time to see just how to get at those resources. There are four ways to go about this:

➤ **Access the resources directly** You do this by opening **My Network Places**, opening **Computers Near Me**, and then opening a computer. As you can see in the following figure, Windows 2000 then shows the shared resources for that computer. (To see the Comment column, select **View**, **Details**.) Now just open the shared folders and drives and work with them the same way you would a local folder or drive (depending on what level of permission you have, of course).

Opening a workgroup computer displays that machine's shared resources.

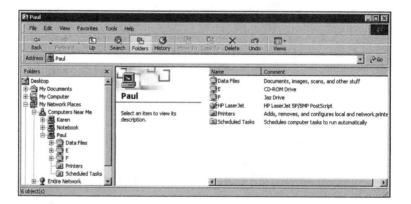

➤ **Define a network place** This is an icon that resides in the My Network Places folder, and it points to a shared resource. This saves you drilling down to the network computer to get to the resource. See "Setting Up Network Places," later in this chapter.

➤ **Map a shared folder or drive** This takes a shared folder or drive and assigns it to an available drive letter on your system. For example, if your hard disk is drive C and your CD-ROM drive is drive D, then you could set up a shared folder or drive as drive E. This gives you even easier access to the shared resource. See "Making Network Folders Look Like Drives on Your Computer," later in this chapter.

➤ **Install a network printer** This enables you to print from your machine and have the hard copy appear on the network printer. (You'll have to pick it up yourself, though. Networks are convenient, but they're not *that* convenient.) Check out "Printing over the Network," a bit later.

Setting Up Network Places

Here are the steps involved in creating a network place for a shared folder or drive:

1. In the **My Network Places** folder, launch the **Add Network Place** icon. The Add Network Place Wizard takes charge.

2. Use either of the following methods to specify which shared folder or drive you want to work with:

➤ Use the text box to enter the location of the shared resource. Type two back-slashes (\\) followed by the computer name, followed by another backslash (\). The wizard helpfully displays a list of the available shares, as shown in the following figure. Select the one you want.

➤ Click **Browse** to arrive at the Browse Network Resources dialog box, highlight the computer that has the resource, and click **OK**. Now type a backslash (\), and then select the share from the list that drops down.

Type a couple of back-slashes, the computer name, and another back-slash, and Windows 2000 displays a list of that computer's shares.

3. The last of the wizard's dialog boxes suggests a name for the new network place, which takes the form *Share Name* on *Computer Name*. Edit the name, if you feel like it, and then click **Finish**.

You end up with a new icon in My Network Places for the shared resource. Windows 2000 is also kind enough to open a window for the resource automatically. In the future, you open the same window by launching the resource's icon in My Network Places.

351

Making Network Folders Look Like Drives on Your Computer

You can avoid the My Network Places folder altogether if you map a network folder or drive so that it takes up a drive letter on your system. Here's how:

1. Using **My Network Places** and its **Computers Near Me** folder, display the shared resources of the workgroup computer you want to work with.

2. Highlight the shared folder or drive you want to map, and then select **File**, **Map Network Drive**. (As you might have guessed by now, you also can right-click the folder or drive and then click **Map Network Drive**.) Up pops the Map Network Drive dialog box, shown here.

Use this dialog box to map a network resource to a drive letter on your computer.

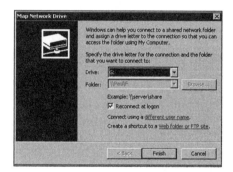

3. Windows 2000 defaults to the first available drive letter. If you'd prefer another, use the **Drive** list to choose it.

4. If you want the resource to get mapped again automatically the next time you crank up Windows 2000, leave the **Reconnect at Logon** check box activated.

5. If you want to ensure that you use the resource with a certain permission level, you might need to connect to the resource using a different username. To set that up, click the **Different User Name** link, enter the appropriate **User Name** and **Password** in the Connect As dialog box that shows up, and then click **OK**.

6. Click **Finish**. Windows 2000 connects to the resource, creates a new drive letter, and then displays a window that shows the contents of the resource.

Printing over the Network

After you connect to a network printer, you can use it just like any local printer on your system. Windows 2000 offers a couple of methods for connecting to a network printer.

Mapping Hidden Shares

Remember when earlier I told you about the hidden shares set up for administrators? To map them, select My Computer's **Tools, Map Network Drive** command. In this case, the **Folder** list is active, and you use it to specify the hidden share. Enter the following: two backslashes (\\), the network name of the computer, a single backslash (\), and the name of the hidden share. Here's an example that points to the hidden share for drive C on a computer named Paul: \\Paul\C$.

The easiest way is to use **My Network Places** to open the computer that has the shared printer, highlight the printer, and then select **File**, **Connect**. (Right-clicking the printer and then clicking **Connect** also can be done.) Windows 2000 installs the printer lickety-split using the remote machine's printer driver files.

If you like using a wizard for these kinds of things, you can do it using the Add Printer Wizard:

1. Select **Start**, **Settings**, **Printers** and launch the **Add Printer** icon to get the Add Printer Wizard to the top of the pile.

2. Click **Next** to get past the introductory dialog box.

3. In the next dialog box, activate the **Network Printer** option and click **Next**.

4. The next dialog box asks you to enter the printer name, but forget that. Instead, click **Next** and use the **Shared Printers** list to highlight the network printer you want to use. (To see a computer's shared printers, double-click the computer name.)

5. Click **Next**. From here, you complete the wizard normally (as described in Chapter 5).

You *Can* Take It with You: Working with Offline Files

In Chapter 23, "Road Scholar: Using Dial-Up Network Connections," I'll show you how to connect to your network via modem when you're on the road. If you're heading out with your notebook and you need some files from another workgroup computer, don't bother copying them to your own machine. Instead, you can tell Windows 2000 to make the shared folder available offline (that is, when you're not connected to the network). Windows 2000 creates a special Offline Files folder and uses it to squirrel away copies of the network files. You work on them at your leisure while offline, and then when you reconnect with the network, you can easily incorporate your changes into the network files to keep everything in sync. (In fact, this process is called *synchronization*.)

Making Network Files Available Offline

The first thing you need to do is tell Windows 2000 which network files are to be made available offline:

1. Use **My Network Places** to open the workgroup computer that has the files you need for the road.

2. Highlight the drive, folder, or file and then select **File**, **Make Available Offline**. (Think, too, about right-clicking the item and then clicking **Make Available Offline**.)

3. The first time you do this, the Offline Files Wizard assumes control of the desktop. Click **Next** to see what happens.

4. The next dialog box asks whether you want to **Automatically Synchronize the Offline Files When I Log On and Log Off My Computer**. If you're dealing with quite a few files, this can slow you down, so leave it deactivated. If you have only a few files to worry about, activate this check box. Either way, click **Next** when you're ready for more.

5. The next wizard dialog box has two check boxes:

   ➤ **Enable reminders** If you leave this option activated, Windows 2000 kindly displays a small banner to remind you if you have offline files that need to be synchronized. This banner appears when you log back on the network and at customizable intervals. This is a good idea, particularly if you elected not to run the automatic synchronization in step 4.

   ➤ **Create a Shortcut to the Offline Files Folder on My Desktop** If you activate this check box, a new Shortcut to Offline Files icon gets velcroed to the desktop. This gives you easy access to your offline files. (The alternative is to open My Network Places and access the files in their usual network locations. Of course, these will be offline versions of the network folders.)

6. Click **Finish**. Windows 2000 synchronizes the network files with your offline files.

Each subsequent time you run the Make Available Offline command, Windows 2000 just jumps directly to the synchronization.

If you need to make changes to any of the offline file setup options, either launch the desktop's **Shortcut to Offline Files** icon (if you elected to create it) or open the shared folder in **My Network Places**. Now select **Tools**, **Folder Options** and display the **Offline Files** tab. This tab lets you change not only the options you set up with the wizard, but also the reminder frequency, and the maximum amount of space devoted to offline files. You also can turn the offline files feature on and off.

Synchronizing the Offline Files with the Network Files

There are two times when you'll want to synchronize your offline files:

➤ While you're still online and you want to be certain that you have the most up-to-date files from the network.

➤ When you've worked on the files offline and have reconnected to the network. In this case, your goal is not only to grab the latest files from the network, but also to update the network files with your changed versions.

Windows 2000 gives you two paths to take when synchronizing:

➤ **Individual Offline Files or Folders**   In this case, highlight the file or folder and then select **File**, **Synchronize**.

➤ **Any or All of the Offline Files**   In this case, select **Tools**, **Synchronize** to display the Items to Synchronize dialog box. The offline items are shown with check boxes, all of which are activated at first. Deactivate the check box beside each item you don't want to update, and then click **Synchronize**.

What happens if you made changes to an offline file *and* the online version has also changed? To handle this sticky wicket, Windows 2000 calls in cavalry in the form of the Resolve File Conflicts dialog box, shown next. You have three choices:

➤ **Keep Both Versions** If you choose this option, Windows 2000 leaves the existing online file as is and puts a renamed copy of your version in the shared folder.

➤ **Keep Only the Version on My Computer** If you choose this option, Windows 2000 gets rid of the online file and replaces it with your version.

➤ **Keep Only the Network Version** If you go with this option, Windows 2000 gets rid of your offline file and replaces it with the online version.

355

You see this dialog box if changes have been made to both the offline and online versions of a file.

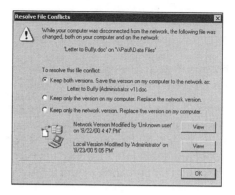

Preventing Files from Being Used Offline

As you can see, working with offline files can get messy. If you have a set of shared files that you simply don't want other people to use offline, it's easy to prevent it. Highlight your shared folder and select **File, Sharing**. In the **Sharing** tab, click **Caching** and then deactivate the **Allow Caching of Files in This Shared Folder** check box.

What Happened

This chapter made the previous chapter's network configuration toil worthwhile. I began by telling you about logging on to your network, and then I showed you the My Network Places folder. From there, you learned about permissions and users. With that info in hand, you found out how to play nicely and share your folders, drives, printers, and Internet connections with your workgroup cohorts. Next up were a few lessons on working with shared resources, including setting up network places, mapping network folders and drives, and setting up a network printer. I closed by showing you how to work with network files offline.

Crib Notes

➤ **Getting to the network** Open **My Network Places** and then launch the **Computers Near Me** icon.

➤ **Sharing your stuff** To share a resource, highlight it, select **File**, **Sharing**, and then activate the **Share this Folder** option.

➤ **Creating a network place** In the **My Network Places** folder, run the **Add Network Place** icon.

➤ **Mapping a network folder or drive** Open the workgroup computer, highlight the folder or drive, and then select **File**, **Map Network Drive**.

➤ **Using a network printer** Open the network computer, highlight the shared printer, and then select **File**, **Connect**.

➤ **Using files offline** Open the computer, highlight the drive, folder, or file, and then select **File**, **Make Available Offline**.

Road Scholar: Using Dial-Up Network Connections

In This Chapter

➤ Setting up a computer to handle incoming calls

➤ Getting a computer ready to dial up the network

➤ Making the call

➤ Adjusting settings to ensure everything works smoothly

➤ All the dial-up know-how you need, sung to the tune of "Goin' Mobile"

Travelers have no shortage of nightmares to fret over (lost luggage, delayed flights, airline food, and so on). For the business traveler, an extra nightmare lurks in the wings: forgetting to pack some crucial network files into your notebook computer. However, it's possible to banish that particular nightmare and always have ready access to whatever you need off the network. The solution is to set up one workgroup computer to accept a "dial-up" network connection. This enables far-flung folks to use their modem to connect to that computer and so gain access to the network. This chapter shows you not only how to make that connection, but also how to set up the dial-up computer. Now all you have to do is remember to pack your modem!

Setting Up a Network Computer to Accept Incoming Calls

You can't dial up your network unless you have something to dial up *to*. So, your first chore is to convert one of your workgroup computers into a machine that's only too happy to accept incoming calls. The next couple of sections show you how it's done.

Running the Network Connection Wizard

Before getting started on this, you need to be sure of two things:

➤ Any users who might do the dial-up thing are set up as users on the computer.

➤ The machine you'll be using has a modem installed and ready to serve.

With all that in place, follow these steps:

Cross Reference

To set up users on a computer, check out the section in Chapter 22 titled "Workgroupies: Notes About Permissions and Users," p. 342.

1. Select **Start**, **Settings**, **Network and Dial-Up Connections**.

2. What you do next depends on whether you have any existing connections (such as a dial-up Internet connection) defined:

   ➤ If you have no other connections defined, the Network and Dial-Up Connections window appears. In this case, launch the **Make New Connection** icon.

Cross Reference

Modem setup is discussed in Chapter 9. See "Getting Your Modem Ready for Action," p. 136.

   ➤ If you have other connections defined, a submenu appears. In this case, select **Make New Connection**.

3. The Network Connection Wizard hoists itself onto the screen. Click **Next** to sidestep the initial dialog box. The wizard displays a list of connection choices, as shown here.

4. Activate **Accept Incoming Connections** and click **Next**. The wizard sets out a list of connection devices for your selecting pleasure.

5. Activate the check box beside your modem, deactivate any other check boxes, and then click **Next**. Now the wizard muses about "virtual private connections." Say, "Yeah, I wish!" and be sure that the **Do Not Allow Virtual Private Connections** option is activated. Click **Next** at your earliest convenience. The wizard waves a list of users in your face.

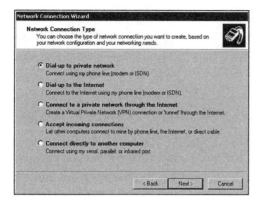

Use this dialog box to pick out the type of connection you want to set up.

6. Activate the check box beside the name of each user to whom you're willing to grant dial-up access to the computer. (Note, too, that you can click **Add** to set up more users from here.) Feel free to click **Next** when that's done. The wizard's seemingly inexhaustible supply of check box lists continues with a list of networking components.

7. You don't have to worry about any of this, so click **Next** to keep things moving.

8. Mission accomplished! In the last dialog box, click **Finish**. The wizard returns you to the Network and Dial-Up Connections window and displays a new icon (usually called Incoming Connections, as shown in the following figure).

That's all you need to do for this machine. Windows 2000 will now monitor the modem to listen for incoming calls, and will automatically answer any that come in.

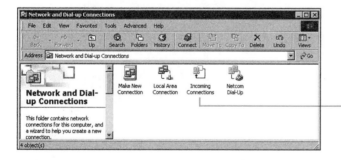

When the wizard's labors are complete, it adds a new icon to the Network and Dial-up Connections folder.

Here's the new icon.

Making Adjustments for Incoming Connections

If you add another modem to your system, or if you want to change which users can dial up the computer, you don't need to run the Network Connection Wizard all over again. Instead, the Incoming Connections icon has a properties dialog box that lets you mess around with the settings.

To get to that dialog box, use either of the following techniques:

➤ If the Network and Dial-Up Connections window is still open, either highlight the **Incoming Connections** icon and select **File**, **Properties**, or right-click the icon and then click **Properties**.

➤ If the window isn't open, select **Start**, **Settings**, **Network and Dial-Up Connections**, **Incoming Connections**.

Either way, you end up eyeballing the Incoming Connections Properties dialog box, shown in the following figure. There are three tabs:

➤ **General**   Use the **Devices** list to specify which device the incoming connections will be using. (This will almost always be your modem. Note, too, that you can highlight the modem and click **Properties** to tweak the modem's settings.)

➤ **Users**   Use this tab to choose which users can make dial-up connections. You can also add **New** users, **Delete** users, and change a user's **Properties** (such as their password).

➤ **Networking**   This tab controls the networking components used during the dial-up connection. The standard components are fine, so you shouldn't have to mess with anything here.

Use this dialog box to adjust some settings related to the Incoming Connections icon.

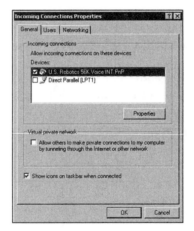

Creating a Dial-Up Connection to Your Network

Okay, so that's stage one. Stage two involves setting up the would-be traveling computer to connect to the network using a modem. As you'll see in the next section, this involves another session with the Network Connection Wizard.

The Network Connection Wizard Redux

Again, your first chore is to ensure that this computer has a working modem. After you've done that, follow these steps to run through a few more Network Connection Wizard shenanigans:

1. Select **Start**, **Settings**, **Network and Dial-Up Connections**.

2. Again, your next move depends on whether you have any existing connections defined:

   ➤ If you have no other connections defined, the Network and Dial-Up Connections window appears. In this case, launch the **Make New Connection** icon.

   ➤ If you have other connections defined, a submenu appears. In this case, select **Make New Connection**.

3. Click **Next** to get to the list of connection types.

4. Activate **Dial-Up to Private Network** and click **Next**. (If you happen to have multiple modems, the wizard will ask you to choose one. Make your choice and click **Next**.) The wizard puzzles over the phone number to use when dialing.

5. Enter the **Phone number**. If it's not a local call, activate the **Use Dialing Rules** check box, and then fill in the **Area Code** and **Country/Region Code**. Click **Next** to forge ahead. The wizard displays the Connection Availability dialog box.

6. If you want every user of the computer to be able to dial up the network, leave **For All Users** activated. If you'd prefer that only you can do it, activate **Only for Myself**, instead. Click **Next**.

7. In the final wizard dialog box, click **Finish**. (Before doing so, you might consider activating the **Add a Shortcut to My Desktop** check box. This tells the wizard to put a connection shortcut on the desktop, which, as you'll see, is a convenience you might like.)

Once again, you're dropped off at the Network and Dial-Up Connections window, where you'll see a new icon (usually named Dial-Up Connection). Windows 2000 will also prompt you to connect to the network. Let's skip this, for now, so click **Cancel**.

Making Adjustments for the Dial-Up Connection

If you need to change the phone number, work with dialing rules, or nudge some other settings for the dial-up connection, the Dial-Up Connection icon also has its own properties dialog box that you can play with. To get there, you have three choices:

➤ If the Network and Dial-Up Connections window is still open, either highlight the **Dial-Up Connection** icon and select **File**, **Properties**, or right-click the icon and then click **Properties**.

➤ If the window isn't open, select **Start**, **Settings**, **Network and Dial-Up Connections**, **Dial-Up Connection**, and then click **Properties** in the dialog box that pops up.

➤ If the window isn't open, select **Start**, **Settings**, **Network and Dial-Up Connections**, right-click the **Dial-Up Connection** icon, and then click **Properties**.

In the end, Windows 2000 levitates the Dial-Up Connection Properties dialog box, shown next.

Use this dialog box to make changes to the dial-up connection.

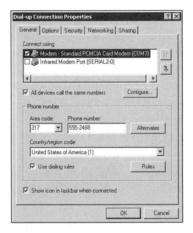

The General tab offers the following tidbits:

➤ **Connect Using**   This box shows the modem you'll be using to make the connection. If you have multiple modems, this box turns into a check box list where you can activate the check box beside the modem you want to use. You shouldn't need to monkey with the modem, but just in case you do, you can click **Configure** to see a dialog box of options.

Cross Reference

I explained dialing locations in Chapter 9. See "Where You're At: Setting Up Dialing Locations," p. 143.

➤ **Phone Number**   Use this group to edit the **Area Code**, **Phone Number**, and **Country/Region Code**. If you want to use dialing locations (a good possibility if you'll be traveling), activate the **Use Dialing Rules** check box and then click the **Rules** button.

➤ **Show Icon in Taskbar When Connected** When this check box is activated, Windows 2000 crams an icon in the taskbar's system tray after the connection has been established. It's a good idea to leave this activated because the icon gives you a quick disconnect route (by right-clicking, as described in the next section).

The **Options** tab, shown in the following figure, is loaded with mostly useful goodies:

➤ **Display Progress While Connecting** When this check box is activated, Windows 2000 displays a dialog box during the connection which gives you feedback on what's happening. This is good for troubleshooting (if the connection fails, you can at least see where it failed), but can be annoying if you're connecting successfully each time.

➤ **Prompt for Name and Password, Certificate, Etc.** If you deactivate this check box, Windows 2000 doesn't ask you for your username and password before connecting. If that data never changes, then deactivating this check box presents you with a simpler dialog box while connecting.

➤ **Include Windows Logon Domain** You don't use domains in your small network, so feel free to leave this check box deactivated.

➤ **Prompt for Phone Number** Again, if you don't need to ever change the phone number before connecting, you can deactivate this option.

➤ **Redial Attempts** This spin box sets the number of times Windows 2000 should redial if it can't get a connection going.

➤ **Time Between Redial Attempts** Use this list to specify how much time Windows 2000 should cool its jets before attempting the next redial.

➤ **Idle Time Before Hanging Up** Use this list to specify the maximum amount of time that the connection can have no activity before Windows 2000 automatically disconnects. If you'll be calling long distance, it's a good idea to choose a relatively short time (such as five minutes).

➤ **Redial If Line Is Dropped** If you activate this check box, Windows 2000 will redial if the connection is lost due to line noise or some other not-under-your-control phenomenon.

The Options tab has a wealth of, well, options.

The rest of the tabs in the Dial-up Connection Properties dialog box contain advanced settings that life's too short to worry about.

Making the Connection

After all that wizardry, you're now set to make the connection. Assuming your modem is connected and ready for action, here's what you do:

1. Select **Start**, **Settings**, **Network and Dial-Up Connections**, **Dial-Up Connection**. (Alternatively, if you elected to have a shortcut for the connection placed on the desktop, double-click that shortcut.) Windows 2000 displays a Connect dialog box something like the one shown here.

Use this dialog box to launch your dial-up connection.

2. Be sure your **User Name** is correct and enter your **Password**. If you want Windows 2000 to include your password automatically in the future, activate the **Save Password** check box.

3. Be sure the correct phone number is shown in the **Dial** text box.

4. If you want to use dialing rules or make other changes (as described in the previous section), click **Properties**. (If you've already activated dialing rules for this connection, use the **Dialing From** list to choose a location or click **Dialing Rules** to make changes.)

5. When you're ready, click **Dial** to get jiggy with it. Windows 2000 dials your modem and connects with the computer you set up to handle incoming calls.

6. When the connection is made, a dialog box pops by to let you know. Click **OK**.

From here, you use the network just like you do when you have a physical connection.

Startup Dial-Up

You can also make the connection during the Windows 2000 startup. When the Log On to Windows dialog box greets you, activate the **Log On Using Dial-Up Connection** check box. When you click **OK**, the Dial-Up Networking dialog box is called in. Use this dialog box to select the connection you want to use (this will be the **Dial-Up Connection** item) and click **Dial**. From here, you follow the preceding steps 2–6.

When your networking duties are complete, you can disconnect by using either of the following methods:

➤ Select **Start**, **Settings**, **Network and Dial-Up Connections**, right-click **Dial-Up Connection**, and then click **Disconnect**.

➤ Right-click the connection icon that Windows 2000 shoehorned into the taskbar's system tray, and then click **Disconnect**.

When Windows 2000 asks for confirmation, click **Yes**.

What Happened

This chapter closed your look at Windows 2000 networking by showing you how to connect to your network using a modem. The first part of the chapter went through the procedure for setting up a computer to accept incoming calls. You then learned how to set up the soon-to-be-remote computer to dial up the network. I finished by showing you how to make the connection.

Crib Notes

➤ **Dial-up wizardry**   You use the Network Connection Wizard to configure computers to accept and make dial-up network connections. To get this wizard on the case, select **Start, Settings, Network and Dial-Up Connections** and then launch the **Make New Connection** icon.

➤ **The dial-up-ee**   To set up a computer to accept dial-up connections, run the Network Connection Wizard and choose the **Accept Incoming Connections** option.

➤ **The dial-up-er**   To set up a computer to make dial-up connections, run the Network Connection Wizard and choose the **Dial-Up to Private Network** option.

➤ **Set up the users**   All the users who will be connecting remotely need to be added to the computer that will be accepting the dial-ups.

➤ **Connecting**   Select **Start, Settings, Network and Dial-Up Connections, Dial-Up Connection**.

➤ **Disconnecting**   Either select **Start, Settings, Network and Dial-Up Connections**, right-click **Dial-Up Connection**, and then click **Disconnect**, or right-click the connection icon in the system tray, and then click **Disconnect**.

The Jargon Jar: The Complete Archive

annotate   To add comments, graphics, highlights, or "rubber stamps" to a received fax.

attachment   A file that latches onto an email message and is sent to the recipient.

Auto Hide   A feature that hides the taskbar until you move the mouse to the bottom of the screen.

AutoRun   A feature that automatically launches a program's setup routine after you insert its CD-ROM or DVD-ROM disc.

backplate   A piece of metal that covers a hole in the back of a computer beside an internal *circuit board* slot.

backup job   A file that specifies a few particulars about a backup: the files you want backed up, the location where the files will be backed up, and any backup options.

Bcc   A blind courtesy (or carbon) copy email message. These are copies of the message that get sent to other people, but their addresses aren't shown to the other recipients. See also *Cc*.

bit   Short for "binary digit," and it represents the most basic unit of computer information. Within your computer, data is stored using tiny electronic devices called *gates*, each of which holds a single bit. These gates can be either on (which means electricity flows through the gate) or off (no electricity flows through the gate). For the likes of you and me, the number 1 represents a gate that's on, and the number 0 represents a gate that's off.

boot   To start your computer.

bps   Stands for bits per second, and it's used to measure the speed at which the modem spews data through a phone line.

bus structure   A network structure in which each *network interface card* is connected to the network interface card in the computer "beside" it via *coaxial cable*. See also *star structure*.

byte   Eight *bits* strung together, which represents a single character of data. For example, the letter "X" is represented by the following byte: 1011000. Weird, I know. Further, the mathematicians tell us that a byte can have 256 possible combinations of ones and zeros (prove it for yourself by raising 2 to the power of 8), and those combinations represent all possible characters: lowercase letters, uppercase letters, numbers, symbols, and so on.

cable connection   Your external modem will be useless until you connect it to your PC. Connecting the *modem cable* is straightforward (as far as these things go, anyway) if you remember one thing: There's usually only one possible place for each end of the cable to plug into. On the modem side, the port is wide and has 25 holes arranged in two rows, and the modem cable will have a plug that has a similar shape with 25 pins arranged in two rows. On the computer side, the *serial port* will be narrower with only 9 pins arranged in two rows, and the corresponding modem cable plug will have the same shape with nine holes arranged in two rows.

Cc   A courtesy (or carbon) copy. These are copies of the message that get sent to other people. See also *Bcc*.

circuit board   A device that fits into a slot inside your computer.

coaxial cable   A cable that uses a bayonet-style connector to attach to a T-connector, which then attaches to a BNC port in the *network interface card*. See also *twisted-pair cable*.

color depth   The number of colors Windows 2000 uses to display stuff on your screen. See also *screen area*.

compression   A standard *protocol* where the sending modem squeezes data into a smaller size, and the receiving modem restores the data to its normal size. Because the data being sent is smaller, this improves data transfer times.

connection settings   A collection of communications settings that both your modem and the remote modem must have in common to establish a successful connection. There are three connection settings to consider: *data bits*, *parity*, and *stop bit*.

cutout   A selected section of a Paint drawing.

daily backup   A backup type that includes only files that were changed on the day you run the backup. See also *incremental backup*.

data bits The number of *bits* in a character, as defined by the remote system. Yes, I know I said earlier that a *byte* represents a character and that there are eight bits in a byte. However, that applies only to PCs. If the remote modem is attached to a non-PC (such as a big mainframe job), the number of bits in a character might be different (seven is common). See also *parity* and *stop bit*.

data transfer rate The maximum (theoretical) speed at which a modem can send data, and it's measured in *bps*. Most modern modems support one of the following data transfer rates: 28,800bps, 33,600bps, or 56,000bps. If you're looking to buy a modem, get one that supports 56,000bps (which is sometimes called V.90, for reasons too geeky to go into here).

defragment To rearrange the contents of a hard disk so that each file's sectors run consecutively. See also *fragmented*.

demodulation The opposite of *modulation*. That is, it's the process that the modem uses to convert the incoming tones back into the original digital data.

desktop The sea of blue that takes up the bulk of the Windows 2000 screen. It's called a "desktop" because it's where your documents and tools appear.

device driver A wee chunk of software that enables Windows 2000 to operate a device.

dial-up A connection to a network (or an *Internet service provider*) that occurs via a modem over a phone line.

dialog box A box that shows up when Windows 2000 or a program requires more information from you.

digital camera A film camera-like device that takes pictures of the outside world and stores them digitally for later downloading to a hard disk.

docking station A box into which you can plug a notebook and that offers expansion room in the form of extra PC Card sockets, drive bays, plugs for external accessories, and ports for other devices.

document scanner A photocopier-like device that creates a digital image of a flat surface such as a piece of paper or a photograph.

download To receive data from a remote computer. See also *upload*.

error correction A standard *protocol* that enables the two modems to determine whether incoming data contains errors and should be re-sent. If you find the remote system is terminating the connection unexpectedly, try disabling error correction.

Explorer bar A pane that shows up on the left side of the My Computer window, and that's used to display bars (such as the handy Folders bar).

favorite   A *Web page* name and address saved within Internet Explorer for easy recall down the road.

fax modem   A special type of modem (although it's by far the most common type these days) that can handle fax transmissions in addition to its usual data duties.

female   A port or plug that has holes. See also *male*.

file transfer protocol   A *protocol* that enables two computers to properly coordinate file *downloads* and *uploads*.

flow control   A procedure that enables the modem and the computer to interact so that incoming data is received properly if the computer is ready, or is put off temporarily if the computer is busy with some other chore.

folder   A storage location for files and other folders (subfolders).

folder template   A file that tells Windows 2000 how to display a *folder* in *Web view*.

font   A style of text that includes the typeface (a unique design applied to every character), the type style (such as **bold** or *italic*), the *type size*, and possibly some type effects (such as underline).

fragmented   When a file is stored on the hard disk using multiple sectors that are scattered throughout the disk. See also *defragment*.

hot swapping   Inserting and removing *PC Card* devices without having to shut down Windows 2000.

hub   A central network connection point used in the *star structure*.

idle time   Time during which a network or Internet connection isn't used.

incremental backup   A backup type that includes only files that have changed since the last normal or incremental backup. See also *daily backup*.

Internet service provider   A company that takes your money in exchange for an Internet account, which is what you need to get online.

IP address   An address (which will look something like 123.234.45.67) that serves as the location of your computer while you're connected to the Internet.

ISP   See *Internet service provider*.

Kbps   Kilobits per second, or thousands of bits per second. *Data transfer rates* are often measured this way, so the three main rates are also written as 28.8Kbps, 33.6Kbps, and 56Kbps.

LAN   See *local area network*.

link   In a *Web page*, a chunk of text or an image that, when clicked, takes you to another Web page.

local area network   A group of computers located relatively close together and that are connected via network cable.

log on   To provide your *Internet service provider* with your user name and password, and so gain access to the wonder that is the Internet.

mail server   A computer that your ISP uses to store and send your email messages.

male   A port or plug that has pins. See also *female*.

map   To set up a shared network folder or disk drive so that it has its own drive letter on your system. See also *shared resource*.

message body   The text of an email message.

MIDI   See *Musical Instrument Digital Interface*.

modem   An electronic device that somehow manages to transmit and receive computer data over telephone lines. The word *modem* was coined by taking the "mo" of *modulation* and stitching it together with the "dem" of *demodulation*. Modems come in three flavors: external, internal, and *PC Card*.

modem cable   A special data cable that connects an external modem to a PC. The cable attaches to a port in the back of the modem on one end, and to a *serial port* in the back of the computer on the other end.

modulation   The process that the modem uses to get computer data ready for transmission along a phone line. That is, the digital commands and data—in the form of *bits*—are converted into tones that the phone system understands. Those tones are the caterwauling and wailing that you hear when the modems first try to connect. See also *demodulation*.

multimedia   Using a computer to play, edit, and record sounds, animations, and movies.

multitasking   The capability to run two or more programs at the same time.

Musical Instrument Digital Interface   A sound file that plays music generated by electronic synthesizers.

network interface card   A *circuit board*, *PC Card* device, or USB device into which the network cable is plugged.

network place   A *shared resource* that has its own icon in your My Network Places folder.

newsgroup   An online discussion forum devoted to a particular topic.

373

NIC   See *network interface card*.

null-modem cable   A special communications cable designed for direct connections between two computers.

offline files   Local copies of network files that you can work with while not connected to the network.

page   See *Web page*.

parity   An extra *bit* that tags along for the ride if the remote system uses fewer than eight *data bits*. This extra bit is used for error checking to see whether the data the modem just received was corrupted on its journey. See also *stop bit*.

PC Card   A small, credit card-sized device that slips into a special socket on your notebook. There are PC Card devices for modems, network adapters, hard disks, and much more.

peer-to-peer   A network configuration in which all the computers have equal status.

permissions   The users, groups, and computers that can access a shared network resource, and the type of access granted to that resource.

Personalized Menus   A new Windows 2000 feature that displays only those Start menu commands that you use most often.

pixels   The individual pinpoints of light that make up a Paint drawing (and, for that matter, everything you see on your screen).

port   A receptacle in the back of a computer into which you plug the cable used by an external device. See also *modem cable*, *printer port*, and *serial port*.

post   To send a message to a newsgroup.

print job   A document for which the Print command has been issued.

print queue   The list of pending *print jobs*.

printer port   On the back of the computer, the receptacle into which you plug the printer cable. On most systems, the printer port is named LPT1.

protocol   A standard method by which your modem and the remote modem exchange data. Just as following the correct protocol is crucial in human diplomatic circles, so is agreeing to use the same electronic protocol in modem diplomacy.

ransom note effect   The messy look given to a document that uses too many *fonts*.

Recycle Bin   The place where Windows 2000 stores deleted files. If you trash a file accidentally, you can use the Recycle Bin to recover it.

sans serif   A *font* that doesn't have cross strokes at its extremities. This type of font is most often used for titles and headings that require a larger type size. See also *serif*.

screen area   The number of columns and rows in the grid of pixels that Windows 2000 uses to display screen images. See also *color depth*.

screen shot   A copy of the current screen image.

sector   A storage area on your hard disk.

separator   In a toolbar, a vertical bar that separates groups of related buttons.

serial port   A plug in the back of your computer into which you insert the *modem cable*. If you have an internal modem, the serial port is built into the modem's circuit board, so you never have to worry about it and there's no cable to run. On most computers, the serial port is named COM1.

serif   A *font* that has small cross strokes at the extremities of each character. Serif fonts are good for regular text in a document. See also *sans serif*.

shared resource   A local folder, disk drive, or printer that has been set up so that people on the network can use it.

shortcut   A file that points to another file. Also, another name for most of the commands on the various Start menus.

signal-to-noise ratio   In a *newsgroup*, the ratio of useful, on-topic *posts* to useless, off-topic posts.

signature   A snippet of text that appears at the bottom of an email message.

spam   Unsolicited commercial email, and the scourge of the Internet. To avoid spam, don't put your real email address in your news account.

spooling   The process by which Windows 2000 farms out a document to the printer after you run the Print command.

star structure   A network structure in which each *network interface card* is connected to a central *hub* via *twisted-pair cable*. See also *bus structure*.

Start Menu folder   A folder on your hard disk that holds the various Start menu shortcuts and folders. It's usually C:\Documents and_Settings*User*\Start Menu\ (where *User* is your Windows 2000 username).

stop bit   Yet another extra *bit* that's sent during modem transmissions. This one goes at the end of the *data bits*, and it marks the end of the character. See also *parity*.

subject line   A line of text that describes what an email message is about.

surf   To jump from *Web page* to Web page.

system standby   A power mode that shuts everything down temporarily until you press a key, move the mouse, or poke the power button.

System State data The crucial configuration files that are the lifeblood of Windows 2000.

tab stop A spot on the WordPad ruler at which the cursor stops when you press the **Tab** key.

tape drive A device that backs up data to tape. Unless you have a spare hard disk, this is the best kind of backup medium to use.

taskbar The gray strip along the bottom of the Windows 2000 screen that's used to switch between running programs.

thumbnail A preview of an image or HTML file (*Web page*).

TSID The Transmitting Station Identifier, which is a short bit of text that identifies your fax modem to the recipient.

twisted-pair cable A cable that uses RJ-45 jacks to connect to an RJ-45 port in the NIC. See also *coaxial cable*, *hub*, and *star structure*.

uniform resource locator See *URL*.

uninstall To completely remove a program from your computer.

upload To send data to a remote computer. See also *download*.

URL The address of a *Web page*.

video adapter An internal *circuit board* that grabs display instructions from the processor and then tells the monitor what to show on the screen.

wallpaper An image or design that covers the screen background.

wave file A standard Windows sound file.

waves How sounds are transmitted through a telephone line. When you talk, you create a sound wave that vibrates a diaphragm in the phone's mouthpiece. The vibration converts the sound wave into an equivalent electromagnetic wave, which is then sent along the phone line. At the other end, the wave vibrates a diaphragm in the earpiece, which reproduces the original sound wave, and your voice is heard loud and clear.

Web integration The use of Web-like features within the Windows 2000 interface.

Web page A document on the Web that contains text, images, and usually a few links.

Web view A folder view that displays a folder as though it were a *Web page*.

Index

A

Active Desktops, 237-239
Add Network Place Wizard,
 341, 351
Add Printer Wizard, 73-75
Add/Remove Hardware
 Wizard, 282-284
Add/Remove Programs
 icon, 274-275
adding new devices, 282
adding. *See* creating
Address
 Books, 200-203
 list, 46
 toolbar, 256, 260
Administrative Tools (Start
 menu) 247
Alt key, 241
animation file formats,
 115
answering phone calls, 161
appearance schemes,
 236-237
Appearance tab, 236
application sharing, 227

archive flags, 294
attachments, 202-203, 207
Audio Tuning Wizard,
 NetMeeting, 223
audio. *See* sound
Auto Arrange command,
 265
AutoRun, 274
AVI file format, 115

B

Back buttons, 45
backgrounds, desktops,
 232-235
Backup command (System
 Tools menu), 295
Backup tab, 297
Backup Wizard, 295-299
backups, 291-300, 304
 advanced settings, 296,
 299
 archive flags, 294
 jobs, 295

copy, 294
daily, 294
define jobs, 298
destinations, 296
differential, 294
end of schedule, 300
everything, 296
floppy disks, 292
frequency, 300
Hard disks, 293
Hardware Compatibility
 List, 293
incremental, 294-295
Jaz disks, 293
jobs, 295, 298
labels, 297, 300
media options, 297
media type selection,
 296
My Documents folder,
 293, 296
names, 300
network, 293
normal, 294-295
recovery, 302-303
Restore Wizard, 302-303

saving jobs, 298
scheduling, 297,
    299-300
selected files, 296
start time, 300
strategy, 294
System State data, 296
tab, 297
tape drives, 293
Task Scheduler, 314
types, 294
Wizards, 295-297, 299
zip disks, 293
bad sectors, 309, 311
batteries
    alarms, 85
    Scheduled Tasks, 316
Bcc addresses, 198
bits, 133
BNC port, 327
bolding text, 64
bookmarks, 193
booting, 18
bps (bits per second), 133
Briefcases, 87, 89, 94
bullets, 66
bus structures, 329-330
buttons
    adding, 263
    Back, 45
    Cancel, 22, 29, 37
    close, 31
    fonts, 63
    Forward, 45
    label in toolbar, 45
    Maximize, 32
    Minimize, 32
    Move To, 49
    Print, 79
    removing, 263
    Start, 20
    taskbar, 254
    text, 263

toolbar, 28
Up, 46
bytes, 133

C

cables
    category 5, 326
    coaxial, 327-328, 330
    disk drives, 279
    modems, 134
    networks, 326
    NICs, 325
    phone to modem,
        138-139
    thinnet, 327
    twisted-pair, 326
cameras, digital, 108-109,
    111
Cancel button, 22, 29, 37
category 5 cabling, 326
cc addresses, 198
CD Player, 117-120
    advanced options, 120
    Internet features, 119
CD-ROM drives, 279
    connecting to sound
        card, 119
    installing programs
        from, 274
    sharing, 343
change permissions, 346
changing icons, 239
Character Map, 69
Chat feature (NetMeeting),
    227
check boxes, 29
Check Disk, 308, 310, 314
child, 46
cleanup, hard disk,
    305-308
clicking, 22

client/server networks, 324
Clipboard, 36
clock, 255
Close button, 31
closing
    Active Desktop items, 239
coaxial cables, 327-328,
    330
colors, screen, 242-243
COM1, 134, 138
combo boxes, 30
command buttons, 29
commands
    Edit menu
        Copy To Folder, 49
        Move To Folder, 49
        Paste, 35
        Select All, 48
        Undo, 36
    File menu
        Delete, 52
        Exit, 31
        Make Available
            Offline, 354
        Map Network Drive,
            352
        New, 33, 47
        Open, 34
        Open With, 59
        Print, 77
        Properties, 308
        Rename, 51
        Restore, 52
        Save, 34
        Save As, 34
        Send To, 50
        Sharing, 344
        Use Printer Offline,
            80
    Settings menu
        Network and Dial-up
            Connections, 360

Start menu
Search, 53
Shut Down, 37
Windows Update, 317
System Tools menu
Backup, 295
Disk Cleanup, 308
Disk Defragmenter,
311
Scheduled Tasks, 314
Tools menu
Folder Options, 55
View menu
Explorer Bar, 261
Folders, 46
Go To, 45
Status Bar, 260
Toolbars, 260
Zoom, 104
comments, folder, 268-269
compatibility, Windows
2000, 278
computer names, 331,
334-335
Computer permissions,
342, 346
Computers Near Me icon,
333, 341, 350
Connect to Internet icon,
168
connection icon, 220
connections, creating,
92-94
Control Panel
Add/Remove Hardware
Wizard, 282
Add/Remove Programs
icon, 274-275
Display icon, 232
Startup menu, 248
Users and Passwords
icon, 340, 342
controls, 28-30

copy backups, 294
Copy To Folder command
(Edit menu), 49
copying
documents, 34
files, 49-51
folders, 49-51
text, 35
Create Shortcut Wizard,
250
creating
Briefcases, 87
connections, 92-94
documents, 33
Emergency Repair Disks,
301
files, 47
folders, 47
text files, 59
Web pages, 58
Ctrl+Alt+Delete, 340
Customize Toolbar dialog
box, 262
customizing desktop. *See*
desktops
cutouts, 104-106
cutting text, 35

D

daily backups, 294
dates, displaying, 21
Defragmenter, 310-313
Delete command (File
menu), 52
Deleted Items folder, 208
deleting, 51-52
email, 208
files, 51
folders, 51
programs, 275
restoring deleted files,
52

scheduled tasks, 316
text, 36
demodulation, 133
Desktop toolbar, 256
desktops, 231
Active Desktops,
237-238
aligning icons, 241
Appearance tab, 236
backgrounds, 232-233
color selection, 236
components, 18-20
creating patterns, 234
Display Properties dialog
box, 232, 235-238
dragging speed, 241
Effects tab, 239
fonts, 237
icons, 8, 239-241
look-and-feel, 8
My Computer icon, 42
navigation indicators,
241
patterns, 234-235
quick launch icons, 20
schemes, 236-237
Screen area slider,
243-244
screen colors, 242-243
screen savers, 235
Settings tab, 242
Show Desktop icon, 232
sizing items, 236
Start button, 20
system tray, 21
transition effects, 240
type sizes, 237
Visual Effects group, 240
wallpapers, 232-234
Details view, 264, 266
device drivers, 281-284
getting, 285
printers, 348
upgrading, 284-286

Device Manager, 284
devices. *See* hardware
Dial-up Connection icon, 363
dial-up connections, 359, 365, 367
  activating, 360
  connecting, 366-367
  Dial-up Connection icon, 363
  dialing locations, 364
  disconnecting, 367
  display progress, 365
  domains, 365
  General tab, 362
  icon, 363
  Incoming Connections icon, 361-362
  Network Connection Wizard, 360, 363
  Networking tab, 362
  offline setup, 363-366
  passwords, 365-366
  Properties, 364
  redial attempts, 365
  setup, 360-361
  Users tab, 362
dialing. *See* Phone Dialer
dialog boxes, 28-30
differential backups, 294
digital cameras, 108-109, 111
direct connections, 91-95
DirectParallel cables, 92
disconnecting from hosts, 95
discussion forums. *See* newsgroups
Disk Cleanup, 306, 308, 314
Disk Cleanup command (System Tools menu), 308

Disk Defragmenter, 310-314
Disk Defragmenter command (System Tools menu), 311
disk drives. See floppy disks; hard disks
Display Properties dialog box, 232
  Appearance tab, 236
  Background tab, 233
  Effects tab, 239
  Screen Saver tab, 235
  Settings tab, 242
  Visual Effects group, 240
  Web tab, 237-238
displays. *See* desktops; screens
documents, 33-36
  adding to Start menu, 250-251
  backups, 293
  copying, 34
  creating, 33
  formatted, 58
  highlighting text, 35
  opening, 34
  plain text, 58
  printing. *See* printing
  saving, 34
  selecting text, 35
Documents and Settings folder, 251
domain names, 221
domains, 331, 334, 365
double-clicking, 22
downloading, 136
  backing up, 293
  device drivers, 285
  newsgroup message lists, 218-219
  program files, 307

Web pages, 191
Windows updates, 318
drag-and-drop
  files, 50-51
  printing, 79
dragging, 22, 241
drive bays, 279
drivers. *See* device drivers
drop-down list boxes, 30
DVD
  drives, 279
  format, 115
  Player, 120-122

E

echo sound, 127
Edit menu commands
  Copy To Folder, 49
  Move To Folder, 49
  Paste, 35
  Select All, 48
  Undo, 36
email, 195-208. *See also* Outlook Express
  Address Books, 200-201, 203
  attachments, 202-203, 205, 207
  Bcc addresses, 198
  blocking, 209
  Cc box, 198
  conversations, group by, 207
  creating, 197-200
  deleting, 208
  faxes in inbox, 161
  flags, 205
  folders, moving to, 208
  format options, 203
  forward message, 207
  From field, 205

groups, 201
Inbox, 197, 206
including message in
    reply, 203
mailing lists, 204
message body, 199
NetMeeting, 223
notification of Web
    page changes, 192
Outlook Express, 176
paper clip icon, 207
primer, 196
priority, 205
reading, 205-206
receive messages, 205
received date, 205
reply format options,
    203
replying to, 207
Rich Text (HTML), 199
rules, setting, 209
sending messages, 199
sending options, 203
Sent Items folder, 203
setup Internet connec-
    tion, 173-174
signatures, 201
spam, 209, 215
spelling checker, 199
subject, 198, 205
threads, 206
To box, 198
Emergency Repair Disks,
    301
Entire Network icon, 341
Ethernet, 325
events, sound settings,
    124-125
Everyone permission, 342,
    345
Exit command (File
    menu), 31
Explore command, 252
Explorer Bar, 261

Explorer Bar command
    (View menu), 261
external plug-in devices,
    278

F

Favorites bar, 261
faxes, 153
    annotating, 163-164
    archive outgoing, 165
    banners, 165
    cover page creation,
        156-159
    creating, 153-155
    dialing options, 155
    Fax Service
        Management, 165
    name assignment, 155
    options, 165
    Page menu, 163
    properties, 165
    receiving, 159-160,
        162-163
    retries, 165
    save incoming, 160
    saving to email inbox,
        161
    shared fax line, 161
    TSID, 155
    user information, 153,
        157-159
    zooming, 162
file and printer sharing,
    336
File menu commands
    Delete, 52
    Exit, 31
    Make Available Offline,
        354
    Map Network Drive, 352
    New, 33, 47
    Open, 34

Open With, 59
Print, 77
Properties, 308
Rename, 51
Restore, 52
Save, 34
Save As, 34
Send To, 50
Sharing, 344
Use Printer Offline, 80
File Transfer Protocol
    (FTP), 136
files, 41
    accessing shared, 350
    adding to Start menu,
        250-251
    attachments, 202
    backups, 293, 295
    copying, 49-51
    creating, 47
    deleting, 51
    drag-and-drop, 50-51
    file and printer sharing,
        336
    highlighting, 44
    lassoing, 48
    moving, 49-51
    naming, 53
    NTFS file system, 347
    organizing, 52
    renaming, 51
    selecting, 47, 49
    sharing, 336, 350
    shortcut menu, 56
    sorting, 265
    storage system, 310
    transferring, 227
finding
    files, 53-54
    text in documents,
        68-69
flames, 214
floppy disks, backups, 292

Folder Options command (Tools menu) , 55
folders, 41
  accessing shared, 350
  adding to Start menu, 250-251
  Address list, 46
  backgrounds, 267-268
  bar, 261
  child, 46
  comments, 268-269
  copying, 49-51
  creating, 47
  customizing, 271
  deleting, 51
  Go To command, 45
  lassoing, 48
  links to, 43
  map to drives, 352
  My Computer, 42-46
  My Network Places, 341
  navigating, 44
  opening, 43
  parent, 46
  program, 274
  Quick Launch, 255
  removing from Start menu, 251
  renaming, 51
  sharing, 344-345, 350
  shortcut menu, 56
  sorting, 265
  templates, 269-270
  viewing subfolders, 46
  WINNT, 44
Folders bar, 261
Folders command (View Menu), 46
Folders list, 46, 50
fonts
  desktop, 237
  installing, 65
  Notepad, 60
  serifs, 63
  size, 63
  toolbar buttons, 63
  typefaces, 63
  WordPad, 62, 64
footers, 77
foreign characters, 69
formatting text, 62
Forward buttons, 45
Found New Hardware box, 72
Found New Hardware Wizard, 281
fragmented disks. *See* Disk Defragmenter
free space, hard disk, 306
FTP (File Transfer Protocol), 136
Full Control permissions, 347

G

Gates, Bill, 52
Getting Started box, 18
Go To command (View menu), 45
graphics, 97. *See also* Paint
  color mode conversion, 107
  digital cameras, 109
  image attributes, 107
  scanners, 108-111
  sizing, 107
graphics cards
  installing, 280-281
  name of, 242
Groups permissions, 342, 346
guest computer, 92-93

H

hard disks, 43
  accessing shared, 350
  backups, as, 293
  bad sectors, 309, 311
  Check Disk, 308, 310
  cleaning up, 305-308
  Disk Cleanup, 306, 308
  Disk Defragmenter, 310-313
  errors, 308, 310
  file storage system, 310
  free space, 306
  installing, 278, 280
  map to local drives, 352
  Properties command, 308
  sectors, 309-310
  sharing, 343-344
  Tools tab, 309, 319
hardware
  Add/Remove Hardware Wizard, 282-284
  compatibility, Windows 2000, 278
  device drivers, 281-286
  Device Manager, 284
  external plug-in devices, 278
  Found New Hardware Wizard, 281
  graphics cards, 280-281
  installing, 277, 280-284
  internal, 278
  network cards, 280-281
  networking, 324
  NICs, 325-326
  PC Card devices, 278
  Plug-and-Play, 277
  removing, 286
  searching for, 282
  slots, 280

sound cards, 280-281
support, new features,
    14-15
troubleshooting,
    284-286
types of, 278
uninstalling, 286
upgrading device
    drivers, 284-286
Hardware Compatibility
List
    backup devices, 293
    NICs, 325
headers, 76
hidden shares, 344, 353
highlighting, 35
History bar, 261
history lists, 188-189
Home Networking News
    Web site, 326
host computer, 92-93
hot swapping, 90-91
HTML, learning, 269
http, 182
hubs, 329-330
hyperlinks. *See* links

I

icons, 19. *See also* buttons
    adding to Start menu,
        252
    aligning on desktop,
        241
    changing desktop, 239
    colors, 240
    large, use, 240
    new, 8
    printer, 75
    quick launch, 20
    shared resource, 345
    Start menu arrange-
        ment, 249-251

text files, 59
underlining options, 55
View command, 256
WordPad files, 61
idle, setting minimum for
    scheduled tasks, 316
images. *See* graphics; Paint
Imaging program, 109-110
Inbox, 197, 206
Incoming Connections
    icon, 361-362
incremental backups, 294-
    295
Indexing Service, 54, 307
Install file, 274
installing, 273, 287
    CD-ROM drives, 279
    circuit boards, 280-281
    device drivers, 281-284
    disk drives, 278, 280
    DVD drives, 279
    fonts, 65
    graphics cards, 280-281
    hardware, 277, 281-284
    modems, 137-138
    network
        cards, 280-281, 325
        hardware, 325-326,
            329
        printers, 351
        protocols, 336
        software, 332,
            334-337
    NICs, 280-281, 325
    Plug-and-Play, 277
    programs, 273-275
    sound cards, 280-281
interfaces. *See* desktops
Internet
    advanced settings, 172
    automatic connections,
        175
    CD Player, 119

communications meth-
    ods, 213
Connect command, 174
Connect to Internet
    icon, 168, 220
connections, 167-168
disconnecting, 175
DNS address, 173
email setup, 173-174
Enable on demand, 349
IP addresses, 171, 173
ISP, choosing, 169
logon procedure, 173
manual setup, 170-174
meetings. *See*
    NetMeeting
new account setup,
    168-169
program sharing, 227
programs from, 274
protocol, 337
shared connections,
    344, 349-350
TCP/IP, 337
telephone calls, 220-226
temporary files, 307
tools, 12
Internet Accounts dialog
    box, 214
    opening, 174-175
    passwords, 174
    setup options, 168
    transfer existing
        account, 170
Internet Explorer. *See*
    Microsoft Internet
    Explorer
Internet Options dialog
    box, 189
IP addresses, 171, 220-221
ISPs (Internet service
    providers), 167-169
italic text, 64

J

jack, RJ-45, 326
Jaz disks, 293, 311

K

Kbps (Kilobits per second), 134
keyboard shortcuts
  deleting, 208
  email messages, 207
  Favorites bar, 262
  History bar, 262
  Media Player, 117
  open file, 116
  printing, 77
  Search bar, 262
  show taskbar, 255
  Undo, 100

L

LAN (local area network).
  See networks
landscape orientation, 76
laptops. *See* notebooks
lasso, 48
launching. *See* opening
Line-In audio volume, 124
links, 43, 181
Links toolbar, 256, 260
list boxes, 29
list view, 264
Local Area Connection
  icon, 332-333
local area network (LAN).
  See networks
log off option, 37
Log Off User command, 248
logons, network, 340

look-and-feel, 8
lurkers, 219

M

mailing lists, 204
mainstream hierarchies, 216
Make Available Offline
  command (File menu), 354
Make New Connections
  command, 93
Map Network Drive com-
  mand (File menu), 352
mapping, 350-352
margins, 76
masks, 104-106
Maximize buttons, 32
maximizing windows, 32
Media Player, 115-117
meeting, Internet. *See*
  NetMeeting
menu bar, 26
menus, 26. *See also* commands
    commands, 26
    hidden items, 24
    personalized, 24
    submenus, 27
message rules, 209
messages, email, reading, 206
Microsoft Internet
  Explorer, 180
    Address Bar, 181, 188
    address suggestions, 182
    Back button, 182
    bookmarks, 193
    Favorites, 183, 185, 190-193
    Forward button, 182
    history lists, 188-189

icon, 20
launching, 174, 180
links, 181
opening, 174, 180
Organize Favorites com-
  mand, 184
page title, 181
Search feature, 185, 187
start page, 183
starting, 180
Synchronize, 190-192
Web addresses, 182
Windows Update, 317
Microsoft NetMeeting
  Wizard, 222
Microsoft Windows 2000
  Server, 324
Microsoft Word, 61
MIDI file format, 114, 124
Minimize buttons, 32
minimizing windows, 32
mistakes, undoing, 36
modems, 131-132
  area code rules, 145-146
  cables, 134
  call waiting, 144
  calling card dialing, 146
  checking for, 136-137
  compression, 136, 142
  connection icon, 220
  data bits, 135
  data protocol, 142
  demodulation, 133
  diagnostic test, 139
  dial-tone detection, 140
  dial-up connections, 364
  dialing locations, 143-146
  Dialing Rules tab, 143
  dialing speed, 141
  disconnect if idle set-
    ting, 141
  Enable on demand, 349

error correction, 136
external, 132
extra initialization commands, 141
faxing, 149, 153-159
flow control, 135, 142
installing, 137-138
internal, 132
Internet Explorer, 180
long distance calls, 147-148
modulation, 133
parity, 135
PC Card, 132
phone cables, 138-139
Phone Dialer, 150
port speed, 140
ports, 134, 138
properties, 140, 142
protocols, 136
receiving faxes, 159-163
settings, 135-136, 139-146
stop bit, 135
transfer rate, 133
volume, 140
XON/XOFF, 142
modulation, 133
monitors
names of, 242
screen area capacity, 244
mouse, 21
drag-and-drop, 50-51
highlighting with, 35
lassoing with, 48
pointers, 21, 32
Move To button, 49
Move To Folder command (Edit menu), 49
movies, 115
moving
files, 49-51
windows, 31
MP3 file format, 114

MPEG file format, 115
multimedia, 113. *See also* sound
animation files, 115
CD Player, 117-120
DVD Player, 120-122
Media Player, 115-117
movies, 115
playing files, 114-115
recording sound, 125-127
sound files, 114
volume controls, 122, 124
multitasking, 24-25, 31
My Computer, 9-10, 42-46, 259-260
adding toolbar buttons, 263
Address toolbar, 260
Auto Arrange command, 265
contents, 43
create file, 47
Customize Toolbar dialog box, 262
Details view, 264, 266
Explorer Bar, 261
Favorites bar, 261
folders, 267-270
Folders bar, 261
Folders list, 46
History bar, 261
information panel, 43
keyboard shortcut, 262
Links toolbar, 260
list view, 264
printing with, 79
Radio toolbar, 260
Search Bar, 261
sorting files and folders, 265
Standard Buttons toolbar, 260-261, 263

Thumbnails view, 264
Tip of the Day, 261
toggling toolbars, 260
toolbars, 260
views, all folders, 266
views button, 264
Web integration, 55
My Current Home Page, 237
My Documents, 52, 248
My Documents folder
backups, 293, 296
My Network Places, 333, 341, 350-351

N

names, computer, 331
navigation indicators, 241
NetBEUI protocol, 337
NetMeeting, 222
accepting all calls, 226
anonymity, 223
Audio Tuning Wizard, 223
calling, 225
Chat feature, 227
configuring, 222, 224
directories, 222, 224
Do Not Disturb command, 226
file transferring, 227
hang up, 226
program sharing, 227
receiving calls, 225
recording volume, 224
SpeedDialing, 226
Start Collaborating command, 228
Whiteboard feature, 227
wizard, 222
Netscape Navigator, 192-193

network
    backups, 293
    starting from, 18
network adapters. *See* network cards
Network and Dial-up
    Connections command
    (Settings menu), 360
network cards (NICs),
    280-281, 325-326, 332
Network Connection
    Wizard, 360, 363
Network Identification tab,
    334
Network Interface Cards
    (NICs), 280-281, 325-326,
    332
network places, 351
networks, 323-324,
    338-339, 356. *See also*
    dial-up connections
    Add Network Place icon,
        341
    automatic setup, 332
    BNC port, 327
    bus structures, 329-330
    cables, 326
    category 5, 326
    client/server, 324
    clients, 335-336
    coaxial cables, 327-328,
        330
    computer names,
        334-335
    Computers Near Me
        icon, 333, 341, 350
    Computers permissions,
        342, 346
    detecting NICs, 332
    domains, 331, 334
    Entire Network icon,
        341
    Ethernet, 325

Everyone permission,
    342, 345
file and printer sharing,
    336
Groups permissions,
    342, 346
hardware, 324
hidden shares, 344, 353
Home Networking News
    Web site, 326
hubs, 329-330
installing printers, 351
Internet connections,
    349-350
Local Area Connection
    icon, 332-333
logons, 340
manual setup, 333-337
mapping, 350, 352
My Network Places, 341,
    350-351
My Network Places icon,
    333
Network Identification
    tab, 334
network places, 351
new features, 15-16
NICs, 280-281, 325-326,
    332
offline files, 307,
    354-355
passwords, 340
peer-to-peer, 324
permissions, 342,
    345-347
printers, 352-353
protocols, 336
RJ-45 jack, 326
secure boots, 340
security, 342
setting permissions,
    345-347

shares
    folders, 343-345
    Internet connections,
        344
    names, 344
    printers, 347-348
    resources, 339, 343,
        345, 350
star structures, 329-330
structures, 328-329
synchronization,
    354-356
TCP/IP, 337
terminators, 329
thinnet cables, 327
topologies, 328-329
twisted-pair cables, 326
Users permissions, 342,
    346
Windows 2000 setup,
    331-332
wireless, 326
workgroup names,
    334-335
workgroups, 331-332,
    341-342
New command (File
    menu), 33, 47
new features
    CD Player, 11
    desktop, 8
    DVD Player, 11
    hardware support, 14-15
    Internet tools, 12
    Media Player, 10
    networks, 15-16
    notebook computer fea-
        tures, 13-14
    Plug and Play, 14
    Quick Launch toolbar, 8
    Web integration, 9
    Windows Update, 12
New Hardware Found dia-
    log box, 90

newsgroups, 214
asterisk icon, 218
categories, 216
downloading message
lists, 218-219
headers downloaded
option, 219
lurkers, 219
names of, 216
newspaper icon, 218
NNTP servers, 215
Outlook Express, 176,
214
plus signs (+), 219
responding messages,
219
sending new message,
219
setup, 214-215
signal-to-noise ratio,
214
spam, 215
subscribing to, 217
threads, 219
topics, 216
Usenet, 216
NIC (Network Interface
Card), 280-281, 325-326,
332
NNTP servers, 215
normal backups, 294-295
notebooks, 13-14, 83
battery alarms, 85
Briefcases, 87, 89, 94
cable connections,
91-95
creating connections,
92-94
DirectParallel cables, 92
disconnecting from
hosts, 95
hot swapping, 90-91
New Hardware Found
dialog box, 90

null-modem cables, 92
PC Cards, 84, 89-91
power management,
84-86
Power Meter icon, 85,
95
Power Options icon, 84
sockets, 89
synchronizing files,
86-87, 89
Unplug or Eject
Hardware icon, 90
Notepad, 31, 58-60
creating files, 59
dates, insert, 60
editing, 36
fonts, 60
opening, 59
printing, 76
symbols in, 69
Unicode, 60
wrapping text, 60
NTFS file system, 347
null-modem cables, 92

O

offline files, 307
Offline Files folder, 354
Open command (File
menu), 34
Open With command (File
menu), 59
opening
documents, 34, 61
email, 205-206
folders, 43
Internet connections,
174
Internet Explorer, 174
Media Player, 115
Notepad, 59
Outlook Express, 196

Paint, 98
Phone Dialer, 150
programs, 23
single-click option, 55
OpenType typefaces, 63
option buttons, 29
Outlook Express, 176
Address Books, 200-201,
203
attachments, 202-203,
207
blocking senders, 209
conversations, group by,
207
creating email, 197,
199-200
Deleted Items folder,
208
downloading newsgroup
message lists, 218-219
folder, moving email to,
208
groups, 201
icon, 21
Inbox, 197, 206
including message in
reply, 203
Internet Accounts dialog
box, 214
launching, 196
message rules, 209
New Message command,
197, 199-200
newsgroups, 214-215,
217
paper clip icon, 207
reading email, 205
receiving messages, 205
responding to news-
group messages, 219
send messages immedi-
ately option, 203
Send/Recv button, 205

sending messages, 199, 203, 219
Sent Items folder, 203
signatures, 201
startup screen options, 197
subscribing to news-groups, 217

P

pages, Web, 179, 181
Paint, 98
　Airbrush tool, 101
　background colors, 99
　canvas, 99
　Clear Image command, 100
　Color Box, 99
　color mode conversion, 107
　cutouts, 104-106
　digital cameras, 109
　drawing area, 99
　foreground colors, 99
　hide tool boxes, 107
　image attributes, 107
　masks, 104-106
　opening, 98
　Pencil tool, 100
　scanning to, 109
　Shift key, 111
　sizing, 107
　Text tool, 102
　Tool Box, 98-99
　Tool Styles, 99
　tools, 99-100, 102
　Transparent style, 105
　undo mistakes, 100
　view full graphic, 106
　wallpaper, set as, 234
　Zooming, 104
Parallel Technologies, 92

parent, 46
parity, 135
passwords, 340, 365-366
Paste command (Edit menu), 35
pasting text, 35
patterns for desktops, 234
PC Cards, 84, 89-91, 278
　modems, 132
　NICs, 325
PCI slots, NICs, 326
PCMCIA cards. *See* PC Cards
peer-to-peer networks, 324
Pencil tool, 100
permissions, 342
　adding, 343
　allow, 346
　change, 346
　deny, 346
　full control, 346
　name list, 345
　read, 346
　setting, 345-347
Personalized Menus, 246, 249
Phone Dialer, 150, 220
　answering, 161
　dialing, 151
　directories, 151
　Enable on demand, 349
　exiting, 152
　Internet telephoning, 220-221
　opening, 150
　redial, 151
　Speed Dial List, 151-152
pictures. *See* graphics
pixels, 243
playing. *See* CD Player; DVD Player; Media Player
Plug-and-Play, 14, 72, 277
pointing, 21

portrait orientation, 76
ports, 278, 325
posting, 214
power management, 84-86
Power Meter icon, 85, 95
Power Options icon, 84
power supply cables
　disk drives, 279
Print button, 79
printing, 71-72, 77
　automatic printer detection, 73
　cables, 72
　canceling, 81
　collation, 78
　command, 77
　compatible printers, 74
　copies, number of, 78
　default printer, 75
　deferring, 80
　drag-and-drop, 79
　drivers, 348
　Fax as printer, 156
　file and printer sharing, 336
　headers and footers, 76
　installation, 72-75
　installing network, 351
　jobs, 80-81
　keyboard shortcut, 77
　margins, 76
　My Computer, 79
　naming printers, 75
　networking, 352-353
　Notepad, 76
　orientation, 76, 79
　page range, 78
　page setup, 76
　pages per sheet, 79
　paper size, 76
　pausing, 81
　Plug-and-Play printers, 72

previewing, 77
printer icons, 75
Printers folder, 72
queue, 80
restarting, 81
screen, 108
selecting printers, 78
sharing, 344, 347-348
source of paper, 76, 79
status, 80
WordPad documents, 76
privileges, 140
program sharing, Internet, 227
programs
   Add/Remove Programs icon, 274-275
   adding to Start menu, 250-251
   installing, 273-275
   Internet downloads, 274
   multiple, 24
   opening, 23
   shutting down, 31
   uninstalling, 275, 277
Properties, Start Menu, 247
Properties command (File menu), 308
protocols, 136, 336
pull-down menus. *See* menus

Q

Quick Launch toolbar, 8, 255-256
   adding shortcuts, 255
   placement, 257
   Show Desktop icon, 232
QuickTime format, 115

R

Radio toolbar, 260
read permissions, 346
reading email, 205-206
Readme files, 59
recording sound, 125-127
recovering bad sectors, 311
recovery, system, 301
Recycle Bin, 52, 307
removing
   buttons, 263
   hardware, 286
   programs, 275
Rename command (File menu), 51
renaming files and folders, 51
Replace All feature, 69
resource sharing, 356
restarting, 37
Restore command (File menu), 52
Restore Wizard, 302-303
restoring files, 52, 302-303
Rich Text Format, 61
right-clicking, 22
RJ-45 jack, 326
RTF (Rich Text Format), 61

S

Save As command (File menu), 34
Save command (File menu), 34, 291
saving
   backup jobs, 298
   documents, 34
scanners, 108-109, 111
Scheduled Task Wizard, 314-316

Scheduled Tasks command (System Tools menu), 314
scheduling system mainte-nance, 313
schemes, 236-237
screens. *See also* desktops
   area slider, 243-244
   capture, 108
   colors, setting, 242-243
   components, 18-20
   savers, 235
scrollbars, 32
scrolling, 23, 32
Search Bar, 261
Search command (Start menu), 53-54
search engines, 187
Search Options, 54
searching
   for files, 53-54
   hardware, 282
   options, 54
   World Wide Web, 185, 187
sectors, 309-310
secure boots, 340
security, permissions, 342
Select All command (Edit menu), 48
selecting
   files, 47, 49
   no-click option, 55
   printers, 78
   text, 35
   windows, 25
   WordPad text, 62
selection areas, 62
Send To command (File menu), 50
Send To menu, 50
Sent Items folder, 203
serial ports, 134

servers, 324
settings, Start menu, 247
Settings menu commands, 360
setup, networks, 331-332
Setup file, 274-275
setup programs, 273-275
shares
    Internet connections, 349-350
    names, 344
    printers, 353
    resources, 339, 343, 350
Sharing command (File menu), 344
shortcut menu, 56
shortcuts
    adding to Start menu, 250, 252
    keyboard. *See* keyboard shortcuts
    Quick Launch toolbar, 255
    quick Start menu, 253
    removing from Start menu, 251
Show Desktop icon, 20
Show Text command, 256
Show Title command, 256
Shut Down command (Start menu), 37
shutting down
    programs, 31
    Windows 2000, 36
signatures, 201
sizing
    graphics, 107
    windows, 32
slots, 280
sorting
    Details view, 266
    files, 265

sound
    cards, 114
        connecting to CD-ROM drive, 119
        installing, 280-281
    CD quality, 126
    CD track files, 115
    echo effect, 127
    Effects menu, 127
    file formats, 114
    hardware, 114
    lack of, 119
    Line-In volume, 124
    mixing, 127
    previews, 125
    radio quality, 126
    recording, 125-127
    schemes, 125
    settings, 124-125
    telephone quality, 126
    volume controls, 122, 124
    Windows events, 124-125
Sound Recorder, 125-127
spam, 209, 215
special characters, 69
Speed Dial List, 151-152
SpeedDialing, 226
spin boxes, 30
Standard Buttons toolbar, 260-263
standby mode, 86
star structures, 329-330
Start button, 20, 23
Start Collaborating command, 228
Start menu, 23, 246-247
    adding icons, 249-252
    adding shortcuts, 252
    Administrative Tools, 247
    Advanced tab, 252

bypassed windows, 248
clear Documents menu, 253
Connections submenu, 248
Control Panel, 248
directory, 251
double arrow, 246-247
drag-and-drop rearranging, 253
Expand My Documents box, 248
Explore command, 252
Favorites, 247
folders, 250-251
hidden items, 246-247
icon arrangement, 249-251
Log Off User command, 248
Personalized Menus, 246, 249
Properties, 247
quick shortcuts, 253
removing items from, 251
right-clicking, 253
settings, 247
show small icons setting, 249
shrinking, 8
sorting, 253
submenus, 252
uninstalling programs, 277
Start menu commands
    Search, 53
    Shut Down, 37
    Windows Update, 317
starting, 18. *See also* opening
    Internet Explorer, 180
    programs, 23

startup
  desktop, 232
  icons, 19-20
Status Bar command (View menu), 260
stop bit, 135
storage devices, 42
subfolders, 46, 52
subject, email, 198
subscribing to newsgroups, 217
switching programs, 24-25
symbols, 69
sync copies, 87
synchronization, 86-87, 89, 354-356
Synchronize, Internet Explorer, 190-192
system maintenance, 313-314
system recovery, 301
system standby mode, 86
System State data, 296
System Tools menu commands
  Disk Cleanup, 308
  Disk Defragmenter, 311
  Scheduled Tasks, 314
system tray, 21

T

tabs
  control, 29
  WordPad, 67
tape drives, 293
Task Scheduler, 314-316
Taskbar and Start Menu Properties dialog box, 247
taskbars, 20, 253, 258
  Address toolbar, 256
  always on top option, 255
  auto hide option, 255
  buttons, 254

clock, 255
Desktop toolbar, 256
dial-up connections icon, 364
expanding, 254
General tab, 255
hiding, 255
Links toolbar, 256
placement on screen, 253
properties, 254
Quick Launch toolbar, 256
rows, number of, 254
Show Desktop icon, 232
showing, 255
switching active window, 24
toolbars, showing, 256
TCP/IP, 337
telephone calls. *See* NetMeeting; Phone Dialer
terminators, 329
text
  bolding, 64
  boxes, 29
  copying, 35
  cutting, 35
  deleting, 36
  files, 58-60
    creating, 59
    fonts, 60
    icons, 59
    WordPad, 61
  formatting, 62
  highlighting, 35
  italic, 64
  underlining, 64
Text tool, 102
thinnet cables, 327
threads, 206, 219
Thumbnails view, 264
time, display, 255
Tip of the Day, 261

toolbars, 27, 256, 258, 271
  Address, 260
  creating, 257
  hiding, 28
  label buttons, 45
  Links, 260
  My Computer. *See* My Computer
  placement, 257
  Radio, 260
  removing buttons, 263
  Reset command, 264
  separators, 263
  Show Text command, 256
  Show Title command, 256
  Standard Buttons, 260
  toggling, 260
  View command, 256
Toolbars command (View menu), 260
Tools menu commands, Folder Options, 55
Tools tab, 309, 319
ToolTips, 8
topologies, network, 328-329
transition effects, desktop, 240
troubleshooting hardware devices, 284-286
twisted-pair cables, 326
type size, desktops, 237
typefaces, 63

U

underlining text, 64
Undo command (Edit menu), 36
Unicode
  Notepad, 60
  WordPad, 61

uninstalling, 273, 287
  hardware, 286
  programs, 275, 277
Universal Serial Bus (USB), 325
Unplug or Eject Hardware icon, 90
Up button, 46
Update command, 88
Update Wizard, 318
updating Windows 2000, 317-318
upload, 136
URLs. *See* Web addresses, 182
USB (Universal Serial Bus), 325
Use Printer Offline command (File menu), 80
Usenet. *See* newsgroups
Users and Passwords icon, 340, 342
Users permissions, 342, 346

V

video adapter, name of, 242
View menu commands
  Explorer Bar, 261
  Folders, 46
  Go To, 45
  Status Bar, 260
  Toolbars, 260
  Zoom, 104
viewing subfolders, 46
volume controls, 122, 124

W-Z

wallpapers, 232-234
WAV file format, 114, 124
Web addresses, 182

Web browsers. *See also* Microsoft Internet Explorer
  Netscape Navigator, 192-193
  setting default, 193
Web integration, 55
Web pages, 179, 181
  Active Desktops, 237
  creating, 58
  Favorites bar, 261
  HTML, 269
  links, 181
  My Current Home Page, 237
  reading offline, 190
Web sites
  Home Networking News, 326
  Windows Update, 317
Whiteboards, 227
windows, 31
  dragging speed, 241
  maximize, 32
  minimizing, 32
  moving, 31
  multiple, 24
  scrolling inside, 32
  selecting, 25
  sizing, 32
Windows 2000 Server, 324
Windows Update command (Start menu), 317
Windows Update Web site, 317
WINNT folder, 44
wireless networks, 326
word processing, 24, 57, 60-61. *See also* Microsoft Word
  files, 58
  selection areas, 62
  WordPad, 24, 58-61
Word. *See* Microsoft Word

WordPad, 28, 58-61
  aligning text, 65
  bullets, 66
  file types supported, 61
  find text, 68-69
  fonts, 62, 64
  formatting text, 62
  icons, file, 61
  indenting text, 65
  margins, 76
  multiple windows, 62
  opening documents, 61
  paragraph formatting, 64-65
  printing, 76-79
  replace text, 68-69
  Rich Text Format, 61
  ruler, 67
  selecting text, 62
  starting, 24, 60
  symbols in, 69
  tabs, 67
  text files, 61
  Unicode format, 61
  Word 6 format, 61
workgroups, 331-332, 341
  names, 334-335
  permissions, 342
World Wide Web, 179. *See also* Internet
  addresses, 182
  links, 181
  search engines, 187
writing tools. *See* Notepad; WordPad
writing. *See* word processing, 57
Zip disks, 293, 311
Zoom command (View menu), 104